The Parent
of the
Handicapped Child

Publication Number 696
AMERICAN LECTURE SERIES®

A Monograph in
The BANNERSTONE DIVISION *of*
AMERICAN LECTURES IN SPECIAL EDUCATION

Edited by
MORRIS VAL JONES, Ph.D.
Speech and Hearing Center
Sacramento State College
Sacramento, California

The Parent
of the
Handicapped Child

The Study of Child-rearing Practices

Second Printing

By

RAY H. BARSCH, Ph.D.

CHARLES C THOMAS · PUBLISHER
Springfield · Illinois · U.S.A.

Published and Distributed Throughout the World by
CHARLES C THOMAS • PUBLISHER
Bannerstone House
301-327 East Lawrence Avenue, Springfield, Illinois, U.S.A.

© *1968, by* CHARLES C THOMAS • PUBLISHER
ISBN 0-398-00097-2 (cloth)
ISBN 0-398-03559-8 (paper)
Library of Congress Catalog Card Number: 67-25701

First Printing, 1968
Second Printing, 1976

With THOMAS BOOKS *careful attention is given to all details of manufacturing and design. It is the Publisher's desire to present books that are satisfactory as to their physical qualities and artistic possibilities and appropriate for their particular use.* THOMAS BOOKS *will be true to those laws of quality that assure a good name and good will.*

Printed in the United States of America
R-1

*To my wife who patiently endured
the manuscript period*

PREFACE

SINCE SIGMUND FREUD awakened us to the importance of early childhood experience, especially parent-child relationships, professional workers have been giving additional emphasis to parental guidance. Writers in professional journals, such as Dorothea McCarthy, have delineated the influence of the home environment upon the language development of the child. More recently professional articles have emphasized the child-rearing practices of parents who have handicapped children; a number of such articles have appeared in *Exceptional Children*, the Journal of the Council for Exceptional Children.

In 1962 Stanwix House published *Understand Those Feelings* by Eugene T. McDonald. In several hundred parent interviews and in conducting group sessions for parents of handicapped children, Dr. McDonald found that unless feelings about handicapped children are understood, handicapped families tend to develop around handicapped children. But parents, if they are given guidance and encouragement, can work through their feelings, organize their thoughts, and begin to participate in a positive action program. He suggests that handicapped children will be accepted more readily by neighbors and playmates as their behavior and appearance improve. Parents must accept the responsibility for increasing the acceptability of their handicapped children in the community.

In 1965 Macmillan brought out *Caring for your Disabled Child* by Benjamin Spock and Marion Lerrigo, both of whom have written numerous books and articles on child rearing practices. This book is promoted by the publishers as "the first complete guide for parents in understanding and helping their mentally, physically or emotionally handicapped children." The authors continue their stress upon the parents' responsibility for discipline, for education in conduct and control. The handicapped child, like the normal child, needs to strive for independence. The adults who plan programs for him must help him move toward adulthood and independence—as much independence as he is capable of achieving.

Most of the writings in the past have been based upon the personal experience and clinical observation of the authors. Research has been lacking upon which to base concrete suggestions for the parents of handicapped children. In the present volume, Dr. Ray Barsch has made a significant contribution toward removing this limitation. Combining the precision of research techniques with the writing skills of a novelist, he translates his findings into highly readable information for the parents of handicapped children and for professional workers who attempt to guide these parents. Dr. Barsch, who recently transferred his research activities from Wisconsin to the DeWitt Reading Clinic in San Rafael, California, has established a research program in learning disabilities. We can anticipate that this book is only the first in a series from the pen of this eminent educator, researcher, and humanitarian.

MORRIS VAL JONES, PH.D.

ACKNOWLEDGMENTS

A SPECIAL DEBT of gratitude is owed to Dr. Robert Sears who generously agreed to permit the use and modification of the original interview used in his study and to Dr. Bernard Farber for his permission to use and modify several instruments which he had previously employed in his study of parents of severely retarded children. Dr. Seymour Sarason provided a definite inspiration for this study and his guidance during the early stages of the project proved to be invaluable.

The two clinical interviewers Mrs. Anne Ewart and Mr. Daniel McCarthy conducted the interviews with sensitivity and sympathy. Mrs. Belle Golden with customary efficiency was a most vital administrative coordinator for the entire project.

Dr. John Cook deserves a warm acknowledgment for his statistical management of the data from the Parent Attitude Rating Inventory and the California Psychological Inventory and for his narrative descriptions of the data process.

Finally, a very special "thank you" is extended to the mothers and fathers who made this study possible. The many long hours they spent in filling out questionnaires and answering thousands of questions about themselves and their children are a reflection of their own dedication to helping others "in the future."

RAY H. BARSCH, PH.D.

The contents of this book are based in part upon the research data derived from Project M3750 under a grant from the National Institute of Mental Health (1959-1963).

This project was conducted at the Easter Seal Child Development Center in Milwaukee, Wisconsin.

CONTENTS

The Parent
of the
Handicapped Child

Chapter 1

INTRODUCTION

THIS IS A BOOK about parents and the child-rearing practices they employ. It is specifically a book about parents of handicapped children although the content has far reaching implications for all parents. It is a frank attempt to achieve some perspective on the dynamics of parenthood—particularly within the family that contains a handicapped child.

Motherhood and fatherhood may be viewed as biologic achievements, but parenthood is a learned process of experimentation enacted daily in the laboratory of the home, the neighborhood and the community. Hypotheses are developed, experiments are devised and tested, and results are analyzed. The laboratory analogy cannot perhaps stand the test of careful scientific inspection, but may stand nonetheless, when one considers the frequency with which a parent goes through the behavioral or mental gymnastics of seeking a technique to accomplish a specific change in their child's behavior.

Undoubtedly, few parents regard themselves as scientists for this label assumes careful and intensive training, highly organized and astute thinking, and a large measure of creativity and dedicatoin. However, they are in a state of continual experimentation, seeking to find answers. They hypothesize, they speculate, they ponder and they analyze. Some manage this better than others. When one technique does not produce results, they try another and another and another. At times they are successful and at times they fail. Experience over a period of time with a number of different subjects may increase their success potential.

In this laboratory of developmental experience, the parent learns to move the child from the bottle to the cup, from the diaper to the training pants, from the babble to the clear sentence, from the stroller to the tricycle, from the spoon to the fork and from the crib to the bed. Parents also learn to manage the emergency of a bruised knee, a cut finger, a siege of measles, the virus infections, the broken leg and the many traumas of disappointment and hurt feelings.

They observe and react to their child's excitement over his accomplishments and empathize with his limitations when his goals out-distance his abilities. They admire the kindergarten drawing, marvel at the oral reading of the first book, drill on the words for the Friday spelling test and help organize the book report that is due on Monday. They may eagerly or reluctantly become involved in Indian Guides, Cub Scouts, Brownies, Boy Scouts and Little League baseball. Their child's development is replete with momentary crises, new adventure and progressive gains.

In the midst of the busy daily schedule of living, they must help the child to differentiate good from evil, teach him to respect the rights of others, teach him whom to trust and whom to fear, how to share with others and how to protect his belongings. They must admonish, direct, cajole, guide, insist, demand, encourage, reward, approve, reject, improve and above all, teach. Within the general pattern of their culture, society will expect their child to walk, to talk, to wash and toilet himself, to respect the flower bed and fruit trees of the neighbors, attend school daily and learn to read before he or she is seven years of age. Furthermore, the child will be expected to be polite, courteous and patient.

For the child's physical welfare, he must learn that knives are sharp, certain liquids are poison, water may be too deep, the tree limb may be too high, puddles are to be avoided, the traffic moves swiftly. All these and many more lessons are learned well or not well in the daily teaching relationship, and with the help of other members of the family, the parent establishes a pattern of expected and approved behavior in the family circle, the neighborhood, the church, school and community. The rules and regulations, the code and the mores are transmitted in the laboratory of parenthood. Some parents teach well. Some do not. Society accepts few excuses.

The parent is truly the "conveyor belt of society" as Sears (1957) has stated, producing an eventual adult to contribute, participate and improve the welfare of that society.

Some parents "convey" their children to society in the form of adults from a stable well-defined efficient constructional period of sixteen to eighteen years. They must be judged as having efficiently fulfilled their obligation to the society in which they live. The adult life of the child becomes a continual reflection of credit upon the "constructional efficiency" of the parent. Some children make their entry into the adult space of living as a haphazard escape from a parental milieu of inconsistency, questionable values, rejection, indecision, neglect and confusion. Their adult lives may be regarded as a credit to their own powers of survival but can scarcely be considered as reflecting credit upon the developmental efficiency of their parents. For some of these "escapees" the adult terrain becomes one of turmoil and turbulence which requires the establishment of an immense corps of remedial services.

Between these two extremes of the extremely efficient child-rearers and the extremely inefficient child-rearers the vast majority of American parents find their positions. Some are to be found on the efficient side more or less distant from the optimal. Some are positioned more or less distant from the negative extreme of inefficiency.

The strength of a society is drawn from those parents who rate positions on the positive side of the child-rearing efficiency continuum and the weakness of a society is, in final analysis, attributable to negative side of that continuum.

The American parent has been subjected to a great deal of authoritative criticism on many fronts and accused of many subtle forms of social neglect as his society continues to be plagued with social ills of one form or another. The small percentage of parents who clearly deserve a rating of gross inefficiency have become the perceptual model for parent-accusers who are apparently convinced that the small percentage is simply an open and obvious symptom of a basic generalized condition.

The rearing of a child in the complex and often chaotic structure of American society is a far from simple matter. On all sides a parent is bombarded with conflicting theories, authoritative warnings, constant admonitions and questionable research. Value systems vary. Customs change. Technology makes today obsolete almost before tomorrow comes. National concern is expressed over declines in moral standards. Popular advertising continues to warn parents that they are contributing to their child's social, moral, physical or physiologic delinquency if they fail to supply him with the proper products. Parents are urged to note early signs of thousands of behaviors and conditions. Whatever their children may do which does not match someone's set of criteria will be attributed to their parental inadequacies. When their children conform to expectancy it will be taken for granted by their society that the parents merely fulfilled an expected obligation.

If one were to list the diagnostic acumen expected of parents, the number of moral concepts to be taught, the lessons of interpersonal relationships which should be comfortably set, the stress tolerances to be built, the defense mechanisms to be built, the confidences to be established and the number of conformities which must be nurtured while making certain that individualities emerge—the list of obligations would overwhelm the average parent.

Fortunately the parents of history have not carefully read the list before embarking upon their parental journey. Faced with so formidable a listing of obligations they might well have chosen to reject the list and the parental process. The biology of mankind has taken care of that remote possibility and the race has continued. Most parents survive this list of obligations by developing some degree of efficiency as child-rearers. Their efficiency rates may not be nearly as high as the optimal benefit to society requires but the overwhelming majority throughout history have worked diligently at the task of meeting their parental obligations.

They have watched their infant take his first steps, master the tricycle, manipulate the first ice cream cone and eat his first hamburger. They have marvelled at his drawings at the PTA open house, proudly attended his installation as a Scout, frowned at his report card and bid him farewell in the parking lot of the summer camp. They have sat besides his bed during his illnesses, applied Merthiolate® to his bruised knee, put the fairy quarter under his pillow when the first tooth fell out and stood in line with him for hours to see a Disney special. They have watched him hit a double with the bases loaded, run over right tackle for a touchdown and come in second in the bag race at the picnic. They have annually organized an "unforgettable" birthday party, provided the gifts at Christmas that were listed by him and somehow managed to get him the big gift when he wanted it. In the midst of thousands upon thousands of experiences, lessons in kindness, sharing, consideration, bearing disappointments, love, courage and confidence were interwoven.

All that happens between a parent and a child from the time of the birth cry to the casting of the first vote in the November election may, in some manner, be construed under the composite heading of child-rearing. It is the business of parenthood.

If a metabolic error, an extra chromosome, a viral infection, a congenital anomaly, a set of antibodies, a toxic process, excessive oxygen, a neural disruption or some other vague agent adventitiously introduces a handicapped child on the terrain of parenthood the business of parenthood continues. The societal obligations remain the same.

Each minute of the day, a young couple in a maternity ward, in a hospital clinic or in a physician's office, somewhere in the world, is confronted with the traumatic news that their child has a handicap. They must absorb, assimilate, recognize and accept the fact that perhaps their child will never walk as other children do, talk as others do, see or hear as others do, learn as others do or grow as others do. New words are suddenly thrust into their vocabulary—words which perhaps were previously associated with others in their past experience or only represented a child on a poster during a campaign. Now the words belong to their child—cerebral palsy, mongolism, blind, deaf, mentally retarded, epileptic, emotionally disturbed. One of these labels describe their child's problem—perhaps more than one label applies.

For some there will be disbelief which will prompt a round of searching visits to other clinics and other physicians. For some there will be quick efforts to place the child in a residential institution. Of the thousands who will be confronted with such news today, few will choose the residential placement. Most will return home and go about the business of rearing this child in the best manner they can.

For some parents such knowledge is learned before the infant is discharged from the maternity ward, but for others a year or more of suspicion, doubt, anxiety and tension precedes the confrontation. Consequently, some parents have their anxieties confirmed very soon after the birth of the child, while others live for years in a state of uncertainty. For some there is the daily waiting for some sign which might indicate that the child is overcoming or outgrowing the feature which causes the parent anxiety—any little sign of improvement may be maximized in the parents' perception. For others there is a resignation to the futility of seeking any miraculous change.

Some parents feel personally responsible for the child's defect. Others are relieved in the knowledge that an accident over which they could not possibly have control is the responsible agent. Some accept their problem, some will learn to accept it and some will never accept it.

Whether or not the parent is classified as "accepting" is usually an evaluative judgment offered by a professional. If the parent is militantly aggressive in seeking to obtain therapeutic services for his child he may be accused of not realistically accepting his child's limitations. If he does not concern himself with efforts to improve or obtain services he may be accused of apathetic rejection of his child. If he questions too much he has a "reaction formation" and may be overprotective and oversolicitous. If he questions too little he is branded as disinterested and insensitive.

The problem with classifying a parent as "accepting" or "unaccepting" is one of defining the label. Each professional may list any set of criteria he desires under each heading and tally the parents according to those criteria. Unfortunately parents are rarely acquainted with criteria in advance.

Regardless of their anxieties, feelings, attitudes, regardless of etiology, therapy and prognosis and regardless of whether the diagnosis is precise, specific and understandable, the parent remains charged with the obligation of society to transmit a culture pattern, to teach a language, to establish social adequacy, to help the child differentiate right from wrong, etc. In short, the identification of the child as handicapped does not serve to absolve the parent from the obligations imposed by society. Society still expects the child to talk, to toilet himself, to dress himself and to generally conform in his social behavior. It seems that a certain leeway is allowed; some delay in such acquisitions, in comparison with the nonhandicapped child is acceptable, but the demand for conformity is still there.

Based upon the clinical records of parents over a fifteen-year period, it seems clear that while society's members may be sympathetic to the young blind child, they also expect that child to talk. Despite the fact that eventually the vast majority of these young children will become eligible for some form of school service their entry to a class may hinge on whether or not the child is bladder-trained and bowel-trained. The school services may be available, but unless the child has learned to tolerate the absence of his mother from his side, he may present an unmanageable problem to the school personnel.

Some degree of behavioral control must also be established. In fact each school and each clinic is likely to have a list of several criteria which must be met by the child before acceptance for service. It is automatically assumed by school people that a good deal of the foundations for learning what the school has to offer have already been laid by the parents during the period from infancy to school age. The parent who has failed to match up to the expectations of school or clinic personnel may readily be classified as overprotective, oversolicitous, rejecting, disinterested, apathetic, guilt-ridden, etc. The labels simply serve as terms of value judgment by a segment of society that for one reason or another indicts the parents for having failed to discharge their obligations.

This, then, appears to be the course for the parent of the handicapped child: First, accept the shock of having a child who is different from other children and yet the same; second, set in motion through child-rearing practices those actions and activities which will build a foundation of physical, social, emotional, intellectual achievements to serve as a base for future services of therapists and teachers; and finally, develop conformity behaviors at progressive levels of complexity.

No parent is ever prepared to be the parent of a handicapped child. The identification of a mother and a father in that role always comes as a painful surprise. Whatever have been the individual parental attitudes toward handicapped people throughout their preparental lives provides a certain textile to be woven into that fabric of role identification. Whatever degree of psychological and social maturity have been developed in each party becomes another textile in the fabric. The textiles are many—socioeconomic status, size of family, neighbors' and relatives' attitude, severity of the handicap, demand for care—these and many more must be woven into that identification. It is an identification which cannot be escaped. It may become psychologically blurred and perhaps even socially suppressed—but it is persistently realistic and demanding. No matter what shading and nuance may be woven into the fabric of such identification by the parent the obligation to fulfill the role of child-rearer is still realistically imposed upon the parent by society.

Confronted with that obligation how does the parent proceed? The answer to that question is the major concern of this book.

Since no parent is truly prepared to assume such a role without some degree of guidance it is inevitable that the mother and father must enter the domain of society's rehabilitation milieu. It is in this context that the natural inclinations of the parent are mixed and mingled with the professional knowledge currently available.

THE PARENT AND THE REHABILITATION MILIEU

The rehabilitation landscape across the nation is an exceptionally variable terrain. In large metropolitan communities clinics for diagnosis and treatment of dozens of differing handicap types exist in prolific number. Each is well staffed and each is dedicated to optimal service. Each clinic, however, becomes a member of a chorus chanting a demanding refrain for more space, more staff, better facilities and the opportunity to intensify service. A waiting list for diagnostic and therapeutic services is a common characteristic. Each agency seeks to define its particular segment of the rehabilitation landscape in as precise terminology as possible. Each agency defines its service population. One serves only the deaf preschool child, another serves only the postadolescent trainable, one only the seriously disturbed, one only the low-income group, the next only the high-income group and so on.

The criteria may be set according to age span, type of handicap, parental income, degree of impairment, source of referral and nature of manifest behavior. The criteria vary from clinic to clinic and agency to agency—but always exist in some form. Some agencies operate within a total psychological framework—some within a medical framework—and others are directed according to social work theory. If the handicapped child and his parents meet the criteria of the respective agency an eligibility for diagnosis or for therapy is established.

The entire organizational structure of clinics and agencies operates to the advantage of certain clusters of children and their parents and to the disadvantage of others. Any parent of a handicapped child in a metropolitan center, is, first of all, confronted with criteria. At any given moment a child might be too young, too old, too severe, not severe enough, too bright, too retarded, at too high an income level or not high enough. Even within a metropolitan community when the welfare roster is lengthy it is possible for the parent of the handicapped child to be faced with a situation of qualifying for *none* of the existing programs.

It is well recognized that despite the apparent abundance of clinical services, each metropolitan community fails a certain percentage of its handicapped in one way or another. All parents of handicapped children are aware of the fact that diagnostic services in metropolitan communities tend to be very good in all areas of disability. The same high quality of available professionals is drastically reduced when the issue of therapy is raised. Comparatively speaking the parent experiences little difficulty in obtaining a diagnosis. The major problems are encountered in the area of availability of therapeutic services. Even in metropolitan centers it is not unusual for the parent of the preschool deaf or blind child to have no place to turn for therapeutic service.

The parent of a handicapped child in a metropolitan center may be able to find a diagnosis, therapy for his child and guidance for the child-rearing process from infancy to adulthood—only if the community has found it wise to organize such services.

It is also true that many metropolitan families are dependent upon the knowledge of the early consultants to insure referral to appropriate therapeutic services. The parent of a child with a single handicap is likely to fare better than one whose child has a combination of handicaps.

Regional diagnostic centers holding a national reputation also tend to attract parents from metropolitan communities seeking classification of their child's problems. Despite a reasonably adequate network of community services it is likely that a certain percentage of parents will find it advisable for their own needs and those of the child to journey to distant places searching for advice and consultation. Many communities have turned to multiple-disability orientations in setting their criteria for service and this has undoubtedly yielded advantages to the parents and the children.

The parent of the nonmetropolitan child is at a more serious disadvantage. Diagnostic centers may be located from fifty to three hundred miles from their homes. A diagnostic visit may be well within range but when consideration must be given to regular commuting for purposes of treatment the parent must often decline. Those who choose to commute for treatment find the process exceptionally tiring and progressively wearing. The rural handicapped child or the remotely located urban child are frequently "therapy-disadvantaged."

In many instances the metropolitan center, the regional center or even the local center must be ignored because the parent cannot manage the transportation. Even among the metropolitan agencies provision of transportation is a rarity. The parent must find a way to bring and fetch the child for both diagnosis and treatment. Most parents manage this demand but some do not.

In spite of an extensive pattern of services within a metropolitan community comparatively few areas can boast of a coverage of its handicapped population from birth to maturity. Many excellent services have been established but the setting of criteria to avoid community duplication has a tendency to result in "gapping." Such gaps, occasioned by criteria, often place a child and his family in the position of being located in the gap area—in a limbo of community service. Under these conditions the child must grow into the next existing set of criteria before receiving the advantages of treatment. Many communities are working diligently to close the gaps and many are succeeding, but the communities which can actually offer a continuum of care are relatively rare. The more typical condition is for the gaps to continue to exist.

In remote areas the intervals between community services are even more widely spaced. In a rehabilitation sense a significant percentage of the nation's handicapped children could be classified as "therapeutically disadvantaged."

The second type of edifice on the rehabilitation landscape is the special education program of the community school system. Here again the metropolitan communities may offer an extensive array of programs but each contains an inevitable set of criteria. Only in unusual instances does the community school provide services to children before the age of five and in many places the typical age for entry of handicapped children into the school system is at six years or even later. A well-organized school program offers educational services to the blind, deaf, partially seeing, partially hearing, trainable and educable, mentally retarded, emotionally disturbed, physically handicapped, neurologically impaired, educationally handicapped, cardiac cases, and so, on but the vast majority of school systems are not as extensive in their offerings.

Many parents of nonmetropolitan handicapped children discover that their local school system does not have provisions for their kind of child. Under such circumstances a parent may be required to decide upon a boarding school away from home, out-of-state schooling, periodic home-bound tutoring or a simple process of waiting until facilities become available. Again the metropolitan child is in a more favorable setting than the rural or remote child.

If the parent does have a child eligible for school services there is always the question of length of stay within the special classes and the inevitable time when the child outgrows the program.

The parent of the handicapped children may occupy a very favorable location on the rehabilitation landscape or one that is not so favorable. His position and that of his child on this terrain will be determined by: (1) the community clinical and agency structure in the town where he resides; (2) the age of the child; (3) the income level of his family; (4) the severity of the child's disorder; (5) availability of transportation; (6) the singularity of handicap; (7) willingness of the parent to coparticipate in therapy; (8) the ability of the child to meet existing criteria for admission to a program; (9) availability of the specifically required program; and (10) the orientation of a particular program. All of these points may stand in the path of some parents or only a few points may apply.

It is important, however, to recognize that the bewildered parent searching for guidance in this new role as the parent of a handicapped child must contend with the *available* rehabilitation milieu. While a great deal of professional knowledge exists, the availability of that knowledge to the parent as he or she seeks to efficiently rear a handicapped child is dependent upon many factors.

The parent always finds a way to diagnosis but the road to treatment is often a rocky one filled with obstacles and detours. The acquisition of child-rearing efficiency for the most part rests squarely upon the shoulders of the parents of the handicapped child.

The parents described in this book probably fall within the classification of fortunate because of the many facilities available in Milwaukee County but even among these parents there was a percentage who encountered one or more of the obstacles referred to above. The story of child-rearing reported in these chapters does not cover those parents who live in outlying areas or in less prolific communities. Their general story may be the same or different.

The parent on the rehabilitation terrain, fortunate or unfortunate, represents a person seeking guidance in establishing a comfortable and helpful identification. It is another significant shading which must be brushed into the portrait of child-rearing.

THE PARENT AND THE PROFESSIONAL

Each parent of a handicapped child encounters professionally trained specialists at many points along the way. It is likely that each parent could put together a sizable list of professionals who have, in some manner, been related to them or their child. The pediatrician, neurologist, psychiatrist, obstetrician, otologist, opthalmalogist, osteopath, orthopedic surgeon, audiologist, clinical psychologist, school psychologist, physical therapist, occupational therapist, speech therapist, social worker, nursery teacher and a classroom teacher may all be included on the list. Some parents have been exposed to all of these and some parents to only a few. Some parents have had the benefit of a team approach in a single setting while others have developed their own team approach by collecting data from various unrelated sources.

Each professional is the product of a prescribed course of specialized training in his respective field. Training programs for professionals are college and university oriented and vary in length from four to eight years. In addition to the collegiate orientation the professional has served some form of apprenticeship under approved supervision. Each one in turn has learned something about "these kinds of children."

University programs are characterized by particular orientations in given fields. Each body of knowledge includes many principles and laws which are incontestably documented by research evidence but it also contains much space for opinion, conjecture, speculation and hypothesis. There is always a variety of theories in existence on any topic. The collegian is exposed to these variations in gradations of intensity and emerges from his training with a set of theories and a philosophy. The shaping of that philosophy which has taken place in his university experience is clear and direct in some instances and vague and diffuse in others.

One may look hard and long before any listing of courses devoted to understanding of parenthood of a handicapped child is found to be a formal part of the professional preparation. Not only do professionals from hundreds of university programs holding varying and differing orientations enter the fields of rehabilitation and special education each year but they also enter the fields with little or no preparation for their encounters with parents.

Each of these professionals in turn will exert some degree of influence upon the parent of the handicapped child. Many times parents are distressed by the lack of agreement among professionals. One believes in bracing, another does not. One believes in surgery, another does not. A wide variety of opinions are expressed to parents in the form of dichotomies: rock—do not rock the baby; rigid schedule—flexible schedule; intensive therapy—sporadic therapy; begin early—wait for development; work with the child—work with the parent; ready for school—wait another year; a passing phase—an embedded characteristic, and on and on. Some parents swirl under the impact of diametrically opposed viewpoints and some feel as though they are personally responsible for achieving a synthesis among these many viewpoints—at least in their own case.

Some parents are blissfully unaware of the many different viewpoints while others are painfully sensitive to the discrepancies. Simple inspection of the literature in each field will provide the student with the controversies in each province. They do exist. There are many different ways of looking at something. When that something is identified as a handicapped child all parties concerned must recognize that here, too, there are many ways of looking at him.

The professional wears one kind of lens ground in the laboratory of his collegiate orientation and the experiential background which he can call upon in making his observations. The parent of the handicapped child wears another kind of lens ground in the laboratory of prosaic daily living, hopes, ambitions, personal complexity and sophistication. The lenses are not identical. They have been ground for different purposes and refract illuminating information accordingly.

These two different kinds of perceptual lenses cause each respective observer to view the child differently. In other words the parent cannot be expected to perceive the child in the same manner as the professional does. These two inevitably different perceptions have often been the cause of misinterpretations, distrust and loss of respect. It is really a problem of perceptual incompatibility.

At each point along the way the parent of the handicapped child presents his child for diagnosis, treatment or therapy to an individual professional who may have a variety of reactions. The child may be recognized as possessing similar characteristics to hundreds and even thousands of children who have been seen before. For some professionals *this* child may represent an unusual case against a background of many cases. Other professionals may never have seen or worked with a child like this. Still other professionals may recognize this child from textbook or lecture descriptions but will actually be seeing a live model for the first time. The parent may be assured, however, that the child is being professionally perceived according to a particular orientation. Symptoms and behaviors will be weighted and categorized according to that particular orientation. The professional may speak from a generalized background of knowledge gained from many similar cases—the parent knows only one—his own.

The perceptions held by the professional world regarding children in each disability group have been abundantly documented in the literature. That perceptual side of the story must be regarded as well defined. The other side of the story—the perception of the parent—is not so clear.

Each parent also employs some form of theoretical orientation—not so clearly defined as the professional's but nonetheless operative. It is this context which constitutes the body of this book. It is the parent side of the story which needs to be told to obtain a balanced perspective in the general domain of handicapped children. The imbalance caused by an almost exclusive documentation of the professional side has created developmental problems for the organism called "child rehabilitation."

This study serves in a small way to illuminate the perceptual side of the parent in this rehabilitation dichotomy by asking parents to discuss their child-rearing practices. It is an opportunity to come to balance and may help professionals to find perceptual compatibility with the parent-world to the continuing advantage of the child.

THE PARENT AND THE RESEARCHER

The most popular parent-research subject has unquestionably been the mother of the emotionally disturbed child. Although an abundant literature exists to delineate the personality dynamics of the disturbed child's mother the emphasis has been placed upon tracing the components in the mother's makeup which could account for the behavioral status of the child. Little attention has been devoted to describing the specific nature of the child-rearing practices, which such mothers might employ in their day-by-day contacts with their child.

The parents of handicapped children have not fared as well in capturing the interest of the researcher. If a rank ordering is considered on the basis of frequency of researcher-interest in a given population, the parents of the mentally retarded child merit the second rank with cerebral palsy, deaf and blind following in order.

Two major topics seem to have interested the parent investigators in the field of mental retardation. One topic may be described as the parental attitude toward institutionalization represented in the discussions of Katz (1946) and Walker (1949), and the other may be considered as the parental attitude toward the mentally retarded child. On this second topic Grebler (1952), Wardell (1947), Schonell and Watts (1956), Rosen (1955), Stone (1948), and Goldstein (1956) have devoted attention to the parent attitudes.

Thorne and Andrews (1946) studied the incidence of what they called "unworthy" attitudes of parents towards mental defectives. Weingold and Hormuth (1935) and Coleman (1953) have contributed descriptions of counseling programs with parents of the mentally retarded.

Farber (1959), studying the parents of severely retarded children in relation to marital integration indices, concluded that among lower class parents there was a higher level of marital integration among families containing a severely retarded girl than in those containing a retarded boy. At middle-class level marital integration scores were not significantly influenced by the sex of the retarded child. Farber also showed that the mother's perception of the degree of dependence-independence in the child bore no relationship to marital integration. However, if the mother regards the retarded child as dependent there is an increased likelihood that adverse tensions will be noted in the normal siblings.

It is probably safe to state that, even among the parents of the mentally retarded, the family containing the severely retarded child has been favored over the parents of the moderately or mildly retarded child.

The same general approach seems to have been employed in reporting on the parents of the other disability groups with a concentration upon the attitudes, and not upon the actions, of parents. In the field of cerebral palsy the study of Shere (1954) has perhaps been the most frequently cited bit of research on parents. Shere found that parents of twins, one of whom had cerebral palsy tended to overprotect the handicapped twin and to make him a central figure in the family. There was also a tendency to expect the non-handicapped twin to assume more responsibility and to act more grown-up.

As a general commentary on the state of affairs in the area of research related to the parent of the handicapped child it must be noted that only a few studies dot the terrain of parenthood and the landscape is virtually barren.

OVERALL CONSIDERATIONS IN DESIGN

The first major question which prompted the design of the present study was simply, "What are the child-rearing practices among parents of handicapped children?" In a sense this simply became a matter of asking parents of handicapped children the same set of questions the Sears' group had asked of the mothers of non-handicapped kindergartners. This was a simple, straightforward search for basic information.

A second point of interest centered on the possibility that specific patterns in child-rearing might be associated with a given disability group. The questions might be phrased, "Is there a characteristic pattern among parents of deaf children which is significantly different from the parents of children with cerebral palsy or mongolism?" "Does the fact that a child has a severe muscular incoordination, such as cerebral palsy, cause a parent to do something different in basic practices from what a parent of a blind child might do?"

A third question might be stated, "What kind of parents use what kind of practices?" Here the interest lies in detailing some of the particular traits among parents which hopefully allow for some explanation as to why they might behave in the manner they have described in their protocols.

In making this broad survey of parental responses to questions on child-rearing and various related matters, the prospecting nature of such a venture was also contemplated. What promising veins might be located among this vast acreage of data which the assay of careful inspection might help define as claims to be staked out for deeper exploration? It was recognized that this first turning of the soil in the land of child-rearing among parents of handicapped children barely scratched the surface, but when one is prospecting, many diggings in many places offer greater potential than a few diggings in depth. Deeper and more intensive explorations can be made at some later date according to the promise obtained by first inspections.

While the emphasis is upon child-rearing practices, those actions or procedures initiated by parents to establish or change patterns of behavior in their children, it is believed that other considerations must be woven into the fabric to set these practices into proper perspective. The attitudes held by parents on a variety of topics were investigated for the possible relationship of these attitudes to motivating parents to take a particular way at a particular time. The regard that each spouse has for the other, the agreement that exists between parents on many questions, the happiness of a marriage and the role interpretation of each become a milieu in which child-rearing decisions take place.

The feelings and attitudes towards religion and expressed practices may add another shading. The possible influence of negative or positive attitudes of maternal and paternal relatives upon the rearing practices must also be considered. The differences between practices used for the handicapped child and those used for his normal siblings hold promise for defining the unique position of the handicapped child in the family portrait.

Consequently, the specific practice has been viewed as an expression of beliefs and attitudes from a composite background made up of the total experiential and cultural life-space of two parents. Many topics included in the investigation sequence may appear to bear little relationship to child-rearing even when a broad surround is considered. Perhaps, final analysis will show this impression to be true. Hunches, guesses, speculations and clinical recall prompted the inclusion of the broad spectrum included in this study.

In conducting research a standard strategy involves the formulation of one or more hypotheses which are constructed to be tested. The second step becomes a matter of designing some form of experiment to determine support or negation of the stated hypothesis. This approach characterizes most of the research study of today and the area of parent research has not escaped from this strategy. Consequently, most of the research has been designed to confirm or deny a preformulated hypothesis and, as such, has been a reflection of some theoretical bias. Construction and testing of hypotheses is generally considered to be a sophisticated level of research. At a primal level research is initiated by a simple question which an investigator is curious to have answered. It is this primary level of research which is reflected in this study. No particular hypothesis motivated the choice of instruments or the design of the questions. The only questions posed in this study were simply straightforward curiosities.

The first simple question is: "What *are* the child-rearing practices of parents of handicapped children?" The second question is related to the arbitrary selection of five major disability groups: "What differences, if any, exist between these groups?" A third question referred to the possibility of interviewing both the mother and the father and was stated as: "How similar or how different are mothers and fathers in their child-rearing decisions within each group and among groups?"

It was decided that questions at a higher level of sophistication might well evolve as data accumulated but that the initial effort should be a direct frontal approach to seeking answers to those simple questions. From one perspective this proved to be a wise choice for it permitted a full surge across many fronts on the parent terrain in a bombardment of inquiry. This in turn resulted in a massive collection of data which in some respects became an avalanche.

From a second perspective the simplicity of the initial set of questions proved to have been unwise. Inundated with thousands of bits of information the task of developing an organization for the data and the search to find meaningful ways to relate one bit to another became a monumental task. It must be admitted, at the outset that the task was not resolved to a high level of satisfaction. There are many segments of data which defied efforts to organize them into units for presentation. Other questions produced such a degree of variation in response that interpretive effort became an entangled confusing pursuit ending with a frustrated discontinuation.

Faced with the mass of data, reactions of joy and of frustration have swung on a pendulum during the past several years. There have been moments of happines in playing with the data but there have also been many moments of frustration and recrimination that hypotheses had not been more carefully thought out earlier in the game. The initial questions were simple in their naiveté. The eventual answers became exceedingly complex. It is prosaic to state but yet painfully true that the initiation, conduct and description of this study has been a significant learning experience for all concerned. Many times in jest, but progressively more in earnest, the thought has occurred that the wisest course of action would have been to devote these chapters to the trials and tribulations of the project or the "Odyssey of M-3750." It is a story which could have considerable significance to other researchers—but it must be postponed.

The target for fixation is the description of child-rearing practices and tangential temptations must be resisted. The effort is merely descriptive and represents a "first pass" at the data. The lode will be workable for many years to come. The professionals in the fields of special education and rehabilitation will find much to interest them.

This project was conceived on a hot August afternoon in 1959 and began the long, hard, "uterine-cortical" development of being shaped into an acceptable document ready for delivery into life if all the perinatal and postnatal circumstances of national decision were favorable. Fortunately, the project's pregnancy was rewarded with a thumping, brisk, live birth. This was only the beginning, however. It had to be nourished by warmth and empathy and guided carefully through its infant stages. Sometimes harshness was called for, some tendencies had to be curbed, some directions had to be detoured and some negative sanctions had to be enforced.

Its initial locomotive efforts eventually became a reasonably adequate gait. Its early vocal efforts eventually emerged as fully formed sentences and interrogations. It has painfully, joyfully, timidly and courageously moved along through its life being shaped by criticism and praise, some mild rejections, and much insistence. It has now reached an adolescent stage—not fully refined, not as mature as desired, but, nevertheless, ready to move into the cold, cruel world for better or worse.

From a parental standpoint, there is doubt that all has been done that could have been done, there is hesitancy that perhaps it is not quite ready to face the world, but despite all these feelings there is the recognition of the compelling and impelling momentum of development which inevitably thrusts the adolescent into the world. Here, then, is the offspring clothed in tables, comments and discussions, somewhat weak, somewhat strong—accompanied in its ventures by a fond parental hope, a feeling of cautious pride—and a quiet prayer.

Chapter 2

CONDUCTING THE STUDY

THIS STUDY was conducted during a three-year period from 1960 to 1962. Parents, known to have a handicapped child labeled as one of the five diagnostic categories, and whose child was between the ages of four and ten years were considered potential participants. The study was limited to families living within the geographical limits of Milwaukee County.

PROCEDURE

A special letter describing the nature of the project, its aims and objectives was prepared. This letter described in general terms the demand which would be made upon the parents, and was composed in such manner as to be useful throughout the study for all groups.

A medical data card was designed for mailing to the child's attending physician, requesting several items of diagnostic information. To avoid the problem of requesting information from a variety of medical specialists, each parent was asked to identify "the doctor who knows most about your child." While case files at the agency frequently contained extensive medical reports from which such information might have been drawn, the uniformity of a simple data card for all cases was considered more economical.

This procedure was also viewed as an opportunity to acquaint the child's physician with the nature of the investigation. Doctors were invited to request further information about the project if they so desired. Many doctors *did* express interest, and were given a more detailed description. No effort was made to arrange for a current medical examination on each case, since the principal interest was centered on the diagnostic label of the child and not upon current health status.

Letters of invitation were sent to the families, inviting the mother to participate in the research study. A return card indicating parental agreement was enclosed for parent signature and mailing. The original effort was not directed at obtaining both mother and father consent since it was felt that a more successful attempt could be made to gain father participation if the mother could serve to prepare a father for his involvement after she had completed her effort.

When affirmative replies were received, appointments were scheduled. Personal phone calls were made to those cases who did not reply to the first invitation. Some had misplaced the invitation; others had forgotten to mail it, and still others requested further information before agreeing to participate.

The First Phase

The affirmative groups were then scheduled for participation in the first phase of the investigation—the completion of self-administered questionnaires, tests, and a variety of scales. This was arranged in group sessions of four to ten mothers. During the first session they received a further orientation regarding the nature of the investigation, goals and aims of the project, and the extent of desired participation. The group sessions were usually scheduled to cover a two hour period. The number of self-administered forms involved in the study usually required two sessions before completion. Because of variations in time availability of the mothers and differences in speed of completion, some mothers completed all the forms at one sitting, while others returned for additional periods.

The test materials were presented and described to the mothers by two experienced group test administrators. The group person was always available to the individual mothers of the group to clarify any difficulties encountered as they filled out the many forms.

The Second Phase

As soon as a mother completed the group series, a schedule was arranged for the clinical interview. Most mothers completed the interview in three to four hours, scheduled in time blocks most convenient to them. Whenever possible the research appointment schedule was arranged to coincide with the mother's regular visits to the clinic for her child's physical, occupational, and speech therapy sessions.

The Inclusion of the Fathers

In the original design of the project it was considered to be extremely important that the fathers would be included in the study of child-rearing practices. During the initial stages of the project the letter inviting the parents to participate was directed to both parents. It soon became apparent that the mothers had to be enlisted as allies in gaining the active participation of their spouses.

The fathers seemed quite willing at the outset to delegate the data-giving process to the mothers. A change in strategy vastly improved the extent of father participation. During the course of the clinical interview the interviewer discussed with the mother the importance of gaining the father's viewpoint in order to place the child-rearing data in proper perspective. The mothers then became the actual recruiters of the father populations. In general, one might say that the mothers did a creditable job of recruiting.

In ten cases the father was not available for participation. Three fathers were deceased, two were separated from the family, three moved out of city to other employment before the study was completed and one was working in another town during the time of the study. One father was omitted because the wife reported that he could only respond to a manual sign language and none of the interviewers held such competency. One father suffered a heart attack shortly before he was invited to participate so the invitation was withdrawn. Consequently, ten fathers could be classified as unavailable for study.

Seventy-three per cent of the available fathers (121) participated in the study. Sixteen fathers flatly refused to participate in any manner. Eight fathers were unable to participate because they operated small businesses or were working at two jobs, and consequently were free from work only after 9 P.M. or 10 P.M. daily or on Saturday evenings or Sundays. No effort was made to intrude upon this limited free time. Three fathers agreed to participate, and consistently failed to appear at appointment times. Two stepfathers completed the group form sequence, but were not invited to the intensive interview.

Considering the sixteen fathers who flatly refused and the three who refused passively by consistently failing appointments, only eleven per cent of the fathers were uncooperative.

Extent of Father Participation

The highest percentage of father participation occurred in the organic, mongoloid and deaf groups where four out of five fathers completed the two sequences in the study. The recruitment of fathers in the cerebral palsy group was not as high. In some measure, the lesser percentage may be attributed to the fact that the parents of children with cerebral palsy were the first study group of the project and the invitational procedures for fathers were improved for subsequent groups. The comparatively reduced percentage in the blind group does not yield a specific explanation when all of the facts are studied. The limited participation of blind group fathers was felt to be accidental and not significant of any particular factor (Table 1).

TABLE 1

PERCENTAGE OF FATHERS IN EACH POPULATION
WHO PARTICIPATED IN THE PROJECT

Cerebral Palsy	Organic	Mongoloid	Blind	Deaf	Total
66%	78%	80%	57%	80%	73%

THE INTERVIEW AND QUESTIONNAIRES

Source and Composition

The basic model on which the clinical interview was based was that used by Sears, Maccoby and Levin (1957) in their study of child-rearing among 379 mothers of kindergarten children in the New England area. In large measure the interview used in the present study was a direct replication of the Sears' interview complete to exact language. Barsch (1959) utilized a questionnaire technique to elicit information of various sorts from the parents of 119 "brain-injured" children. General forms, concepts and areas of investigation which were believed to be pertinent for this study were extracted and modified. In addition to these two sources a number of areas were introduced which were judged to hold particular pertinence for the general area of the handicapped.

A basic interview and questionnaire sequence was agreed upon and utilized in collecting data on both the mothers and fathers of children with cerebral palsy. Analysis of the interview protocols led to the elimination of certain items and the remodeling of some questions into checklists for group administration. Once the revisions had been made the final form was used for the other four populations.

Several scales employed by Farber (1959) in his study of parents of mentally retarded children were also included in the final instrument series. Those forms utilized in this study which are not specifically borrowed *in toto* from a previous investigator were originated for this study.

Structure of Interview

The first portion of the interview was devoted to questions of a routine, mechanical and factual nature reviewing the general infancy background information which have been elicited many times from the parents at each new clinic, school, dispensary, etc. This was judged to be nonthreatening in content and at a stage of memorization where its recital had been practiced on many occasions. It was felt that this series would introduce a general perceptual set for the interview, suggest the nature of things to come, and serve as a vehicle for the clinical interviewer and the parent to establish a relationship.

The second segment of the interview concerned itself with questions related to immediate past practices in relation to feeding, sleep, toileting, play, etc. Wherever it seemed feasible the parent was asked to compare such practices with those employed with siblings so that a general pattern of similarities and differences might be drawn. In this section parents were asked to specify techniques, explore their motivations, account for their modifications and evaluate their actions. Mothers were asked to comment on the father's role in immediate past practices and fathers were asked to comment on their role as well as to evaluate their wives in these areas. The responses tapped areas of unrehearsed thought and represented the first plunge into feelings which were not so readily verbalized. This first invasion of privacy called for a critical evaluation of what practices had been tried, why they had been tried, what results had been attained and the parental feeling of effectiveness of the various procedures.

The final portion of the interview posed questions about current practices, attitudes and personal feelings on specific topics. Here the parents were asked to comment on how the general business of daily living was being managed today, to describe and evaluate their spouses, to talk about religion and child sex behavior, their expectations for the future, their own feelings of adequacy and other more intimate content.

Each successive stage was structured to probe more deeply into the personal dynamics of the parent relying upon the growing relationship of confidence, trust and intimacy between the clinical interviewer and the parent, to free the parents for a more intimate exploration of themselves and their feelings.

The analysis of the interview records, interviewers' impressions and general evaluative discussion by the research staff indicated that this progressive phenomenon did, in fact, take place. The relationship between interviewer and parent did become stronger, more confidential and trusting as the sessions continued and bonds of empathy grew between them. Almost all parents looked upon the interviewer as a close friend by the time the entire sequence was completed.

For many of the parents the perceptual set of giving information in a research project became a secondary consideration to the personal dynamics, to the excitement and threat of systematic self-appraisal, to the revelations being experienced in relation to their own feelings and to the eagerness with which they reported changes in thinking which had taken place during the intervals between interview sessions.

There was a general characteristic of unfolding or release in almost all of the interviews when they were evaluated in terms of the three levels of response depth. Some parents openly expressed this release by commenting that they had "never been so confidential with anyone before" or "have never talked over such things with anyone before" or "I've never told this to anyone before."

The clinical interviewers, empathically identifying with the parent, sharing the various moments of truth and the self-exposure or self-accusation progressively from start to finish, were understandably distressed by the necessity to code a response in some arbitrary manner and convert it mechanically to some statistical form. It left a feeling that the lifeblood of the response had been drained out, the tone had gone and the empty barren statistic remained.

The Father Interview and Checklist Sequence

The interview structure employed with the fathers was essentially a duplication of the mother interview, asking the same set of questions to ascertain the extent of agreement between the husband and wife on common topics. The same set of checklists were also administered to the fathers with some minor revisions in pronouns to make the forms applicable to the husband. No forms were completed by the fathers which did not have a counterpart among the forms employed with the mothers.

Consequently the general investigative set was not one of establishing portraits of fathers as unique individuals in their own right, but rather to define relative extents of agreements and disagreements. It is recognized that the structure of the interview did not do justice to the portrait of identity for fathers. The father has essentially been neglected in most studies of child-rearing. It is unlikely that investigators have minimized his potential but have rather found it difficult to capture him for research purposes. Some of the naiveté which will be noted in the general handling of the fathers as research subjects must be attributed to the absence of guidelines in the field. To cast him only in the role of "agree-disagree" may set him as an assistant to the mother in child-rearing, as a subordinate or secondary individual. Such was not the original intent, but when the final data were assembled it seemed clear that the slant had been in this direction.

In the original planning there was little disagreement among the research staff that the mothers would tolerate a time consuming process more readily than the fathers. There was never any doubt that a large number of mothers would accept the invitation but the extent of father participation was open to wide speculation. The actual number represented in the final tabulations exceeded expectations even though many readers may regard this as a small percentage.

Consequently the father interview was initially structured as a reduced version of the mother interview. This would take less time and might insure fuller participation. The actual experience in the interviewing clearly proved the fallacy of this reasoning. The fathers were as ready to talk as were the mothers. For many of them, the experience was the first opportunity they had received to "tell their side of the story." They welcomed the chance and would gladly have "given" more if the structure had called for it.

Range of Questionnaires

The group form sequence consisted of seventeen questionnaires described below. Each was designed to allow the parent to place a check mark next to the statement or item which pertained to their situation. In addition to these questionnaires the California Psychological Inventory and the Parent Attitude Research Inventory were completed by each parent.

Socio-economic Form: This form covered areas of income, home ownership, number of siblings, etc.

Family History—Mother/Father: A form relating to the family background of the mother and father was included in the battery.

Family Social Patterns: This form was comprised of statements related to the extent of family togetherness. Family visiting, rituals, recreations, etc. were included, and parents were asked to indicate the frequency with which each activity occurred.

Courtship and Marriage: The same form used by Farber (1959) in his study of parents was inserted into this battery.

Neighbor Relationships: This form was also identical to that used in the Farber study and related to the general attitudes and practices of parents in relation to neighbors.

Explanation of Neighbors: This form contained a series of statements related to various ways parents might discuss the problems of this child with the neighbors. The form was previously used by Barsch (1959) in a study of parents of brain-damaged children.

Child's Activities—Hobbies—Interests: A series of child interests and organizational affiliations were included to tap the area of leisure time behavior. This form was specifically designed for this study.

Hobby, Activity and Interests of Mother and Father: These two forms were devised for this study to attain some finding on the range and character of the general outside interest patterns of mothers and fathers.

My Relatives and My Husband's Relatives: These two checklists were modified from the previous study by Barsch and were a means of determining the attitudes of relatives on both sides of the family in relation to this child.

Child Behavior Checklists: This form represents a modification of one used by Farber, and lists a series of achievements and behaviors in children.

Play Behavior with Others: This form contains a series of statements related to a child's response in play situations with other children, and attempts to evaluate the general play adjustment which has been observed by parents.

Sibling Attitudes: A series of statements reflecting various attitudes, behaviors and reactions on the part of brothers and sisters was given to parents, to allow for checking of those statements which were pertinent to their particular family situations.

Communication Patterns: This form, devised for this study, contained a series of descriptive statements related to reception, expression and association of language. Parents were asked to check those statements which applied to their child.

Chores: This form contained a series of questions related to parent attitudes towards teaching children a sense of responsibility by assigning household chores and listed a series of possibilities. It also contained questions related to the practices of giving a regular weekly allowance.

Changes in Mother Since the Birth of this Child: This form was modified in four different versions to allow the mother and father to evaluate each other as well as themselves. This form was first used by Farber (1959).

Attitudes Towards Animals: To determine the incidence of pets, the child's fearfulness or acceptance, and the child's responsibility toward the pet, a series of questions and statements in this area were devised for parent checking. This form has been dropped from the battery for subsequent groups.

Handicap Ranking Form: Ten handicapping conditions were listed and parents were asked to rank order each handicap on the basis of "Which handicap do you feel is the most serious handicap a child might have?" The rank order of their child's handicap was the major concern. This form has also been administered to two thousand other people, including parents of normal children, nurses, therapists, college students and teachers. Comparative analysis has been conducted. This form was designed especially for this study (see Chapter 16).

Definitions of a Child-Rearing Practice

For purposes of this investigation, an operational definition of a child-rearing practice was employed as follows:

A technique devised by a parent and employed actively or passively in relationship to the child, in order to accomplish a specific change in the child which the parent deems desirable.

When a parent is confronted with the need to alter a child's behavior, to halt a given piece of objectionable behavior, to bring about a more complex behavior, teach a skill or initiate a pattern, the parent chooses a particular course of action to accomplish this goal. The parent's original hypothesis is that a particular effort will bring about the desired change. Whether or not this necessarily results in the achievement of a goal, the parental effort constitutes a rearing practice. Implied in such consideration is the component of conscious choice on the part of a parent. To remain passive in the face of certain dilemmas is considered as fulfilling the criteria of a practice as well as if the parent acts (provided that the parent chooses passivity as a means to an end). The goal is always determined by the parent.

While parents in the interviews at times left the impression that they had given little or no thought to a particular practice, it has been assumed that some conscious process, not currently recalled, did, in fact, govern their behavior at the time.

Setting

With few exceptions, the interviews were conducted in individual offices of the Milwaukee Easter Seal Child Development Center in a series of sessions. Most of the mothers who had children enrolled in various therapy programs at the Center were interviewed and tested at times when they brought their child to the Center. Few cases were able to complete the data sequences in one setting for either the group forms or the clinical interview. In those instances where it was attempted, the four-hour process was found to be excessively exhausting to both the interviewer and the parent.

As a general rule, the group forms were completed in two sessions of an hour and a half each, and the interviews spanned four or five one-hour sessions. While the actual data collection process via interview was estimated at an average of four hours per parent approximately 35 per cent of the cases spent more than eight hours in the interview sequence. This additional time was occasioned by the specific use of interview time to seek personal counseling on matters generated by particular questions in the interview.

Source of the Populations

A large percentage of the cases (81 per cent) could be classified as a "captive—beholden" population since they were the mothers and fathers of children who were either currently being served by the center or had been served in the recent past. The entire case file was screened to select cases who were within the desired age range and represented one of the diagnostic groups involved. Once this screening had taken place an invitation was sent to every case, and 95 per cent of these cases agreed to participate.

During the second and third years of the project, it became necessary to recruit cases to bring some of the categories to a suitable number. Two resources were used for this purpose. The day camp roster for 1960 of the Easter Seal Holler Park Day Camp was screened for age and category and invitations were sent to parents. Next, the directors of special education departments in five school systems of metropolitan Milwaukee were asked to help in recruiting populations of parents of deaf and blind children. All agreed to write a covering letter endorsing the project, to be included in the invitation letter, to all parents in classes for the deaf or the visually handicapped. The letters were mailed by the administrative offices of the schools with requests to return agreement cards to the research project office. In this manner an additional thirty-six cases were obtained.

The cases recruited from the day camp roster and the public and parochial school special classes represent the nineteen per cent of unknown cases. None of these children had ever received service from the center.

Interview Personnel

In the early stages of organization, the possibility of obtaining the data by using graduate students or people with interviewing experience in other fields was entertained. A pilot venture in this vein suggested that certain therapeutic aspects were inherent in the interview situation. The role of the interviewer was reconstructed to allow for clinical response to such dynamics. This required the employment of clinically sophisticated interviewers.

In the restructuring process, the interviewer was expected to be sensitive to parental anxieties, to deal with these anxieties as they were noted if clinical judgment dictated for the best interests of the interview, to allow the parent to explore certain feelings generated by the questions, to permit tangential material to be introduced by the parent and generally to respond clinically if, in the best judgment of the interviewer, such response was warranted. This reformulation of the interviewer role required the assignment of clinically oriented and trained professionals to this project.

This modification required a reconsideration of the total time sequence for each interview. Because the clinically trained people had more experience in working with various nuances in personal response, the interviews became more dynamic and less mechanical. It became obvious that more and more parents began to use the interview situation therapeutically. This occasioned some delay in the mechanical process of moving quickly from one question to the next throughout the series and increased the total time necessary to complete each case. The general enrichment of the data, the on-the-spot service to the parent, and the highly positive evaluation of the total experience by a large majority of the parents, indicates that this decision to reformulate the interviewer role was mutually profitable—to the project and to the parent.

The bulk of the final interviewing was conducted by two persons, a medical social worker, male; and a clinical psychologist, female. In order to accommodate the fathers and conduct interviews during evening hours, four additional people were added to the research staff for part-time work. Two school social workers and two psychologists were added for this purpose. Training in this particular interview method, and orientation to the needs of this project, were carried out by the medical social worker. The two full time interviewers participated in all planning, review, and revision conferences throughout the project and assisted in the analysis of data.

Interview Procedure

For the 177 cases who participated in the full interview sequence, the assigned clinical interviewer studied the completed group forms on each case, noting omissions, inconsistencies and response areas suggesting a need for further probing before scheduling the interview appointments. In this manner, during the first session, the omissions were fulfilled, the inconsistencies clarified and the necessary probing accomplished before the actual interview began. This procedure also allowed the interviewer to acquire the broad tone of the case and to familiarize himself with general background data.

It has been stated that hindsight is remarkably accurate at 20/20 and this is especially pertinent to a number of revisions which were made in basic procedures in collecting these data. In retrospect, the decision to forego the tape recording of verbatim response in favor of interviewers manually transcribing responses proved economically wise but "data poor."

Many times during the course of the study, the interviewers expressed their great concern that a valuable piece of datum had been lost because the parent talked too fast, pouring forth multiple paragraphs to express a particular thought at a pace which the interviewer could not transcribe. Such was the continual frustration of the interviewers throughout the study. Their concern was for the loss of shadings and nuances which they felt necessary to the painting of a realistic portrait of the parent of the handicapped child. Their concern was genuine and the loss did, in fact, occur. It is, however, a loss which must be accepted in view of the decisions which had to be made.

Clinically oriented interviewers were constantly frustrated by a need to code a response and prepare it for statistical treatment. They resisted forging a dynamic response into a neat category. Despite the resistance and the frustrations, the forging process took place. If, in the process, some of the human richness has been squeezed out of the ore of the response, this also must be suffered as a loss.

Some data were lost because of a word. Despite endless hours of refining semantics to avoid ambiguity or distortion, and to maintain simple grammatical constructions which would not be perceived differentially by parents, the assembly line of protocols which began to develop during the intense period of the study gradually revealed semantic flaws in various portions of the interviews. The revision activity could actually have continued up to the final moment of data collection, but the painful exercise of strict discipline saved the instruments from being tampered with once the final form had been set after the Cerebral Palsy group was completed.

There were also a number of other losses, but the recounting of such details represents a painful retrospective analysis and is best left dormant. These losses have finally been balanced into some state of comfort by a shrug of the shoulders, a flick of the wrist and the gay statement, *"C'est le research."*

None of the mothers or fathers openly refused to answer any question in the entire group form and interview sequence. There was no apparent perception that the questions represented an invasion of privacy. While some parents hedged or rambled on, sometimes missing the point of the question, we did not feel that these were deliberate efforts to evade the implications of any of the questions.

Cooperation of Parents

The cooperative attitude of the parents was impressive. On the whole, the parents were unusually faithful in maintaining their appointment schedules. A minimum amount of cancellations occurred. The parents gave freely of their time and appeared to be genuinely interested in providing information. Most of them openly expressed their motivation to contribute to a better understanding in the future. Many indicated that they felt a debt of gratitude for past services rendered by the agency and consider their voluntary research effort as a form of payment on the debt.

Only one mother was encountered who could be classified as openly hostile to the entire interview situation. It was later learned that her husband had forced her to volunteer after she had initially rejected the invitation!

Some parents commented that this was the first time in the life of the child that they had ever sat down and systematically talked about the child's problem from so many vantage points. In some instances, the experience caused both a mother and a father to review their responses to similar questions in the quiet evening hours in their own home, and to find new depths of understanding and empathy between them that they had not experienced before in relation to the child's problem.

Some parents have expressed interest in the findings of this study in the months or years that have passed since their participation, but for the most part, the parents seem to feel that they have discharged an obligation, and rarely discuss or question the eventual results of the total study. Throughout the years of actual interviewing, almost all parents accepted the explanation that the results of their personal contribution would be submerged into the totality of the scientific investigation and that they would never actually learn their own scorings on any of the tests, or how their own responses compared with those of other parents.

The two instruments which provoked the greatest interest, and perhaps the greatest anxiety, were the Parent Attitude Research Instrument and the California Psychological Inventory. These were the two instruments which held no direct relationship to their child and were perceived by all of the parents as tests. The questions of the parents always centered on the same topic, that of questioning if their performance on these two tests had shown whether or not "they were normal."

Analysis of the general dynamics of the total set of interview records revealed that parents had used the interview experience in a variety of ways. Some found the interview to be an opportunity to discharge a great deal of hostile feeling towards physicians, schools, therapists and, in some instances, their spouses. Others found the interview to be a convenient setting for working through doubts and anxieties about specific aspects of their child's problem. Still others, used the systematic process of reviewing practices, beliefs and attitudes as a means of formulating and expressing some generalizations about various aspects of family dynamics which they had never before perceived to be related.

The unscrambling of various interpretations of their child's problem, and the clarification of some misconceptions, became a dynamic of the interview for other parents. Several parents expressed the feeling that the interview had served to "recharge their own batteries." Taking a systematic and organized look at their problem after many years of prosaic living caused them to look anew at their problems in a more positive manner. Since the vast majority of parents who participated had been served in some manner by the agency conducting the study there was a certain feeling of discharging an obligation involved in their cooperation.

Several mothers who were aware that their husbands would also participate used the interview opportunity to express the hope that the husband's experience would serve to resolve many of the dilemmas which existed between them and their spouses—not only about issues related to the handicapped child, but also other personal marital problems.

In the same vein, it soon became clear that some of the fathers had agreed to participate in the hope that they would be able to present their side of the story and enlist the help of the interviewer in "straightening out" their wives. Some fathers expressed this thought openly during the interview, but others cloaked the expression in many ways which allowed for interpreting the same request by clinically reading between the lines. While this was not the basic motivation for all fathers, it happened often enough to deserve special comment.

There was a marked difference in the quality of responses obtained from the parents of the deaf and the blind in the interview sequence. There were no refusals to respond to any of the questions asked, but the response pattern was more mechanical, showing less depth of feeling and less groping for meaning. Several explanations may be offered to account for this.

Parents of the deaf and the blind generally have little occasion to become acquainted with a clinical orientation to their problem, i.e., they have not learned to explore their feelings in an interview process as have the parents of the cerebral palsied, the organic, and the mongol. For almost all parents of the deaf and blind, the diagnosis of the child's problem was very specific, direct, and early. The problem is clear-cut and obvious, and is not beclouded by many intangibles. In the other groups, the problem is complicated by anxieties over mental retardation, perceptual disturbances, behavior disorders, delays in diagnosis, seizures, etc.

Another explanation lies in the fact that the parents of the deaf and blind in most cases represented an unknown population to the agency conducting the investigation. A few cases had been psychologically evaluated and worked with at some point in their development, but all others in these two groups have been specially recruited for this study. The parents knew of the agency from general community reputation, but had not previously had personal contact. Consequently, their response to the invitation to participate was perhaps more broadly philanthropic than that of the others. Almost all others came, in part, because they held positive feelings towards the professional clinicians associated with the study based upon helpful contacts in the past. This was not true of the deaf and blind population who came, in most cases, because the project was personally endorsed by school authorities whom they admired and respected.

The Five Populations

The general spectrum of handicapping conditions in childhood is composed of many different disease levels. An investigation of the child-rearing practices among sample groups of parents representing a large number of the spectrum was considered impractical. Five populations, considered to be the most representative of the total disability firmament, were selected for study. The populations are not sharply defined. Those who demand such precision will, undoubtedly, be disappointed.

During the early stages of the project there was a fond hope that the five populations might be secured in reasonably equal numbers. Unfortunately, this hope was never realized. The variability in the numbers of cases representing each handicapped presented some problems in the interpretation of the data and must be taken into account.

The category of "mental retardation" was not considered as a group title since reduced intellectual functioning might be associated with any of the five populations. Further elaboration on each of the populations follows.

The Organic Group

The definition of *brain-injury in* children has been the subject of much controversy during the past fifteen years. The question of whether or not a specific set of behavior characteristics are associated with a specific form of brain-injury remains unanswered. Various terms are preferred in various clinics and among various groups. In some quarters, *neurologically impaired* is favored. In other quarters, *children with psychoneurologic learning disorders* is applied. *Children with perceptual handicaps, organically damaged, brain-damaged, neurologically handicapped,* and *brain-injured* are all terms which have found some usage. Specific neurologic damage is frequently difficult to assess.

In view of the nationwide controversy over the terms and the associated characteristics, some operational definitions were demanded for purposes of this study. First, it was established that each case assigned to the organic group had been diagnosed as brain-injured by a physician. No effort was made to ascertain specific neurologic findings since the variability in this area would tend to pose a severe classification problem. Second, it was established that the parent was operating under the impression that such was the child's diagnosis. Whatever the accuracy of the term or the diagnosis might be, and despite the professional controversy, the fact remained that the parent perceived the child as brain-injured and presumably acted in accord with that perception in the child-rearing process.

None of the children of this group had significant problems in sight or hearing and none had a neuromuscular problem of sufficient intensity to warrant a diagnosis of cerebral palsy. Some were very hyperactive, some were not. An inspection of the clinical case files revealed that all of the children had some form of perceptual disturbance in varying degrees and all were described by examining psychologists as having significant learning problems which interfered with school learning in whatever school situation they were enrolled, or would be expected to experience major adjustment difficulties when they became eligible for school enrollment.

While this scarcely represents a clean set of characteristics for scientific purposes, the broad survey component of the objectives of this study must be kept in mind. The emphasis was upon the *parent*. Perhaps a more precise grouping may have yielded more profound results. It was felt, however, that a broad sweep across the category would produce a number of promising leads among this group which might prompt a more detailed and precise investigation at some later time.

According to these definitions 123 cases were assigned to this group. Sixty-five of these cases were fully interviewed while the remaining fifty-eight contributed data only to the questionnaire and group testing sequence.

The Blind Group

This sample is the smallest number of the five populations. A total of twenty cases in which the child was medically and educationally classified as blind responded favorably to the invitation to participate in the project. Since the recruitment process occurred in cooperation with public school personnel responsible for classes for the blind a specific selection factor operated in obtaining this sample. As nearly as could be determined from community estimates of incidence, the obtained cases represented about 70 per cent of the potential population of family resident blind children attending public school in Milwaukee County.

No effort was made to invite parents of blind children who had been enrolled in the State School for the Blind since this represented a population of handicapped children living away from home. The decreasing incidence of retrolental fibroplasia has dramatically reduced the number of potential cases in the community. Only fourteen cases participated in the full sequence of both interview and checklists.

The Cerebral Palsy Group

The main reference point for the identification of the seventy total cases in the cerebral palsy group was the child's case file in the Cerebral Palsy Clinic of Milwaukee. The case files were inspected to obtain the specific classification and degree of severity as it had been recorded in the child's case history. No more precise methods were considered. If the child's case file indicated that the child had been seen for a diagnostic examination and a diagnosis of cerebral palsy had been ruled out by the examining physician, the case was shifted to one of the other applicable categories in keeping with the diagnostic conclusions of the physicians. No effort was made to obtain specific numbers of each major type of cerebral palsy. The distribution of types in the final sample was accidental.

The Mongoloid Group

The diagnosis of mongolism usually presents little problem to the physician and the condition has been carefully studied for many years. In general, one might view this condition as being precisely defined.

Historically, the child with mongolism has been considered as an institutional entity and parents have traditionally sought to place the child in such a setting at a relatively early age. However, the present generation has come to accept the possibility that the mongoloid child might well remain in the home and thrive within the community. The pendulum of social thought now appears to be swinging to an opposite position from traditional thought, and increasing efforts are being made to retain the child within the community. Community programs at a preschool level, and the emergence of the educational concept of public school programs for the trainable child, have done much to support the pendulum swing.

Thirty-nine mothers of mongoloid children agreed to participate in the present study. Twenty-five of these completed both the interview and group form sequences, while the remaining fourteen were only able to complete the questionnaires.

No particular effort was made to differentiate any specific trait patterns among the mongoloid group. The attending physician's statement of such diagnosis served as the criteria for assignment to that population. Once again, the major interest was in the fact that the parent was confronted with the rearing of a mongoloid child.

The Deaf Group

All children represented in the deaf group were recruited from public school classes for deaf children and as such students they had already met criteria for enrollment. In this respect, they prepresented the most homogeneous sample of the five.

Twenty such cases were discussed by parents who completed the two data collection units while four additional cases are represented only in the group questionnaire data.

No mother in this group had a hearing problem. One of the fathers was reported to be deaf and able to communicate manually but not orally. Twelve more mothers of deaf children agreed to participate in the project, but they presented a dilemma. All of these indicated that they were deaf and would require an interviewer skilled in manual communication. None of the members of the project staff held such competence, and after some discussion with several authorities in this field, it was agreed that these twelve cases would not be included.

Consequently, the data from the parents of deaf children must be considered to be telling only a half of the child-rearing story. The other half of the story is yet to be learned from parents who themselves are deaf. Just a brief consideration of the possible comparisons between hearing and nonhearing parents offers an intriguing field of investigation.

The data in this study, however, must be evaluated in the light of the fact that all parents who testified were not themselves deaf.

Comparisons with Sears (1957) Study

The study of a normal control group was not included within the scope of this present study. The only study found in the literature which has any degree of comparability was the one reported by Sears *et al.* (1957) in which sequences of questions asked of mothers of kindergarten age children had been incorporated directly into the interview utilized with the parents of handicapped children. While no brief is held for the substitution of Sears data, in lieu of a specific control group for the present study, some comparisons with the Sears data will afford some perspective to the findings among the parents of the handicapped. From time to time, throughout the text, the findings of Sears will be compared to these findings where the statements of questions were identical.

Interviewed and Partial Cases

One hundred and seventy-seven mothers completed the full interview sequence. An additional ninety-eight cases completed the group form and questionnaire sequence. During the early stages of the study, major revisions were made in the organization of the clinical interview, which made it impossible to equate the interview questions used on the pilot groups to those used subsequently with final groups. This required the deletion of seventy-eight interviews from the final tabulation and analysis. The remaining twenty mothers did not complete the interview sequence because of illness, new child deliveries, change of residence, etc. However, since the group forms and questionnaires remained stable throughout the study, the responses of these ninety-eight mothers were included in the tabulation and analysis of data obtained from group forms.

Two general populations of varying size are utilized throughout this text to present the data. A basic sample of 177 cases plus an expanded sample of 275 cases were included in the final analysis of data where appropriate.

PROCESSING OF DATA

The information contained in the interview battery received differential handling depending on the source. The responses to the interpersonal interview itself were categorized, coded, and tallied. On the group forms, composite scores were derived wherever possible or else a straightforward tally was done on various items.

Interpersonal Interview

Processing of Data

The initial reading of a representative sample of responses to a given item provided a preliminary series of categories for the item. These categories were added to, if a sufficient number of noncategorizeable responses warranted this; or, the categories were reduced if a different conceptualization of the underlying scheme of categorizing made such a course more meaningful. Data such as birth weight, age of achieving a certain skill, etc., were categorized on an *a priori* basis.

Two people independently categorized a response to a given item. When agreement was obtained, the classification of response stood as categorized. When the two workers did not independently agree on how to categorize the response, a third person (a research assistant) discussed the discrepancy with the two until complete agreement was reached.

Group Forms

Two of the group forms, the CPI and the PARI, were standardized instruments and were scored in the manner dictated by the respective instructions. The responses to a certain number of the group forms such as those pertaining to demographic group memberships, parent groups, etc., were amenable to a simple description using frequency distributions or tables. The group forms were reduced to a composite score based on *a priori* assumptions regarding the underlying dimension or dimensions. Still other group forms of an experimental nature had been used previously by other workers and a composite score based on the author's scoring scheme was computed.

Analysis of Data

Responses to interview items and other discreet data were tabulated in contingency tables. Where it was deemed important and was possible, means and standard deviations or medians and ranges were reported. The type of measurement and the shape of underlying distribution dictated the use of either parametric or nonparametric statistics in testing hypotheses.

Chapter 3

THE DEMOGRAPHY OF THE FIVE POPULATIONS

THE SCENIC BACKGROUND to the interpretation of these data on child-rearing practices must be sketched on a canvas of demographic characteristics for both the parents and the children represented in this study. Since the simple identification that a child has a handicap has little meaning unless the details of the impairment to function are carefully described, a number of descriptive tables related to defining the child populations will be presented and discussed.

The limitations of language in presenting a clear picture of a handicapped child are well recognized. These demographic elaborations may at least serve the same purpose as a rough charcoal sketch— as a working model to which the actual data adds the color, shading and tone that will make the children emerge as dynamic beings. The same rationale is offered for the extensive detailing of characteristics of the parents. The sketching of the children can start the mural.

THE CHILDREN

Mean Ages of the Children

During the early stages of the study it was decided to narrow the age range for the total population to a six year span from ages four to ten. This span was selected for a number of reasons. First, this span permitted a coverage of the early years of schooling and suggested that all parents were probably fully aware of the diagnosis by that time. Secondly, the major events in child-rearing would either be current or comparatively recent and parental recall and report were more likely to be accurate. This decision on the age range necessitated the elimination of a number of cases in each population because the children were over age.

The fifty-three cases in the cerebral palsy group, the sixty-five cases in the organic group and the twenty cases in the deaf group yielded a uniform mean age for the children (Table 2). The fourteen cases in the blind group represented a slightly older group. The incidence of nine- and ten-year-olds was minimal in all age groups. The concentration was clearly within the four to eight year range. Statistical analysis on all tables reported in this text has shown that variations in findings were never significantly related to differences in age between eight- and ten-year-olds in any of the populations.

TABLE 2
MEAN AGES OF THE CHILDREN REPRESENTED IN THE
FIVE STUDY POPULATIONS

	Cerebral Palsy	Organic	Mongoloid	Blind	Deaf
Mean ages	6.3	6.7	5.2	7.9	6.4

Number of Children in Each Family

Little or no difference existed among the five groups on the mean number of children within these families. The average family for all groups consisted of three children (Table 3). Consequently, no particular handicap appeared to be of any significance in relation to family size.

TABLE 3
MEAN NUMBER OF CHILDREN IN EACH FAMILY

	Cerebral Palsy	Organic	Mongoloid	Blind	Deaf
Mean No. of children in each family	3.1	3.0	3.5	3.8	3.5

Ordinal Position of the Handicapped Child

One third of the cases were first children, one third were second born children and one third were third or fourth born. Only in the organic group did there appear to be any shifting of the distribution into thirds and here there was some tendency toward first born (Table 4). It was of interest to note that nine of the twenty-five mothers in the mongoloid group delivered a normal child in a pregnancy subsequent to the mongoloid child and two of these delivered two normal children from subsequent pregnancies.

TABLE 4
DISTRIBUTION OF STUDY POPULATIONS (177 CASES)
ON ORDINAL POSITION OF THIS CHILD

Ordinal Position	Cerebral Palsy	Organic	Mongoloid	Blind	Deaf	Total
Only Child	5	6	1	1	2	8%
First	12	20	3	2	4	23%
Second	20	22	6	2	5	31%
Third	9	10	6	5	6	20%
Fourth	7	5	5	2	3	12%
Fifth		1	4	1		3%
Sixth				1		1%
Eighth		1				1%
No. in group	53	65	25	14	20	

Male-Female Ratio in the Study Population

The incidence of boys was twice as great as that of girls among the 177 cases. The cerebral palsy, mongoloid and deaf held a 2:1 ratio in favor of boys. The blind group was evenly divided and the organic group showed a 3:1 ratio in favor of boys. These figures are in accord with generally accepted incidence ratios (Table 5).

TABLE 5
MALE-FEMALE RATIO IN THE STUDY POPULATIONS

	Cerebral Palsy	Organic	Mongoloid	Blind	Deaf	Total
Male	33 62%	49 75%	16 64%	7 50%	13 65%	118 65%
Female	20 38%	16 25%	9 36%	7 50%	7 35%	59 35%
No. in group	53	65	25	14	20	177

Incidence of Seizures and Convulsions

The incidence of convulsions or seizures was not a significant problem for the total study population. As might be expected the highest incidence of seizure problems occurred in the organic group (Table 6). The cerebral palsy and organic groups reported a small incidence of infant convulsions with no repetition since infancy, but the organic group reported about one fourth of the group which might now be classified as seizure problems and who were currently on a medication schedule to reduce seizure possibility. None of the mongoloid group reported infant convulsons or any incidence of seizures. Only

TABLE 6

INCIDENCE OF CONVULSIONS AMONG THE FIVE
HANDICAP POPULATIONS

	Cerebral Palsy	Organic	Mongoloid*	Blind	Deaf	Total
Only infancy	13%	11%			5%	8%
Infancy and cont.		11%		7%	15%	6%
Post 2 years	15%	15%			10%	11%
Total	28%	37%		7%	30%	27%

*There was no incidence in the Mongoloid group.

one case in the blind group was reported to be a seizure problem. The deaf group presented a surprise finding of five of the twenty cases being seizure problems. Considering the incidence of convulsions or seizures at any time during the child's life, the mongoloid and blind groups were significantly different from the other three.

When the seizure cases were separated from each of the groups and compared analytically across the variance in all of the various tabulations, the fact that a child had a seizure problem was not found to be significantly related to child-rearing practices or attitudes among the parents. While some mothers appeared to be influenced in their attitudes by the fact that their child had a seizure problem, this finding was felt to be unique to a particular mother and not characteristic of the seizure group.

Severity of Handicaps

The judgment of the extent of handicap into three possible classifications, "mild," "moderate," and "severe" was based upon the rating given to the case by the child's attending physician on the medical data card. Since the underlying conception of severity differed in each of the diagnostic categories, no uniformity can be attributed to the rankings. They are of some interest, however, to show the distribution within each group.

The profundity of deafness in terms of decibel loss accounted for three in four deaf children being classified as severe. In the blind category, the total absence of sight accounted for slightly more than half of these children being classified as severe. In both groups the presence of some acuity led to a moderate classification by the medical specialists. The organic group appeared to have been categorized

on the basis of behavioral disturbances. The cerebral palsy classifications appear to have been based on the lack of independent movement
(Table 7). In general, the "mild" and "moderate" rankings pre-
vailed.

TABLE 7
SEVERITY OF HANDICAP DISTRIBUTION

	Cerebral Palsy	Organic	Mongoloid	Blind	Deaf	Total	
Severe	17	20	10	8	15	70	39%
Moderate	36	45	15	6	5	107	61%

Types of Therapy Received by Children

A wide variation occurred among the five groups in the matter
of the types of therapy which had been administered to the children.
Five types of therapy were defined: physical, occupational and speech
therapy, and visual and auditory training. In each group a sizeable
percentage had received *no* form of therapy. This was most pronounced in the mongoloid, organic, and blind groups (Table 8).
Nine out of ten mongoloid children received no form of therapy, and
those few who did had been enrolled in a program of occupational
therapy. In the cerebral palsy group, those who received therapy at
all, received all three traditional forms. To some extent, this was
due to the orientation of the clinic.

TABLE 8
TYPES OF THERAPY RECEIVED BY 177 CASES

	Cerebral Palsy	Organic	Mongoloid	Blind	Deaf
No therapy	39%	62%	90%	57%	21%
Speech therapy		16%		28%	42%
PT - OT - ST	61%	10%		7%	
VT				7%	
AT		12%			37%
OT only			10%		

However, it was interesting to note that four out of ten did not
receive any form of therapy. One blind child had received physical
and occupational therapy, and one had received visual training;
several had received speech therapy, but more than half had received
no therapy. In the deaf group, the children either had received
speech therapy or auditory training, but one in five had not been

seen for any form of help. In the organic group all therapies were represented except visual training, but the majority of cases had not received any formal therapy.

On an overall basis, the finding is that only in the deaf group were most children reported to have received therapy—most of the other children did not. Some of the cases in the cerebral palsy group had been judged to be so minimally handicapped that no therapy was advisable. The organic cases who had received physical therapy were so mildly handicapped that no classification of cerebral palsy had been made by the orthopedic specialist.

The area of therapy is frequently a matter of therapeutic orientation of pertinent physicians, availability of agency resources, and ability of parents to transport a child for therapy. Consequently, no judgment or interpretation can be made on the absence of therapy or the extent of therapy among these handicapped children.

Incidence of Electroencephalogram, Pneumoencephalogram, and Spinal Tap in Diagnostic Process

Among a handicapped population there is always a question of the type of diagnostic instrumentation employed in ascertaining the nature and extent of the child's disorder. Where some question of neurologic involvement exists, the electroencephalograph, pneumoencephalograph, and the spinal tap represent the three major instruments or techniques employed beyond the standard neurological examination.

Half of the composite group received EEGs with three out of four children in the organic group representing the highest incidence. Each group had some incidence of EEG administration including the mongoloid group where one child was listed. In the cerebral palsy and the deaf group nearly half had been given an EEG. The pneumoencephalograph had been administered only to a few cases in the organic and the blind. A spinal tap had been taken of a small percentage of cases in each group except the mongoloid (Table 9).

Instrumentation for detailing of possible neurologic impairment had been principally employed, as might be expected, in the cerebral palsy and the organic groups. The finding that 45 per cent of the

TABLE 9

INCIDENCE OF EEG, PEG AND SPINAL TAP PROCEDURES
IN DIAGNOSTIC PROCESS*

	Cerebral Palsy	Organic	Mongoloid	Blind	Deaf	Total
EEG	45%	75%	4%	21%	45%	49%
PEG		11%		14%		6%
Spinal tap	15%	26%		21%	10%	17%
None	40%	25%	96%	79%	55%	

*Cases with EEG also may have had other procedures.

deaf had received an EEG was unexpected. The least incidence of neurologic study occurred in the mongoloid and blind groups.

Intellectual Ranges for the Children

The administration of specific intelligence tests to each of the children represented in this study was not within the scope of this project. However, to gain some perspective on the general levels of intellectual distribution, the effort was made to identify the intellectual level of each child through indirect means. Since four out of five cases were known to the agency conducting the investigation, the case files were inspected for test results. For those cases who were not known to the agency as active cases, the intelligence test scores were obtained from pertinent school authorities.

Since many of the cerebral palsied and organic children had been classified by the clinic psychologist as being untestable with standardized instruments, the impression of the intellectual level stated in the child's record was used to categorize the case. Precision in terms of means, medians, etc. was not intended.

The general distribution within ranges was sought to determine possible factors of consideration in assessing the parental responses to the entire investigation. Consequently, four levels of function were arbitrarily defined and the cases were grouped accordingly (Table 10). The most meaningful grouping suggested was that of classification according to educational terminology of *average, educable mentally handicapped, trainable mentally handicapped* and *subtrainable*. Each was interpreted within the customary ranges for those classifications.

In the cerebral palsy group two out of three children were considered to be retarded with the majority of these falling in the trainable

TABLE 10

INTELLECTUAL RANGES FOR THE FIVE STUDY POPULATIONS

	Cerebral Palsy		Organic		Mongoloid		Blind		Deaf		Total	
Average												
Educable mentally handicapped	19	36%	17	26%			10	71%	16	80%	62	35%
Trainable mentally handicapped	10	19%	27	42%	23	92%	4	29%	4	20%	45	25%
Subtrainable mentally handicapped	12	23%	17	26%	2	8%					52	29%
	12	23%	4	6%							18	11%

and subtrainable levels. Three out of four organic children were classified in one of the three retardation categories with the preponderance located within the educable category. Except for two mongoloid cases, who were judged to be functioning at subtrainable levels, all of these children were placed in the trainable category.

In the blind and deaf groups none were at the two lowest levels and only a few cases were in the educable group. Consequently, the blind and deaf groups are largely composed of parents whose children have average intelligence and conversely the cerebral palsy, organic and mongoloid groups are composed mainly of parents whose children are classified as retarded.

The concentration at the subtrainable level of 23 per cent of the cerebral palsy group is also associated with a concentration of the most severely physically handicapped children.

Seventy cases were classified as "severe" in extent or degree of handicap. When these are separately distributed across the five populations, according to intellectual levels, the majority of those rated severe in the blind and deaf groups are in the average classification in intellectual range (Table 11).

TABLE 11

INTELLECTUAL DISTRIBUTION OF THE 70 SEVERELY HANDICAPPED CASES

	Cerebral Palsy	Organic	Mongoloid	Blind	Deaf	Total Per Cent
Average		3		7	13	33%
Educable mentally handicapped	4	6		1	2	19%
Trainable mentally handicapped	5	8	8			30%
Subtrainable mentally handicapped	8	3	2			19%
No. in group	17	20	10	8	15	

The three other populations show an incidence almost entirely classified below the average intellectual range. In the cerebral palsy, organic and mongoloid groups there is a positive relationship between reduced intellectual level and a ranking of severe in extent of handicap. Further meaning cannot be elaborated because of the differing criteria employed in the severity rankings.

School Placements

All children in the deaf group were enrolled in public school classes for the deaf (Table 12). This uniformity was due to the recruitment process in which the total population of this group was drawn from the enrollment files of the public schools. The same explanation is true for the blind group, with the exception of three cases, who were enrolled in the preschool program of the Easter Seal Child Development Center. Fifty-two of the 177 cases were being served in the preschool programs of the Easter Seal Center at the time of the study. The high incidence of organic children in this preschool distribution may be accounted for on the basis of program emphasis at the Center. In general, the entire enrollment of the Easter Seal Center was composed of approximately 50 per cent of the cases holding or suspected of having a diagnosis of brain-injury.

TABLE 12

DISTRIBUTION OF SCHOOL PLACEMENTS FOR 177 CHILDREN

	Cerebral Palsy		Organic		Mongoloid		Blind		Deaf		Total	
Preschool	14	26%	30	46%	5	20%	3	21%			52	29%
Orthopedic classes	10	19%									10	6%
EMH or TMH	1	2%	10	15%							11	6%
Regular	12	23%	13	20%							25	14%
Special sensory class							11	79%	20	100%	31	18%
No. in group	53		65		25		14		20		177	

The fourteen cases in the cerebral palsy group, who were receiving preschool services, were also enrolled at the Easter Seal Center. The twenty cases in the mongoloid group, who were classified as "no school," were all on the waiting list for the Easter Seal program, and have since been enrolled for service. Since all of the mongoloid cases had been drawn from the clinical files of the Easter Seal, the placement of cases in terms of school was readily understandable.

Only in the cerebral palsy and the organic group can any semblance of distribution be truly considered. Only one in five children with cerebral palsy were attending an orthopedic school, but all of the cases classified as severely retarded and severely physically involved were not attending any form of schooling. Considering those children with cerebral palsy who were attending the preschool programs of the Easter Seal Center, and those not enrolled in any form of schooling as a non-formal schooling group, more than half of the cerebral palsy group were not in school. Roughly, about one in four of this group were attending regular elementary school programs with no specialized services within the school program. In the organic group one in three cases were attending school with a nearly equal distribution of cases in the regular elementary classes and the classes for the retarded.

Considering those in the cerebral palsy and organic groups, who were attending regular school, and seven of the ten cases attending orthopedic school, to be on a par with the blind and the deaf who were attending special classes, holding an orientation which might generally be classified as a normal elementary school curriculum, one-third of the total group were being educationally treated as average children. One in four cases were attending no school, and one in four were enrolled in preschool. A small percentage of organic and cerebral palsy were attending classes for the educable mentally handicapped.

All possible school relationships are accounted for in the distribution. By and large, the distribution of school placements was directly in accord with the policies and procedures of the seven Milwaukee County school systems in which these families resided. The criteria for admission to special or regular classes in terms of age, acuity loss, muscular dysfunction, intellectual level, etc., could explain a given child's inclusion or exclusion. In consideration of mean ages, intellectual levels, severity classifications, and school policies, the 177 cases were considered to be a representative sampling of the communities' handicapped children within the four to ten year age range.

THE PARENTS

All parents lived within the boundaries of Milwaukee County and their children attended urban or suburban public or parochial schools in the metropolitan complex. Milwaukee is essentially an industrial town with both light and heavy industry.

Socioeconomic Factors

More than three fourths of the 275 families owned their own homes, with the parents of the deaf (90 per cent) showing the highest incidence of home ownership (Table 14). The median income level for each group was between $6000 and $7000, with the parents of the mongoloid group having the highest median ($7050) of the five populations (Table 13).

TABLE 13
MEDIAN INCOMES FOR THE 177 INTERVIEWED CASES

Cerebral Palsy $6113	Organic $6520	Mongoloid $7050	Blind $6050	Deaf $6259

TABLE 14
DISTRIBUTION OF LIVING SITUATIONS

	Cerebral Palsy	Organic	Mongoloid	Blind	Deaf	Total
Own	71%	76%	60%	85%	90%	76%
Rent	29%	24%	40%	15%	10%	24%

Almost every family in the study held a religious group affiliation; with the two major religions, Catholic and Protestant, accounting for almost all of the parents. A small percentage of families were Jewish and a few held affiliations in church groups which are nationally in small percentages. In general, the Catholic and Protestant affiliations were equally represented in each of the five study groups. One per cent of the total group indicated that they professed no religion (Table 15). Those who professed no religion were in the organic and cerebral palsy groups with the other three groups showing every family to profess some religion. The expression of those beliefs in religious practices will be discussed in a subsequent chapter.

TABLE 15
RELIGIOUS PREFERENCES OF THE 177 MOTHERS

	Cerebral Palsy	Organic	Mongoloid	Blind	Deaf	Total
None	3%	2%				1%
Jewish	1%	11%	3%	5%		6%
Protestant	37%	37%	28%	26%	42%	36%
Catholic	54%	50%	62%	69%	46%	54%
Other	4%		7%		12%	3%

Mean Ages of Mothers and Fathers

Fathers as a group were two to three years older than the mothers in general conformity to cultural standards (Table 16). The cerebral palsy group contained the youngest group of parents with the blind and mongoloid having the oldest groups among the five populations. The mean age for the total group of mothers was 36.1 years and for the fathers 38.6 years.

TABLE 16

MEAN AGE OF PARENTS AT TIME OF STUDY

	Cerebral Palsy	Organic	Mongoloid	Blind	Deaf
Mothers	32.7	35.1	38.7	38.4	35.8
Fathers	35.1	37.6	40.7	41.7	38.2

Most mothers were between the ages of twenty and thirty years when they gave birth to the child represented in this study (Table 17). A small percentage were below twenty years or above forty years with the majority in the youngest extreme being in the organic group and the majority in the oldest extreme being in the mongoloid group. The highest concentration in terms of age in the cerebral palsy, blind and deaf groups was in the range twenty-five to twenty-nine years. In the organic group the largest percentage was in the range from twenty to twenty-four years and the range from thirty-five to forty years showed the highest incidence for the mongoloid group.

TABLE 17

DISTRIBUTION OF MOTHERS' AGES AT BIRTH OF THIS CHILD

Years	Cerebral Palsy	Organic	Mongoloid	Blind	Deaf	Total
17 - 19	4%	10%			6%	7%
20 - 24	20%	35%	15%	15%	33%	28%
25 - 29	39%	28%	15%	43%	38%	31%
30 - 34	22%	15%	22%	21%	8%	17%
35 - 40	4%	10%	37%	21%	8%	13%
41 - 45	2%	2%	10%		6%	4%

Since the age range among children in the study was from four to ten years, the age at the birth of the handicapped child represents a different finding. Three-fourths of the mothers in the cerebral palsy, organic and deaf groups gave birth to this child before their thirtieth birthday. In the mongoloid and blind, the incidence was shifted towards being past thirty.

Educational Level of Mothers

Only twelve mothers in the total sample did not receive a formal education beyond the eighth grade. All others were exposed to high school programs, most of them completed a secondary program (Table 18) and ten per cent of the total were college graduates. None had pursued courses leading to graduate degrees. When the levels of educational attainment of these mothers was compared to the level attained by their own mothers and fathers, the general level of attainment was higher.

TABLE 18

EDUCATION OF MOTHER AND MOTHER'S FATHER AND MOTHER*

Educational Level	Mother		Mother's Father		Mother's Mother	
Did not attend school			2	1%	4	3%
Grades 1 - 4			13	8%	11	7%
Grades 5 - 8	12	7%	79	52%	86	55%
Grades 9 - 12	126	70%	34	22%	40	25%
Some college or university	24	13%	9	6%	8	5%
BA degree	18	10%	11	7%	8	5%
College or university beyond BA	5	4%	2	2%		
	Mdn 9-12		Mdn 5-8		Mdn 5-8	

*For all groups.

This finding was expected in view of the general advances which have taken place in the educational opportunities and programming during the past thirty years. The principal difference is in the matter of the increased incidence of high school graduates within the mothers' group over their own parents' schooling. Although there were more mothers in this group who had completed college work, as compared to their own parents, the differences were not great. The increased incidence of high school graduations within this generation was not matched by a comparable increase in college educations over the previous generations, which is in contradiction to the general pattern in the nation.

Educational Level of Fathers

The fathers in these groups had achieved a higher level of formal education than their own mothers and fathers, largely in the direction of a greater incidence of high school graduations. Two thirds of the paternal mothers and fathers had no formal education beyond the eighth grade. Among the fathers in this study, there was a significant difference between themselves and their own parents, on the matter of college work and between their wives and their parents. While the percentage of fathers who have attended college represents a sizable rise over the previous generation, most of the fathers who entered college did not complete their college course. Only one out of three fathers who attended college earned the bachelor degree.

Mothers in this group appeared to have been more persistent in regard to college completion, since three out of four mothers who started college, earned their bachelor degrees. The fathers outdistanced the mothers on the question of working toward graduate degrees; five fathers were reported to either be currently working toward a master's degree or to have already completed such work (Table 19).

TABLE 19

EDUCATION OF FATHER AND FATHER'S FATHER AND MOTHER*

Educational Level	Father		Father's Father		Father's Mother	
Did not attend school			1	1%	1	1%
Grades 1 - 4			7	7%	4	4%
Grades 5 - 8	12	9%	60	57%	65	60%
Grades 9 - 12	64	50%	27	25%	31	28%
Some college	31	24%	7	7%	6	5%
University (but not BA) BA degree	16	13%	2	2%	2	2%
College or University beyond BA	5	4%	2	2%		
	Mdn	9-12	Mdn	5-8	Mdn	5-8

*For all groups.

In general, the parents of the handicapped children were better educated than their own parents, and by a slight shading, the fathers were better educated than the mothers.

Levels of Occupation of Fathers

The occupational level of the 177 fathers represented in the interviewed population revealed no particular concentration (Table 20). Skilled factory workers, professional and technical workers, and cler-

TABLE 20

OCCUPATION OF FATHER AND FATHER'S FATHER
AND MOTHER'S FATHER

Occupational Level	Father %	Father's Father %	Mother's Father %
Business oriented, proprietor or managerial	10	8	8
Professional and high-level technical	25	9	13
Clerical, sales and white-collar service	22	17	14
Blue-collar, factory skilled	26	26	36
Blue-collar, factory semi-skilled	12	21	13
Blue-collar, factory unskilled or laboring	4	18	15
Total	99	99	99
Median of Fathers	3		
Median of Father's Father	4		
Median of Mother's Father	4		

ical, sales and white-collar service workers each accounted for one fourth of the group; 10 per cent were owners of businesses and 15 per cent were semiskilled and unskilled. As a total group, they represented a higher occupational level than had been attained by their own fathers and their wives' fathers. The median for the fathers of handicapped children was at the third level while the median for both the husband's and wife's fathers was at level four.

Stability of Father Employment

The fathers in this study represented a high level of stability in terms of employment with 50 to 60 per cent having held the same job for ten or more years (Table 21), and 25 to 38 per cent had been employed at the same job for five to ten years. Taking five years of employment in one setting to represent stability, four out of five fathers in this study were considered to be stable in terms of employment. Despite the fact that 20 per cent reported that they had been holding their present job for less than five years, further investigation of the specific records indicated that some fathers had interpreted promotions within their own companies to positions of greater responsibility as different jobs, and actually could be considered highly stable. Only 3 per cent of the total group had changed types of work or companies within a two year period preceding the study.

TABLE 21

EXTENT OF STABILITY OF FATHER'S EMPLOYMENT

	Cerebral Palsy		Organic		Mongoloid		Blind		Deaf	
More than 15 years on the same job	8)		6)		4)		2)		5)	
		50%		43%		40%		63%		50%
More than 10 years on the same job	10)		14)		4)		3)		3)	
More than 5 years on the same job	9	25%	18	38%	7	35%	3	38%	4	25%
Less than 5 years on the same job	7		9		5				4	
Deceased or retired	2									
	—		—		—		—		16	
Total	36		47		20		8		—	

Employment Levels of Mothers

With the national increase in working mothers, there was some interest in determining the extent of mothers in this population who were working at full or part-time jobs (Table 22). Only one fourth of the total sample reported that they were employed for work outside the home at the time of this study. The percentage was highest among the mongoloid and deaf groups where four out of ten were working. Except for the blind group, the tendency was for the mother to be employed on a part-time job for less than twenty hours per week. Most of the mothers in this study were not employed in community jobs.

TABLE 22

PERCENTAGE OF MOTHERS IN EACH GROUP CURRENTLY
EMPLOYED IN FULL OR PART-TIME JOBS

	Cerebral Palsy	Organic	Mongoloid	Blind	Deaf	Total
Less than 20 hours per week	11%	12%	32%	7%	25%	15%
More than 20 hours per week	9%	6%	12%	14%	15%	10%
	20%	18%	44%	21%	40%	25%

Most of the couples were married after an engagement period of less than twelve months (Table 23). This was particularly true in the cerebral palsy and organic groups. The mongoloid and the blind groups showed a nearly even split between those married after long or short engagement periods. Only a few couples were married in civil ceremonies, with the vast majority having repeated their marriage vows in religious ceremony (Table 24).

TABLE 23

EXTENT OF ENGAGEMENT PERIOD REPORTED BY MOTHERS

	Cerebral Palsy	Organic	Mongoloid	Blind	Deaf	Total
Long engagement (More than 12 mos)	31%	27%	48%	44%	37%	34%
Short engagement (Less than 12 mos)	69%	73%	52%	56%	63%	66%

TABLE 24

EXTENT OF COUPLES MARRIED IN RELIGIOUS OR CIVIL CEREMONIES

	Cerebral Palsy	Organic	Mongoloid	Blind	Deaf	Total
Religious	89%	89%	87%	88%	88%	89%
Civil	7%	11%	5%	6%	12%	9%
Not ascertained	4%		8%	6%		2%

In response to a four point scale, asking mothers to rate the quality of their relationship to their own mothers, 85 per cent of the total group indicated that they held a very or fairly close relationship. A small percentage indicated that the relationship to their own mothers was not close at all (Table 25). The mothers in the cerebral palsy and the mongoloid groups showed the greatest extent of closeness, while the mothers in the organic group suggested the greatest extent of negative relationship. Most mothers felt a close relationship to

TABLE 25

MOTHERS' PERCEPTION OF THEIR RELATIONSHIP TO THEIR OWN MOTHERS*

	Cerebral Palsy	Organic	Mongoloid	Blind	Deaf	Total
Very close	47%	36%	51%	44%	33%	42%
Fairly close	35%	47%	43%	50%	50%	43%
Not very close	14%	14%	6%	6%	8%	11%
Not close at all	4%	3%			8%	4%

*Based on 275 cases responding.

their own mothers. The same degree of closeness with their fathers was not found in any of the groups, although the percentage of mothers who felt a fairly close relationship to their fathers is equal to the percentage who felt fairly close to their own mothers. Again, a small percentage of the total group indicated that their relationship to their father was not at all close (Table 26).

TABLE 26
EXTENT OF CLOSENESS TO OWN FATHER
AS PERCEIVED BY MOTHERS

	Cerebral Palsy	Organic	Mongoloid	Blind	Deaf	Total
Very close	38%	27%	39%	27%	38%	33%
Fairly close	43%	43%	35%	53%	33%	42%
Not very close	17%	19%	19%	20%	17%	18%
Not close at all	2%	11%	7%		12%	7%

THE BIRTH DEMOGRAPHY

A third element in demography, which seems a necessity in a study of handicapped populations, is the presentation of factors associated with pregnancy, labor, delivery, and early infancy. The historical pattern of study for each of these conditions has focussed on the many issues arising from prematurity, blood incompatibilities, prolonged labor, and a variety of other circumstances which may be associated with birth trauma.

To add other nuances to the general portrait of these families, questions about pregnancy, Rh factor, birth weight, term of birth, etc., were asked of the mothers. They were also asked to make some form of evaluation on a comparative basis to the birth events of their other children.

Distribution of Birth Weights

The distribution of birth weights among the total population was set into four two-pound range groupings, with nearly half of the total group reporting a birth weight between six to eight pounds. The cerebral palsy and organic groups accounted for two thirds of the cases with birth weights below six pounds, and the cerebral palsy group accounted for half of the twenty-one cases who were below four pounds at birth (Table 27).

TABLE 27

BIRTH WEIGHTS OF HANDICAPPED CHILDREN WHOSE
PARENTS WERE INTERVIEWED

Weight	Cerebral Palsy	Organic	Mongoloid	Blind	Deaf	Total	
8 lb to 9 lb 15 oz	9	17	3	3	6	38	21%
6 lb to 7 lb 15 oz	21	32	10	5	13	81	46%
4 lb to 5 lb 15 oz	11	16	6	1	1	35	20%
2 lb to 3 lb 15 oz	11		5	5		21	12%
Can't say	1		1			2	2%
No. in group	53	65	25	14	20	177	

*One mother reported weight of 1 lb 9 oz at birth.

Pregnancy Terms

The incidence of prematurity was greatest among the blind and cerebral palsy groups where 43 to 50 per cent reported premature births (Table 28). One third of the mongoloid group also reported prematurities. While the overall incidence of postmature births was minimal, the deaf and organic groups reported one in four births to have been postmature. Only half of the total population studied were delivered at term. One of each two children were either post or premature with prematurity more prevalent.

TABLE 28

PERCENTAGES OF MOTHERS IN EACH POPULATION
ACCORDING TO TERMS OF PREGNANCY

	Cerebral Palsy	Organic	Mongoloid	Blind	Deaf	Total
Full term	51%	49%	56%	43%	62%	52%
Post term	6%	26%	8%	7%	25%	17%
Premature	43%	25%	36%	50%	13%	31%

Hours of Labor

The bulk of the study population reported a labor period ranging from three to fifteen hours with *this* child with the tendency being toward a three to eight hour labor in all groups but the blind. Very brief labor periods or those extended for a day or longer accounted for a small percentage of the study population. Only in the cerebral palsy group was there any incidence of exceptionally prolonged labor periods and here five mothers indicated that they labored more than thirty hours with their child. These five cases were all classified as severely handicapped and retarded children (Table 29).

TABLE 29
HOURS OF LABOR BEFORE DELIVERY OF THIS CHILD*

	Cerebral Palsy	Organic	Mongoloid	Blind	Deaf	Total
Less than 3 hours	15%	14%	12%	7%	17%	13%
3 - 8 hours	45%	44%	60%	29%	46%	46%
9 - 15 hours	9%	21%	24%	50%	17%	24%
16 - 30 hours	13%	21%	4%	14%	20%	14%
More than 30 hours	9%					2%
Not ascertained	9%					2%

*As reported by the mothers.

Miscarriage, Stillbirths, and Abortions

The problem of miscarriages, stillbirths, and abortions were present for one out of four mothers in this study. For most of the mothers such problems did not enter the picture of their pregnancies (Table 30). For those who had such problems a single occurrence was the usual experience. Few had two or three of such happenings. The general finding is that a comparatively small percentage of mothers in this study experienced such pregnancy and delivery difficulties.

TABLE 30
NUMBER OF CHILDREN LOST PRIOR TO BIRTH OF
HANDICAPPED CHILD*

	Cerebral Palsy	Organic	Mongoloid	Blind	Deaf	Total	
None	41	53	16	8	15	133	75%
One	5	8	4	4	4	24	14%
Two	4	1	5	1	1	12	7%
Three plus	2	2		1		5	3%
No information	1	1				2	1%
	—	—	—	—	—	—	
No. in group	53	65	25	14	20	177	

*Through miscarriage, abortion or stillbirth, as reported by the mothers.

Rh Factor

Twenty-five of the 177 mothers reported an Rh blood incompatibility problem with thirteen having awareness of such problem existing before their pregnancy, and twelve learning of the problem during the course of *this* pregnancy. Fifteen of these twenty-five mothers were in the cerebral palsy and organic groups, six were in the mongoloid group and two each in the deaf and blind groups (Table 31).

TABLE 31

RH FACTOR IN PREGNANCY OF HANDICAPPED CHILD

	Cerebral Palsy	Organic	Mongoloid	Blind	Deaf	Total
No Rh problem	43	60	19	12	18	152 (85%)
Rh problem known before pregnancy	4	3	3	1	2	13 (8%)
Rh problem found out during pregnancy	6	2	3	1		12 (7%)
No. in group	53	65	25	14	20	177

Methods of Delivery Utilized with the Handicapped Child

For two thirds of the deliveries the presentation was in normal position. For a very small percentage of the children cesarean sections were employed. It was interesting to note that each population, except the cerebral palsy group, reported some incidence of natural childbirth with the highest frequency in the organic group. Considering these three methods to be comparatively uncomplicated, the birth process presented no unusual problems to 85 per cent of the mothers in this study. Breech, transverse, or other complications were reported in one in seven cases (Table 32).

TABLE 32

MOTHERS' REPORTS OF METHOD OF DELIVERY
OF HANDICAPPED CHILD

	Cerebral Palsy	Organic	Mongoloid	Blind	Deaf	Total	
Cesarean	2	4			1	7	4%
Head first	46	34	17	7	15	119	68%
Breech transverse instrument	5	16	2	4	1	28	15%
Natural childbirth		11	6	3	3	23	13%
No. in group	53	65	25	14	20	177	

The highest incidence of complications was reported in the organic group where 25 per cent experienced some unusual problems. Once again, these findings suggest that the incidence of delivery complications was not significantly related to any of the handicap groups. If such problems existed, they were unique to an individual case and not representative of any group.

Use of Obstetric Specialist

All populations are nearly evenly divided on the extent of utilization of obstetric specialists to attend the birth of the handicapped child. In only two cases was an obstetrician specifically sought for the delivery of the child represented in this study. Those parents who reported using the services of an obstetrician did so routinely for all of their pregnancies. No differences existed among the groups on this question (Table 33).

TABLE 33

EXTENT OF UTILIZATION OF OBSTETRICAL SPECIALIST
IN DELIVERY OF THIS CHILD

	Cerebral Palsy	Organic	Mongoloid	Blind	Deaf	Total
Obstetrician	38%	40%	40%	50%	46%	41%
General practitioner	58%	56%	56%	50%	50%	55%
Other	4%	4%	4%		4%	4%

Condition of the Child at Birth

Conditions of jaundice were principally noted in the cerebral palsy, organic and mongoloid groups where a total of twenty-three cases were reported (Table 34). Fifteen cases were cyanotic and eleven were misshapen. Of interest, is the finding that one fourth of the total group received oxygen after birth. Nine cases in the blind group with retrolental fibroplasia were among that group. Thirteen organic cases and twelve cerebral palsy cases had received oxygen. These three groupings held most of the cases who had received oxygen.

TABLE 34

CONDITION OF HANDICAPPED CHILD AT BIRTH*

	Cerebral Palsy	Organic	Mongoloid	Blind	Deaf	Total
Jaundiced	23%	20%	29%	7%	7%	20%
Blue or discolored	23%	12%	3%	7%	20%	13%
Given oxygen	39%	52%	23%	60%	33%	39%
Feeding problem in hospital	7%	12%	32%	27%	20%	19%
Misshapen head	3%		7%		20%	5%
Physically disfigured	7%	4%	7%			4%

*Some cases listed in multiple categories

Mothers' Comparison of this Pregnancy With Others

When mothers were asked to compare the pregnancy with this child to other pregnancies which they had experienced, in terms of more or less problems, only one of each four mothers felt that *this* pregnancy was marked by more problems. All others viewed this pregnancy to have been about the same as others or even easier than others. Only in the cerebral palsy and organic groups was there a significant extent of more problems cited with this pregnancy than others. In all other groups relatively few mothers viewed this pregnancy as unusual (Table 35).

TABLE 35
MOTHERS' FEELINGS ABOUT COMPARATIVE DIFFICULTY
OF PREGNANCY OF HANDICAPPED CHILD*

	Cerebral Palsy	Organic	Mongoloid	Blind	Deaf	Total	
Fewer problems	15)	11)	2)	1)	3)	32	20%
	)63%	)73%	)79%	)92%	)84%		
About the same	12)	33)	17)	11)	13)	86	54%
More problems	16	16	5	1	3	41	26%
Not applicable	7	3	1	1	1	13	
No response	3	2				5	
No. in group	53	65	25	14	20	177	

*Percentage based upon the 159 cases on whom such information was obtained and where mother had a basis for comparison.

Mothers' Impressions of Delivery Difficulty

To gain some information on the perception mothers held of their delivery of *this* child, they were asked to rate their delivery on a four point scale in terms of easy or difficult delivery. The question of possible complications during delivery is a standard one included in the investigation or collection of case history information in most clinics serving a handicapped child population. This is also of interest because of the many complications in delivery which have been associated with the incidence of handicaps among children. Another point of interest stems from the possibility that complications in delivery might be a source of initial anxiety which might influence a mother's general attitude of protectiveness or rejection of the child.

The ratings, which the mothers gave to this delivery, showed that two out of three mothers in the total group perceived this delivery as easy or very easy, with the highest extent of perceptions of delivery ease reported by the deaf and organic groups where four out of five mothers rated *this* as an easy delivery (Table 36). Only 8 per cent of the total group viewed their delivery of this child as being very difficult.

TABLE 36

MOTHERS' IMPRESSION OF DIFFICULTY OF DELIVERY

	Cerebral Palsy	Organic	Mongoloid	Blind	Deaf	Total
Very easy	7)	13)	8)	1)	4)	33)
	)66%	)79%	)66%	)64%	)79%	)69%
Easy	26)	31)	9)	8)	11)	85)
Difficult	14)	12)	7)	4)	3)	40)
	)33%	)21%	)33%	)36%	)21%	)31%
Very difficult	3)	8)	1)	1)	1)	14)
No response	3	1			1	5
No. in group	53	65	25	14	20	177

The findings suggest that the clinical questionnaires are more likely than not to record no significant information in this area, and the suggestion from these data is that delivery complications may not be as prevalent in association with handicaps as has often been suspected. Finally, these data suggest that only a small percentage of parents may be suspect in terms of relating current negative attitudes toward the child to painful or disturbing complications in the delivery process.

Mothers' Ratings of Ease of this Delivery

One of each three mothers viewed the delivery of the handicapped child to be the easiest of those she had experiencd (Table 37). Nearly half of the total group felt that the delivery of this child was about the same as their other deliveries. Only one in four viewed this delivery to be the most difficult she had experienced. The highest incidence of "most difficult" ratings occurred in the cerebral palsy group where 40 per cent rated this delivery as such. The blind and organic groups revealed a 24 per cent rating of "most difficult." The

TABLE 37

MOTHERS' FEELINGS ABOUT *COMPARATIVE* DIFFICULTY
OF DELIVERY OF HANDICAPPED CHILD

	Cerebral Palsy		Organic		Mongoloid		Blind		Deaf		Total	
Easiest	11	29%	17	29%	9	38%	5	38%	6	33%	48	32%
About the same	12	31%	28	47%	12	50%	5	38%	10	56%	67	44%
Most difficult	15	40%	14	24%	3	12%	3	24%	2	11%	37	24%
Not applicable	7		3		1		1		1		13	
No response	8		3						1		12	
No. in group	53		65		25		14		20		177	

findings here were similar to those found when the mothers rated the delivery of the handicapped child as a single experience.

The general feeling expressed by the mothers is that this delivery was at least similar to, if not easier, than their other deliveries. The incidence of ratings of this delivery being the most difficult is significantly related to the cerebral palsy group, and is more likely to be a factor in cerebral palsy than any of the other groups. Apparently, where severe difficulties were encountered in the other populations in this study, the dynamics were unique unto a particular mother and not to the group as a whole.

Infancy Feeding Problems

The highest incidence of feeding problems during early infancy was reported by the mothers of the cerebral palsy group (Table 38). This finding is in accord with the general dynamics of cerebral palsy where the neuromuscular involvement of tongue, jaw, lips, etc., is often a component of the child's overall problem. The least extent of problem in this area was reported by the blind group.

TABLE 38

INCIDENCE IN PERCENTAGE OF FEEDING PROBLEM
DURING THE INFANCY OF THIS CHILD

Cerebral Palsy	Organic	Mongoloid	Blind	Deaf
60%	40%	44%	25%	30%

Although a small percentage in each group reported that they had also been confronted with an infancy feeding problem in one or more siblings of *this* child, this finding was not significantly related to the incidence of feeding problems in the handicapped group.

While the emotional surround of *this* child's feeding problem undoubtedly generated various degrees of anxiety within the mother,
the feeding problem seems to have been unique to the particular
child and not necessarily related to the dynamics of deviancy except
in the cerebral palsy group where two out of three cases reported
infancy feeding difficulties.

COMMENTARY ON THESE DEMOGRAPHIC FINDINGS

The mean age for the total population involved in the study was
6.5 with the only significant variants existing in the mongoloid group
where the mean age was 1.3 years below the full group mean and
the blind group where the subgroup mean was 1.4 above the full
mean. Although the mean of the study sample and the general
distribution of cases clearly established a four to eight year age range
there is a strong probability that the findings to be reported in regard to specific questions have applicability to children somewhat
younger as well as somewhat older.

Clinical experience with children aged three, nine, ten, eleven and
twelve and their parents has indicated that the same general findings
might be anticipated. Only as the young child is emerging from the
infant period and the preadolescent is advancing into the domain of
physiologic change does clinical experience suggest that these findings would have to be viewed with caution.

In the years before and since the formality of the study clinical
contacts with parents have continued to verify the notion that although the data are precisely applicable to the handicapped children aged four to eight in these five groups and their parents, it is a
comfortable clinical step to broaden the scope of the data to an age
range from three to twelve years thereby covering a nine year span.

Although the proprieties of research dictate a faithful adherence
to the procured data the persistent clinical finding of the same general results in the nine to twelve year group in the past four years
lends an air of confidence to the notion of claiming application to
a wider age range. As a consequence of this confidence, "liberties
of extension" will be exercised within the commentaries on each of
the respective topics. It must be recognized, however, that this con-

fidence is derived from subsequent clinical experience and there is no violation of data when the extensions are discussed.

The finding of an average family of five (two parents and three children) suggest an overall impression that the average couple are not deterred in their desire or ability to produce more children. Since the reference is to *mean* number of children in each group a sizable percentage of families had four, five and six children. In accord with generally reported ratios there were two handicapped boys represented for each handicapped girl. Some investigators have reported a 3:1 ratio in some disability populations. Consequently this finding of incidence was expected.

In only 8 per cent of the families was the handicapped child an *only* child. Consequently all other handicapped children in this study had either younger or older siblings as a part of their family constellation. The average family consisted of two siblings to join the child with the handicap. The next breakdown of the total population into ordinal thirds was a fortuitous circumstance; 31 per cent were first or only children, 31 per cent were second born and 32 per cent were third or fourth born. A very small percentage (4 per cent) were fifth and sixth born children. Nearly two thirds of the group were first or second born children. The general conclusion to be drawn from this finding is that the ordinal position of the handicapped child is not a mechanically significant factor.

Unfortunately no real significance can be attributed to the severity rankings since each physician employed a different set of criteria in making the ratings. There can be no generic classification strain when ranking both cerebral palsy and deafness on the same continuum. In spite of this lack of classification precision the composite group of physicians did provide for a differential permitting a conclusion that except for the deaf population the rating of mild or moderate characterized the group. Throughout the study there were only a few instances where the severity of the handicap, severe versus moderate, seemed to generate a significant difference in the child-rearing practices.

There is an automatic expectation of variance in regard to therapies received among these five disability groups since the nature of their problems normally require different approaches. Psychological or educational therapy were not included by operational definition under the classification. The incidence of "no therapy" was somewhat of a surprise finding in a community where many therapeutic agencies exist.

Since the orientation of a referrant is probably a significant factor in whether a child receives any of the listed therapies the data do not allow for an expanded discussion. It is of some interest however to note that four out of ten children with cerebral palsy received no therapy, six out of ten organic cases received no therapy, nine out of ten mongoloid children, six out of ten blind children and one in five deaf children received no therapy. Only in the cerebral palsy and the deaf group was there a significant number who had received therapy.

A general understanding of the professional background in the various disciplines represented in this list of therapies suggests that the physical, occupational and speech therapist, and the auditory clinician might well have a great deal to offer to those populations which are not typically within their therapeutic province. It is possible that this finding, that a majority of organic, mongoloid and blind cases received no therapy in a metropolitan community, may have been peculiar to the nature of this sample. One cannot help but wonder however whether this finding might be, to some degree, nationally representative.

Milwaukee County is comparatively well equipped with sources. Rural communities where therapeutic services are distantly located would conceivably reflect even less incidence of therapy. If the findings of this particular sample are to be considered representative— even to some degree—the net finding implies that half of the parents in this nation have received no direct therapeutic services for their child. The fact that professional therapies are unavailable, unprescribed or restricted to certain groups is a significant factor with which most parents of handicapped children must contend. Most parents seek some form of help for their child and frequently are in no position to evaluate the adequacy of therapy or the true "professionally perceived" need for therapy.

An extension of each of the listed therapies into provinces not typically entered might well provide new frontiers for each of the disciplines represented. These findings at least suggest that each professional group might well give consideration to such extensions. Physical therapists might well find there is much they can bring to a deaf, blind, mongoloid or organic child from their wealthy experiential backgrounds.

Occupational therapy and speech professionals may find much within their own disciplinary backgrounds which could be of value to disability groups who are not now referred to them. It is recognized that there are many individual therapists in these four fields who are in fact dealing with all five types of children but these are in a minority.

It would seem logical to assume that each handicapped child and his parents should be afforded the benefit of the immensely valuable bodies of knowledge encompassed by these four fields. Perhaps the general state of mental health of the parental population in the field of rehabilitation might be positively influenced by the simple incidence of therapy for the child. It is worth consideration, in spite of the host of problems which seem attendant upon such a suggestion.

All ranges of intelligence were represented within the five groups, but approximately two thirds of the total group were classified at some level of retardation. Since the blind and deaf had been recruited from a population which was attending school, and the other three groups had been recruited from a clinical population, it was inevitable that a higher incidence of children of tested average intelligence would be found in the deaf and blind groups. The major concern in delineating the intellectual levels of each child centered around the possibility that parents whose children were of average or better than average ability might differ in their child-rearing practices from those whose children were retarded.

As a general rule very few occasions of significant differences were noted in the comparison of parental responses when the data were reviewed on an average-retarded distribution. Where such differences seemed to be attributable to a variation in intellectual levels of the child the comments on the data will account for this. Since a massive portion of the composite data were reviewed on this basis the absence of a comment on this significant point of difference should be taken to imply that the intellectual variance among the children was not an important consideration in a given area.

There is a widespread belief that the retarded child requires a specialized handling from teachers, parents, therapists, physicians and so on. There is also the general belief the child of average intelligence requires no specialized consideration in regard to intellectual matters. Unfortunately the parents of these handicapped children do not have the benefit of research findings on such topics, clinical techniques or even the professional perspective on the day by day meaning of intellectual variance.

It is probably safe to say that a professional practitioner's understanding of mental retardation based upon clinical experience, training, analysis of research, an objective vantage point and performance perspective can never have the same understanding of this condition that the parent holds. Some parents were aware that their children were classified as retarded, in addition to the primary handicap, and others were aware that their children had been classified as intellectually average or above average. The concern of this study was not directed at defining the intellectual levels of the groups as a child-oriented research technique but was rather directed toward the possibility that parents might approach child-rearing practices somewhat differently if they had a retarded handicapped child.

Dividing the group into intellectual levels was only a strategy for viewing the parental data from a different perspective seeking to catch a nuance in child-rearing if such existed. As will be noted in the various sections which follow, the anxieties related to mental retardation were certainly present among a large percentage of the parents, but these anxieties were not an automatic influence upon rearing practices. In general, one might conclude that the presence of mental retardation is far less a factor in child-rearing than might be suspected or expected.

The parent must learn in the laboratory of daily behaviors what meaning the term, mental retardation, might hold for their child. Particularly is this true in relation to setting goals and expectancies. It seems from these data, that the parent continues to regard the child as average for purpose of child-rearing techniques, in spite of intellectual acceptance of the designation of the child as mentally retarded, and only in the prosaic course of daily effort to gain conformity behavior does the dynamic meaning of this term come to a state of awareness.

This is a negative point perhaps from a professional's consideration but seems to be a logical consequence of the mysteriousness of the term from the vantage point of the parents. Parents perceive their child as being of average intelligence in spite of the severity of his other handicaps until their personal parental experience causes them to modify that perception. Consequently the parental effort at child-rearing is governed by the parental perception of the child's intellectual level, accurate or inaccurate, and not by the measured state of intellectual organization in the child.

Three fourths of the total group were enrolled in some form of educational program either in a specialized nursery program or in public school regular or special programs. If the twenty cases in the mongoloid group who are awaiting placement in a preschool program at the time of this study are excluded, only 16 per cent of the total group had been considered as ineligible for an educational program. Essentially the majority of the parents were in a perceptual context of viewing their child as capable of learning and, furthermore, were assured that some form of teaching effort was being extended in their child's behalf. Consequently only a small percentage of parents were confronted with the fact that their child could not currently benefit from teaching. Such parents learned the dynamics of mental retardation more dramatically and perhaps painfully.

A number of social and economic characteristics can be shaded into the group portrait of these 177 families. The median income for each of the five groups was approximately equal and three fourths or more in each group owned their own homes. Ninety-nine per cent of the families professed a religious affiliation. The average mother was thirty-six years of age and the father was thirty-eight years. Only 7 per cent of the mothers did not complete high school and only 9 per cent of the fathers did not complete their secondary education. Four per cent of the fathers could be classified as occupationally unskilled but all others were distributed in varying ranges of skilled occupations. Over 85 per cent of the fathers had held the same job for five or more years with more than half of the group holding the same job for ten or more years.

The portrait is one of a middle class group of home-owning, church-affiliated people with at least a high school education and stability in employment. One-fourth of the mothers were currently employed at either full time or part-time jobs but the majority of the mothers were not employed. The majority of these couples were married in a religious ceremony after a courtship and engagement period of less than one year. As a generality the mothers in this study expressed a description of a close relationship to their own mothers and a close relationship to their fathers.

In terms of income, education, home ownership, religious affiliation, parental closeness, father's occupational stability, length of engagement, type of wedding ceremony, age, family size, severity of handicap, intellectual levels of children and educational services for the child, these five groups show a consistently matched distribution. The portrait of the parental groups is a rather clearly defined picture of similarity.

The multiples of demography which have been discussed thus far reveal five comparatively similar groups of parents distinguishable at this moment only by the artificial groupings based upon their child's handicap label. This high degree of similarity enhances the study of the manner in which each family reared their handicapped child because it places the handicapped child in the position of being the *critical variable.*

Having defined the general characteristics of the families involved the data related to the demography of the birth of the handicapped child deserve some commentary before delineating the child-rearing practices.

Heavy babies (eight to ten pounds) were most noted in the organic group and premature babies were most prevalent in the cerebral palsy and blind groups. Only 50 per cent of the mothers delivered a child in the traditionally average birth weight range. Birth weights at either extreme, as well as the premature and postmature pregnancy terms, were potential anxiety agents for half of this population of 177 mothers. Brief labor periods were equally distributed among all five groups. Lengthy labors were also equally distributed except for the mongoloid group showing a very small percentage of enduring labor periods.

The majority of these mothers had suffered no miscarriages and only a small percentage reported more than one miscarriage, still-birth or abortion. Only 20 per cent of the total group of mothers reported some blood incompatibility problem. The majority of deliveries were accomplished in the head first position. All groups were equally distributed on the question of an obstetric specialist versus a general practitioner. Only two parents especially sought an obstetric specialist for *this* child.

All groups reported some negative features in the condition of the child at birth. The majority of mothers rated the delivery of this child as easy or very easy and those who had delivered other children presented a fairly even distribution of ratings on the comparison of this delivery with others. Some reported it to be their easiest, some their most difficult and some regarded it to be the same as others. The distribution of ratings was the same for all five groups. They also presented a five group majority opinion that *this* pregnancy was the same as others or even less troublesome than others.

The pregnancy, labor, delivery, and birth complications were evenly distributed among the five groups. There are only minor points of differences among the populations except for a significant finding that the organic and blind groups showed a high evidence of requiring oxygen for the baby after birth. A general cross-sectional inspection shows that in each group about one third of the mothers had reason to be anxious about the birth of this child. Since the finding is present in each group the specific disability is discounted as holding any significant bearing on this anxiety incidence.

All of the factors which have thus far been discussed may be taken as a set of descriptive characteristics of these mothers *before* they became the parent of a handicapped child. The data review up to this point may be regarded as mechanical information, descriptive of the mother before she assumed an identity as a child-rearer. Returning from the hospital and introducing the baby into the home established her identity as a child-rearer. The awareness of handicap is yet to come.

Chapter 4

INITIAL CONCERN AND ACTION

THE DYNAMIC STORY of the parenthood of a handicapped child must start in the early moments when the parent first becomes aware that the child is different. For some parents this awareness gradually increases as expected developmental milestones pass with little change in the child, while for others the awareness is present within minutes after the child's birth. These are the moments of adjustment.

What does the parent notice first? What action is taken? To whom do they turn and where do they go?

For approximately 30 per cent of the total group of parents their initial concern for possible negatives in their child's development was attendant upon traumatic circumstances surrounding the labor and delivery complications. Others became concerned when the child did not feed properly or when rolling or sitting up did not take place. Except for the organic group, all parents reported that they became concerned about their child within the first six months if they did not have reason to be concerned at the time of birth. Some parents worried but did nothing—waiting to see if observations they had made would be negated with the passage of time. Others were afraid to go to the doctor lest they have their suspicions painfully confirmed.

In the organic group minor pecularities were often observed but frequently ignored because of their minor nature. The standards of expectancy were operative for all parents. Concerns stemmed entirely from observations that certain expected behaviors were not occurring within their child at expected times. Motor delays were the principal focus. Failure to develop speech patterns was the second major focus.

The plan of action was similar for all—the first step was to seek medical opinion from their pediatrician or their family doctor. Some parents acted quickly; some delayed. Each of the five groups contained both types of parents.

DIAGNOSIS

Extent of Search for Diagnosis

One of the criticisms frequently levelled against the general population of parents of handicapped children is directed at their tendency to refuse to accept the opinions of physicians and continue to search for an answer for their child's problem. A sincere appraisal of the field of rehabilitation will reveal that many differences of opinion exist among all pertinent disciplines regarding philosophy, theory, diagnostic methods, treatment recommendations, etc. To a certain extent these disagreements form a solid wall of evidence to suggest to a parent that "perhaps someone else will have a different opinion." The truth of the matter appears to be that differences can be found. Clinical sophistication, experience, advanced training all serve to sharpen diagnostic sensitivity. Usually, however, the parent seems to be seeking a more positive prognosis or a wishful reduction of the handicap.

Whether further diagnostic search represents a positive or a negative approach by a given parent is beyond the scope of these data. Interest here is centered simply on determining the extent of search for diagnosis undertaken by these 177 cases in the hope of ascertaining general similarities and differences among these groups (Table 39).

TABLE 39
EXTENT OF MEDICAL SEARCH IN TERMS OF NUMBER
OF DOCTORS SEEN FOR DIAGNOSTIC SERVICE

	Cerebral Palsy	Organic	Mongoloid	Blind	Deaf
Saw only one MD	8%	20%	30%	39%	15%
Sought a second MD	80%	15%	33%	44%	25%
Sought a third MD	6%	27%	20%	6%	15%
Sought a fourth MD	6%	10%	13%	11%	15%
Sought five or more MD's		28%	3%		30%

The least amount of search was undertaken by the cerebral palsy group who seem to have settled for the diagnosis of the second doctor to whom they took the child. This is understandable when one remembers that this population was recruited from the case files of the Cerebral Palsy Clinic of Milwaukee. Almost all of these cases were referred to the clinic by the original examining physician for consultation and therapy. The presence of a medical specialist with specific advanced training in cerebral palsy and the program of physical, occupational and speech therapy undoubtedly accounted for the limited search in this group.

The same limitation in the searching process was found in the blind group where most of the cases looked no further than the second physician. The pediatrician or general practitioner customarily referred parents to an ophthalmologist for verification, and the parents did not look for further diagnostic clarification.

The greatest amount of search occurred in the organic and the deaf groups with approximately three out of ten parents in each group reporting that five or more physicians had conducted diagnostic studies on the child before the parent discontinued seeking further clarification. In the mongoloid group one to three doctors was the pattern for the majority.

The general diagnostic problem in identifying brain-injury in children can account for the extensive searching among the organic group, but the incidence of multiple diagnostic examinations for the deaf is not readily explainable. Perhaps, the need to precisely determine the extent of acuity loss, rather than the question of its existence, prompted these parents to seek multiple consultations.

If a majority report is identified for each group, the usual procedure was to consult one or two additional physicians beyond the first one to whom the child was taken. Generally, the parents were referred to the second doctor by the original physician to whom they came, and in almost every instance, the second physician was a recognized specialist in a pertinent area of medical practice. The selection of a third physician or more, usually stemmed from parental initiative based upon recommendations of friends and relatives, other parents, books, magazines, or newspaper publicity.

When the concept of search is regarded as an expression of parental dissatisfaction with the accuracy or adequacy of the diagnostic interpretation, then only those parents who sought additional examinations beyond the second physician may be considered to have engaged in any form of diagnostic search.

Age of Child at Diagnosis

The age of the child when the parent learned of the diagnosis varied considerably across all of the populations, with the mongoloid group reporting that eight out of ten cases were so diagnosed during the first year of life. The cerebral palsy group reached the same proportion by the time the child was two years of age. For the deaf it took slightly longer to reach an eight out of ten ratio and it occurred sometime during the third year. The most surprising response to this question came from one case in the organic, and two in the blind, who denied that they had ever received a diagnostic clarification (Table 40).

TABLE 40

AGE OF CHILD WHEN PARENT RECEIVED
DIAGNOSIS OF CHILD'S CONDITION

	Cerebral Palsy	Organic	Mongoloid	Blind	Deaf
At birth	9%	1%	10%	11%	10%
Before 6 months	22%	5%	50%	33%	15%
6 - 12 months	35%	11%	20%	17%	15%
12 - 24 months	22%	3%	7%	11%	30%
24 - 36 months	6%	9%	3%	11%	20%
36 - 48 months	4%	25%	3%		5%
48 months or more	2%	38%	7%	6%	5%
No diagnosis yet		9%		11%	

The greatest amount of delay occurred in the organic group where three out of four cases did not receive a diagnosis until the child was three or more years of age. It must follow then that the organic group experienced the longest period of uncertainty before their anxieties were crystallized around a diagnostic label. The waiting period was least for the mongoloid group and this is understandable in view of the physical stigmata associated with the condition. All other conditions are not so readily apparent and usually require a variety of developmental failures before they can be accurately identified. Diagnostic anxiety seeking for confirmation or negation of observed irregularities, on a purely temporal basis, is most protracted for the organic and most compacted for the mongoloid group.

The age of the child at diagnosis is related to the multiplicity of medical search. The earlier diagnosed cases engaged in the least amount of search.

The Physician's Time and Attitude

In day-by-day clinical practice, many parents have expressed open hostility to the medical profession for the manner in which doctors have hesitated in defining the child's problem, related to them as parents, treated the child, etc. Because this has come to be an expected pattern of clinical behavior among parents of handicapped children, and in the belief that clinicians tend to overestimate the prevalence of such critical expression, the parents were asked to evaluate the diagnostic interpretation session they held with the physician who diagnosed the child from two viewpoints.

First, they were asked to comment on whether they felt the doctor had spent enough time with them and second, to comment on the doctor's attitude during the interpretation session. Since some of the parents had seen only a pediatrician or a general practitioner, and others had seen from two to five specialists, the definition of the "doctor who interpreted the diagnosis" represents a wide variety of medical specialties.

Responses were frankly subjective and represented the idiosyncratic perception of each parent. Each parent, however, holds a positive or negative impression of the experience, whatever the reasons may be for such perception, and expresses this perception to other professionals and the general community. The two questions were included to determine the extent of positive or negative perceptions among these five populations so as to reinforce or negate a general clinical belief.

The majority of the parents were critical of the amount of time spent by the physician in interpreting the diagnosis (Table 41). No matter what reality factors, such as the physician's own time demands, time of day, private office or hospital, were attendant upon the situation, the perception of the parent was a negative one, largely concerned with the matter of not being given sufficient time to fully comprehend, question, and process the information which was presented. This was most pronounced among parents in the cerebral palsy group where only two of the fifty-three cases felt that the physician had spent adequate time explaining the details of their child's problem. The parents in the blind group were also much concerned about this.

TABLE 41

PARENTAL EVALUATION OF AMOUNT OF TIME PHYSICIAN
SPENT IN DISCUSSING DIAGNOSIS

	Cerebral Palsy	Organic	Mongoloid	Blind	Deaf
Spent inadequate amount of time	96%	63%	59%	75%	69%
Spent adequate amount of time	4%	37%	41%	25%	31%

When the question of the doctor's attitude toward them was posed, the parental responses lent themselves to grouping in three categories. About one third of the total group felt that the physician was abrupt, blunt, and completely objective showing little concern for the individuality of their problem (Table 42).

TABLE 42

PARENTAL EVALUATION OF PHYSICIAN'S
ATTITUDE IN DISCUSSING DIAGNOSIS

	Cerebral Palsy	Organic	Mongoloid	Blind	Deaf
Abrupt, blunt, unconcerned	31%	25%	40%	32%	35%
Satisfactory	15%	25%	12%	42%	20%
Patient, warm, kind, supportive	53%	50%	48%	26%	45%

(Time factor a different form of criticism from attitude)

A middle group of responses, in which the parent stated in a matter-of-fact manner, projecting no emotional tone of either positive or negative connotation, that the physician's attitude was satisfactory accounted for another quarter of the group as a whole. The third category was composed of parental statements of a positive nature with affective tones of warmth, support, patience, and understanding.

As a general rule, the majority of these parents gave a response which could be classified as being on the positive side of the scale with about half of the members in each group, except the blind, expressing a highly positive perception of the physician's attitude.

The general conclusion gained from these two questions is that parents were favorably impressed by the physicians' interpersonal attitude toward them, but resented the *brevity* of the encounter. About one third of the group gave negative responses to both questions. For full appreciation of these data the individual dynamics of the physician-patient-parent triad in each negative instance would have to be explored. For now, however, the group findings suggest that a generalization of negativism on the part of parents is unwarranted. Perhaps, in view of the complexities of refined diagnosis, an acknowledged state of comparative ignorance in many fields of medical knowledge, the general anxiety state of the perplexed and the general cultural pattern of "too little time," such incidence of negativism is inevitable.

Father Participation

Since the sketching of the father role in the child-rearing process was one of the objectives in the study, it was of interest to ascertain whether or not the father participated in the diagnostic interpretation conference or whether the mother experienced this alone. Only in the blind group was there a clear majority of fathers who went to the physician's conference with their wives. The organic fathers revealed that a greater percentage went than did not go, but on all other groups the fathers are nearly evenly split between those who did, and did not, go (Table 43).

TABLE 43

PERCENTAGE OF HUSBANDS IN EACH GROUP WHO
ACCOMPANIED THEIR WIVES TO THE DIAGNOSING PHYSICIAN

Response	Cerebral Palsy	Organic	Mongoloid	Blind	Deaf	Total
Yes	55%	64%	52%	71%	58%	60%
No	45%	36%	48%	29%	42%	40%

The reasons why the father did not did not go were not ascertained and may well be explained simply on the basis of freedom from working obligations. On the other hand, the personal dynamics of each father may serve as a better source of exploration.

Father Reaction to Deviancy

Almost all of the fathers became aware of the child's problems at the same time as the mother. While some fathers tended to dismiss their wives' concerns as exaggerations and minimized the significance of the wife's observation, the husbands *did* share their wife's concern. None of them made any efforts to block the wife's efforts to find out what was wrong. Fathers, however, seemed to suffer in silence with their anxieties, while wives were more openly expressive.

Whether fathers became suspicious of deviations before the mothers did could not be ascertained. The mother was clearly the first to give voice to her concerns. Many mothers commented that it "took a while before he could see what I was talking about" but there were only a few instances where the husband refused or did not see, and agree with the wife in concern for, some aspect of child behavior which was not operating in the expected manner.

By and large the impression has been gained that only a few fathers were not deeply invested in their concerns for the infant at the same time as the mothers.

EARLY INFANCY

Extent of Father Participation During Infancy

The early infancy period is a time of formula, diapering, bathing, rocking, holding, and watchfulness. With the decline in breast feeding, the necessity to make formula, heat the bottle, and take the time to feed the infant occupies a great deal of the daily schedule; frequent change of clothing also occupies time. In the midst of preparing meals for the family, cleaning the house, marketing, and many other duties within the role of the mother, there is some question of what role the father plays in relation to the infant during this period. To find out how actively these fathers participated during this infancy period, a series of questions pertaining to this area were asked of the mothers.

The percentages listed in Table 44 indicate that all of the groups presented a picture of majority action on the part of the fathers. Most of them were quite active in helping to feed and diaper the infant. Bathing the baby appeared to be the province of the mothers, although each group showed that some of the fathers were also active in this performance.

The mothers in the blind and deaf groups presented the best image

TABLE 44

EXTENT OF FATHER HELPFULNESS DURING
INFANCY OF THIS CHILD

	Cerebral Palsy	Organic	Mongoloid	Blind	Deaf
Fed the infant	70%	66%	68%	84%	78%
Diapered the infant	69%	65%	62%	84%	74%
Bathed the infant	31%	33%	50%	34%	48%
Generally helpful	63%	92%	97%	92%	86%

of husband helpfulness during the feeding and diapering period. When mothers were asked to comment on whether their husband had been more helpful during the infancy of this child as compared to those of the siblings, the response again showed the husbands in a generally favorable light. Only in the cerebral palsy group did the mothers express a group finding that their husbands were significantly less helpful during the infancy of the handicapped child. The mothers in the mongoloid group felt that their husbands were more helpful with *this* child than with others, while the other three groups stated that the husband had been at least as helpful as with the siblings.

On an overall judgment of helpfulness beyond the three specific acts of feeding, diapering, and bathing, such activities as warming the bottle, holding the baby, fetching a diaper, watching the infant were included in the concept of participation. Here the mothers revealed that only a few fathers, in the total population, were not active participants. On an overall basis, only the fathers in the cerebral palsy group show a significant number of ratings on the negative side.

Almost all of the mothers reported favorably on father participation in infant activities. The general finding is that *both* parents were acting together in the early infancy period of child-rearing.

Questions on Motor Development

It seemed obvious at the outset of the study that this investigation required some probing into developmental questions pertaining to sitting up, crawling, walking, etc. This series is almost an inevitable component in the clinical interview wherever parents attempt to secure service. A series of questions on motor development were structured into the interview in the hope of obtaining such data on these handicapped children.

Parents were asked to bring baby books wherein they had recorded important milestones in the infant's development. Many omissions were noted in the books that were brought and the parents had extreme difficulty in recalling the specific details in behavior of the child which caused them to record a particular entry. More than half of the total group had never recorded such data on the child.

In formulating the questions on motor development the entire area seemed to lend itself readily to a series of straightforward questions which appeared to be clear and direct. The responses of the parents, however, soon revealed a tremendous variability on specifics of behavior which constituted achievement in any of the areas. Even when the interviewer probed a response to determine whether the parent version matched with the operational definition of independent sitting for instance, the nuances in parental interpretation of independence yielded a degree of variation which defied distribution of the responses on any workable scale.

While it was not felt that the data obtained in the area of motor development could be tabulated and treated from any meaningful base, the analysis of responses did yield a number of observations which hold some interest for future investigators in the study of childrearing.

The recall of specific delays or achievements in motor behavior was most accurate and vivid among the parents of children whose early infancy was marked by some obvious manifestation of muscular difficulty. The emotional investment in the issue of independent walking made by the parent of a child with cerebral palsy brought about a clarity of detail on this point which far surpassed the recall of other parents whose children experienced little difficulty in learning to walk.

Asking a parent to recall specific times and experiences six to nine years after the events transpired when they had no particular reason to perceive the initial situation as being in any way "out of the ordinary" produced a very vague and unreliable set of responses. Since most parents seem perceptually to emphasize the specific disability of the child, matters pertaining to early audition were clearest in the recall of parents of the deaf, early vision in the clarity of recall for the parents of the blind, etc.

While it is likely that every parent observes the early stages of hand usage, walking, talking, etc. in each of their children, and may even experience some anxiety over minor delays, the progressive continuation of new achievements in their child causes yesterday's victories to be forgotten in the concentration upon the achievements of today. As one mother put it, "If I had only known how many times someone was going to ask me all these questions about walking and crawling and sitting in the past five years, I would have paid more attention and would have remembered better." Very often the parents seemed to be in the position of the college student who discovers when confronted by the examination questions that he has studied the wrong chapter. The parents knew a great deal about their child's development, but had never expected to be asked to reply in such detail.

There were other parents who did not receive a diagnosis of their child's problems until four or five years after birth. The general course of questioning to which they were exposed at various diagnostic clinics caused them to try to recall and reevaluate the significance of specific behaviors which they had given little attention at the time of occurrence. This process of retrospective analysis produced all sorts of distortions and exaggeration. At the time the actual motor-sensory-symbolic stages were taking place, the parent did not identify a significant deviation. Now, some years later, their recall is essentially being challenged to report accurately on events which are underscored by a professional, but which were not perceived by the parent as significant at the time. The result became a memory scramble of vague responses.

Clinical Implications

The discrepancies found in parental recall on these developmental motor questions suggest that clinicians who rely upon a developmental questionnaire as a significant component in building a diagnostic formulation on a child would do well to sharply define a precise wording for motor questions which would allow for parental accuracy. Another way to achieve accuracy would be a matter of asking a parent to carefully describe the manner in which a child crawled or rolled or sat by himself. Usually clinic questionnaires presuppose a common operational definition for the descriptive terms which are employed between the respondent and the clinician. The results in this study indicate that this is a false supposition. In the interests of clear interviewing operational definitions seem to be a necessity.

COMMENTARY ON THIS EARLY PERIOD

Some parents started their relationship with their child on a note of anxiety. The complications of the birth, delivery, labor and so on were sufficiently traumatic that they *knew* with an impact of immediacy that something was wrong with this child. About one-third of the total group received that *immediate* awareness. This group tended to regard the baby's survival as a major victory and literally started rearing a handicapped child as soon as they returned from the hospital. The others may have held some anxieties from the hospital period but returned to their homes essentially unaware of their child's difficulty.

As the mothers discussed their early anxieties in motor achievements and language developments it was clear that the typical reaction was one of delay. So much literature has been presented on the topic of individual differences in development, and ranges in achievement of developmental milestones, that the mothers tended to play a waiting game. After all they were surrounded with evidence from their other children, children of relatives and friends and neighbors which all comes under the heading of, "Give him time—the same thing happened with Aunt Clara's second child and look at him now." When mothers could no longer contain their anxieties they took action. For some the action was deliberate and related to their specific anxiety while for others the action was taken in the form of questioning the physician during a routine visit.

Two courses of action seemed typically to follow in the wake of maternal anxiety about some deviations in development. If the pediatrician or general practitioner alleviated the anxiety by suggesting that "we give the child time," the mother returned home and abided by the physician's advice unless her anxiety continued at a high level. If such was the case she sought for another physician to examine the child. In the event that the original physician agreed with the mother, she may have received a definite diagnosis at that time or was referred to a specialist for further examination.

There is a widespread belief that parents of handicapped children are nomadic searchers for diagnostic clarification. The findings of this study suggest that this belief is without real foundation.

When the range of medical contacts made by parents in diagnostic search were investigated, the curious fact that some parents saw two doctors while others saw as many as twelve aroused concern. The most obvious explanation would seem to lie in some variables of the parent personality. The stereotype of the anxious, frustrated, guilty parent comes to mind. Analysis of personality profiles and clinical impressions did not bear this out. No significant differences emerged between the personality profiles of those parents who had a limited search and those who visited many different doctors. As this matter was studied further, it became clear that the searching parent is not so much seeking diagnostic confirmation or clarification, but rather, seems to be seeking an understanding and empathetic physician who accepts and recognizes their feelings and attitudes.

The physician holds a unique place in the life story of a family containing a child with a handicap. There are likely to be frequent diagnostic examinations, a shorter interval between progress evaluations, and a more directive role in the life planning and management.

The parent of the handicapped child seeks the best possible medical service for the child. The parent seeks authoritative competency, diagnostic sensitivity, experienced security and realism—all of these they expect in their doctor, plus an all important attribute which supersedes all others—empathy: empathy for their child; empathy for themselves as individuals. In the climate of empathy, the physician, the child, and the parent offer to each other the greatest contribution toward enriched developmental progress.

On the basis of these data and from deeper analysis of parental comments, a number of conclusions seem warranted on the topic of diagnostic search.

1. Once the parent has selected or been referred to a particular physician in the search for diagnosis of the child's problem, the level of acceptance of diagnosis and prognosis is dependent upon the degree to which the physician communicates his positive acceptance of the parent as a person. It appears that the general practitioner who communicates empathically with

the parent arouses no strong desire in the parent to seek the consultation of a specialist.

2. Since most parents during diagnostic search and subsequent years of medical care are exposed to a number of specialists, the parent comes to rely on a single physician eventually who makes *them* feel most comfortable in the discussion and management of their problems.

3. Despite the fact that the diagnostic subject is the child, the physician must become aware that the parent is the *actual* patient with whom the relationship must be established.

4. Some effort must be made by the physician to include the father in the communication of diagnostic and therapeutic interpretations. The fathers of handicapped children, as a group, must rely upon second-hand information which has already been filtered through the perceptual matrix of the mother.

5. The parent expects the physician to show a *continuing* interest in the child's problems, even though the physician upon initial examination may justifiably indicate that no change can be expected, the parent still expects periodic visits. Furthermore, the parent expects subsequent contact to be initiated by the doctor.

6. Further consideration must be given to techniques for helping the parent develop a realistic understanding of the nature of the child's problem. Sophisticated neurological explanations are seldom assimilated by the parent with any meaning. Oversimplified explanations frequently result in no understanding at all. Since achievement of a realistic understanding requires an educational effort frequently impaired by anxieties and perceptual distortions, it becomes all the more important to develop economical techniques for achieving such understanding.

7. As a general rule, the parent perceives the problem as more serious than the physician does. Many times the negative attitudes of physicians toward parent, and parent toward physician, have their roots in this form of discrepancy. The effort to equalize the perceptions may well have a significantly beneficial effect upon the physician-parent relationship.

8. While parents express a feeling of respect for the physician

who truthfully indicates that he does not have a specific answer for their question, they still expect some action. The parent can accept an experimental effort, can accept a speculation, can accept a limited prognosis, but cannot accept the expression that nothing can be done for their child.

9. The continued analysis of the physician-child-parent triad has brought us to the conviction that the child merely serves as a dynamic stage for the parent and the physician to form a mutually satisfying relationship.

This initial period of anxiety must culminate in a diagnostic label—to give a name to what is wrong with the child's development. Those 30 per cent of the mothers who experienced the immediacy of impact knew that something was wrong but they did not have a name for the wrong. That was yet to come.

The timetable for receiving the diagnostic label varied for each group. One-third of the cerebral palsy group received a diagnosis before six months, another third by the time the child reached his first birthday and the final third waited two or more years. The organic group showed the greatest variance. Nearly two thirds of these parents waited until the child's fourth or fifth year before receiving a diagnostic statement from a physician. The mongoloid group had, in the majority, a label within the first year. The report that 13 per cent of the mongoloid group did not receive a diagnosis until the child was more than two years old is a surprising finding.

Similarly the incidence of delay in the diagnosis of blindness beyond two years in 28 per cent of the cases came as a surprise. The 11 per cent of the blind group who reported no diagnosis of blindness indicated that, although the child met legal criteria for admission to classes for the blind, the parents did not feel that the physician had truly classified the child as blind.

Diagnostic precision in all of these groups may be difficult to achieve and some delay may be attributed to the nature of a particular child's problem. Then, too, parental delay must be taken into account. Rarely does a parent visit one or more physicians with an insistent day by day consecutivity. Parents delay in arranging the next appointment, wait until conditions are right at home, other children become ill—dozens of explanations intervene between diagnostic appointments. The delay in diagnosis is essentially a temporal problem of intervals between appointments—parentally occasioned or physician directed.

It is of interest however to consider the fact that the initial concern of the mother which prompts the diagnostic quest does not produce a diagnostic label for the majority of these parents until a year or more after the first expression of concern. Whatever vague anxieties the parent of the infant may have, these anxieties will not be composited under some diagnostic label for a considerable length of time.

Meanwhile the parent discharges the child-rearing obligation in a climate of anxiety and diagnostic hope. It is unfortunately the same story for all five groups and represents an intangible factor which cannot be placed in the child-rearing matrix with any degree of confidence. Discussing child-rearing techniques retrospectively with a parent four to eight years after this critical initial period has passed does not readily permit an interpretation of the impact of diagnostic delay upon child-rearing practices.

The period of initial concern is considered to be the single, most critical period in the life of the parent of a handicapped child. It is within this period that the major adjustment probably takes place. By the time a child usually arrives at an age where some form of therapy is begun the parent is already a veteran of deviancy. The data suggest that the parent is aware of deviancy from one to four years *before* someone establishes a diagnostic label to characterize the parental concern.

This critical period is essentially an unexplored area among researchers concerned with the field of rehabilitation. The best information available is retrospective since the child rarely becomes a research subject until he is of school age. By the time his parent is reached, whatever have been the dynamics of those early moments, the feelings and reactions of the initial signs of deviation have historically been interwoven into the parental personality with the individual fibers indiscernible within the total fabric.

The doubts, hesitations, hopes, fears, questions, and anxieties which have accompanied each observation of the parent have been lost to the researcher in the canyons of time. Memory has a way of exaggerating or diminishing the reactions of the past and the tricks played upon the view of the observer by the shadows of memory interfere with the attainment of a clear picture. The quiet moments when neither parent dared to talk with each other for fear of unveiling their anxieties about the child, the bed pillows damp with the tears of painful information, the hundreds of deliberate cognitive efforts to erase the frustrating day-by-day observations, and the thousands of prayers which have been offered to plead for the vital developmental changes to take place, are but part of the crucial parental dynamics in those early days.

The poignancy of those moments—so critical to the understanding of the nature of family dynamics—must somehow be captured by the researchers of the future of the full parental story is to be unravelled. This study made a brief sally into this vital terrain of understanding, retrospectively—with admittedly sketchy results. Those parents who were verbally fluent were able to detail the feelings of those moments of initial concern but most parents could only give a practiced recital of those early days which somehow hinted at the poignancy but never quite expressed it.

Some researcher of the future will have to structure all-illuminating interpretation of the psychological dynamics of dynamic difference between those parents who have an immediacy of deviation impact in the maternity ward and those who gradually acquire an awareness of deviancy as developmental milestones fail to materialize. It seems to be a logical belief that the parental dynamics in these two extremes would differ significantly. Unfortunately, neither the data from this study nor the extensiveness of clinical experience can shed any bright light on this picture. Some dimly lighted speculations are the only illumination which can be offered.

The parent who is confronted with an immediacy of impact in the hospital appears to build an adjustment based upon a survival principle continually pointing out to themselves and all others that the survival of the child was miraculous. Therefore, whatever form of deviancy may be the residual the parent perceives it as a bonus against the possibility that the child might have died. Against that black negative side of the ledger any residual becomes an asset entry on the ledger of life. Clinical experience suggests that such parents evaluate *anything* the child does in terms of, "We are thankful that he is alive—he might have died." In their perceptual schema all data fall on the positive side. Even when the child is nine years old and has not been accepted in school, the parents comfort themselves with the vitality of the child in contrast to traumatic struggle for survival at birth.

Some psychologists tend to place such perception in the category of a delusional effort. The parents who have clinically presented this picture have rarely failed to recognize the deviancy of the child— they do not delude themselves on that score. They do, however, seem to have a constant buffer zone which allows them to balance any negative against a lifelong positive of the child's survival. In view of the dynamic realities of day-by-day living which characterize their efforts to stimulate the development of the handicapped child, this buffer zone may actually serve as a psychological zone to insure the survival of the parent in a complex society.

Among the parents who have such a "buffer zone" built in the vineyard of trauma there are those who face a continuity of nursing service to the child, but there are also those parents who become a jubilant audience to a child who achieves a degree of normalcy, eventually attending school, holding a job and even marrying. The painful parental pacing of the corridors of death in the maternity ward may open upon a hallway of life with varying degrees of life-long brightness.

The continuum of development from severe handicap to mild handicap, or absence of any impairment, is dotted at all points with children who survived miraculously from a neonatal struggle for life. In any community there is probably a representative sample of living refutations of a dismal prognosis given in the neonatal time period. It is imperative that clinicians in all professions who deal with the parents of handicapped children become cognizant of the possible significance of this buffer zone in evaluating the pluses and minuses of a particular couple's child-rearing proficiency and their perception of the child.

The adaptive responses of the parent who assumes that the infant brought home from the hospital will develop along a normal course, and then begins to notice soft or hard signs of deviancy, have also not been delineated. The retrospective inquiry into that period of parenthood evoked an affective introspective report from only a few parents. The slimness of the data on this topic is partially due to the structure of the questions in the parent interview and partially due to the retrospective diminution of feeling intensity. Discussion of this area must be drawn from comments made by a few verbally expressive parents and from clinical counseling experiences with thousands of parents. The story of this period in the life of a parent who gradually becomes aware of the child's deviation must be pieced together from many fragments and be bound into a composite with the glue of subjective impressions gained over the years.

The paragraphs to follow are an attempt to narrate this dynamic acquisition of awareness and delineate a composite. Not all parents of handicapped children experience in the same manner. Allowances must always be made for the personality of the parent and the nature and severity of the child's problem but it is likely that clinicians will be able to place many of their parents somewhere within this picture.

Perhaps the first major and continuing anxiety is related to the possible significance of any complication or deviation in the pregnancy, labor, delivery and neonatal period. When the infant is delivered without blemish and appears to feed, sleep and wake normally, the mother is relieved but does not ignore the possibility that whatever difficulties may have been present may yet take some subtle toll. Reassuring answers from the attending physicians, nurses, husband, relatives and friends may bring partial comfort to the mother but the gnawing doubt still remains in the quiet hours when the reassuring bombardment has ceased. Only the continuity of development without signs of difficulty can dim the doubts. Only the optimal behavior of the growing child can bring the reassurance the mother desires.

In general conversation among women one will continue to overhear remarks which indicate that such doubts persist among mothers of nonhandicapped children well into the child's development. If some event or circumstance brought a complication in the prenatal or postnatal period even the solid normal course of development does not serve to erase the mother's concern. She has seen, heard and read too much in popular press and conversations to dismiss the possibility of a relationship between a birth negative and some aspect of later development. There is almost always a quiet constancy of a search for correlation between later behavior and incidents of birth.

The genuine fact that birth complications are frequently relegated to the status of mysteries when one tries to tie in specific correlations to later behavior does not comfort the mother. The apparently established fact that birth complications do not inevitably presage some developmental deviation also adds to the anxiety. If a simple one to one relationship had been established between each complication and some later behavioral manifestation the mother's burden would be lessened. The fact that the complication may have little or no bearing on the child's future places the mother in the mid-space of waiting to see whether her case is one where there is or is not a correlation.

Mothers laden with varying degrees of anxiety regarding the possible relationship of jaundice, cyanosis, prematurity, blood incompatibilities, lengthy labors, pregnancy difficulties, and so on, to the later development of the child engage in a scientific process of daily observation in much the same manner as a laboratory technician. Each movement or change in the infant is observed and cognitively recorded as a positive or a negative in building a correlation matrix. Response to formulas, to handling, bathing, noises, lights must all be observed, not simply as developmental occurrences, but always in terms of whether such behavioral responses suggest a negative or positive.

Those mothers start the child-rearing process from a different base than do those who have the immediate impact of deviation. The first group *knows* there is something wrong; the second group *suspects* that something *might* be wrong. Among all other factors which make a contribution to the initial attitude toward rearing *this* child the knowledge or suspicion of deviation must be considered as a vital part of this early pattern.

There are two more characterizing patterns which can be defined among mothers in this area of initial concern. Those mothers whose pregnancy, labor and delivery were experienced as uneventful, and where no special circumstances occurred within the early hospital period, compose the two other categories. Most mothers in this study regarded their pregnancies with these children as less complex or at least similar to their other pregnancies. Most mothers regarded the delivery as easy or very easy. Most mothers reported a labor of less than eight hours. Judging from the maternal reporting in this study the percentage of mothers who experience minimal complications in the birth of the handicapped child is much greater than the percentage of those who have significant difficulties.

The traditional belief that each handicapped child has been the product of a stormy pregnancy and delivery must be relegated to the status of myth rather than fact. While it is entirely possible that any disturbance in a natural course from conception to delivery may be a factor in a handicapped product, the general body of evidence to support the notion of an inevitable consequence is building very slowly. An impressive by-product of this line of questioning of the mothers was the surprising incidence of volunteered comments by mothers that the pregnancy and deliveries of one or more of the nonhandicapped siblings had been far more traumatic than that of the handicapped child.

The data from this study suggest that the majority of parents of these children begin their child-rearing relationship to this infant under the assumption of complete normalcy and only gradually come to an awareness of deviation. The parents of the mongoloid group reported the earliest point of concern and, in the majority, had received a diagnostic confirmation of their concern within the first year of life. It is important to note that in spite of the usual striking physical characteristics of mongolism 70 per cent of the mothers in that group reported that diagnostic information was not given to them in the hospital and was received only as they expressed their concern by seeking medical help. The traditional belief that the parents of mongoloid children have an immediate awareness was not borne out by these reports.

In the blind group 61 per cent were diagnosed by the age of one year, but for 50 per cent of that group the awareness began to develop after the infant was home from the hospital. The remainder of that group waited from one to four years for a diagnosis which implies that they were relating to the child in the home situation as a fully-sighted child for child-rearing purposes.

The deaf group reported that 80 per cent of their group lived with *this* child from post-hospital days to three years of age in varying states of awareness of the child's acuity loss. The knowledge of neurologic impairment is perhaps the slowest to develop, with nearly three fourths of the group coming to that awareness *after* the child was three years of age. In this respect the cerebral palsy group was more fortunate. Similar to the mongoloid group it achieved an awareness of diagnosis for the majority by the time the first year had passed.

A cumulative state of awareness was acquired by these mothers from the developmental timetables. Whether they employed formalized tables presented in books, used their other children as models or relied upon comments from friends and neighbors, they all operated within a framework of developmental expectancy. When an expected bit of behavior was not forthcoming, its absence became an anxiety trigger.

Therefore, those mothers who brought their children home from the hospital with little concern for their welfare learned day by day or week by week—or even month by month—one bit at a time— that there was something different about this child. The popular conception that children are "often delayed in these things" could temporarily assuage the mother's anxiety but not for long. Sooner or later the absence of advancing complexity caused the parent to act.

Since the neonate is a small package of life to be fondled, fed and bathed, several months pass before a significant behavioral change is naturally expected. Consequently these mothers fixated upon motoric advancements and speech development as the major concerns. When the child did not sit, lift, lift, turn over and so on—when he did not move as expected there was cause for alarm.

Developmental timetables have verified that the typical course of motoric advancement is one of intervals with new achievements spaced weeks or even months apart. Consequently the time intervals in normal development become a factor in prolonging or alleviating the parental anxieties. The importance of each delay does not strike the parent except as evidence accumulates.

While the child with cerebral palsy may be obvious to all at the age of five years, he is not as obvious when he is only five *months* old. It is apparent that most parents become aware of handicap only as expected behaviors do not emerge. It seems fair to conclude that most parents of handicapped children do not know they *are* the parents of a handicapped child for at least a year or more.

While some differences were noted among the five disability groups, these differences in initial anxieties and subsequent achievement of a diagnostic label could not be attributed to the parents. It was rather a matter of the manifesting nature of each disability that accounted for delay. Consequently no significant correlations can be drawn in regard to child-rearing practices among these five groups. Every group had representatives in each category. Every group was faced with the same struggle of coming to an identification of themselves as parents of a handicapped child. Even those parents who had an immediate awareness of deviation in the child still had to come to an awareness of the meaning of that deviation in identifying themselves.

The fourth group deserving of comment are those parents who seem to be unaware that their child has a problem until school authorities indicate that the child is having a learning or an adjustment problem. This news precipitates a diagnostic search where none has previously taken place. This particular group, mostly in the organic, was of special interest because the characteristics of the children were so obvious to professionals that it was difficult to imagine that such deviations, even though minor, had not been observed by the parents during the previous five or six years.

Intensive probing on this topic in the clinical interviews brought about by some clarification. The behaviors which interest professionals in terms of conformity are not the same set of behaviors which interest the parent. Often parents commented that the aggressiveness which concerned the professional was simply regarded as, "that's the way boys are" in the eyes of a parent. Difficulties in coordination were regarded as "part of growing up." Parents had found a way of normalizing those behaviors as they lived with the child day-by-day. It was not a question of whether or not the behavior had been observed. It was rather a question of whether the parent attached any significance to the behavior. It is probably true that any behavior noted in an organic child can be found among other children at some age if one searches enough, without evidence of organicity.

If a child walks and talks, the shadings and nuances of perceptual disturbances, difficulties in concept formation, problems in language synthesis, distractibility, acuity losses, etc., as significant indicators of handicap may be noted by parents in the early stages of development but the evidence seems clearly to indicate that the parent fails to attach the proper significance to these shadings.

It is this notion of an accumulating awareness which needs to be stressed again and again in setting the perspective for interpreting the child-rearing practices of the parent. It seems quite clear that the parent *arrives* at a self-identification and a child-identification of handicap in the vineyard of child-rearing—not prior to initiating such practices.

It also seems clear that the degree of severity and the nature of each disability in each child, despite a common label, hasten or retard the development of such awareness. The period of initial concern is a time of dual discovery for the parent. One discovery is made in terms of the mechanics of development in the child and the other discovery is made in terms of parental self. For some parents this comes early while for others it takes years.

Despite the findings of some group patterns in this study it seems wiser to view this topic from an individualized perspective. Each parent, regardless of type of disability, makes these two discoveries in their personalized time span. The obvious characteristics, so glaring in the school-age child, were far less obvious in his infant life.

The tendency of some clinicians to castigate the parents for their retrospective ambiguity and seeming insensitivity might well be tempered by this conclusion. The early signs are not as clear as later signs.

As previously indicated it is felt that the dynamic portrait of the parent of the handicapped child could have been positively enhanced by the shadings and nuances which might have been blended in from accurate data in the area of initial concern. The loss must be regarded as a significant limitation upon the composite picture. The loss, however, was an inevitable product of time delay in reaching the parent.

Astute researchers in the future who become interested in this area of investigation will undoubtedly devise a methodology to derive such data. In some manner it must be possible to detail those early moments of trauma when the stark realization of deviancy strikes the parent. Perhaps the hospital psychologists may find a way to study those early parental responses.

It is also vital that some delineation is made of the constructional dynamics of awareness for those parents who come to the realization of handicap over a period of years. As if the parent were building a bank account of awareness each behavioral deposit must some day be recorded and descriptively analyzed if rehabilitation specialists are to achieve a profound understanding of parental dynamics.

The present study and the years of clinical experience have only served to turn the knob and perhaps open the door of understanding to a small crack of light, but future investigators must push the door to its full opening. This study and clinical experience have built a firm conviction that the area of initial and growing concern represents the mother lode in the understanding of the rehabilitation parent.

The portrait of the father in the parental duo begins with some attempt to understand the parental role in initial concern and the early infancy period. It is clear from the data that most fathers share the early concern in simultaneity with the mother. The father may express his concern in a different manner, he may attempt to minimize his concern and even deliberately seek to dismiss his own concern and that of his wife, but the temporal contiguity of concern is present. The dynamics of the "ostrich father" who buries his head in the sands of apathy are probably triggered by this initial concern.

Despite the fact that every rehabilitation clinician is probably well acquainted with maternal narratives about fathers who have "refused" to share the problem, the evidence from the present study clearly supports the notion that the father of the handicapped child *does* share an initial concern. While his feelings may not be the equal of the mother's, there is no question of his observational awareness of deviation. He is there. He may turn away but *before he turns away, he has perceived.*

Not only is the majority picture one of simultaneity of awareness in the two parents but it is also a picture of father helpfulness in the management of the many details of infant management. No effort was made in this study to ascertain whether such helpfulness was a daily occurrence, irregular or sporadic. Interest was mainly focussed upon the question of whether the fathers of handicapped children participated in the early mechanics of child-rearing. Only a small percentage of the mothers expressed significantly negative attitudes towards their mates on this topic. This area must be classified as a "shared area of concern" for both parents in all five groups. While each father may have displayed greater or lesser frequence he *did* participate.

Such a finding is generally in keeping with changes which have occurred in the paternal role in modern family life. Fathers have become more actively involved with problems of early management. The fathers of these children were very much a part of the early child-rearing scene. Failures to participate more actively in the medical-diagnostic process could usually be attributed to economic factors.

Chapter 5

PATTERNS OF COMMUNICATION

THE DAY-BY-DAY business of child-rearing is accompanied by a heavy reliance upon oral communication. The parent, in the course of helping the child to conform to expected patterns of behavior, to move in proper directions, to refrain from touching, and to gain some understanding of the world about him, depends for the most part on the spoken word to accomplish such goals.

In the American culture spoken words are more important than in many other cultures. Americans are very verbal. Most parents surround their children with a verbal barrage of "Dos" and "Don'ts" as the major frontal attack in transmitting the rules of behavior, culture patterns, and moral standards. This reliance upon the spoken word carries with it the implicit assumption that the child at whom the words are directed has the capacity for comprehending the words and translating these words into patterns of meaning for his own actions.

Being surrounded by a verbal environment, the child gradually refines his vocal explorations to imitate the sound patterns he hears about him and under the careful tutelage of parents and others, learns to speak words in the same manner. Developmentally, he gradually acquires a precise pattern of articulating sounds with progressive skill. Quite early in life the child begins using words to convey his thoughts, and desires, and fits his communicative pattern into the mold cast by his parents.

To learn to imitate and modify the articulations, he must acquire a skill at discriminating differences among various gross sounds and those which appear to have a relative similarity. He must become a listener. He must listen and talk, listen and talk, and continue to listen and talk throughout his lifetime in order to exchange his thoughts with those of others in the practical business of conversation. He must learn to wait patiently for his turn to talk while others are talking. Parents teach their children with varying degrees of success to avoid interrupting adult conversations with unrelated requests or comments. The child must learn to verbalize his explanations for his actions to present evidence for parental decision-making. These are but a few of the ingredients which go into the building of a communication pattern between parents and children, and children and others in their world.

Casual observations of mother-child conversations will reflect a parental tendency to talk in simple, direct, and brief sentence structures to very young children and to progressively complicate the sentence formulations as the child grows older. This appears to occur without a great deal of conscious planning on the part of a parent to match the expression of directives to the progressive increase in language capacity as a child grows older. It just happens. Observation will also reveal that parents restructure their original expression in a regressive direction if child comprehension and action is not quickly evident.

If the child does not grasp the first utterance, the parent will say it again, altering the rhythm so as to seemingly underline key words. Unconsciously, the attempt to reach the child takes the form of progressive simplification and emphasis.

Chronologic age appears to culturally infer capacity for complexity. Most adults talk to young children in different sentence structure and emphasis than they do to older children. There is a cultural recognition that vocabulary, length of sentence, compounding, and abstraction must be scaled downward for the young child while the older child is expected to deal receptively with more complicated oral formulations.

Consequently, the question might be raised regarding the possible tendency in parents of handicapped children to rely upon simpler expression when confronted with a deaf child, a blind child, a mongoloid, a cerebral palsied, or a brain-damaged child regardless of chronologic age. Do they tend to reflect a high degree of modification in their communicative effort by resorting to slower speech, increased volume, shorter sentences, and multiple expressions of the same thought?

While there are undoubtedly hundreds of ways statements might be formulated to tap the many variations which might be utilized by a parent in modifying their communicative effort, eight statements were devised to secure data in this area. Statements were formulated which might have some general application to all of the groups involved.

To gain a general appraisal of the nature of the *communication* milieu among these families with particular reference to the handicapped child's receptive and expressive problems, and the manner in which the parents may, or may not, have modified their communication with the child in recognition of such problems, a series of seventy-three statements were devised to cover these three areas. The statements were organized into the Communication Patterns form (see Appendix) placed in random order and presented to parents during the group testing sequence of the study.

The form directed the parent to read each statement and place a check mark in the designated space if that statement applied to them or their child.

The form contained forty-two statements which referred to some aspect of expressive language or speech, and twenty-one statements related to the child's receptive behavior in the communication process.

The statements listed on the Communication Patterns form referring to modifications which might be employed by parents in their day-by-day efforts to communicate with their handicapped children were as follows:

--------The easiest way to get through to him is by gestures.
--------We talk louder to this child.
--------We talk slower to this child.
--------We frequently have to say things different ways before he understands.
--------We use shorter sentences when we talk to him.
--------We talk differently to him than to our other children.
--------We talk to him in the same way as we talk to our other children.
--------We make sure that he's looking at us when we talk to him.
--------I have to repeat things I say before he seems to catch on.
--------We try to teach him to say words clearly.
--------We have given up trying to teach him to say words clearly.

Since the emphasis in this study was upon the parental attitudes and techniques of child-rearing, the statements regarding receptive and expressive communication traits among the children were considered secondary to the ten statements concerned with specific parental practices. Consequently, the items checked by parents in the receptive and expressive categories reflected a state of awareness and an expression of the general problem with which they were confronted. The ten statements of parental modification were used to divide the parents into a high and low group in the extent of modification.

Parents who indicated that they talked differently to this child from how they talked to siblings, and checked three of the five statements, were classified as "high modifiers." All others were considered to be making no modifications or only minor changes, in order to communicate with their handicapped child. Almost all of those rated as "low modifiers" indicated that they talked to this child in the same manner as they did to their other children.

A number of questions come to mind in contemplating the review of these data. To what extent did parents of deaf children modify their effort? How did parents report the oral speech of their deaf children in a community where the educators of the deaf are devoted to the oral method? What differences existed among the mild, moderately and severely involved children with cerebral palsy and their parents? Were any patterns of communication peculiar to one or the other of the diagnostic groups? Did parental perceptions generally conform to accepted clinical pictures in each group. What types of differences, if any, were reflected in the father responses versus the mother responses? Were any differences noted among parents of hyperactive children and those with children who were comparatively docile? These and many other questions might be asked of the data obtained from the communication questionnaire.

THE CEREBRAL PALSY GROUP

Parental Modification

Most of the mothers of cerebral palsied children (84 per cent) indicated that they talked to the handicapped child in the same manner as they talked to their other children (Table 45). If any modification was indicated, it was usually to talk slower to the handicapped child. When the intellectual levels of the cases are taken into consideration in evaluating this incidence of low modification of parental communicative effort, the fact that 63 per cent of the

TABLE 45

PERCENTAGES OF PARENTS IN EACH GROUP CLASSIFIED AS
HIGH OR LOW MODIFIERS OF COMMUNICATION PATTERNS

	Cerebral Palsy	Organic	Mongoloid	Blind	Deaf
High use of modification	16%	39%	50%	5%	70%
Low use of modification	84%	61%	50%	95%	30%

children were of average intelligence, or moderately retarded, suggests that the parents probably had little need to be significantly concerned about their child's inability to comprehend what was spoken to him.

Only one mother indicated that she talked louder to this child than to her other children. Of those techniques available for selection, by virtue of their inclusion on the form, the combination of talking slower, using shorter sentences, and saying something in several different ways was the usual modification. Three mothers of severely retarded children indicated that their child responded best when the parents used gestures to communicate with him. These same three cases were also rated as being severe receptive and expressive problems.

Receptive Communication

Most of the mothers (69 per cent) indicated that their children had no difficulty in understanding what was said to them. Three of the twenty-one cases who indicated some form of receptive problem checked the item stating that the child understood nothing that was said to him (Table 46).

To ascertain the general concurrence of the mothers' indications of severe expressive problems with professional evaluations, the speech

TABLE 46

CHARACTERISTICS OF RECEPTIVE COMMUNICATION AMONG
THE FIVE POPULATIONS AS REPORTED BY PARENTS

	Cerebral Palsy	Organic	Mongoloid	Blind	Deaf
No problem	69%	39%	34%	84%	0%
Reception varies	21%	48%	66%	16%	50%
Receives gestures better than speech	10%	13%			50%

therapists' reports in the clinical case files were searched for ratings
of severe expressive problems. Thirty-five of the seventy cases (50
per cent) had been designated as severe problems by the speech
therapists. Only one of these thirty-five mothers had *not* indicated
a similar rating in the items checked on the communication form.
This appears to reflect evidence for reality perception in these thirty-
two mothers, at least on this particular question.

The majority of the cerebral palsied cases (72 per cent) were
identified by their parents as having difficulties in expressive communication ranging from moderate to severe degrees. All children
described by their mothers as having no problem in expressive communication were of average intelligence or in the moderately retarded
group, and those who were of school age were attending school either
in regular or orthopedic units.

Only six of the thirty-five severe expressive cases were attending
school, with five at the orthopedic school, and one in a class for the
educable mentally handicapped. The six who were attending school
were all classified as moderately retarded. All twenty-three cases,
who had been classified as severely retarded, were also classifid as
severe expressive problems. The remaining seven cases, in the severe
expressive category, were moderately retarded and not old enough for
special class eligibility. While a severe expressive problem did not
necessarily eliminate a child from school enrollment, if severe retardation was also present, he was not acceptable for school attendance.

Ten of the mothers whose children were rated by them, and by
the therapists, as severe expressive problems, attributed this difficulty
to an involvement of tongue-musculature.

The items inserted to attempt an evaluation of maternal perception
of that expressive language phenomena which is professionally labeled
perseveration and echolalia, evoked minimal response from the parents of the children with cerebral palsy. Only eight mothers checked
items which might reflect perseveration, and only two cases checked
the "little Sir Echo" item.

THE ORGANIC GROUP

Parental Modifications

Parents in the organic group reported that only one third felt any need to modify their pattern of communication for their brain-damaged child. Most parents talked to *this* child in the same manner as they talked to their other children. Those who talked differently to this child all reported a similar pattern of modification—they spoke at a slower pace, used shorter sentences, and found themselves giving directives in several different formulations before they achieved results with the child.

Despite the report that 79 per cent of the organic children presented special problems of understanding parent speech, the incidence of significant modifications in the parents' communication to the child is much less than might be expected.

Expressive Pattern

Three in each four children in this group were considered by their parents to have difficulty with expressive speech. Ten children were reported to have no words. Nineteen others preferred to make their wants known by gesturing rather than vocal effort. Forty-five children perseverated in their speech and twenty were echolalic.

Receptive Patterns

Approximately two thirds of the organic group were reported to experience some difficulty in receiving and comprehending language. Sometimes the child understood the directions or the words being used, at other times the child gave no manifestation of recognition. Some parents felt that the child understood better if the parent held visual contact during the communication effort. Some felt that their child responded better to gestural language than to spoken words. It is interesting to note that although two thirds of the children were reported to have a receptive problem, only one third of the parents made any attempt to modify their communication pattern.

THE DEAF GROUP

Parental Modifications

The parents of these deaf children were confronted with the problem of communicating the thousands of directives, commands, and comments which make up the business of daily living over a period of time to a child who was in the transitional stage of substituting oral symbols for a more primitive pattern of gestural language. The word-fluent parent accustomed to communicating in oral speech to other children, friends, relatives, etc., is faced with a child who sometimes understands and sometimes does not. The child may become confused if the speech is delivered too quickly.

It apparently becomes necessary to insure that the child is looking at the speaker for optimum efficiency, and this must present problems in terms of distance from the speaker or type of separations, such as from room to room in a house. The child's attention must be disengaged from a point of concentration in order that his receptive channels are freed to receive parental speech.

Projection of these various potential problem areas suggest that perhaps the necessity for parental modification in communication patterns in this group is greater than among the four groups in this study. This belief was substantiated in the findings which show that 70 per cent of the parents in the deaf group were classified as high modifiers of communication.

The principal form of modification among these parents was the use of gestures instead of oral speech and the insistence upon visual contact with the child during the speaking act. Shorter sentences and simpler language were also used. All of the parents still emphasized an oral approach and were attempting to teach their children words.

Patterns of Reception

Parents might well be expected to encounter considerable difficulty in the day by day process of communicating demands, requests, directives, and comments to their deaf children when the parental modality of oral speech represents the main communicative channel. It was then of interest to ascertain the particular frequency with which these parents checked items on the Communication Patterns form which reflected some dilemma in prosaic daily oral intercourse.

Half of the mothers in this group indicated that their deaf child responded better to gestured directives than to oral speech. A small percentage reported that their child experienced no difficulty in understanding parental speech, but the majority indicated that the child's reception of speech was sporadically efficient. About half of the group noted that their child was a nonlistener if he or she were concentrating on something else, and for three fourths of the group visual contact with the parent was necessary to insure reception. Nearly half of the group indicated that the child's receptive efficiency was reduced if people talked fast.

Patterns of Expression

The twenty-four children in the deaf group were all enrolled in public school classes for the deaf where the teaching philosophy is dominantly one of emphasizing oral communications. Since all of the parents of these children were nondeaf adults, the probability that the children were receiving an emphasis on oral communication both at home and at school exists. This would represent a milieu in which the spoken word would be most highly valued as a mode of communication.

It was not surprising, therefore, to find that only one child in this group was reported as having no oral speech. All others used some form of oral communication. For more than half the group, however, according to the parents, the children preferred to use gestures in their efforts to communicate. None of the children in this group could be classified as noncommunicators since each was reported to be trying to communicate with parents and peers on some level of oral speech and two thirds of the parents felt that the children were learning to talk clearly. It is very likely that the preference for gestures in some of the children may represent a transitional stage to a higher level of communication since the majority of this group were in the five to seven year age range.

The incidence of probable difficulties with monitoring of sound in terms of speaking too loudly or too softly was noted by 45 per cent of the parents with the greater tendency being one of talking too loudly.

THE MONGOLOID GROUP

Parental Modifications

Two forms of modification were employed by parents of mongoloid children. They talked slower to this child, and phrased their speech in several different ways in order to reach the child. The use of shorter sentences or increased volume was checked by only a few parents, and only one indicated that gestures were employed in communicating with the child. Those rated low in modification reported that they talked to the mongoloid child in the same manner as to their other children. Since these parents showed the second greatest frequency of high modification (50 per cent), it must be pointed out that this finding is regarded as a chance factor and significance is attached to this in terms of relating this comparatively high incidence of modification.

The net conclusion in this case is that some parents do modify their communication and some do not. The specificity of the child's immaturity in receptive and expressive areas as reported by parents and professionals does not appear to occasion a parental adaptation except in certain parents. Certain constellations of traits might be found among the high modifiers as other data on parents are related to these findings, but it seems clear that it is not the diagnostic category which prompts the adaptation.

Receptive Problems

The majority in this group were reported to have some difficulty in understanding what was said to them with the indication that reception varied a great deal. One third of the mothers felt that their children experienced little or no difficulty in understanding spoken language. The same comments made about parents and their evaluation of the receptive processes in the section on the cerebral palsied were felt to be equally applicable to the parents of mongoloid children. While a few parents rated to be high in the use of modifications were found to report the absence of a receptive problem, the bulk of those rated high in modification identified a receptive problem in the child. The presence of the receptive problem was unrelated to the child's chronologic age, with findings revealing a scattering at all age levels. Again there was a high degree of concordance on this point in both parents.

Expressive Problems

The paucity of language in the mongoloid child, which has been reported in the general literature in the field of mental retardation, was corroboratively reflected in the type of items checked by the parents of these children. One mother indicated that her child talked clearly in sentences, but all the others reported their child to have a moderate to severe problem in verbal expression. Twenty-three cases were stated to be learning to talk clearly while fourteen cases were checked as being "jargoneers" with expressive speech limited to unintelligible sounds.

In none of the records was there any indication that the child was not actively attempting oral communication. The child's chronologic age was not found to be significant in relation to the severity of his expressive problem. It has been fairly well established at this point that the mongoloid child eventually acquires a limited oral speech-pattern with variations in the chronological time in which such clarity might come about, and these findings from parents are in general accord with professional observations. The mothers and fathers of these children were in high agreement on this area.

THE BLIND GROUP

Patterns of Reception

Only three parents suggested that their blind child experienced any form of difficulty in understanding whatever parents had to say. The general impression gained is that the parents of the blind did not perceive the reception of language as any form of problem for their children.

Patterns of Expression

The area of expressive speech was also viewed very positively by the parents of the blind children with only two cases indicating that the child's speech was poor and difficult to understand. All others were either talking clearly or were acquiring clearer patterns with advancing age.

Parent Modification

Only two cases indicated that they introduced any form of modification in their communicative efforts with their blind child. Seeing no expressive or receptive problem in their children almost all of the parents felt no need to modify their communicative patterns.

EVALUATION OF RESPONSE

No brief is held here for the comprehensiveness of these data in representing the true picture of communication patterns within all these families. Adequate study of parental communication requires some systematic recording of on-the-spot conversations, directives, admonitions, and exhortations with trained observers or electronic revices of some kind. While this is regarded as a vital area of investigation for those concerned with child-rearing, the scope of the present study did not permit other than a preliminary and tentative entry into this domain by means of a checklist questionnaire.

Several questions can be posed in evaluating whether or not the check marks made by parents in response to given statements have some semblance of relationship to the reality of the communication situation as it exists in their families. First, one might ask whether the completed forms reflected any kind of consistency of response. Did parents check items which were in contradiction with one another, such as checking the statement that the child talked clearly in sentences and then on another page indicating that the child had no intelligible words? Fortunately every parent was consistent within the form. While a number of items in each area were neglected by some parents whose interview records indicated that the items applied in their case, each parent checked enough items to indicate their perceptions of the receptive and expressive levels of their child and their own modifications.

The second question regarding consistency may be raised in relation to the extent of agreement between mothers and fathers. Did fathers and mothers tend to reflect the same communication status? As a general rule, the answer must be in the affirmative. Some interesting differences were found in certain populations which will be discussed later but these differences were attributable to perceptual variations in mothers and fathers concerning the severities of expressive and receptive problems and not due to gross dissimilarities. In no instance did a mother report clear speech while her spouse reported absence of speech. Mothers, on the whole, checked more statements on the total form than did fathers. Since this difference in volume of response characterized the fathers throughout all areas of investigation, no specific interpretation will be attempted in regard to communication patterns.

The third question can be referred to the concordance with clinical findings on the children. Did the patterns of receptive and expressive problems reflected by parents bear any relationship to the problems described by therapists, teachers, and psychologists contained in the child's clinical case file? Since more than 80 per cent of the cases were known to the investigators, it was possible to check the case files on the majority of the study population. When clinical expressions of receptive or expressive severity were compared with parental perceptions, the findings revealed a reasonably high degree of correlation.

Professionals tended to view the problem as more severe than did the parent, but rarely did a parent perceive no problem where a therapist indicated that a serious expressive or receptive problem existed. Parents generally reflected less awareness of receptive problems than they had for expressive problems but this finding is not surprising. Empirical clinical evidence will support the observation that parents impute receptive comprehension to their child as a matter of routine unless they suspect or have confirmed some auditory acuity loss. The more subtle manifestations of receptive inefficiency found in aphasia tend to escape detection by parents in the general dynamics of daily living. For that matter, these same subtle receptive problems escape detection by many professionals.

Many times parents impute comprehension to an attentive child so long as it appears that the child is listening. Parents are also inclined to attribute inadequacies in comprehension to stubbornness, orneriness, and negativism, and to attach some deliberate significance to the child when he does not catch on. Parents voice this in the form of statements such as, "He just refuses to listen" or "When he gets a stubborn streak, it's like talking to a brick wall."

Consequently, the general finding that parents in this study were less aware of receptive problems is interpreted as a normal response. Clinical expressions of receptive severity were generally at variance with parental reporting in all of the study populations. It is felt that this variance is attributable to a general parental factor of less sensitivity in this area which would hold true for all parents regardless of whether the child were normal or handicapped. This was not a matter of a parent denying the existence of a problem, but rather perceiving it from a different bias.

The three evaluative questions concerned with (1) parental consistency within the form, (2) mother-father agreement on the nature of the problem and (3) concordance with clinical findings, can all be answered in the affirmative. Parent perceptions as reflected in the Communication Patterns form were not significantly at variance per parent, between parents, and with clinical findings. Some degree of validity may be attributed to the findings to be discussed in subsequent paragraphs, albeit limited.

Expressive Summary

The statements which were inserted to tap the phenomenon of perseveration and echolalia failed to attract any appreciable responses except in the organic group. While the general literature related to organic children leads one to expect a greater incidence of such behavior among the general distribution of intellectual levels represented in the organic groups than was reflected by the parents, the failing is more likely attributable to vagueness in semantic organization on the form than to the implied failure of the parent to be sensitive and responsive to such behavior.

The parents of blind children were most positive among all the groups in indicating the absence of an expressive problem (Table 47). The blind child was perceived as having little or no difficulty in speech expression. They were viewed as talking clearly or making good progress in the acquisition of speech. The deaf group was also perceived very positively by the parents with three-fourths of the group reported as making good progress in learning how to talk clearly. There was a marked tendency for parents of deaf children to indicate that, despite oral progress, the child preferred to use gestures to communicate with the parents. This observation falls in the category of an expected finding. The highest incidence of expressive difficulty was reported by the parents in the cerebral palsy group with the concentration of difficulty lodged in the severe cases.

TABLE 47

CHARACTERISTICS OF EXPRESSIVE COMMUNICATION AMONG
THE FIVE POPULATIONS AS REPORTED BY PARENTS

	Cerebral Palsy	Organic	Mongoloid	Blind	Deaf
Talks clearly	28%	38%	12%	79%	10%
Has no words	26%	8%	36%		5%
Jargon use	18%	20%	20%		35%
Learning to talk clearly	28%	34%	42%	21%	50%

The entire population of parents expressed a majority opinion that expressive speech was not a severe handicap. Either the child talked clearly or was making progress in acquiring speech, and the parents felt no compulsion to check other negative statements in the expressive series. The totality of these perceptions was taken as a reflection of optimism among the parents, and for the most part was in accord with the intellectual ratings, professional judgments, degree of severity found among the children. While individual cases in all groups were reported to have extreme expressive difficulty, the general group finding revealed that the majority of cases were not experiencing any unusual difficulty.

Receptive Summary

The most favorable commentary on reception of language was made by the parents of blind children. Only 16 per cent of this group checked any of the negative items in the receptive series. The majority of cerebral palsy cases were also placed in a favorable light by their parents. The deaf group reported the greatest amount of difficulty in this area and the organic group was comparatively evenly divided on a "no problem-problem" split. Only among the parents of the deaf was there a significant indication that the child received gestures more meaningfully than he responded to words.

In general, the findings were felt to conform to expectancy; the shading of parental positivism in this area was accepted as common naiveté, due to their unawareness of all the implications hidden in the receptive statements. The parent of the deaf child perceived a direct relationship between the child's acuity problem and his receptive difficulty. In all other groups there was no significant relationship between parental perception of the extent of receptive problem and the child's labeled handicap.

Parental Modification

As a general rule all of the parents talked to their handicapped child in the same manner as to their other children. Only when there was an obvious obstacle to reception in the form of acuity loss was there a significant modification in parental communication. For specific cases in the cerebral palsy and organic groups there were notable modifications reported by parents, but these were not in large percentage.

Mothers and fathers in all five populations were in a high state of agreement on their perceptions of the child's expressive and receptive problems and their own use of modified communicative effort. Only in the organic group was there a notable incidence of disagreement among mothers and fathers. The direction of disagreement is of interest because mothers were more inclined to see a problem in receptive areas than were the fathers and the fathers were more likely to see an expressive problem where the mothers did not.

All cases, with the exception of some parents of severely handicapped and retarded children with cerebral palsy, indicated that they were actively attempting to teach the child to say words properly in the daily course of family living. Shorter sentences and saying things in several different ways represented the major forms of modifications employed by parents.

Clinical Implications

While the series of statements employed in the Communication Patterns form are not considered to represent a refined probe into the true nature of the communicative milieu in these families, there are a number of emergents from these cursory samples which are worthy of note for clinical practice.

The extent of parental modification is believed to be related to the general level of communication sensitivity in any parent. The findings have suggested that parents err most frequently in their perception of the child's receptive problems. Difficulties with reception are frequently misjudged as stubbornness, willfulness, playfulness, and other behavioral traits.

Clinicians might well serve the child's development by the concentrated effort to help the parent differentiate between the true problems in handling receptive language versus the true problems of negativism, playfulness, etc. Expressive problems are more obviously manifest and recognized. Receptive problems tend to be obscured. Clinical programs devoted to helping parents become sensitive to the many nuances in reception of language, and emphasis upon teaching parents specific forms of communicative modifications to ameliorate such receptive problems, may aid to reinforce speech and language therapy programs for optimum benefit to the child.

COMMENTARY ON COMMUNICATION

The technique of using a group questionnaire to investigate this significant area of parent-child interactions' is admittedly open to criticism. Methodology directed towards samples of live conversation would undoubtedly provide greater precision on this topic. The evidence obtained simply indicated that parents reported certain types of modification in their pattern of communication. When a parent checked the statement of using simpler sentences there was no way of obtaining a comparative sample of such simplification. The study, however, was not intended to study communication in detail.

A number of points, however, deserve further comment to suggest possible directions for future study:

1. Parents develop whatever modifications they employ as a function of the day-by-day child-rearing effort. They change their own expressions in order to communicate with their child. Only three sets of parents in this study commented that the modification of their communicative patterns was based upon professional advice from a psychologist, physician, therapist or language specialist. All others adapted their language as their own parental experience dictated. Modification was therefore parentally oriented. In view of the tremendous body of knowledge which exists in the field of child reception and expression of language it is reasonable to assume that professional specialists would have taken special pains to communicate such research and understanding to the parent where it could be put to use in the home setting. The evidence is to the contrary. Each parent seems to

go about the business of developing a communication pattern with their handicapped child on a day-by-day basis in the child-rearing milieu and not according to the principles of communication which have been delineated by the various professional groups in each field.

2. As a consequence of this apparent "do-it-yourself" process the parental affirmation that the "child understands anything that is said to him" must immediately be suspect. In clinical practice it has often been observed that the parent who indicates that the child has good understanding of spoken language is an expert gesticulator, frequently without awareness that each directive is unconsciously accompanied by a gesture which gives emphasis to the oral formulation.

3. The textbooks on language and communication often refer to the language development obligation of the parent of any child. From his parent the child learns the lauguage of his culture. The parent is automatically cast in the role of a language instructor with the obligation to achieve a sufficient competency in each student-child to satisfy the demands of the educational society. Despite some probing in this area it was not possible to ascertain whether any of these parents held a conscious awareness of their role as a language instructor. From clinical experience it seems safe to conclude that few parents view themselves with any degree of formality as consciously enacting the role which the language theorists have assigned to them. The teaching aspect of parent-child communication was a remote consideration. The accomplishment of day-by-day management of behavior was the primary focus.

4. It was of interest to note that all parents cast an optimistic vote regarding their child's expressive fluency. Where articulation problems or expressive formulation difficulties were known to exist the parent perceived a continuing state of improvement. Even in regard to receptive problems the parents expressed a favorable note of improvement. Regardless of the difficulties experienced by either the child or the parent in the area of communication parents tended to view the difficulties lessening through time.

5. The major reason for modification in each group, other than the deaf, was related to assumptions or knowledge of reduced intelligence in the child. Where the assumption of average intelligence was held there was little effort to modify. It is apparent that the parental perception of intellectual level, and not the professional measurement of level, is the significant factor. Long before a parent has the benefit of a medical or psychological assessment the communicative patterns are established. It seems reasonable to conclude that the parent develops a communication line with the child, not because of a disability, but because he or she is their child living in their home. They assign whatever intellectual level they deem advisable and very often are just as accurate as eventual testing may measure—if their own scale of modification could be quantified.

6. A more detailed study of this area of parent-child interaction is required if the child-rearing process for any group of children and parents is to be fully understood. In the prosaic situation of child-rearing the expression of directives, correctives, remonstrations, admonitions, advising, coaxing, urging, rewarding and punishing is primarily verbal. The way a parent uses words to derive desired behavioral change represents a significant focus for research. The use of parental language in the child-rearing process is even more deserving of investigation among groups of handicapped children because of the many difficulties in language reception and expression which have been detailed in the rehabilitation literature. While this study barely scratched the surface in this area, a start has been made. The phenomenon of language in the interpersonal relationships among people looms as a progressively more critical area for research. In the immense effort of linguists, semanticists, psychologists and aphasic therapists there must be some way to insert a wedge on behalf of the parent of the handicapped child. If American parenthood is so heavily reliant upon words in conducting its child-rearing obligation then "child-rearing words" become an automatically critical variable in understanding the rearing process. Language space is the major domain of child-rearing—it is time that research specialists recognized this fact.

Chapter 6

PATTERNS OF TOILET TRAINING

Toilet training represents an important element in the curriculum of child-rearing. Three perspectives may be considered in discussing the reason and the manner in which parents go about the business of teaching their children independently to respond to bladder and bowel urges in the pattern prescribed by the culture. One perspective may be termed "sociological" and refers to the standards set down by the culture.

Society expects a parent to have achieved the child's bowel training by the age of two or three years and any delay beyond this age requires a constant explanation to other parents. Bladder control is expected to be achieved first for waking hours and then later for sleeping hours. The invention of training pants to serve as a transition between the diaper stage and regular underpants represents a social expression of this cultural demand. Training pants for children above the age of three are difficult to purchase as many parents of handicapped children have testified.

Parents who have not been successful within the prescribed time limits feel an urgency to explain reasons for such delay to friends and relatives as an accounting for their failure to conform to this societal demand. While a certain range of tolerance may be granted to the parent of the handicapped child the expectancy is nonetheless present. Even though there appears to be some acceptance of delay there are still upper limits for the attainment of toilet competency. Rarely is a child acceptable in a school setting unless the criteria of toilet training has been met.

In those schools that deal with the physically handicapped there may be an understandable excuse from personal competency, but there is still a demand for the child to somehow indicate a toileting need which can be managed by a matron or attendant. Since the schools set toilet competence as a criteria for admission the parent of a handicapped child has a "social range" from birth to school enrollment to accomplish this goal. The upper limits of the range are determined by the customary age for accepting children with given disabilities. Where children are customarily accepted at four or five years of age the parent has that period of time available.

The pressure to achieve toilet competency becomes a matter of essentially insuring or postponing the child's admission to school. Intellectual level or severity of handicap may be far less a barrier to school enrollment than failure to manage toileting. The school demand is a societal demand. Some parents may achieve this well within the prescribed limits and others may fail—but the limits have been defined. Those who do not conform to those limits accept some form of social penalty for such failure.

A second perspective on toilet training may be termed "psychological" and is rooted in various theories of dynamic personality linking the toilet training to sexual anxieties of various types. In this perspective the emphasis is placed upon the parental anxieties in relation to anal behavior, pressing the parent to resolve the anxiety at the earliest possible moment by ridding themselves of continuing anxiety in this area.

In this frame of reference the taboos of history for preoccupation with urinary and defecation processes mingle with varied sexual insecurities. The anxieties thus generated must be resolved by speedy achievement of independence.

A third perspective, and frequently a most compelling one, may be labeled "reality factors." This perspective enters the domain of general housekeeping and causes a mother to wilt under the constant demand to wash clothes and bed sheets, to become weary of diaper pails, to seek relief from constant changing and to long for the day when she can cease her hypervigilant status. When children are borne in rapid succession each child trained reduces the total demand. Pretty pinafores and suits appear far more attractive when the bulging encumberance of diapers and rubber pants have been removed. As one mother stated, "I'd have a lot more time to play with my child and enjoy him if I didn't have to spend so much time washing his diapers and messy clothes and sheets, and watching him constantly for any little sign that would mean a rush to the bathroom."

It is likely that all three of these perspectives are aligned in some rank order for all parents in creating the urgency to achieve toilet training for their children. A series of questions were posed in the interview to gain some information in this area.

TRAINING TECHNIQUES AND TIMING

The mothers were divided in all groups on the question of a timetable for bowel training between the feeling that such training should be accomplished before the child was two years of age and those who felt that the child's readiness for such learning should be the determining factor. The "readiness" belief was most pronounced in the organic and the mongoloid groups and "before two years" was preferred in the blind and deaf. All mothers agreed that training should be accomplished by age four except for a few mothers who were unwilling to commit themselves to any definite statement (Table 48).

TABLE 48
MOTHERS' BELIEFS REGARDING AGE OF CHILD FOR INITIATING BOWEL TRAINING

	Cerebral Palsy*	Organic	Mongoloid	Blind	Deaf
Before 2 years		34%	35%	40%	45%
Before 3 years		4%	10%	7%	19%
Before 4 years			3%	7%	
Whenever they are ready		57%	48%	33%	36%
Have no set belief		4%	3%	13%	

*Question not asked.

When these findings are compared with those of Sears (1957) on a similar question there is a considerable variance between the mothers of normal kindergartners and the mothers of the handicapped. Almost all of the mothers in the Sears study initiated bowel training before their child was two years of age. Among the mothers of the handicapped the belief that training should begin "when the child is ready," accounts for a sizable percentage in each group and tends to distort a comparison.

Whereas the question in this study asked mothers to state their belief, the Sears study requested the mothers to indicate the age of the child when they did in fact begin. Even granting that some of the mothers of the handicapped who expressed the "readiness" concept did, in fact, initiate training before two years of age there is a considerable difference between the two groups. As a group the mothers of the handicapped children tended to start the bowel training procedure at a later age than did the Sears' mothers.

There was virtually no variation among the mothers on the question of how they happened to begin bowel training this child at the particular time they started. Very few parents relied upon a physician's recommendation, "expert" advice from a pamphlet or book about children, advice from a friend or relative, or imitation of others to initiate the training. Almost every mother stated she made an independent decision to begin at the time she did (Table 49).

TABLE 49

PERCENTAGE DISTRIBUTION OF MOTHERS' ACCOUNTING
FOR INITIATION OF BOWEL TRAINING

	Cerebral Palsy*	Organic	Mongoloid	Blind	Deaf
I decided for myself		93%	100%	100%	87%
The doctor advised me to begin		3%			4%
A relative or friend suggested I begin		4%			
Read in a book					8%

*Question not asked.

Response to "Accidents"

All parents agree that there are moments during the later stages of the toilet training period in which the child sometimes forgets the lessons he has learned and experiences a slip-up in control. These are often moments when the mother is disappointed because what appeared to be accomplished fact is, by virtue of the accident, evidence that independence has not yet been attained and there is more to do. When such "accidents" occur a mother is confronted with a demand for some kind of reaction. Should she ignore the accident or reprimand the child for failure to heed the bowel or bladder signals? The mothers were asked to indicate what their reaction had been or was when such slip-ups occurred (Table 50).

The mothers of the blind, deaf and organic presented a majority expression that such accidents were ignored by them or at worst were met with a mild verbal reminder. Their statements indicated

TABLE 50

MOTHERS' RESPONSES TO "ACCIDENTS"
AFTER CHILDREN ARE TRAINED

	Cerebral Palsy	Organic	Mongoloid	Blind	Deaf
Let it go by, not concerned, gentle pat on rear	48%	59%	40%	83%	65%
General reaction of doing something to child: punishment physical or verbal, disciplining	52%	33%	55%	17%	24%
Got furious or angry		8%	5%		11%

that they accepted such possibilities as a necessary and expected part of the learning process. Among the mothers in the cerebral palsy and mongoloid groups, however, the balance was shifted in the direction of aggressive action toward the child either as physical punishment or sharp verbal reprimand at those times. All sets of mothers had a sizable representation in the active and passive response categories, with only the mothers of the blind indicating an overwhelming tendency toward an accepting-passive reaction.

Techniques Used in Bowel and Bladder Training

The favored technique for achieving bowel training was to place the child on "potty chair," or on a specially constructed seat which fits on a commode, at regular intervals and to help the child gain the idea of desired elimination by verbal encouragement from the parent. This technique served the majority of parents in each group except the mongoloid and the blind. More than one fourth of the mothers in the blind group indicated the child had learned this act by himself and presumably required no definable effort on the part of the mother. One case in each of the deaf and mongoloid group was also reported to have learned this independently.

The high incidence of self-trained children in the blind group requires some explanation. Working from the verbatim statements of mothers there was a clear indication in their own words that they fully believed their children had trained themselves with no help from the parent. This appears to be a broad conclusion on the part of the mothers implying no effort on their part (Table 51).

In the Sears report some mothers indicated that their children

TABLE 51

METHODS USED IN BOWEL TRAINING

	Cerebral Palsy	Organic	Mongoloid	Blind	Deaf
Sat on potty regularly	85%	69%	43%	47%	61%
Caught him or tried to anticipate		12%	22%	12%	
Punished, made him wash out own pants		3%			
Explained		5%	8%		17%
Praised	15%	9%	16%	6%	4%
Learned by himself			3%	29%	4%
Gave enema, prune juice, etc.			3%		9%
Other		2%	5%	6%	4%

had learned bowel training from imitation of siblings but not to the extent reported by the blind group. Further analysis of individual cases will be required to extract the meaning of this finding.

Some mothers stated that they had employed what might be termed an "anticipation process." In this method they watched their child at play and the moment the child began to squirm or show signs which the mother interpreted to be a bowel urge she would intervene to take him to the toilet and hopefully achieve results. If she was lucky in this technique, she would praise the child and verbally point out that in the future the child should move to the bathroom voluntarily when such urges occurred. After a number of such fortunate happenings the child caught the idea. This technique served only a few people but those who used it felt that success had been achieved. The method, however, requires a hypervigilant state in the mother.

Only one of the mothers reported a frank punishment process. Verbal explanation and the high use of praise for appropriate effort and response were used by the other mothers to achieve bowel training. No particular technique was more pronounced in one group than among the others. Regular routine by roughly ascertaining the usual time of bowel movements was clearly the dominant procedure.

The procedures for bladder training were no different than those used for bowel training (Table 52). Most mothers sat the child on the toilet on a regular schedule and praised him for the urination if it occurred. Again, the blind group was at variance with the other

TABLE 52

METHODS USED FOR BLADDER TRAINING

	Cerebral Palsy	Organic	Mongoloid	Blind	Deaf
Put on potty at regular times	63%	74%	74%	44%	59%
Praised him	16%	8%	26%		5%
Punished him	3%	5%			
Explained to him	8%	2%			18%
Caught him at right time	3%			19%	
Let him train himself, just left diapers on		8%		29%	9%
Other	7%	2%		8%	9%

groups because one quarter reported that the child had trained himself and there was no need for a maternal program. Here, the blind group also varied because one-fifth of the group employed an anticipation process and caught the child at the right time.

In general the methods employed by the mothers of the handicapped did not differ from those used by the mothers of the nonhandicapped (Sears, p. 114-119). No specific methods emerged as being unique to any one handicap group and there was generally little difference among the groups on any method.

None of the mothers in the cerebral palsy group told of any special procedures that might be indicative of specifical modifications because of the child's neuromuscular involvement. As a matter of interest none of the mothers expressed any modification in procedures which might be considered as a concession to the child's handicap.

Father Involvement

Toilet training was the province of the mother in all groups but the majority of fathers became involved to some extent by helping when the mothers were busy or by reminding the child to go to the bathroom. Some fathers were quite helpful according to the mothers but the role was always that of an assistant. Some fathers were especially assigned the role of teaching the boy child to stand for urination. Fathers were least involved in the cerebral palsy group where most of the mothers managed the toilet training process with no help from the fathers. In all other groups six out of ten fathers were active participants as assistants and substitutes but there were still a sizable number of fathers who were not involved at all (Table 53).

TABLE 53

INVOLVEMENT OF FATHER IN THE TOILET TRAINING
PROCESS OF THIS CHILD

	Cerebral Palsy	Organic	Mongoloid	Blind	Deaf
Mother did it all	59%	38%	37%	33%	40%
Helped a little, showed how, did it when mother was busy	36%	49%	15%	42%	50%
Helped a little, reminded, help work out a technique	5%	13%	48%	25%	10%

Achievement of Bowel and Bladder Control

More children in the deaf group had achieved bowel control by age three than was true in any of the other groups. For the deaf, three out of four children were trained before they reached their third birthdays as compared to six out of ten in the organic, cerebral palsy, and blind groups, and five out of ten in the mongoloid group. The remainder of the blind group achieved this by age six (Table 54). Other groups showed scattered incidence of achievement at four, five, and six years of age. By six years of age all parents had achieved success in bowel training their child except for those cases in each group who were still struggling with the task. It must be pointed out that the children represented in the percentages of "not yet trained" in the various groups were four and five years of age and had not yet reached the upper limits suggested by the successful group.

Here there is a clear difference between the nonhandicapped of

TABLE 54

AGES AT COMPLETION OF BOWEL TRAINING

	Cerebral Palsy	Organic	Mongoloid	Blind	Deaf
Not trained yet	7%	12%	45%		5%
Before 1 year		12%	10%	8%	20%
Between 1 and 2 years		21%	17%	17%	30%
Between 2 and 3 years	66%	27%	24%	33%	25%
Between 3 and 4 years		10%			15%
Between 4 and 5 years	27%	14%		25%	5%
Between 5 and 6 years		4%	4%	17%	
Over 7 years					

Sears and these groups. Where the mothers of the normal kindergartners reported that 80 per cent had achieved bowel training by
age two and the other 20 per cent managed within the next year,
none of the handicapped groups presented any comparable percentages. Every group reported significant delays when compared to
the reports on the nonhandicapped. Individual cases in each group
managed this in keeping with the ages of nonhandicapped but the
percentages are too small to represent the characteristics of the respective handicap group. Only in the deaf group was there any
degree of comparability.

While 100 per cent of the mothers of the nonhandicapped group
reported the task of bowel training completed by age three, the
mothers of the handicapped did not fare as well. Four out of ten
mothers in the organic and blind, half of the mongoloid, one third
of the cerebral palsy and one-quarter of the deaf continued to struggle through this period from one to three years more.

The deaf also reported the highest incidence of bladder control
achievement by the time the child was three, followed in rank order
by the blind, organic and mongoloid groups. As a group finding
phenomenon bladder control was achieved in greater incidence by
age three than bowel control. A few cases in the deaf and organic
stated that their child had achieved bladder control before his first
birthday. One mother of a mongoloid child also stated that her
child had been trained for bladder control before one year (Table
55).

In the data reported by Sears, the mothers who started the toilet
training procedures after the child was twenty to twenty-four months

TABLE 55

AGES OF CHILDREN UPON COMPLETION OF BLADDER TRAINING

	Cerebral Palsy*	Organic	Mongoloid	Blind	Deaf
Not trained yet		3%	38%		5%
Before 1 year		11%	4%		20%
Between 1 and 2 years		25%	24%	9%	30%
Between 2 and 3 years		32%	29%	64%	30%
Between 3 and 4 years		10%			5%
Between 4 and 5 years		14%		9%	10%
Between 5 and 6 years		3%	4%	18%	
Over 7 years		2%			

*Question not asked.

accomplished the task in half the time span as those who had started at an earlier age. The general tendency among the mothers of the handicapped to initiate the toilet training effort at a later age than the Sears mothers did not result in a shorter period of time between initiation and completion. A later start did not shorten the time span as was true in the Sears data. While some mothers among the handicapped compared favorably with the Sears mothers in the number of months before independence was attained, the majority were forced to teach over a longer period of time.

Similarity to Sibling Practices

Since the focus of this study is upon differences and similarities in child-rearing practices among and within groups of parents of handicapped children, the question of whether the parent went about the business of toilet training with this child in the same manner as with the nonhandicapped siblings is pertinent.

For the most of the mothers the procedures employed were the same for the handicapped child as for the nonhandicapped siblings. Slightly more than one quarter of the organic, deaf and blind groups stated that they had to think of different procedures for the handicapped child and the mongoloid group was evenly divided between those who used the same and different methods (Table 56).

The exact variations employed by those who went about this differently with the handicapped child were not ascertained. Untallied comments from the mothers, however, indicate that variations

TABLE 56
SIMILARITY OF TOILET TRAINING PROCEDURES TO
THOSE EMPLOYED WITH SIBLINGS

	Cerebral Palsy*	Organic	Mongoloid	Blind	Deaf
I had to think of a different way with this child		26%	45%	31%	26%
I did it in the same way as with my other children		66%	52%	56%	61%
Have only one child or other child too young to compare		8%	3%	13%	13%

*Question not asked.

were mainly of a temporal and verbal nature. The mothers were more concerned about time and more frequently sat the child on the toilet or tried different temporal arrangements. They were also more pressed to find words to communicate the meaning of independence to the child. It is interesting to note, however, that a modification of procedure represents a minority report.

When mothers were asked to compare the toilet training of this child with that of their other children in terms of the rate of learning, the cerebral palsy, organic and mongoloid groups were in agreement that this child learned slower. In the deaf and blind groups the mothers were comparatively evenly divided between those who felt that this child learned slower and those who regarded the rate of learning to be about the same as for their other children. A small percentage in each group felt that the handicapped child had learned faster than the nonhandicapped siblings. Among those reported to have learned faster, the organic group showed a significantly higher percentage than the other four groups.

In general, however, toilet training was viewed as a slower process for *this* child than for siblings except in the sensory-handicapped groups where the child was either faster or the same as his siblings (Table 57). The highest incidence of slow learners was reported in the mongoloid group.

TABLE 57

MOTHERS' COMPARISONS OF THE RATE OF LEARNING FOR TOILET TRAINING BETWEEN THIS CHILD AND SIBLINGS

	Cerebral Palsy	Organic	Mongoloid	Blind	Deaf
Learned slower	57%	63%	87%	44%	43%
Learned faster	9%	17%	3%	6%	10%
About the same rate	34%	20%	10%	50%	47%

Few children in any of the groups remained continent during the day at an earlier age than their nonhandicapped siblings. In the blind and deaf groups about half of the group were reported to have achieved "day dryness" at about the same age as their siblings. Among the blind children, except for a few earlier ones, the other half were delayed beyond their brothers and sisters. Among the mongoloid group more than half achieve dryness at a later age than their siblings and another quarter of this group had not yet achieved this at the time of this study. A few deaf and organic children had also not achieved this. The deaf group showed the least delay and the mongoloid group showed the highest percentage of delay. Daytime continence presented the greatest problem to the mothers of the mongoloid group but a sizeable percentage in each group reported significant delays (Table 58).

TABLE 58

COMPARISON OF THIS CHILD WITH SIBLINGS ON AGE OF
MAINTAINING CONTINENCE DURING THE DAY*

	Cerebral Palsy[†]	Organic	Mongoloid	Blind	Deaf
At an earlier age than my other children		15%		6%	10%
At a later age than my other children		41%	54%	47%	38%
About the same age as others		32%	18%	47%	48%
Does not yet stay dry regularly during the day		12%	28%		4%

*Tally includes only those cases with siblings.
†Question not asked.

Toilet Independence

Toilet independence is the term applied to the total activity ensuing after a child receives a bowel or bladder urge, such as seeking out the bathroom, managing his own clothing before, during and after the act of defecation or urination—accomplishing the entire act without the help of either parent. A point of interest was to determine what variations existed among these groups as well as a general comparison to the same achievement in their siblings.

The high incidence of untrained children in the mongoloid and organic accounted for the major variations among the groups (Table 59). All groups reported a sizable percentage of cases who had achieved independence much later than their siblings. Only in the deaf and blind was there a significant percentage of cases where independence had been achieved at about the same age as other children in the family. A few children had managed this at an earlier age than the siblings but the general tendency across the groups was to be delayed. While each group showed approximately 60/40 split toward delay, the organic and mongoloid groups were clearly delayed while the blind and deaf compared favorably with the siblings.

TABLE 59

RATE OF ACHIEVEMENT OF TOILET INDEPENDENCE IN
THE HANDICAPPED AS COMPARED TO SIBLINGS*

	Cerebral Palsy[†]	Organic	Mongoloid	Blind	Deaf
At an earlier age than my other children		9%		7%	5%
At a later age than my other children		41%	43%	33%	40%
At about the same age as my others		31%	10%	53%	50%
Does not yet manage by self		19%	47%	7%	5%

*Tally includes only cases with siblings.
†Question not asked.

Since delay as well as similarity were reported in each group in sizable percentages, the variations cannot be directly ascribed to the child's handicap, level of intelligence or sex. When these factors were checked for possible complicity none were found to be significantly related. The source of such variation lies within other factors yet to be related.

Explanations for Delay

The explanations given for the delay in achieving toilet training by those mothers who said *these* children took a longer time than their siblings centered around two main points. The mothers in the cerebral palsy, organic, mongoloid and blind groups attributed the delay to the child's handicap or his retardation, indicating that he or she was generally slower at learning most things and that little more could be expected. The deaf group concentrated their explanations in the area of communications, indicating that the major problem was a matter of getting the meaning across to the child in words or gestures.

While this matter of communication was the predominant explanation by the deaf, all other groups complained to some degree that their child's delay stemmed from an inability to understand what was expected. A few mothers frankly stated that they felt the delay was caused by their own inability to devote as much time and effort to the training as they had to the teaching of the siblings (Table 60).

Here was an area where the mothers felt that their child's handi-

TABLE 60

EXPLANATIONS GIVEN BY MOTHERS TO ACCOUNT FOR
REPORTED DELAYS IN TOILET TRAINING SUCCESS

	Cerebral Palsy	Organic	Mongoloid	Blind	Deaf
Didn't have as much time	6%		5%	17%	
He was retarded, brain-injured, etc.	50%	55%	60%	50%	13%
Didn't understand as easily	44%	45%	35%	33%	88%

cap or communication problems clearly were factors in delaying
the achievement of toilet competence. This explanation, however,
was offered only by those mothers whose children had been delayed
or had not yet achieved. Those who had been successful on the same
general timetable as with siblings or even earlier made no mention
of the child's handicap as a deterrent. Since the successful group
represented near or more than half of the organic, blind and deaf
group the first search was to find whether the children in each group
differed sufficiently from one another to account for these explanations. No significant difference existed between the children in terms
of age, sex or severity of handicap. The mongoloid group, however,
was uniform in their concern for the child's retardation.

The unanimity of opinion suggests that the child's retardation
was definitely a factor but in all of the other groups some factors
other than the generic handicap were at work. The specific analysis
of individual mothers on a number of other dimensions will perhaps
afford a more adequate accounting for this differential among the
mothers.

Mothers' Perceptions of Self

Most mothers felt that they had been too lenient or lax in their
efforts to toilet train this child and conveyed the idea that any delay in such achievement was probably due to their own laxity rather
than to some factor within the child. A small percentage in each
group felt that they had been too strict. None of the groups reflected
any real difference from the others. The mothers in the blind group
expressed the highest extent of laxity but were closely followed by
the mongoloid and deaf. More mothers in the organic group evaluated themselves as too strict than did any of the others (Table 61).

TABLE 61
MOTHERS' EVALUATIONS OF THEIR OWN STRICTNESS
OR LENIENCY IN TOILET TRAINING PROCESS

	Cerebral Palsy*	Organic	Mongoloid	Blind	Deaf
Much too strict		7%			
Too strict		27%	17%	9%	13%
Too lenient or lax		66%	61%	25%	40%
Much too lenient or lax			22%	66%	47%

*Question not asked.

Another perspective on a mother's feeling of competency in child-rearing can be shaded into the general portrait by ascertaining whether a mother regarded the toilet training process to have been easy or difficult to achieve. Retrospective evaluations can always be maximized or minimized.

The mothers were asked to make an overall evaluation of the process of toilet training in terms of ease or difficulty of achieving success. On this two point scale, each group was divided with the mothers of the blind and deaf tending to consider the toilet training to have been easy to accomplish and the mongoloid group viewing it as difficult to achieve.

The organic mothers were evenly divided among themselves between those who thought it had been easy and those who felt it had been difficult. The high incidence of mongoloid children who were not yet trained can be ascribed to the category of "difficult" in rating since the mothers had not yet managed the process and consequently rate the task a difficult one (Table 62).

During the course of the training process, mothers will frequently seek out other mothers to talk to about the procedure. Sometimes

TABLE 62
MOTHERS' EVALUATIONS OF EASE OF ACCOMPLISHMENT
OF TOILET TRAINING

	Cerebral Palsy*	Organic	Mongoloid	Blind	Deaf
It was easy to accomplish		43%	23%	56%	64%
It was difficult to accomplish		42%	32%	44%	31%
I still haven't accomplished it		15%	45%		5%

*Question not asked.

they talk to women who have already achieved success and sometimes they talk to those who are also suffering through this stage
with children. In the course of ordinary conversation on child-
rearing among mothers, the topic of toilet training will be a favored
topic particularly among mothers who are in the midst of the training procedure. It was felt that these exchanges would allow a mother
to make some comparative estimate of her own success in relation
to other mothers she may have talked to. This was also viewed as
a contributing item to the general portrait of a mother's feeling of
adequacy as a child-rearer (Table 63).

TABLE 63

COMPARISONS OF MOTHERS' FEELINGS OF SUCCESS
IN REGARD TO TOILET TRAINING

	Cerebral Palsy*	Organic	Mongoloid	Blind	Deaf
More successful than others		14%	43%	13%	25%
Less successful than others		32%	28%	27%	29%
About the same as others		54%	28%	60%	46%

*Question not asked.

Unfortunately, this question was not introduced until after the
cerebral palsy group had completed its protocols so only four groups
of mothers were exposed to this question. They were asked to check
whether they felt themselves to be more or less successful or about
as successful as others in the matter of toilet training based upon
their conversations with other mothers. The major problem in evaluating this response stems from a questionable perceptual set. While
it was intended that reference to conversations with "other mothers"
encompassed the mother of a child, the response of some mothers
suggested that they had interpreted the question to refer only to other
mothers of handicapped children. Despite this confusion in set which
occurred in small percentage among all four groups, the spread of
the findings is of interest.

Only a small percentage of mothers of organic, blind and deaf
considered themselves to be more successful than others. Most of
the mothers regarded themselves as less successful or at least as
successful as others. The mongoloid group which reported the great-

est incidence of delay and problems in this area tended to view themselves as more successful. This finding is not in accord with other data on this general question and must be held in abeyance until more detailed case by case analysis can illuminate the meaning of this. The tendency among the other three groups was to express some concern for less success or to place themselves in a general category of "being just about like everyone else" on this matter.

COMMENTARY ON TOILET TRAINING

This chapter lends itself to ten points of summarization to present this area of child-rearing. The results come exclusively from the reports of the mothers in the five groups:

1. *As a total group they were divided between those who believed that toilet training should be initiated before age two and those who subscribed to a concept of beginning when the child gives some evidence of readiness for such training.*

The definition of readiness appeared to be individually interpreted by each mother and few could verbalize the exact behavior which they observed in their child which allowed them to conclude that the child was "ready."

Comments from the mothers at other points in the interviews suggested that the majority of those mothers who held to a belief of "when the child is ready" did in fact believe that such readiness would be expected before two years of age.

2. *The mothers made their own decision as to starting the training procedures and were rarely guided by outside advice.*

This was a surprising finding which was expressed almost in chorus by the four groups questioned. The surprise stemmed from the general clinical notion that parents of handicapped children frequently seek advice on many issues in child management from physicians, social workers, psychologists and therapists. There was a prestudy hypothesis that the answers to that question would reflect a wide variance in reliance upon advisory sources. The concordance of independent decision was therefore an unexpected result.

3. *When children had "accidents" after the training period was well under way, some mothers ignored or passively accepted the accident as an expected happening in the learning process*

and others took a punitive view toward such slip-ups. The direction of response was not related to the diagnostic category and the explanation for a mother's course of action must be searched for in the personality dynamics of each mother.

The blind and deaf groups indicated majority views toward passive acceptance of accidents while the other three groups indicated approximately a 50/50 split between a passive and active response. It was not possible to evolve a significant explanation for the high incidence of passivity in the blind and deaf groups.

In none of the groups was any evidence present that one or the other form of reaction was attributable to the child's handicap, or any feeling on the part of the mothers that the child was "really not responsible" because of retardation, neuromuscular handicap or language difficulty. The general feeling tone was clearly in the direction of an expression that, whichever action a mother reported, her choice was based upon a generalized attitude of, "That's what *should* be done in such circumstances." The belief was a part of each mother's child-rearing composite. It was her way of attempting to accomplish desired results. To seek a deeper explanation of individual responses in terms of personality traits of punitiveness, rejection, apathy or some other term seemed an unwarranted course.

Where such a response might later be sorted as another bit of evidence to support a personality contention about individual mothers it was added to the list. At this point the data on this question can only be interpreted as a specific child-rearing technique choice. In this respect the blind and deaf groups were significantly different from the other three for some obscure reason.

4. *They employed the same techniques of training with the handicapped child as with their other children. Regularity of placement on the toilet, praising successes, and verbal reminders seemed to have been standard procedure. Rarely did any mother describe some ingenious method of training.*

The favored technique for accomplishing both bowel and bladder training was regularity in placing the child on the toilet. Verbal explanations, anticipations, and praise for success were less favored. The mothers of the blind reported an unexpected finding indicating that for both bowel and bladder training 29 per cent of their group required no parental effort—the child achieved competence independently. The same four children were accounted for in each area. These four mothers simply reported that "it just happened." They offered no other explanation for the independence except to record it as an accomplished fact.

The parents employed the same approach to training their nonhandicapped children. No evidence emerged to indicate that a parent employed any form of ingenious device or gimmick to achieve success. The nature of the child's handicap, the language problems which may have existed and the possibility of retardation were unrelated to the parental approach. It is felt that each parent again was expressing a belief that "this is the way to go about it" for any child.

The many methods devised by professionals to condition and reinforce desired behaviors, and to extinguish undesirable behavior, apparently represent a body of knowledge which was unavailable to these parents. It is probably safe to assume that most parents enter this area of training without benefit of reinforcement technology. By the same token, however, it is likely that the advocates of reinforcement theory could readily define that the parent achieved success by unconsciously employing a reinforcement process.

Whatever professional analysis may be pursued it is clear that these parents selected the particular method as a way to do it for all children. Except for the surprising incidence of independence in the blind group all other mothers seemed to rely upon similar patterns. The parent evolves a system for children regardless of the nature of the child. Each couple has its own system for its family.

5. *In general, both bowel and bladder training took a longer time to achieve than among the mothers of nonhandicapped children when age comparisons are made, although many mothers of the handicapped felt that this child had learned independence at about the same rate as his siblings. Some mothers, mostly notably in the deaf and blind group managed the entire procedure without significant delay. Comparative analysis of those who manage a "normal" timetable with such factors as intellectual level, and other traits may reveal an explanation.*

In the Sears study all normal kindergartners were reported to be bowel-trained by age three. In the five handicap groups percentage of accomplishment by age three varied from 51 to 75 per cent with the deaf group reporting the highest percentage. The blind and mongoloid groups reported the lengthiest delays. Only the mongoloid group appeared to report a significant lack of accomplishment. Delays in all groups varied from one to three years after the third birthday with each group except the blind reporting a few cases where such success had not yet been achieved.

Parents of the mongoloid group reported better results on bladder training than bowel training reporting that 57 per cent were trained for bladder by age three. The organic group reported 68 per cent success by age three (Table 54). The blind group (73 per cent) and the deaf group (80 per cent) also had a majority achievement by age three. Bladder training was apparently easier to achieve than bowel training for all of the groups.

When the parents reported a 26 to 45 per cent incidence of employing different techniques with *this* child than with siblings (Table 56) this seemed to be a reflection of a contradiction to what had been previously noted about similarity. In probing the manner in which parents modified their toilet training procedures with this child as different from siblings it was expected that the modifications would involve some techniques which had not previously been cited. Such was not the case.

Probing revealed that when the mother reported that she "had to think of a different way with this child" she was not referring to some ingenious method but was rather indicating that where regularity had served as the major method for the siblings she changed to anticipation for *this* child. "Different way" in the mother's perception simply meant an emphasis upon one of the other forms listed such as punishment, more explanation, more praise, etc.

6. *In the cerebral palsy, blind and deaf groups the mothers were approximately evenly divided in a 50-50 split in their reporting on whether this child was slower than his siblings in achieving, or faster, or the same as his siblings. Each group reported a small percentage of cases where the handicapped*

child achieved toilet training success faster than siblings. The mongoloid and organic groups reported that the majority of their children were slower than siblings.

While to some extent the slowness of the mongoloid and organic groups may be related to mental retardation there is a notable percentage in each group who were judged to be the equal or faster than their nonhandicapped siblings. It is not possible simply to attribute a slower rate to the presence of mental retardation since the individual cases of slower rate did not neatly match those who might be classified as retarded. Some other factors were involved which are obscured in these data.

7. *As a general rule the handicapped child achieved an independence at toileting later than his siblings in each of the four groups questioned. When asked to account for such delays the explanation given by the mother was nearly unanimously directed at some aspect of the child's handicap.*

Even though the mothers reported no significant modifications in toilet training techniques which bore any relationship to the child's handicap they attributed delays in achievement to the dynamics of the handicap. The data, therefore, suggest the parent employs a fairly standard technique and when success is delayed explains this delay on the basis of the handicap. The delay seems to be accepted by the parents as inevitable. The handicap does not generate a different procedure, merely an apparent resignation to delay—if in fact a delay does occur.

It was interesting to note that even when the parent reported that the successful achievement was faster than, or at least at the same rate as, siblings they still accounted for delays with the handicapped child on the basis of a handicap factor. Unfortunately no questions were directed towards accounting for delays among siblings.

8. *Toilet training was, in the main, the province of the mother with some assistance from father.*

This was not felt to infer a lack on the part of the father but rather to imply a time factor. Working fathers simply had less time available during toilet training hours. Most of the fathers played some role in this training but the major responsibility rested in the mothers.

9. *Most mothers retrospectively regarded themselves as "too lenient" in toilet training procedures and implied that a stricter approach would have achieved faster results.*

This perception must be added to the elements of handicap which mothers felt accounted for delays. Unfortunately the question of comparative perceptions of success was subject to a considerable amount of question misinterpretation. It was later learned that some mothers interpreted this question to refer to other mothers of the same type of children, while some took it as referring to other mothers in general. The tabulation was included mainly to indicate the distribution across groups even with the variance in perceptual set.

10. *All groups experienced problems but all groups eventually succeeded in spite of whatever problems were encountered along the way. Techniques were general and standard and delays were present, but success was achieved without professional help.*

Almost all of the mothers who reported lack of success at the time of this study did achieve success within the next year. If the problem persists beyond age six years the case must be regarded as dramatically atypical.

Clinicians confronted with parents who are deep in the throes of the toilet training task might well consider unique approaches which are directly related to the specific problems of the child. For instance, these parents gave little evidence of awareness of receptive language problems among their children and essentially indicated that they used the same general language pattern for all of their children.

Some attention to language patterns, levels of discrimination within the child required to properly interpret cues, sensitivity to behavioral signs indicative of readiness as a part of the clinical counseling relationship, might profitably assist a mother to engage in the training procedure with far less anxiety than seems to be the case.

Delay may be inevitable, but a well-directed approach based upon a unique understanding of the particular child, and the dynamics of disability may significantly reduce such delay.

Chapter 7

REST AND SLEEP PATTERNS

THE MODERN AMERICAN culture pattern has established the fact that the child is placed in, or sent to, bed several hours before his parents retire. The number of hours a child is expected to sleep and the hour at which he is placed or sent to bed varies with advancing age and the particular pattern within a given family. The necessity for the process to occur is without question. The ease with which the process is accomplished is a matter of parental management.

American mothers concerned with the welfare of their child emphasize the need for the proper amount of sleep. This usually includes the practice of taking a nap in the early afternoon. The age at which the nap period is discontinued varies from family to family and from child to child. In some cases continuation of the nap period becomes a highly aggravating matter between a mother and child when the child begins to resist the practice. In other cases mothers account for the fact that a child is continuing the nap period long beyond the time when most of her friends' children have ceased with the statement that their children need more sleep than others.

Many mothers of brain-damaged children have reported in the counseling sessions that the nap period, and the time after the child has been put to bed for the evening, represent the only times of the day when they (the mothers) are able to relax and complete their housework. Sears (1957, p. 294) has described the bedtime process in the following manner:

> For a variety of reasons . . . children may be put to bed when they are not sleepy. This leads to difficulties. A child can be forced to do a number of things he is unwilling to do—pick up a toy, turn off the TV, go outdoors—but he cannot be forced to go to sleep. All a parent can do is arrange surroundings conducive to sleep. The primary conditions seem to be, (1) reducing the level of all kinds of visual and auditory stimulation, and (2) providing a set of familiar surroundings and objects that are associated with going to sleep. The latter are more

[147]

easily arranged than the former, particularly when there are a number of children in the family.

This area of investigation was of interest to ascertain the answers to a number of questions about sleep and bedtime practices.

BEDTIME BEHAVIOR

Regularity of Bedtime

The parents in the cerebral palsy group were almost unanimous in their belief that children should have a regular bedtime. Four out of five parents in the deaf group also held this belief. While two-thirds of each of the other groups favored a regular bedtime there were sizable percentages in each of these groups who felt that bedtimes should vary according to situations, moods, etc. (Table 64). Most of the parents, however, believe in a regular bedtime for all children. They will allow that the hour of such bedtime may be different at varying age levels but agree that a specific hour should be regularly held.

TABLE 64

PERCENTAGES OF CHILDREN WHO HAVE A REGULAR BEDTIME

	Cerebral Palsy	Organic	Mongoloid	Blind	Deaf	Total
Should have regular bedtime	94%	66%	72%	64%	80%	77%

No particular bedtime hour was preferred to any sizable extent among any of the groups. Each population distributed its choices from 6:30 PM to 9 PM and later. By 8:30 PM three of four children have retired with the cerebral palsy and organic showing a high percentage of children who are in bed by 7:30 PM. (Table 65). Ten per cent of the total group were late retirees going to bed after 9 PM.

Parents selected the bedtime hour based upon their conviction that the welfare of the child dictated that particular hour or simply decided upon an hour as a convenience in terms of household management. Whatever their reason for the choice, a regular bedtime allowing for nine to eleven hours of sleep with the waking period set to permit preparing for school attendance appeared to be the typical pattern among these families.

TABLE 65

DISTRIBUTION OF BEDTIME SCHEDULES IN
PERCENTAGES FOR THE HANDICAPPED CHILD

	Cerebral Palsy	Organic	Mongoloid	Blind	Deaf
6:30 - 7:00 PM	11%	1%			
7:00 - 7:30 PM	13%	25%	16%	4%	20%
7:30 - 8:00 PM	17%	23%	28%	43%	25%
8:00 - 8:30 PM	34%	31%	20%	21%	30%
8:30 - 9:00 PM	19%	12%	20%	21%	10%
After 9:00 PM	6%	8%	16%	15%	15%

The Sears' data showed that three out of four children were also in bed by 8:30 PM. In this instance the total group of mothers of the handicapped compared favorably with the mothers of the nonhandicapped. The data suggest that despite the fact that the mean ages of the handicapped group were higher than for the nonhandicapped group, the bedtime hours were essentially the same. While Sears found only 1 per cent of his population reporting a bedtime after 8:30 PM, this study found 10 per cent reporting a bedtime after 9 PM. This greater percentage of late hour children may be due to the older ages among the handicapped.

When these findings on the number of hours of sleep needed were compared to the mothers' reports on whether *this* child needed more or less sleep than others, only the mothers of the cerebral palsy group gave evidence of supporting their contention of more rest by assigning a need for more hours of sleep than the majority opinion. The mothers in the organic and the mongoloid groups who indicated a need for more rest apparently felt that a nine to eleven hour sleep represented "more" than other children.

Uniformity of Bedtime

A sizable percentage in all five groups reported that they held to a single bedtime hour for all of the children in the family (Table 66).

TABLE 66

PERCENTAGE DISTRIBUTION ON QUESTION WHETHER
MOTHER REPORTED ONE REGULAR BEDTIME
FOR ALL CHILDREN IN FAMILY

	Cerebral Palsy	Organic	Mongoloid	Blind	Deaf	Total
Regular bedtime	46%	48%	24%	36%	40%	44%
Irregular bedtime	54%	52%	76%	64%	60%	56%

For example, one mother stated that "eight o'clock is bedtime for all of my children as long as they are going to school." Only in the mongoloid group was there a significant variation. Those parents who did not hold to a single bedtime hour varied the hour according to the age of the child, allowing older children to remain up and active until later in the evening. Some who reported irregular bedtime hours said that it depended somewhat on how tired the child appeared to be.

The presence of visitors, special occasions, such as weekends, parties, visitations, and special TV programs were all listed as reasons for having a variable bedtime. The major reason for variability, however, was child age. Some explanation for the group variations may stem from a consideration of the spread of ages among the siblings. Where children represent a narrow age range, the concept of older children did not seem as pertinent as when the age scatter was from four to fifteen years.

The general finding is that nearly half of the families in this study held to a single bedtime hour for all of their children. The only group to significantly depart from this 50/50 split was the mongoloid.

Similarity of Practices

Most parents managed the bedtime practices with the handicapped children in the same manner as they did with their other children. About one third of the total group, however, reported that they did things differently at the child's bedtime. The differences in effort usually revolved around such tasks as adjusting braces, giving medication, undressing the child, etc., which were not required for their other children. In general, though, the bedtime process was the same in its practices with siblings as with the handicapped child (Table 67).

TABLE 67

PERCENTAGE OF CASES WHO EMPLOYED DIFFERENT
PRACTICES AT BEDTIME WITH THIS CHILD
THAN WITH SIBLINGS*

	Cerebral Palsy	Organic	Mongoloid	Blind	Deaf	Total
Different practices	33%	38%	32%	15%	25%	33%
Same practices	66%	62%	68%	85%	75%	66%

*Cases with no siblings excluded from this tally.

Bedtime Prayers

The bedtime ritual of saying prayers as a forerunner of sleep was observed by nearly all of the families in this study. The blind group showed the highest incidence and the cerebral palsy group the lowest (Table 68). In only a few instances the handicapped child did not say prayers while his siblings did. As a general rule, however, bedtime prayers were said by all children if that was a family practice.

TABLE 68

PERCENTAGE OF CASES WHO SAY PRAYERS AT BEDTIME

Cerebral Palsy	Organic	Mongoloid	Blind	Deaf
77%	83%	85%	92%	85%

The usual method of teaching the prayers to the child according to the parents was by means of repetitive efforts on the part of the mother or father guiding the child to repeat the words after the parent nightly until the child became independent. Fifteen per cent of the 177 cases indicated that their children did not say prayers at bedtime. When these cases were checked against the general family ratings of high or low religiousness, in all instances where the child did not say night prayers the family had been rated as "low religious." Apparently the general attitude toward religious practice and belief carries over into the matter of whether the child will be taught evening prayers.

Bedtime Rituals

Some parents reported that they had organized a specific ritual for bedtime such as going to the child's room to read a story each night before turning off the light and saying a final good night. Some had organized a brief program of a glass of juice or milk at the kitchen table before departing for bed. Others had arranged brief games to be played or a record to be played or a quiet talking period about the day's activities. Those who reported such organized presleep experiences were in the minority. It was further learned that such practices were unique to the family. If such practices were reported for the handicapped child they were also followed for the siblings and represented the idea, "that's the way we do things in this house" (Table 69).

TABLE 69
PERCENTAGE OF CASES WHO EMPLOY SPECIAL
ROUTINES FOR BEDTIME

Cerebral Palsy	Organic	Mongoloid	Blind	Deaf
40%	32%	25%	8%	40%

The majority of the parents limited their activity to tucking the child in, listening to prayers or teaching prayers, kissing the child and saying good night. Some parents in the cerebral palsy group made some sort of game of the business of removing braces or fastening night braces, but for the most part, the bedtime process was very mechanical. Some parents stated that the child went to bed independently with little involvement of either parent.

Where special activities were structured into the bedtime procedure they were unique and bore no apparent relationship to the fact that the child had a handicap. This was a procedure developed by a particular mother for all of her children. The dynamics underlying these rituals were not ascertained.

Security Objects

In the general folklore of child-rearing the belief that children sleep better or feel more secure if they take a favored toy to bed with them has long been held. The general idea behind this is that the child's security is enhanced by the comfort of the favored piece. For some children it may be a stuffed toy, while for others it may be a particular blanket, or some sort of cloth. There was some interest in ascertaining the prevalence of such a practice among these five handicap groups.

In all groups except the organic, the number of children who did not take an object to bed with them was greater than those who did (Table 70). Each group, however, showed a significant percentage of those who did, with the organic group revealing the greatest extent of this behavior with more than half of the group having a bedtime security object. When the mothers were asked if this was also true for their other children, the incidence was almost identical when the mothers reported or recalled sibling practices at the same age.

It seemed reasonably clear that such behavior had virtually no

TABLE 70

PERCENTAGE OF CASES WHERE PARENT REPORTED THAT CHILD TOOK A "SECURITY OBJECT" TO BED AT NIGHT

	Cerebral Palsy	Organic	Mongoloid	Blind	Deaf	Total
Takes an object to bed	36%	52%	28%	20%	40%	41%
Does not take object	64%	48%	72%	80%	60%	59%

relationship to the fact that the child was handicapped, nor did any differences between the groups express a variance which might be attributed to the dynamics of a given handicap.

The negative or affirmative response to this question was a reflection of family patterns and practices. Certain mothers accepted and reinforced such security objects and others never started or encouraged the process with any of their children. Whatever the rationale might be, some families develop and encourage this practice with all of their children and others do not. The explanation for this "do-do not" equation may be buried in the security dynamics of the parents but is not apparent from these data.

The objects were listed as toys, stuffed animals, dolls, favorite pieces of blankets, towels, etc. No particular object emerged as a favorite among any of the populations.

SLEEP

Amount of Sleep Needed

In general conversation all parents will express themselves on the question of how many hours of sleep they feel their children should have each night to insure proper healthful rest. Presumably the parental conviction on the number of hours needed should guide the bedtime practice which they enforce in regard to the hour at which children are prepared for bed.

There was a general agreement among the parents in all five groups that these children required at least nine to eleven hours of sleep each night for proper rest. A small percentage in each group, except the blind, felt that six to nine hours of sleep would be sufficient for their child (Table 71). Two of each five parents in the cerebral palsy group felt that their child needed twelve or more hours of sleep each night.

TABLE 71

MOTHERS' OPINION ON THE NUMBER OF HOURS OF
SLEEP DESIRABLE FOR THEIR CHILD

	Cerebral Palsy	Organic	Mongoloid	Blind	Deaf	Total
6-8 hours	5%	8%	8%		10%	7%
9-11 hours	55%	77%	85%	86%	90%	73%
12 or more	40%	15%	8%	14%		20%

This incidence was particularly influenced by the parents of the severely handicapped and severely retarded children in the group.

No explanation other than parental choice could be found for the 15 per cent of the organic group who were judged to require more than twelve hours of sleep. In this matter then, a significant difference was found among the groups in the incidence of children judged to need more than twelve hours of sleep. In the perception of the parent of a severely handicapped child with cerebral palsy more sleep is necessary than for other children.

It must be pointed out that, in general family practices, the increasing age of the child may allow for more stay-up time before retiring. The age span in each group is from four to ten years but there appears to be an insufficient variation in the opinions of the mothers regarding the required hours of sleep to suggest that the requirement is significantly different for four-year-olds than it is for ten-year-olds among these parents of handicapped children. Only the cerebral palsy group differs from the others and this difference is in the direction of requiring more sleep with no distinctions made for the age of the child.

When the parents were asked whether they felt that the handicapped child needed more rest than other children, the viewpoints were not as positively weighted toward a unanimity of opinion. Half of the mothers in the cerebral palsy, organic and mongoloid groups felt that this child needed about the same amount of rest as other children, but the blind and deaf groups saw an even greater similarity in rest needs between this child and others (Table 72). The other half of the mothers in the first three groups felt that these children needed more rest than other children. This finding supports the unanimity on the question of number of hours of sleep required. Parents felt that the child needed the same or more rest than other children and would probably subscribe to the nine to eleven hour quota for any child in that age range.

TABLE 72
DISTRIBUTION OF MOTHER RESPONSES ON QUESTION
OF WHETHER THIS CHILD NEEDS MORE REST
THAN OTHER CHILDREN

	Cerebral Palsy	Organic	Mongoloid	Blind	Deaf	Total
Needs more	43%	46%	40%	29%	20%	40%
Needs less	6%	3%	8%	7%	10%	6%
Needs same	51%	51%	52%	64%	70%	54%

Afternoon Naps

It is customary for most parents of young children to expect their child to rest during the early afternoon, usually after lunch has been eaten. This practice is carried on for a number of years between infancy and entry into school according to the beliefs of the mother and the child's acceptance of this enforced rest. Except for the mongoloid group most of the children in each group had stopped taking an afternoon nap at the time of this study, but each group still reported a sizable percentage of cases who were continuing to take an afternoon nap (Table 73).

TABLE 73
PERCENTAGE OF CHILDREN IN THIS STUDY WHO
TAKE AFTERNOON NAPS

	Cerebral Palsy	Organic	Mongoloid	Blind	Deaf	Total
Afternoon nap	40%	31%	52%	21%	25%	35%

When parents were asked to recall the age at which the child had ceased taking his daily nap, the responses show that almost all of the blind and deaf group discontinued this practice before the child was four and a half years old (Table 74). The age of stopping naps was five and six years for the other three groups. Considering that more than half of the mongoloid group were still taking naps and that four out of ten in the cerebral palsy group were also napping, these two groups showed the greatest extent of delay. It will be recalled that the mothers in the cerebral palsy group were distinctly different in their opinion that their children needed more rest than other children and the continuation of the afternoon nap period beyond the age when most children have stopped is a method for gaining more rest for the child.

TABLE 74

AGES AT WHICH CHILDREN STOPPED NAPS

Age	Cerebral Palsy	Organic	Mongoloid	Blind	Deaf
2	2 6%	4 9%	1 8%	1 9%	3 20%
2½					
3	3 9%	13 29%	3 25%	3 27%	5 33%
3½					
4	9 28%	14 31%	4 33%	6 55%	4 27%
4½					
5	9 28%	12 27%	3 25%		3 20%
6	8 25%	2 4%		1 9%	
7	1 3%		1 8%		

Father Involvement

As a group the fathers of the blind and deaf groups showed the greatest extent of participation in the process of preparing the child for sleep at bedtime. If the father helped the child undress, helped care for toileting and washing, said prayers with the child or in some manner physically participated beyond the mere contribution of a verbal "good night" he was classified as being actively involved in the bedtime process. In all populations the fathers were reported to be more often active than passive. On an overall basis across five populations three out of four fathers were actively involved in the bedtime routines of the child (Table 75).

TABLE 75

EXTENT OF FATHER INVOLVEMENT IN
PUTTING THIS CHILD TO BED*

	Cerebral Palsy	Organic	Mongoloid	Blind	Deaf
Yes	32 64%	48 75%	18 72%	13 92%	16 80%
No	18 36%	16 25%	7 28%	1 8%	4 20%

*3 cases where father deceased and 1 where divorced not included in tally.

Best Time of Day

To gain some impression of which period of the day was judged to be best or worst for the child according to the parent perception of ease of management, attitudes, pliability, etc., the parents were asked to comment on "best" and "worst" periods for their child.

Morning was considered to be the best time of the day for the child by the majority of the parents, except in the blind group, where the group spread over three time periods (Table 76). It was interesting to note that one fourth of the cerebral palsy group felt that there was no particular time during the day that was best for their child.

While the converse might be expected when parents were asked to identify the period of the day which they felt was the child's worst time the responses did not reflect such a finding. It was true that the parents in the cerebral palsy group indicated in the majority of cases that morning was the best time and that evening was the worst time, but this was not true in the other groups. The prospect of a child "wearing thin" as he approached his bedtime hour is an expected result of an energetic day. The same parents in the cerebral palsy group who identified their child as having no particular time of the day which could be classified as best time also felt that no particular time period could be classified as worst time for their child (Table 76).

TABLE 76

DISTRIBUTION OF OPINIONS OF MOTHERS ON
QUESTION OF WHICH PERIOD OF THE DAY IS
BEST-WORST FOR THIS CHILD

	Cerebral Palsy		Organic		Mongoloid		Blind		Deaf	
	Best	Worst	Best	Worst	Best	Worst	Best	Worst	Best	Worst
Morning	70%		68%	12%	64%	12%	43%	57%	75%	10%
Afternoon	7%	13%	12%	31%	12%	32%	29%	29%	20%	30%
Early evening		64%	12%	46%	12%	44%	21%	14%	5%	40%
No particular time	23%	23%	8%	11%	12%	12%	7%			20%

COMMENTARY

This area of child-rearing seems to be a well-organized practice among most parents. Very few parents expressed comment to indicate that this represented a problem area in their relationship with the handicapped child. Most parents adhered to a regular bedtime for their children and believed that nine to eleven hours of sleep were a necessity. Some felt that their handicapped child needed more rest than other children, but there were a large number who did not agree on this point.

Parents go about bedtime practices with their handicapped children in the same manner as they do with their other children. The differences that were described were largely due to adjustment of braces or delayed independence in undressing. The majority of children said prayers at bedtime. Bedtime rituals, such as stories or games, once in bed were not the general rule. Usually, the procedure was to simply tuck the child in for the night. Some children took security objects to bed with them while others did not.

Generally, the differences found among the groups on these questions showed no variation that could be ascribed to the child's handicap or a parent attitude about the handicap. These practices were idiosyncratic to each family.

On the question of taking afternoon naps, there was a general delay across the groups with the children breaking away from this pattern at somewhat later ages than expected. Fathers appeared to be active participants in bedtime procedure among all groups.

The majority of parents held a strong conviction that a regular bedtime hour should be prescribed for children but each group contained a minority incidence of those who held no conviction on this matter. The two hour span between 7 PM and 9 PM encompasses the regular bedtime hour for these children with only the cerebral palsy group indicating a small percentage of cases having an earlier time. Each group contained a small percentage of cases where children were allowed to remain up after 9 PM. The mothers who departed from the two-hour norm span noted that the children were so exhausted by this time that it would have been unfair to the child to have prolonged his waking period. Those parents who practiced the late extreme also were among those who held no strong conviction about the need for a regular bedtime.

Regularity of bedtime hours is related to age by these parents. Older children have a later bedtime than younger ones. No unusual bedtime rituals were reported by parents which could be construed as being motivated by the child's handicap except for the removal of braces and this was usually a mechanical affair without ceremony. If a mother was a ritual-organizer for *this* child she also organized night time rituals for all children in her family. Evening prayers were the majority ritual. The mothers in the blind group showed the lowest prevalence of special bedtime routines.

Whether or not a child takes a security object to bed is somehow related to the dynamics of a given family and is a pattern probably developed and encouraged for all children in that family.

In spite of the fact that the majority of cases in each group were attending school programs the incidence of afternoon napping was relatively high in each group. Where children were enrolled in morning school programs many of the mothers reported that the child was placed in his bedroom for a rest period in the early afternoon.

There was a general agreement among the parents to all five groups that the morning hours represented the best period of the day for their child. Early evening was generally considered to be the worst period for behavioral control. If these parental expressions of "best" and "worst" periods are considered meaningful the implications to the service professions are clear.

Therapists in treatment clinics and teachers in special education could undoubtedly add their testimony to the fact that morning hours are regarded as best. There is a general feeling that the children are more sensitive and responsive to therapeutic change within those hours. It is likely that the child moves less economically, is less efficient visually and listens less attentively as the afternoon hours wear on.

The reduction in learning efficiency which seems to be associated with later afternoon hours should indicate to parents and teachers that this period of the day is least conducive to learning new concepts of behavior or movement in that time period. As a consequence of these reports, a traditional educational belief and a sizable body of professional literature, the critical period for learning is during morning hours. By implication this must be the period of concentrated teaching effort for significant learning. Later periods offer a less responsive pupil to the teacher—whether the teacher is a professional or a parent. Despite this traditional belief, violations continue to occur. Parents might be well advised however to save the important lessons for the best time.

A surprising number of parents noted no particular differences in the sensitivity of their children which could be characterized as "best" or "worst." Evidence from other sources suggests that the observational sensitivity of the parent in these cases requires some sharpening.

Chapter 8

PATTERNS OF RESTRICTION, DEMAND AND ALLOWANCE

RESTRICTIONS AND DEMANDS

THE DAILY RHYTHM of a child's waking hours from early infancy to adolescence is made up of a tempo, beat, and measure of maternally and paternally voiced "Dos" and "Don'ts." The child must learn what not to do and what to do under the watchful eye and voice of the parent.

The parent of the handicapped child must guard their child against any form of danger which might interfere with health. The parent of the child with cerebral palsy must guard against the child falling against, or on top of, objects which might injure him during the period of time when he is learning his mobility bearings. The parent of the blind child must actively encourage the child to explore his world and at the same time be watchful lest such exploration lead to serious injury. The parent of the deaf child must be mindful of the child's need for visual clueing for danger. Each parent of a handicapped child is perhaps burdened with a heavier responsibility than is the parent of the nonhandicapped when it comes to the matter of teaching basic lessons of safety and care.

These children must learn to look carefully before they cross a street, be cautious of sharp knives, recognize the danger of heights, keep their feet dry, button their coats, respect the belongings of others, and become mindful of possible dangers. They must also learn not to use crayons on the walls, to be polite to the neighbors, to avoid the neighbor's tulip bed, to keep hands off the merchandise displays in the supermarket, and to come home when they are called from play.

The listing of all these minor lessons which progressively build to a pattern of consciously guided self-protective, respectful, healthful behavior of a more mature nature every year can actually become a volume unto itself. When one contemplates a listing of all the "little" lessons a child must learn to survive in a complex society, the task appears endless. Each lesson, however, has import. The sharp knife is a potential danger for the blind child as well as the nonhandicapped child. The little lessons must be learned by all. These little lessons constitute the day by day curriculum of child-rearing.

While the task of ascertaining how mothers went about the business of teaching these countless little lessons was intriguing but not felt to be within the scope of this study, some effort was made to find out, in a general way, what kinds of rules and regulations and restrictions these mothers held for their children. An arbitrary listing was prepared for parental checking and a few direct questions related to this area were included in the clinical interview.

A point of interest was the matter of general rules of behavior which these parents set for their children in some of the common problem areas which confront all parents. Although the list of behaviors presented for their response was far from exhaustive, it, nonetheless, allowed for some measure of discrimination among the groups.

There was common agreement among the parents of all groups that their children were not allowed to climb around on household furniture. It was not possible to determine the extent to which each parent enforced such a rule but there was a unanimity of parent feeling that this was their ruling.

The highest extent of agreement among the mothers occurred on the two questions of allowing the child to talk to strangers and accepting a ride from a stranger (Table 77). Few mothers agreed that this was acceptable behavior. The increased incidence of criminal acts upon young children in American society, with the attendant newspaper accounting, has instilled a cultural anxiety which must be considered by today's parents far more than was true of previous generations.

To prevent the possibility of harm and injury the mother must set a firm rule that the child should not engage in conversation with strangers and present some rationale for this which will guide the child's behavior. Most mothers agreed that talking to a stranger

TABLE 77

MOTHERS' INDICATED AGREEMENT WITH CERTAIN BEHAVIORS

	Cerebral Palsy	Organic	Mongoloid	Blind	Deaf	All Groups
Rough play must be in basement or outdoors		79%	73%	89%	95%	82%
Climbing on furniture allowed	7%	14%	10%	6%	9%	10%
Must hang up own clothes	49%	52%	47%	56%	68%	52%
Must clean own room	46%	29%	33%	22%	32%	31%
Talking after in bed		37%	37%	33%	41%	37%
Must pick up toys	64%	93%	90%	89%	91%	84%
Play limited to certain rooms		38%	37%	89%	23%	42%
Playing in road or alley		22%	7%	11%	18%	17%
Must stay in own yard for play	32%	27%	60%	33%	18%	33%
Play only with own toys		21%	37%	17%	5%	21%
Loud noises only outdoors	71%	45%	47%	56%	45%	54%
Stay near house	58%	22%	100%	78%	86%	56%
Talk to strangers	8%	14%	10%	22%		8%
Accept ride from stranger	7%	15%	3%	11%	5%	7%

was acceptable if the child was in the mother's presence but should be avoided at times when the child was alone on the street. Furthermore, most of the mothers agreed that it was more acceptable to talk to a strange woman than to a strange man. Essentially the same rules applied to the matter of accepting a ride in a car. The mothers were even more emphatic on this point.

Unfortunately, the exact manner in which the parents communicated these two rules to their child was not ascertained. The technique employed by each parent of a deaf or blind child or mongoloid to communicate and rationalize such rules should be studied in greater detail.

Only the parents in the blind group expressed a significant agreement that play should be limited to certain rooms of the house. In the other groups this was a matter of concern to about one third of each group.

The parents in the cerebral palsy group seemed to express the greatest concern that the place for loud noises was out-of-doors and should not be allowed within the house. All other groups were about evenly divided on the import of such a limitation.

Only in the mongoloid group was there a sizable percentage of parents who agreed that a child should stay in his own yard for play. All other groups seemed to regard this as a minor point. The mothers of the mongoloid group were unanimous in agreement that their child should stay near the house and here the majority of mothers in the blind and deaf groups were in accord with them.

Judging the extent of agreement on a given rule of behavior to represent a weighting of consensus on the rule, a rank order of importance can be determined across the groups which might be defined as a basic set of rules among these parents. To bring about a semantic consistency, the rules can all be cast under the heading of maternal agreement that these children should be taught the following:

1. To refuse to accept a ride from strangers.
2. To refuse to talk to strangers when unaccompanied by a parent.
3. To avoid climbing on household furniture.
4. To pick up his own toys.
5. To confine rough play to basement area or out-of-doors.

6. To avoid playing in roads or alleys.

7. To be silent after going to bed at night.

On all other behaviors listed as possible restrictions there was a considerable amount of variance.

On the question of whether or not the children must hang up their own clothes the mothers in the cerebral palsy, organic, mongoloid and blind groups were evenly divided with half of each group listing it as a rule and the other half not listing it at all. The deaf group mothers were a little more convinced of this need because more than two thirds of that group felt it was a rule.

The obligation on the child to pick up his toys and put them away after completing his play was also uniformly regarded as an important rule except in the cerebral palsy group where the mothers having severely handicapped children did not list this as a rule. It is probable that the child's physical limitations upon the act of picking up and returning toys negated the setting of such a rule.

TELEVISION

The impact of television upon American society has been the subject of voluminous discussion on many fronts during recent years. The advent of educational television stations with entry into classroom life has represented a truly remarkable advancement in the use of the medium. Novel advertising with intriguing slogans has brought many a product to the level of continual household vocabulary.

The study of this impact has also generated a great deal of concern in many quarters over the negative influences upon child development. There is concern over the deleterious effect of exposure to violence and various vigilante committees wage zealous campaigns to guard American children from undue exposure to programs which may be construed as injurious to social and moral values.

Some experts express concern that the American youngster is becoming a sedentary individual hypnotized into a state of passive inactivity instead of being a curious, investigative, exploring, active, aggressive youngster exercising gross muscles in vigorous activity. Some talk of TV as a curriculum of training to join the adult ranks of the spectator "fat" American. Mothers speak of being unable to "unglue the child from the viewing chair." Regular bedtime schedules are delayed in favor of "one more program." Mothers suffer exasperations in attempting to pry the child from his spectator spot in order to come to the dinner table on time.

On the positive side mothers will express their thankfulness to the TV screen for helping to pass the time during a child's sojourn with the customary viruses, measles and colds, or for occupying the child during periods of inclement weather. For the typical American parent television appears to be both a monster of conflict and a boon to tranquility. However, it may be perceived there can be no question that it has become a primitive necessity for family living.

When the television question is considered for the handicapped child a number of images come to mind. One can picture the cerebral palsied child in a wheel chair unable to romp and run in vigorous activity with neighborhood peers and unable to occupy time with productive manipulative activity spending many long, passive hours watching the "vast wasteland." The question of what relationship the deaf child holds to the television world certainly is intriguing. The manner in which the blind child relates to TV is also of interest. The hyperactive, brain-damaged child, the mongol child, the receptive or expressive aphasic, the child with visual or auditory perceptual problems all offer a population of child viewers who could be considered as atypical televiewers.

While the particular value which television holds for various disability groups in terms of communication, thought processes, new learning, etc., holds promise as a fertile field of investigation, the temptation to focus this investigation upon the child was staunchly resisted in favor of maintaining a consistent concern for the role of the parent.

Thus disciplined, attention was directed to the expression of control tendencies regarding the extent to which parents limited the child's viewing. The use of television viewing restriction represents a potentially powerful tool for parents to obtain desired behavior from the child. As guardians of the child's physical, social, and emotional welfare, parents have some obligation to reflect on the negative and positive values that the viewing of a single program might hold for their child. In view of the many considerations of physical and perceptual deviation represented among the children in this study, there was interest in ascertaining the extent of restriction exercised by the parents on their child's TV viewing.

To investigate this area a series of questions related to television were included in the clinical interview.

A four point scale emerged from the analysis of responses. Some parents exercised a formal and rigid control of the amount of time which the child was allowed to spend in viewing TV. Some strictly limited the child's viewing to one or two programs per day. Some set a time limit such as one hour of viewing allowed just prior to bedtime. The most prevalent expression was one construed to be *no effort at control.* Some parents felt that the children set their own controls and didn't watch enough to present any need for controls. Others felt that school work, bedtime, eating routines, etc., were so set that there was little time for TV and rarely a need for controls.

Some children were said to show no interest in TV and consequently, no effort at control was necessary. Another segment stated that they exercised some control in the matter of deciding which programs were suitable for child viewing or that only children's programs, interpreted broadly, were allowed, but there was no stringent effort to control for this.

Few mothers and fathers exercised a strict control of the amount of time their children viewed television (Table 78). Half of the mothers and half of the fathers reported that they made no effort to control either the type of program allowed or the amount of time spent watching. Among those parents who exercised a strict control there was little difference between mothers and fathers except that in the mongoloid group fathers were more controlling than the mothers. As a general rule, however, mothers were more controlling than the fathers. This may be due to the fact that most fathers were not at home during the major portion of the child's waking hours.

Each of the groups reported a small percentage of their children as having no interest whatsoever in viewing television and, consequently, had no reason to be concerned about any regulation of time or type of program. Disinterest was most pronounced among the deaf children where one fourth were said to show no interest in the TV screen. In the other groups an average of 10 per cent

TABLE 78

EXTENT OF RESTRICTION ON TELEVISION
VIEWING EXERCISED BY PARENTS

	Cerebral Palsy		Organic		Mongoloid		Blind		Deaf		Total	
	M	F	M	F	M	F	M	F	M	F	M	F
Strict control	17%	11%	21%	15%	4%	16%	14%	12%	10%	0%	16%	12%
Mild control	34%	25%	20%	16%	24%	16%	29%	38%	35%	33%	27%	22%
No control	40%	56%	49%	47%	60%	63%	43%	50%	30%	50%	45%	53%
Not interested	9%	8%	10%	22%	12%	5%	14%	0%	25%	12%	12%	13%

showed no interest. These children were described as being unaware of TV and for the most part were the severely handicapped and severely retarded children.

In the blind group two mothers stated that their blind child paid no particular attention. It would seem that neither the deaf nor blind group should show any concern for TV, but the parents reported a great deal of audio-interest among the blind and a great deal of visual interest among the deaf. While each group may have been handicapped in their appreciation of TV by the loss of the visual or the audio they, nonetheless, did relate meaningfully to the TV set.

Only a few parents among the cerebral palsy group commented on the value of the "constant image" for occupying the child's attention. The impression gained from these parents is that few of these children spent a great deal of time watching television and that in only few instances was television a soporific or a substitute for other activities.

The image of the handicapped child sitting before the set vicariously experiencing many events which might never be a part of his life did not emerge from these responses. As a matter of fact, when the parents were asked to comment on how much the child had learned from TV, they were hard-pressed to come up with a meaningful statement. Most parents felt that the child had learned something but they could not specify. Most also viewed TV as an entertainment medium and said they were not concerned about the learning as long as the child was being entertained.

Some mothers and fathers felt that their child had learned some negatives from TV such as silly commercials or gun-play or anti-social phrases, etc. Only a few parents felt that their child had learned words from TV or how to play games. Television was a medium for entertainment and fun and not viewed as being an educational medium by the majority of parents.

The general finding was that television viewing was not a problem area among the parents of the handicapped children. Fathers and mothers were not wholly in agreement on the question of control of viewing, but it seemed that whatever controlling did occur was more likely to stem from the mother than the father.

This question was also asked in the Sears' study and is available for comparison. The mothers of the nonhandicapped kindergartners exercised far greater control over the amount of time their children watched television and the type of programs which were allowed to be viewed than was apparent among the parents of the handicapped. Some shading of the interpretation of this apparent difference in control may stem from a difference in the year in which the questions were asked of the two groups of mothers. Sears asked the question when TV was a relatively novel, cultural phenomenon as contrasted to 1962 and 1963 when the TV set had achieved the status of a family necessity and some process of selective viewing was being noted generally.

The image of the handicapped child captured by a TV screen to vicariously experience a world in which his own participation might be limited is clearly denied by these findings. While a few children in the cerebral palsy group might fit such an image, this situation was a rarity.

When the parents were asked to define what their children had learned from television few responses indicated any positive values. Some felt that their child had learned some speech and some said that the children's programs had helped the child learn some games. For the most part, the parents seem to have regarded the television viewing as an entertainment experience and to have given little thought to specific educational values.

HOUSEHOLD RESPONSIBILITIES

In the daily course of home living there is a constant demand for little things to be done such as hanging up clothes in proper places, picking up toys, emptying ash trays, washing and drying dishes, carrying out garbage, burning the trash, mowing the lawn, and a list of additional items which for most parents could become an almost endless inventory of minor household tasks. Many of these trivia can be utilized by parents as a training ground for teaching the child a sense of responsibility in doing things for others and gaining a general feeling of contribution to the family operation of the household. This may have the effect of impressing upon the child in progressive stages the importance of doing his share to maintain the neatness and orderliness of the home.

The mothers in the Sears study (p. 287) were divided on this question for their five-year-old kindergartners with half making no demands upon their children for any regular tasks, and the other half having some regular assignments for the child. Few of these, however, insisted upon more than one or two minor assignments and exerted a moderate amount of pressure to enforce the responsibilities.

On this point the mothers of the handicapped were clearly more convinced and each group showed a high percentage of parents who had assigned regular responsibilities to their child (Table 79). The high percentages among the handicapped as contrasted with the mothers of the kindergartners may in part be due to the higher ages of the handicapped children, but there is little doubt that the parents of the handicapped believed in the assignment of household tasks for their children. Only in the cerebral palsy group was there any clear evidence that the child's handicap was a factor in negating such considerations.

TABLE 79

PERCENTAGES OF PARENTS IN EACH GROUP WHO
REPORTED THAT THIS CHILD WAS ASSIGNED
REGULAR TASKS IN THE HOUSEHOLD (N=275)

	Cerebral Palsy	Organic	Mongoloid	Blind	Deaf
Assigned regular tasks	89%	87%	74%	79%	87%
Not assigned regular tasks	11%	13%	26%	21%	13%

The severely physically and mentally retarded segment of the cerebral palsied cases in this study accounted for the percentage in that group who stated that no demands were made upon the child.

The mothers in other groups who reported that they made no such demands upon the child stated that the child was too young or that it was easier for mothers to do the jobs themselves. Other than those in the cerebral palsy group none of the parents accounted for their failure to assign household tasks on the basis of the child's handicap. Apparently, with certain exceptions, the handicapped child is expected to assume certain minor responsibilities just as well as siblings and other members of the household.

To determine specific tasks which might be assigned, parents were asked to affirm or deny whether the tasks specified on an arbitrary list were among those duties which they assigned to their handicapped child. Almost all parents had one or two specific tasks and many parents reported that four or five items on the list were expected of their child (Table 80).

TABLE 80

INCIDENCE OF HOUSEHOLD RESPONSIBILITIES
ASSIGNED TO THIS CHILD*

	Cerebral Palsy	Organic	Mongoloid	Blind	Deaf
Washing dishes	13	10	3	3	4
Drying dishes	15	30	8	6	9
Setting table	24	35	12	8	11
Cleaning own room	14	30	2	8	5
Making bed	13	26	6	3	7
Carry out garbage	11	30	2	4	9
Feeding pet	8	21	3	3	5
Clearing toys	41	77	21	10	18
Emptying wastebasket	11	25	3	4	7
Cutting grass	0	7	0	0	2
Vacuum	5	9	1	2	1
Dust	15	12	8	6	6
Other	10	8	0	2	2

*Tally includes only those who did assign tasks.

First and foremost assignment given to the children was the responsibility for clearing away their own toys upon completion of their activities. The second ranked task was that of setting the table at mealtime. Some responsibility for maintaining the cleanliness of their own room on a regular basis was reported as the third most frequent form of assignment. Drying dishes could be ranked in fourth incidence among all groups. Vacuuming, dusting, feeding pets, emptying waste baskets, making their own beds, washing dishes, cutting grass and a variety of other tasks were all reported in scattered minor incidence.

Parents in the deaf group reported the highest incidence of demand for clearing one's own toys and the blind group were least demanding of the five groups for picking up toys. While the majority of parents demanded picking up toys as one of the assignments, there were some parents in each group who did not list this as a requirement but did list others. It was interesting to note the incidence of blind children who were reported to dry dishes, set the table, and clean their own rooms.

Taking each group in turn, the cerebral palsy group were assigned to clear toys, set table, dry dishes and clean their own rooms. The same series was prevalent in the organic group. The mongoloid group showed the least incidence of assignment with clearing of toys and setting the table being the principal tasks demanded by parents. The blind group seemed to favor clearing toys, setting table and cleaning one's own room. The same was true for the deaf.

In the category of "other tasks" parents inserted comments such as "clean own closet," "burns papers," "stacks papers," "rakes leaves," "piles diapers," and an assortment of other tasks.

The general impression gained from these responses is that although these parents believe that household tasks should be assigned on a regular basis to help the child learn a sense of responsibility, the nature of the task assignments is never of a strenuous or demanding quality. Simple tasks which could be easily performed were characteristic. Furthermore, none of the children appeared to be employed on more than two or three tasks as a general rule, and all of these tasks could be classified as "assistance to mother." Except for the few children who were reported to cut grass or rake leaves, none of the assignments were of a service to the traditional father role. The assignment of responsibilities, therefore, seems to be the province of the mother, directed by her and utilized to decrease demand upon her for home care.

Clinicians might well devote some effort to helping parents study a variety of tasks which might be considered as possible assignments for children in order that the potential for learning such forms of responsibility might be exploited to the fullest according to the intellectual level and within the natural limitations of the handicap.

ALLOWANCES

In some cultural strata in our society parents use the technique of granting the child a weekly monetary allowance as a means of teaching money values, thrift, saving, and responsibilities of handling money. Usually this technique involves progressive increments as the child grows older. Some parents will utilize this method to teach a child to save a portion of the allowance while allowing for free expenditure of the remainder. Others will settle for the single lesson of a regular weekly amount to meet needs which the child might have in the way of candy, gum, comic books, etc.

Since this technique is generally understood to be a middle-class culture and the socioeconomic level of these populations were within the middle class range, it was of interest to ascertain whether parents of the handicapped also employed this system with their children. Parents were asked whether this child was given a monetary allowance and if so, how much.

As a general pattern these parents did not grant allowances to their children. Each group revealed an approximately uniform percentage of those who did so, roughly amounting to three out of ten parents (Table 81). Among those parents who gave allowances, the usual grant was twenty-five cents, with ten cents being the least, and fifty cents being the most.

TABLE 81

PERCENTAGES OF PARENTS IN EACH GROUP WHO
REPORTED THAT THIS CHILD RECEIVED A
REGULAR WEEKLY ALLOWANCE*

	Cerebral Palsy	Organic	Mongoloid	Blind	Deaf
Given an allowance	28%	27%	5%	28%	26%
Do not give an allowance	72%	73%	95%	72%	74%

*N=275

Few of the parents who employed an allowance technique insisted that the child save a portion of the money except among the blind and the deaf groups where, if a parent gave an allowance, there was also an insistence upon partial saving. The mongoloid group showed the least inclination toward this practice. The uniformity of the distribution among 270 parents suggests a relatively common attitude in the negative on the question of allowances.

The data do not allow for any exploration of reasons why these parents were in such close agreement on this point.

COMMENTARY

These three areas of behavior were reported in similar manner across all five groups. In only a few instances could a particular choice of action on the part of a parent be attributed to a consideration for the child's handicap. In regard to restrictions and demands each parent expressed a code of child-rearing practice which applied equally to the handicapped child and his siblings. Except for those cases where the muscular handicap of the child was a significant consideration in setting restrictions the only other factor to influence a differential in restrictions between *this* child and siblings was the matter of age. Younger siblings may have experienced less restrictions and older siblings tended to experience more restrictions. A principle of increased restrictions and demands in accordance with advancing age and presumed levels of greater behavioral complexity seemed to govern the parental practices.

Undoubtedly there are thousands of shadings and nuances which should be added to this picture of how these parents set restrictions, and made demands, if a totally clear picture would be expected. For instance, the matter of the strictness of enforcement, extensiveness of detail involved in each item, frequency of demand and the parental tolerance level for error were not investigated. While such extensions would have clarified the details of these areas the focus remained upon the group characteristics rather than upon individual techniques and accomplishments.

All of these parents had some set of rules for the children. The reasons why some parents were more emphatic about certain rules and others seemed emphatic about different rules must be classified as unique to the parent as a parent and not as the parent of a handicapped child.

The legendary belief that the parents of handicapped children are remiss in imposing restrictions and making demands upon such children gained no support from these data. Each group of parents reflected enough variation on these items within their own group and across groups that few items can be singled out as holding significance to a particular group in contrast to others.

The parental attitude toward television viewing was also held to have little relationship to the child's handicap. These parents had certain beliefs about the value of television for *all* children and acted in accord with those beliefs. There was practically no evidence that these mothers *relied* upon television viewing as a practice for achieving personal freedom. It also seemed clear that only two or three parents regarded TV as therapeutic in the sense of a teaching device. Television did not preempt the teaching responsibility of the parent.

Here again the practices might have been made clearer by asking parents to more clearly define their personal standards on this topic but preliminary interest was squarely fixated upon achieving some global impressions rather than seeking precise detail. Expressed attitudes were considered as general attitudes and not specifically related to their identity as parents of handicapped children. In this regard the possibility that these parents were expressing a popular parental attitude must be entertained.

The exact details of household responsibilities were not ascertained. It is possible that a mother checked the listing that a child "sets the table" and actual inspection of such process within the home would reveal that the child only performed a small detail in the total act of setting the table. Since the full act was not defined for the parents each one held her own personal definition of the total act of behavior which she would consider under each item. If the child believed he was setting the table by placing silverware only, he acted as if he had accomplished the full act and would undoubtedly list such activity as a responsibility if he were given the same check list to indicate his chores. Since the entire group of mothers were at the same disadvantage of lacking a precise job specification for each item, a generalizing effect was assumed.

The practice of granting the child a weekly monetary allowance was clearly not a part of the child-rearing relationship for the majority of these parents. The parents who granted allowances did so for all siblings after a certain age. Those who did not grant allowances indicated that this practice was also not employed for siblings. In this matter the handicap of the child seemed to have little bearing upon the parental practice. If any significance can be noted it comes from the findings that the parents in the mongoloid group showed the lowest incidence of granting allowances and this negation may have some relationship to the child's retardation.

In the areas covered by this line of investigation there was a marked similarity in parental practices among the five groups and even a rather solid conviction among the majority of mothers in regard to certain practices. Practices for siblings were essentially identical to those employed with the handicapped child.

In general there was little evidence to suggest that any of these areas constituted a problem area for most parents. If clinicians are confronted with parents who are problem-laden in these areas, the difficulties stem from personal dynamics not shared by this study group.

Chapter 9

THE PARENT AND CHILD SEX BEHAVIOR

THE SEXUAL BEHAVIOR of children who are handicapped may be reviewed from two perspectives. First, some investigation must be directed toward ascertaining whether or not certain primitive curiosities, self-stimulations, and responses occur in the same manner as has been described by Sears (p. 181-217) for nonhandicapped children. Second, it is important to determine whether parents of handicapped children respond differently to such behavior and if such difference does occur to determine how the response is related to the child's handicap.

The mores of American society are equally applicable to the handicapped child. It is likely that they are even more applicable. People are often overheard ascribing various sexual deviations to handicapped children in general on the premise that their abnormalities automatically extend into the sphere of sexual behavior. While it is true that such expressions scarcely represent a sophisticated viewpoint, it must be remembered that the parent rears the handicapped child in a milieu containing naive as well as sophisticated attitudes both personally as well as from the general community.

Sears (1957, p. 181) discussed the general social problem of sex in American society and described the role of a mother in such areas as follows:

> The task of the mother in our society then, involves training the child to inhibit sex impulses toward family members, avoid erotic play with other children, and avoid sexual self-stimulation. Partly as a means to these ends, and partly as an end in itself, efforts are made to inculcate modesty standards. Some modesty training occurs in all societies; none tolerate complete nudity at all times. There is much variability in Western standards, both from group to group and from time to time as witness taste in adult evening gowns and bathing costumes. But in early childhood modesty is not connected with ritual display.

It is of interest to consider the mother who is confronted with a severely physically handicapped child and the way she might fulfill this role. The mother of the blind child, deaf child, hyperactive organic child, and the mongoloid child all suggest images of maternal confrontation which might conceivably alter the manner in which the mother goes about the business of teaching these taboos and restrictions.

The area of sex training can be examined from a number of vantage points and in varying depths. For the purpose of this study the same three areas of concentration employed by Sears were used, namely modesty, masturbation, and social sex play. This was not an easy topic for expression among the parents and their responses were generally considered to be less direct and less detailed than for other topics.

Parents rarely elaborated on the techniques they employed and did not specifically describe details of sex play among the children. The usual comment in the interviewer's report stated that the introduction of the topic was frequently reacted to with thinly camouflaged surprise. None of the parents refused to answer the questions but many were obviously uncomfortable in such discussion and were happy to move on to another topic.

SEX TYPING

As a general cultural observation there are a number of attitudes and beliefs which are commonly held on the matter of sex typing. Boys are supposed to develop traits and behaviors which have been associated with men while girls must acquire the traits of women. Rugged, aggressive, body-contact play is assigned to males. Quiet, sedentary, refined play is associated with feminine characteristics. Doll play for girls and trucks and airplanes for boys are common associations.

The sex typing process is initiated early in the child's life by the clothes that are worn, toys that are presented, and a general attitude on the part of adults in the environment. Boys are expected to progressively become braver and less sensitive. Crying behavior is expected to be removed from the boy's response pattern but remain socially acceptable for girls at any age. Toys emphasize that girls must imitate the maternal role and play at various domestic chores

and motherhood. Boys are supposed to play with toys which emphasize a vocational role such as being a doctor, a mechanical engineer,
a chemist, etc.

This is the manner in which this society places a developmental
emphasis upon typing the male and female behaviors. Girls who
vary from such culturally defined patterns and engage in boylike
activities may be classed as "tomboys" while boys who engage in
girl-like activities usually earn the name "sissies." Both labels imply
that the child is not behaving in the prescribed manner.

Each parent becomes a sex-typing model to be imitated and each
parent is expected to reinforce the typing by the toys and clothes
that are bought, the experiences that are arranged, and by continually
pointing out to the child that certain behaviors which are expressed
must be sublimated because "boys don't act that way" or "that kind
of thing is only for girls." These statements and many others in a
similar vein are to be used by parents to help the child achieve a
proper image. Each parent must express an attitude on these questions and does so in the child-rearing process.

How do parents of handicapped children feel about holding their
child to culturally expected sex-typed behaviors? Does the existence
of a handicap reduce the concern for sex typing? What response
do parents give to behaviors in the child which are commonly associated with the opposite sex?

The question of parental reaction to doll play among boys and
rough play among girls was asked during the clinical interview.
The question was asked of both parents.

The degree of importance that the parents of the five groups
attached to the belief that boys should act like boys and avoid doll
play and any behavior associated with a feminine identification,
or that girls should do girl things and avoid activities associated with
a masculine identification, produced a distribution of responses which
could be set on a three point scale.

Some felt identification play to be very important, others felt this
was important but did not weigh their answer with any modifiers
which would suggest a high value, and still others felt that this was
not an important issue.

Among the mothers as a composite group, approximately half of

the responses indicated that the mothers saw no reason to be concerned about boys and girls actively engaging in play behavior
traditionally associated with the opposite sex. One fourth of the
mothers in the cerebral palsy, organic and mongoloid groups expressed strong feelings about the importance of sex-identification play,
and their counterparts in the deaf and blind groups were even more
numerous in their valuation of this as a very important consideration.
Why the mothers in the deaf and blind groups should express greater
concern than the mothers in the other three groups is not clear. It
was also true that the fathers in the blind and deaf groups expressed
a greater feeling of concern than did the other fathers (Table 82).

In general, the fathers attached greater import to this question
than the mothers did in all of the groups. The fathers were more
concerned that boys should behave and act like boys and girls should
be ladylike than were the mothers. The mothers and fathers in the
cerebral palsy, organic and mongoloid groups seem least concerned,
and both mothers and fathers of deaf and blind are most concerned.
A considerable amount of disagreement between mothers and fathers
was noted in this area of evaluation of child behavior.

In the Sears (p. 397) study this question was handled somewhat
differently. Two additional questions were asked of the mothers of
the nonhandicapped which were not included in the present study.
These questions asked the mothers to comment on their feelings of
whether there is any difference between the way boys and girls
ought to act at age five and what the mothers had taught their sons
about the treatment that should be accorded to little girls. These
two questions were included in their analysis of maternal responses
and, consequently, the comparison between the two studies cannot
be as direct as on some other issues. In the analysis of these responses,
the Sears group rated the mothers on a seven point scale "that
ranged from a very low expectation of any sex difference in young
children's behavior to a very strong conviction that boys and girls
should be influenced from the very beginning to act manly or lady-
like."

If some interpretive liberties are taken with the Sears data some
comparisons can be attempted. In the present study a three point
scale was possible. If the Sears scales are now interpreted to mean

TABLE 82

EXTENT OF IMPORTANCE ATTRIBUTED TO MATTER OF
BOYS ACTING LIKE "BOYS" AND FOR GIRLS TO BE
"LADY-LIKE" EXPRESSED BY MOTHERS AND FATHERS

	Cerebral Palsy		Organic		Mongoloid		Blind		Deaf		Total	
	M	F	M	F	M	F	M	F	M	F	M	F
Not important	40%	31%	50%	33%	58%	39%	36%	25%	45%	20%	46%	30%
Important	32%	56%	27%	29%	17%	28%	21%	25%	5%		20%	27%
Very important	28%	13%	23%	38%	25%	33%	43%	50%	50%	80%	34%	43%

that the first three levels are equivalent to this study's scale of "not important" then the comparative percentage is 36 per cent. If the midpoint of level four on Sears is taken to be equivalent to "important" on this scale then the comparative percentage is 20 per cent. The final three levels on the Sears scale yield a comparative percentage of 43 per cent.

The mothers of the nonhandicapped expressed a greater extent of concern for behavior associated with sex typing than did the mothers of the handicapped. The Sears mothers showed an equal concern for this manly or ladylike behavior to the concern expressed by the fathers of the handicapped.

Why mothers of the handicapped should be less concerned about sex typing than mothers of the nonhandicapped is not clear.

MODESTY

The culture pattern dictates that children must be clothed while playing out-of-doors or moving about the community. Only in the warmest weather of the summer is there an allowance for near nudity in the form of trunks or shorts with no demand for full coverage. While society imposes certain limitations on nudity out-of-doors each family can set its own rules and patterns on this matter within the privacy of their own home.

To ascertain the attitudes of these parents on the question of modesty they were asked how they felt about the matter of the child running about the house in a naked state. The responses were grouped according to a permission-objection continuum in three categories. The data were also compared to the Sears study where the same question was asked.

The mothers of nonhandicapped children (Sears) expressed a significantly greater incidence of permissiveness for their children to run about without clothes than did any of the five handicapped populations. All five groups expressed a majority opinion of objection to such behavior in their children (Table 83).

The mothers and fathers of the deaf reported to no incidence of unlimited permissiveness and the same was true for the mothers in the mongoloid group and the fathers in the blind group. The highest extent of permissiveness was reported by the mothers of cerebral palsy

TABLE 83

EXTENT OF AGREEMENT BETWEEN FATHERS AND
MOTHERS ON THEIR FEELINGS REGARDING THIS
CHILD RUNNING ABOUT WITHOUT CLOTHES ON

	Cerebral Palsy		Organic		Mongoloid		Blind		Deaf		Sears Mothers
	M	F	M	F	M	F	M	F	M	F	
No objection	25%	15%	15%	15%	36%	6%	13%	13%	30%	18%	46%
Permissible occasionally	16%	7%	17%	24%		23%	20%				30%
Objects to such behavior	58%	78%	68%	61%	64%	71%	66%	87%	71%	82%	30%

children. While nearly half of the mothers of nonhandicapped were permissive in this area the composite finding among mothers of the handicapped was that only 10 per cent were permissive. Only on the rating of occasional permissiveness was there some degree of concordance between the two different mother groups.

Why there should be this large discrepancy in concern for modesty between these two groups is not clear.

The fathers of the handicapped registered a greater incidence of objection to allowing children to run about without their clothes on than did their wives, but there was a generally high state of agreement between fathers and mothers in all groups that such behavior should not be allowed. The incidence of permissiveness was very low for all groups. The mothers of the cerebral palsy and blind groups were more permissive than fathers. Mothers and fathers in organic group expressed the highest level of agreement on all three possible levels of permissiveness but in all other groups the mother tended to be more lenient than the fathers.

MASTURBATION

Information on the topic of masturbation was gained by asking the parents to respond to the question, "What have you done when you have noticed him playing with himself?" and "How important do you feel it is to prevent this in a child?" The word *masturbation* was not used in the questioning because it was felt that most parents might regard this as associated with puberty behavior or might regard the word as a "more severe" situation and therefore deny its existence.

The mothers and fathers in the cerebral palsy, mongoloid and deaf groups were in relatively close accord in their report that they had never observed such behavior in their child but the parents in the other two groups did not show a similar agreement (Table 84). In the organic group half of the fathers stated they had never observed such behavior as compared to only one third of the mothers reporting no such behavior. In the blind group the proportions were reversed. Here the fathers had apparently observed incidence where the mother had not. The overall finding was that more than 40 per cent of the total group reported no observations of such behavior.

TABLE 84

PARENTAL RESPONSES TO OBSERVED MASTURBATORY
BEHAVIOR IN COMPARATIVES PERCENTAGES

	Cerebral Palsy		Organic		Mongoloid		Blind		Deaf		Total		Sears
	M	F	M	F	M	F	M	F	M	F	M	F	
Have ignored such behavior	5%	3%	11%	7%	15%	5%					6%	3%	4%
Physically diverted	16%	21%	15%	2%	8%	11%	7%	13%	5%	9%	10%	11%	
Have expressed mild verbal reproach	25%	18%	42%	29%	23%	32%	50%	63%	20%	27%	32%	34%	49%
Have expressed strong verbal reproach	8%	3%		11%	19%	16%		13%	10%	9%	7%	10%	5%
Have never observed such behavior	46%	55%	32%	51%	35%	36%	43%	10%	65%	55%	44%	42%	41%

The percentages were similar on an overall basis for both mothers and fathers. The deaf group reported the least incidence or observation of masturbatory behavior in their children.

As a general finding across all the group, six out of ten parents reported that they had observed such behavior. The incidence appeared to be highest in the organic and the mongoloid groups according to the mothers and highest in the blind and mongoloid groups according to the fathers. The parents in the mongoloid group reflected the closest extent of agreement on this point.

Since the general findings reflected that such behavior had occurred for 40 to 60 per cent of each group it was of interest to ascertain the manner in which each of these parent groups dealt with the situation when it was observed. Analysis of parental responses to a question directed at their reaction to such behavior allowed for a distribution into four categories. When the verbatim response indicated that the parent had done nothing or had ignored the behavior the classification of "have ignored such behavior" was assigned to the response. If the parental statement indicated that they moved the child's hands, pulled the hands away from the genital area, or quickly initiated some other activity to manipulatively occupy the child, the category of "physically diverted" was employed.

Two levels of verbal reproach could be distinguished. Some parents indicated that they told the child to stop, or suggested another activity, but made no special issue of the behavior since the child discontinued such activity with the mild reproach. Others indicated that they spoke sharply to the child, became angry, forbade the behavior, shamed the child, etc., in a manner that reflected a strong, harsh, verbal reproach.

None of the parents reported spanking the child or using any stringent physical action upon the child. If their child did engage in masturbatory behavior the approach of mild verbal commands to discontinue seemed to be favored by all five groups as the parental response for such situations. A very small percentage of mothers and fathers ignored such behavior, with the blind and deaf groups being most emphatic in reporting that *none* of the mothers or fathers ignored such behavior. Doing something to, or with, the child's hands was most pronounced among the parents of the cerebral palsy group as a response technique although all groups reported some incidence of this approach. A stringent verbal reproach was reported to be more frequent among fathers than mothers in the organic and blind groups where none of the mothers use a strong verbal reproach.

Throughout the analysis, however, it seems clear that a mild verbal reproach was the characteristic response for the mothers and fathers of all five groups. As a secondary group characteristic the cerebral palsy group physically diverted, and the mongoloid group utilized, a strong verbal reproach. Among the other three groups none of the other techniques ascended to a secondary approach. Except for the organic and the blind groups there was a generally high extent of agreement between mothers and fathers on this question. In both instances the greater or lesser observations of the fathers contributed to the disagreements.

When the parents were subsequently asked whether they felt it was important to prevent such behavior in a child the fathers were more in the affirmative on this question than the mothers except in the cerebral palsy group (Table 85). There also seemed to be little doubt as to where the vast majority of both mothers and fathers stood on this question. Very few felt that it was not important to prevent such behavior. The mothers and fathers of the mongoloid group were almost totally in agreement on this issue.

The explanations offered to justify their positions on this issue fell into two categories. Most of the parents felt that such behavior was socially unacceptable and, therefore, worthy of change or prevention. A smaller percentage felt that such behavior might become a "bad habit." Only four fathers in the total sample expressed any concern that masturbatory behavior might have a harmful physical effect upon the child. Two fathers and four mothers frankly stated a personal revulsion at the thought. When the mother and father explanations were compared, the mothers were more concerned about the development of a bad habit while the fathers tended to emphasize the social undesirability. More mothers than fathers (13 per cent compared to 2 per cent) expressed concern for possible physical harm to the child.

To gain some perspective on this question the Sears' data were compared to the response percentages of the parents of the handi-

TABLE 85
EXTENT OF AGREEMENT BETWEEN MOTHERS AND FATHERS ON IMPORTANCE OF PREVENTING MASTURBATION IN A CHILD

	Cerebral Palsy		Organic		Mongoloid		Blind		Deaf	
	M	F	M	F	M	F	M	F	M	F
Important to prevent	82%	75%	75%	82%	92%	95%	79%	100%	77%	82%
Not important to prevent	18%	25%	25%	18%	8%	5%	21%		23%	18%

capped children. The parents of the nonhandicapped are in close accord with these parents on the matter of whether masturbatory behavior should be ignored when it occurs. A negligible percentage in both studies reported that they paid no attention to their child when this behavior was observed.

There was also a concordance between the parents in both studies on the incidence of a stringent approach. Few parents expressed a potent and angry approach to such behavior. A mild reproach was favored in both studies. There was also an equal incidence of reporting that no such behavior had been observed. On this question the parents of the handicapped and the nonhandicapped are in accord: masturbatory behavior requires some sort of intervention by the parent to cause the child to stop, and such intervention is usually in the nature of a mild reproach. Apparently both parent populations feel this technique is effective.

While the data for the parents of the nonhandicapped was not specifically presented for the discrete question of whether or not parents felt it was important to prevent such behavior in a child, the general pattern of response in the Sears study may be taken to reflect an equal intensity of feeling that masturbatory behavior should be prevented.

SEX PLAY WITH OTHER CHILDREN

Children are curious little creatures exploring their worlds in countless ways to find out about more and more. This curiosity may well cause them to investigate the bodies of their playmates in what might generally be called sex play. Whether or not this type of investigation had been noted by the parents of the handicapped among their children was ascertained by posing the question, "How about sex play with other children—has this come up yet?" and "How about children wanting to look at each other or go to the toilet together or giggling together—how do you feel about it when you notice this sort of thing going on among the children?"

In the analysis of the responses the comments on both questions were treated as one and rated in terms of parental objection or acceptance of such behavior.

When the categories of moderate, considerable, and severe pressure are considered as a unit from the Sears report (p. 207) 29 per cent of the mothers of nonhandicapped children felt strongly about preventing or inhibiting sex play among children and were joined in this feeling by a composite 32 per cent of the mothers and 25 per cent of the fathers of the handicapped children. The mothers in the deaf group expressed a greater incidence of concern for inhibition than any other group (Table 86).

As a general finding the fathers in the handicapped group expressed less feeling of objection for this behavior than did the mothers except for the organic group where mothers were less concerned.

For some reason, which is not readily discernible, the parents of handicapped children seemed more inclined to regard such behavior as an expression of normal curiosity than did the parents of the nonhandicapped. Fathers of the cerebral palsy and deaf groups were least concerned among the five father populations while the organic group mothers were least concerned among the five mother populations. When all mothers from both studies are compared to each group there is a commonality of concern among all groups except the mothers in the deaf group who were emphatic in their expression of objection to such behavior.

The same degree of commonality was not found among the mothers in considering curiosity a normal phenomenon of development. Here the organic mothers were most accepting and the mongoloid mothers least accepting. The other three groups of mothers of the handicapped showed some degree of commonality (28 to 33 per cent). Only the mothers of the deaf were less tolerant than the mothers of the nonhandicapped. All other mother groups were more accepting.

A small percentage of parents in each group indicated that such curiosity might be acceptable among younger children but would not be acceptable among older children. Since the Sears data does not report such findings it is not possible to consider this finding comparatively. The mongoloid and deaf group mothers showed the greatest incidence of this qualification in their responses with one fourth of the mongoloid group and one fifth of the deaf group introducing this modification.

Nearly half of the mothers of the five-year-olds in the Sears study stated that they had never noticed such curiosity in their child. None

TABLE 86
COMPARATIVE FINDINGS IN PERCENTAGES BETWEEN FATHERS AND MOTHERS ON THE QUESTION OF THEIR FEELINGS REGARDING SEXUAL CURIOSITY AMONG CHILDREN

	Cerebral Palsy		Organic		Mongoloid		Blind		Deaf		Total		Sears
	M	F	M	F	M	F	M	F	M	F	M	F	
Object to expression of such curiosity—emphasize privacy	33%	18%	20%	31%	32%	22%	27%	27%	50%	27%	32%	25%	29%
Have no concern; consider such curiosity as normal behavior	33%	67%	45%	27%	28%	33%	33%	13%	10%	55%	30%	39%	24%
Consider it acceptable behavior among young children but not among older	4%	3%	6%	5%	24%	12%	7%	25%	20%	9%	12%	8%	1%
Deny any expression of such curiosity from their child	30%	12%	29%	37%	16%	33%	33%	35%	20%	9%	26%	28%	46%

of the mother groups of the handicapped approached this extent of denial. The highest incidence of denial in this study occurred among the mothers and fathers of the blind. The fact that the Sears study was of five-year-olds and the age ranges in this study were from four to ten years suggests the possibility that the handicapped group simply reflected several more years of opportunity to express such curiosity.

On the matter of agreement between mothers and fathers as to whether such behavior had ever been noticed only the parents in the blind group showed a high level of agreement. In all other groups a considerable amount of disagreement was noted. The mothers in the cerebral palsy and deaf groups reported less incidence of sexual curiosity among the children than did their spouses. The mothers in the organic and mongoloid groups reported a greater incidence than did their spouses.

Since the probing of these responses was not pursued to an extent which would allow for interpretation of these variances, the meaning of this state of disagreement among the fathers and mothers must await the more intensive analysis of individual protocols for possible interpretations. The seemingly obvious possibility that fathers have less opportunity to observe children because of working schedules does not explain the variations among the five father groups.

In general, it would seem that the parents of the handicapped have observed more incidents of sexual curiosity among their children than did the mothers of the nonhandicapped but they expressed less concern about such behavior than did the mothers of the kindergartners. The reasons for this difference are not clear. No speculations can be offered at this time as to why the mothers of mongoloid children reported such a high incidence of objection as compared to all of the other groups.

COMMENTARY ON THE FOUR SEX QUESTIONS

Fathers expressed a greater concern that "boys should act like boys" and "girls like girls" than did the mothers. In this respect the fathers expressed the same extent of concern which the mothers of the nonhandicapped group in the Sears' study had expressed. Mothers of the handicapped were less concerned about sex typing in all groups than were the fathers and significantly less concerned about this topic than were the mothers of kindergartners in the Sears study.

The mothers of the nonhandicapped kindergartners were clearly less concerned with modesty behaviors than any of the five mother groups in this study. Both mothers and fathers in these five handicap groups expressed a strong majority objection to child nudity.

The topic of masturbation produced a finding that such behavior had been observed in approximately 50 per cent of each of the five groups of children represented which was approximately the same incidence reported by the Sears study. Only a small percentage of parents reported that they used a strong verbal reproach toward the child for such behavior and a small percentage in each group observed but ignored.

The general impression gained was that all parents, despite some expression of revulsion, had some degree of acceptance of such behavior as normal but only a small percentage felt that if it were ignored it would disappear. There can be no question that the "some action" was compelled in the majority.

It was interesting to note that while the mothers and fathers of the handicapped were less concerned about sex typing than the mothers of the nonhandicapped five-year-olds in the Sears study, and both study populations appeared to be equally concerned about masturbation behavior. The parents of the handicapped children were more concerned about sexual curiosity and sex play with other children than were the Sears mothers. As a general pattern the fathers were less concerned about this than the mothers. If the Sears data are taken as comparable the incidence of such behavior was observed oftener among the handicapped groups than among the nonhandicapped kindergartners. Mothers of the handicapped were more aware of such behavior in their child than were the fathers.

In general, the parents tried to convey the impression that they were no different from other parents when it came to their views and attitudes on sex training. However, the distinct impression was formed from their clinical behavior during that sequence of questions, as well as from their verbalized statements, that most of these parents had carefully compartmentalized this area of thought into the black box of uncertainty and had assigned it for consideration at some future time. They seemed to feel that such matters might be of import at some later stage in a child's development but were of minimal concern at the present time.

The analysis of the respective reactions of these parents could be pursued in relation to each parent's total attitude towards sexual behavior as an area of human behavior. The psychological literature is voluminous on this topic and there are undoubtedly many descriptive pages in that literature which would apply to these adults as marriage partners, children of their own parents, etc. They probably contained the same general distribution of personal attitudes of freedom, bias, prejudice, rejection, acceptance, and so on which would characterize any adult population.

Their respective motivations in regard to their responses to child behaviors are undoubtedly related to their personal dynamics on these questions but no attempt was made to secure sexual attitude data from the parent on any other perspective than the child-rearing viewpoint.

Whatever may be the medieval legendary association between sexual deviation and handicap the child-rearing practices of these parents show no significant differences from those of parents of non-handicapped children.

Unsolicited comments from many of the parents clearly indicated that the expressions they voiced on these topics were equally applicable to their nonhandicapped children. These comments were an expression of belief as parents. Even though the questions were not asked concerning siblings the parents volunteered to comment on the equal applicability.

The responses were parental. Whether these responses are considered in, or out of, agreement with some one else's belief is probably strictly a matter of where each perceiver stands in relation to these questions. The general expression, however, seemed to be one of conservatism. Permissiveness and advanced liberal thought on these matters were not the typical expressions. It was also felt that this entire area was not a problem area for these parents in the day by day course of family life.

Chapter 10

SIBLING ATTITUDES AND THE QUESTION
OF FAMILY LIMITATION

MANY PROFESSIONALS have expressed concern about the lot of the normal siblings in a family containing a handicapped child. What losses are suffered when maternal attention must be given to the braced child who must be taken to a clinic regularly? What resentments build up when one is pushed to become independent too quickly because the handicapped sibling is overly dependent? What explanations can be given to one's peers to explain the presence of the handicapped sibling? These, and many more questions, come to mind when the normal sibling is considered. Since almost all of the parents had more than one child the attitudes of siblings represents a salient dimension for the child-rearing picture.

There is no doubt that the most efficient way to find out what a brother or a sister thinks or feels about a handicapped sibling is to conduct a direct investigation among the siblings themselves which would allow for some analysis and some generalizations. This, however, was not possible within the scope of this study but it was possible to ask the parents to check a list of statements describing possible sibling reactions for those which were pertinent and to allow the findings from such data serve as a preliminary form of investigations.

A series of thirty statements listing various behaviors and attitudes which siblings might manifest in the family relationship to the handicapped child were devised and presented to both the mother and the father during the group test sequence of the study. The directions on the form stated: "Brothers and sisters frequently must make some kind of adjustment. This adjustment varies in each family. Check those items which apply to your particular case."

Seventeen statements were cast to reflect a negative attitude on the part of siblings and ten statements were of a positive quality (see Appendix, Sibling Attitudes Form). Three statements were noncommittal. To qualify the distribution of scores among the total population a simple scoring system was devised.

Table 87 shows the mean scores and standard deviations for the five groups resulting from scoring the questionnaires. The higher the score the greater was the evidence of resentment on the part of the siblings. According to these mean scores the mothers in the organic and deaf groups indicated the greatest extent of sibling resentment of the handicapped child, while the mothers in the cerebral palsy group indicated the least amount of resentment. While the fathers in the organic group matched their wives in indicating sibling resentment, the fathers in the deaf group showed a lesser extent of negative sibling attitudes than had been reported by their wives.

TABLE 87
MEAN SCORES ON SIBLING ATTITUDES

	Mothers			Fathers		
	N	*Mean*	*SD*	*N*	*Mean*	*SD*
Blind	19	8.47	2.85	8	6.38	3.28
Deaf	23	9.09	2.9	13	6.38	1.94
Cerebral Palsy	65	7.18	2.73	30	8.23	2.78
Mongoloid	35	8.69	4.19	19	7.11	2.47
Organic	118	9.41	2.93	47	9.06	3.76

When the data were inspected simply on the question of whether the parent was indicating a generally positive or generally negative picture of the siblings relative to the handicapped child, the feeling was in the positive majority (Table 88). Many of the parents checked items of a positive connotation and also checked some negatives. However, the predominance of positive or negative became the guideline in establishing one or the other viewpoint.

It is undoubtedly true that any sibling will have some moments of resentment during a young lifetime but a parent must generally contend with an overall attitude. The findings that parents tended to view the siblings as generally positive toward the handicapped child must be taken to represent the perceptions held by the parents. A direct approach to the siblings might conceivably reveal a different perspective.

On the basis of these findings, however, it would appear that the general course of everyday living between siblings and a handicapped child is a pleasant one. Only a small percentage of parents in each

TABLE 88

EXTENT OF POSITIVE OR NEGATIVE SIBLING
ATTITUDES AS REPORTED BY 177 MOTHERS

	Cerebral Palsy		Organic		Mongoloid		Blind		Deaf		Total
Positive	41	77%	50	77%	21	84%	11	79%	14	70%	78%
Negative	6	11%	6	9%	3	12%	1	7%	4	20%	11%
Too Young	1	3%	3	5%			1	7%			3%
No siblings	5	9%	6	9%	1	4%	1	7%	2	10%	8%
No. in group	53		65		25		14		20		

group could be considered as confronted with a great deal of negativism and resentment by siblings which posed a serious family problem. The resentments were defined as beliefs that the handicapped child was loved more, given more attention, or given more material things. The expression of these resentments took the form of teasing, overt physical attack, embarrassment among peers, refusal to play with the handicapped child, etc.

Despite the number of items which were stated as mild negativisms which might be expected in any family situation, the parents still presented a positive picture. None of the five groups showed a significant variation from the others. The general impression is that brothers and sisters of the cerebral palsied, mongoloid, organic, deaf and blind seem to accept their handicapped sibling and present no significant continuing problem to their parents in this regard.

FAMILY LIMITATION: INFLUENTIAL FACTORS

In coping with the problems presented by a handicapped child in the family, some modification of modes of adjustment and orientation may be expected. For instance, Farber (1960) has noted that with the entry of a severely retarded child, the following may occur: an arrest in growth through the normal family cycle, degree of mental integration is lessened and brothers and sisters may suffer as the family attempts to cope with the presented problems. Holt's (1958) work has indicated that the constant attention required by the handicapped child may result in an exhausted mother, along with concomitant restrictions in family activities, and a desire to have no more children.

To ascertain the pertinence of this question for these families the parents were asked whether the handicapped child had anything to do with their desire to have more children. While most of the parents commented that this did not influence them one way or the other, there were a number who freely expressed the fact that they limited their families or that they deliberately sought a subsequent pregnancy.

The comments of the parents who indicated that the presence of the handicapped child was a factor in considering further additions to the family were expressed in the positive as well as the negative.

One mother stated, "His condition increased our feeling of urgency to have another for our older normal child. Also, it was a matter of pride. We had to prove to ourselves that we could have another normal child." Another said, "We were at a low ebb. We were fearful to have more yet our desire was to have a normal girl to compensate for this one. Another thing—we didn't want our older boy to grow up with only an abnormal child." These comments were typical of those who expressed a positive feeling toward subsequent pregnancies because of this child.

The following comments are typical of those who indicated that they had limited their families because of the handicapped child:

I don't know if I'd want another one. He takes so much time. Sort of scares you—in a way.

The children I've had have been accidents. I had no desire for more children after this one. Who was to say this would not run through all others (*mongoloid*).

I'm afraid to have children—might be like this one or worse (*deaf*).

I just worry that what happened could happen again (*organic*).

I was afraid that I might have another one like her. Also, if I had another child I might not be able to give her the attention she'd need (*mongoloid*).

I was afraid of having more handicapped—maybe even another mongoloid. At my age I thought I might not be able to cope with any more handicapped.

Because I'm afraid of having another—not just deaf—but maybe a worse handicap. With the Rh factor I wouldn't want to play around with a child's future.

I have no desire. This is it! (*cerebral palsy*).

Mainly I don't have a desire. I don't know if I could take it. He is very demanding. What if something else would happen—then what would I do. I'm no gambler.

Some of these alterations in family orientations may be considered strategies for coping with the problems presented by the child. Clark and Farber (1962) have reviewed the literature pertaining to four of these strategies—withdrawal from community participation, institutionalization, establishment of priorities in family life, and decisions regarding future limitation of the family. While family limitaton may well be an important strategy used by the family, it is readily apparent that a number of additional factors could influence this variable, i.e., religion, education, severity of handicap, and age of mother at the birth of the handicapped child. A previous study (Cook, 1963) has found that of these four factors only the latter two were related to family limitation, which was defined as the number of children born subsequent to the handicapped child.

This previous study (Cook, 1963) used fifty-one families in which there was a cerebral palsied child. The present discussion is an attempt to extend the generality of the previous findings—that age of mother, severity of handicap, and the interaction between these two factors account for most of the variance on the strategy of family limitation. The generality is obtained by analyzing the pertinent information obtained on the five handicapped groups utilized in this project.

Table 89 shows the number of children born subsequent to the birth of the handicapped child as a function of the diagnostic group. Since the cerebral palsied group previously used was also included in the present analysis, it was of some interest to ascertain if diagnostic grouping had a differential effect on our dependent variable family limitation. A chi-square analysis indicated that the null hypothesis could not be rejected ($\chi^2 = 4.63$, p $<$ .20) suggesting that family limitation was not a strategy which differentiated the groups. Such trends which are noticeable, such as greater limitation in the mongoloid groups, would seem to be attributable to the mother's age.

The dependent variable, number of children born subsequent to

TABLE 89

FAMILY LIMITATION IN RELATION TO
HANDICAPPING CONDITION*

Handicapping	None		One		Two or More		No.
Condition	f	%	f	%	f	%	
Blind	4	28	5	36	5	36	14
Deaf	10	50	6	30	4	20	20
Cerebral Palsied	21	40	20	38	12	22	53
Mongoloid	14	55	8	32	3	12	25
Organic	23	36	18	28	23	36	64*
Total	72		57		47		176
Per Cent	41		32		27		

Children Born Subsequent to Birth of Handicapped Child

$\chi^2 = 4.63$, df $= 4$, pα.20

*One organic case not ascertained.

the handicapped child, was cast in a 2 χ 2 analysis of variance format with the factors being age of mother and severity of handicap, each at two levels. Unequal numbers of observations in the cells necessitated the use of an approximate solution using proportionate frequencies, as suggested by Johnson and Jackson (1959, 243-245). The source table for this analysis is shown in Table 90. Both age of mother and the interaction between age of mother and severity of handicap were highly significant, as indicated by the F ratios of 232.77 and 1305.53 (p < .001). The severity factor just approached significance as the required F ratio at the .05 level was 3.90.

Consideration of Table 90 would indicate that when the effect of age of mother and severity of handicap were removed, less than 10 per cent of the sum of squares of the dependent variable remained to be accounted for by other factors.

TABLE 90

SOURCE TABLE FOR THE ANALYSIS OF VARIANCE,
TESTING THE EFFECTS OF AGE OF MOTHER AT BIRTH
OF HANDICAPPED CHILD AND SEVERITY OF THE
HANDICAP ON FAMILY LIMITATION

Source of Variance	df	Sums of Squares*	Mean Squares	F	p
Age	1	30.26	30.26	232.77	<.001
Severity	1	0.45	0.45	3.46	>.05
Interaction	1	169.72	169.72	1305.53	<.001
Among subclasses	3	200.43	66.81	513.92	<.001
Within subclasses	172	21.55	0.13	——	——
Total	173	221.98			

*Adjusted sums of squares for unequal cell analysis of variance.

Table 91 presents the configuration of the significant interaction between age of mother at birth of the handicapped child and the severity of the handicapping condition on the family limitation factor. As was found in the previous study (Cook, 1963) of this question, age of mother and severity of handicap, while potent variables in themselves, interact in such a way that an older mother with a severely handicapped child will be more likely to limit family growth subsequent to the birth of a handicapped child than would a younger mother with a moderately handicapped child.

TABLE 91

MEAN NUMBER (UNADJUSTED) CHILDREN BORN
SUBSEQUENT TO THE HANDICAPPED CHILD AS
A FUNCTION OF MOTHER'S AGE AT BIRTH
AND SEVERITY OF HANDICAPPED CHILD

		Severe	Handicapping Condition Mild or Moderate	N
Age of Mother	Over 30 years	0.27 (N=22)	0.51 (N=41)	113
	Under 30 years	1.28 (N=50)	1.30 (N=63)	
	N	72	106	63

COMMENTARY

The parent of the handicapped reports the attitude of their non-handicapped children to be generally favorable. There may be occasional moments of resentment from the sibling but the majority of the parents report no significant problem from this source. It is possible that these parents were insensitive to the feelings of their other children when it came to discerning the siblings' real attitude toward his handicapped brother or sister. In the general course of intimate family living the naive sibling would be very likely to leave himself unguarded and in some manner would reveal his feelings. The popular belief that a sibling would bear some resentment was, in part, a bias built into the questionnaire offering parents a preponderance of negative statements in contrast to the positive.

While some of the families in this study were simply recruited for purposes of this study the majority of the parents involved had some association with the Easter Seal Center. Because of this there was some opportunity casually to check with clinical records and parent counselors on the staff as to whether the parental report on sibling attitudes represents a faithful report. The result was affirmative. In those cases where it was possible to check there was no doubt that the research parent reported a story on siblings consistent with the general clinical picture he or she had presented during regular counseling sessions.

There is a possibility that the parents report a positive attitude when in fact a negative attitude exists—this, however, seems somewhat remote since most parents were found consistently to report the same findings. If, in fact, a "positively reported" sibling harbored "negative-obscured feelings" the critical point is that his parent perceived it as positive and related to child-rearing practices according to such perceptions.

Whether these reports from parents truly represented the siblings can only be verified by going back to the siblings of this population and investigating this area directly. Therefore, limited by parental data from this study, the attitudes of siblings are regarded to be positive—contrary to popular opinion. The deep resentments which are often cited may be spectacular exceptions to these generalizations.

The highest incidence of reported sibling resentment (20 per cent) was found in the deaf group. In all other groups the incidence was considered to be negligible.

That advanced age of a mother might be a factor in family limitation in a family with a handicapped child really comes as little surprise, as this would be expected in the general population as well. However, with increased age, the additional factor of a severely handicapped child makes subsequent pregnancies even less likely. Thus, it would seem that coupled with the reproductive exhaustion of advanced age, there would also be operating an inhibitory factor having its genesis in other than the basic biological process.

One can conceive of a general state of exhaustion as a result of caring for the severely handicapped child. Factors such as fear of another handicapped child, drain on depleted financial resources, and concern for the effect of the handicapped child on subsequent siblings, may all contribute to family limitation subsequent to the birth of a handicapped child.

In fact, as responses to an interview question, "Did X's problem have anything to do with your desire for more children?" are considered, it is apparent that all the above factors entered into the reasons given for limiting the family. It was apparent also that the stated desire and the actual consequence were not identical in all cases. Some mothers had stated emphatically they wanted no more children, but, in fact, did have one or several children subsequent to the birth of the handicapped child. Interestingly enough, some mothers answered the above question in the affirmative and then went on to explain that they felt another child would compensate for X in their own lives, would provide a normal companion for X to play with and learn from, or it would prove to the parents that they could have a normal child. It is difficult to say with certainty, however, whether or not the latter statements are post priori rationalizations for an accomplished fact.

In summary then, results based on the analysis of the data only indicated that if number of children born subsequent to the birth of the handicapped child is to be used as an index of the strategy of family limitation, then the factors of mother's age at birth of the child and severity of handicap must be controlled or partialled out.

There are, of course, other ways of looking upon this area of family limitation.

The majority of these parents *did not know* they were parents of a handicapped child until two to three years after the birth of this child. The temporal intervals between this birth and that of subsequent siblings often preceded knowledge of the handicapped. The concept of judging family limitation on the basis of the number of subsequent deliveries must be viewed as a dubious indicator of family limitation. The comments of some parents indicated a deliberate attempt at achieving pregnancy for a subsequent child to "make up for this one" or as an effort to obtain a "normal sibling for the previous normal sibling." These statements might well be viewed as negative motivations. Such effort did not *limit* the family but rather served to increase it. The possibility that some parents unconsciously limited but were not able to report such unconscious limitation must also be considered.

The general impression gained from the data given to these questions by the mothers was one of questionability. It must be conceded that the information hoped for in asking the question did not materialize. Only, in the few cases where the parent openly expressed a limiting concept can any credence be given to the data. Such cases were too few in number to suggest any significant findings on this topic. Despite the collection of data and the accumulated findings no significant clarification on this subject can be ascertained from these findings.

Whether the birth of a handicapped child has a significant bearing on future family limitation is no better answered than before this study was initiated. The question requires a more penetrating form of investigation than was possible in this study.

Chapter 11

THE PARENT AND THE COMMUNITY

THE PARENT FUNCTIONS as a member of a community and relates to many people beyond his own home. The father, and in some cases the mother too, works in the community. They attend churches, join clubs, go shopping, and participate in community events.

In this study four areas of questioning were covered to present a general picture of these parents and their community relationships. They were asked to comment on how they explained their child's problem to the neighbors and to others. The general relationship and attitudes of both the mothers' and fathers' relatives were ascertained and compared. The extent of membership in parent organizations devoted to the cause of their child's handicap offers another facet to the parent as a community member. The determination of the extent of neighborliness in these families was obtained from a questionnaire concerning neighbor relationships.

NEIGHBORS

Explanation to Neighbors

Neighbors, friends, sales clerks, passers-by all have a curiosity about the child with a problem and every parent of a handicapped child is often confronted with a need to explain their child's problem. At times parents seem to do this in an anticipation of someone's question and explain about their child's difficulty before any questions are asked. Other parents may say nothing until they are asked directly. Whatever the timing may be there is always a need for a ready explanation. The child's brace or crutch, his apparent lack of hearing, absence of speech, poor coordination all become points of curiosity for many people.

This area of behavior, the explaining of the child's problem, represents another facet of the parents' relationship to the general community (see Appendix).

[204]

The majority in all five populations reported that they talked freely with their neighbors about their child's problem, explaining what doctors have told them and keeping them informed about the child's progress. In each group, except the deaf, there was a small percentage who indicated that they made no effort to discuss their child's condition with neighbors unless they were confronted with a direct question (Table 92).

There was little difference on this matter between the mothers and fathers. Both reported that the majority talked freely to the neighbors about the problem although fathers reflected a greater tendency to explain only when asked directly.

In the cerebral palsy group the general movement into the community accompanied by the child always produced some questions from people about the child's problem, and most parents dealt with such questions on a direct answer naming the child's diagnosis. Mothers commented that most people settled for that single reply but at times people wanted a full explanation and asked many questions. In this group the handicap is obvious and immediately identified by others.

In the organic group a handicap is rarely obvious and the general community can only question certain oddities in the child's behavior. This group of parents probably encounters the greatest difficulty in explaining that certain behaviors are due to a brain-injury. Here the general community appears more likely to attribute such behaviors to naughtiness, stubbornness, or spoiling, and according to the parents seem disinclined to believe that such actions are not caused by parental mishandling.

The mongoloid and blind groups also have children with obvious handicaps. In the mongoloid group parents indicated that they often had to contend with various old wives' tales and superstitions about causative factors.

The parents of the deaf conveyed the idea that the fact that their child might not hear speech directed at him caused the parent to anticipate possible sources of embarrassment for the child and the questioning adult. Consequently, a quick explanation that the child was deaf would immediately set the perception and dictate further behavior. The need to explain the communicative problem might almost be classified as a necessity among parents in the deaf group.

TABLE 92

PARENTAL RESPONSES TO QUESTION REGARDING
EXPLANATION GIVEN ABOUT THIS CHILD

	Cerebral Palsy		Organic		Mongoloid		Blind		Deaf	
	M	F	M	F	M	F	M	F	M	F
Have explained	79%	71%	84%	78%	79%	63%	75%	75%	100%	93%
Only when asked directly	17%	29%	12%	12%	18%	31%	15%	25%		7%
Not ascertained	4%		4%	10%	3%	6%	10%			

Those parents who were classified as being least neighborly according to their reports of neighbor relationships were also those who did not volunteer an explanation of their child's problem. In general, however, these parents seemed to have no difficulty in explaining their child's problem to the community curious. It seemed that only a few parents experienced any embarrassment in this area.

Neighborliness

A questionnaire used by Farber (1959) in his study of parents of mentally retarded children was included in the group form sequence to be completed by the mothers and fathers. This was a multiple choice form covering areas of relationships with neighbors such as: length of time parents had lived in the present neighborhood; whether friendships had been formed; extent of mutual entertaining; extent of other social activities in which neighbors were part of the group, and whether some are disliked (see Appendix).

A simple scoring system was devised for these sixteen questions, and means and standard deviations were calculated for both mothers and fathers. The lower the score the more neighborliness was felt to exist. On this basis the mothers of the cerebral palsy and mongoloid groups appeared to be the most neighborly. (Table 93) The fathers of the same groups also were found to be most neighborly among the fathers. In general, the mothers were found to be more neighborly than the fathers. For the most part, the individual fathers and mothers were in agreement on these questions. However, there were some instances where a mother was judged to be very neighborly while her husband's responses to the same set of questions placed him in a category of being far less neighborly than his wife.

TABLE 93

NEIGHBORLINESS SCORES OF PARENTS OF
HANDICAPPED GROUPS

Group		*Mothers*			*Fathers*	
	N	*Mean*	*SD*	*N*	*Mean*	*SD*
Blind	16	10.94	5.26	8	16.13	10.61
Deaf	23	10.26	5.66	16	13.13	7.56
Mongoloid	36	8.06	5.61	19	9.00	5.81
Cerebral Palsied	66	8.92	5.97	34	10.41	6.91
Organic	79	10.53	6.64	49	12.86	8.05

(The lower the score, the more neighborliness)

This judgment of neighborliness is only a broad measure and the many factors which might influence neighbor relationships such as recent location in a new neighborhood or widely spaced housing, distances away from other houses, etc., were not taken into account.

In all of the groups there were some families that seemed to limit themselves to a nodding acquaintance with neighbors, and at an opposite extreme, some families who held close personal friendships with neighbors which involved constant visiting, social activities, and sharing confidences. The bulk of all the groups, however, rested somewhere in between these two extremes. The variations among the groups on these questions was felt to have no relationship to the presence of a handicapped child in a family.

ATTITUDES OF RELATIVES

In the course of case by case clinical practice and parent group-counseling sessions the topic of the attitudes of relatives such as adult brothers and sisters, mothers, fathers, and various in-laws have often been reviewed by the parents as a negative factor added to the total problem of rearing a handicapped child. Many times parents have complained that certain relatives resented their child, suggested institutionalization, or were openly critical of the general manner in which parents related to the child. On the other hand, round table discussion has as often occasioned a very positive expression from some parents indicating that the relatives were very understanding and helpful.

In the belief that the attitudes of relatives on both sides of the family represented a shading or a nuance which might lend greater depth and meaning to the picture of child-rearing among the parents of handicapped children, an investigation into this area was included in the group form sequence for the parent.

Each parent was asked to complete two forms, one referring to their own relatives and the other referring to the relatives of their spouse. With minor semantic modifications both forms were the same (see Appendix). Each form contained thirty-five statements which pertained to attitudes and actions of relatives. Those which applied to their particular situation were to be checked. Twenty-six statements were phrased in a manner to imply that relatives were critical of parent actions related to the child, blamed parents for the child's handicap, or in some manner rejected the child. Six statements were phrased in positive terms indicating that the relatives were regarded favorably by the parent in relation to the child's problem. Three additional statements were classified as noncommittal.

The procedure did not specify to the parent the exact range of relationships to be included in the perceptual set but rather established a global set. The intention was to secure a general picture of whether or not these parents were contending with critical attitudes of relatives in their rearing of this child, as another potential source of anxiety.

In the evaluation of the completed forms the presence of three or more negative statements was held to be a critical or negative attitude on the part of relatives and the checking of two or more positive statements was considered to represent a supportive or positive attitude. Where the statements that relatives are seldom or never seen were checked these were classified in the no contact category.

TABLE 94

ATTITUDES OF MATERNAL RELATIVES AS
REPORTED BY MOTHERS

	Cerebral Palsy	Organic	Mongoloid	Blind	Deaf	Total
Positive	93%	63%	71%	68%	67%	72%
Negative	6%	33%	26%	21%	21%	23%
No contact	1%	4%	3%	11%	12%	5%

TABLE 95

ATTITUDES OF MATERNAL RELATIVES AS
REPORTED BY FATHERS

	Cerebral Palsy	Organic	Mongoloid	Blind	Deaf	Total
Positive	77%	66%	85%	100%	75%	75%
Negative	14%	32%	10%		12%	19%
No contact	9%	2%	5%		12%	6%

TABLE 96

ATTITUDES OF PATERNAL RELATIVES AS
REPORTED BY MOTHERS

	Cerebral Palsy	Organic	Mongoloid	Blind	Deaf	Total
Positive	77%	56%	56%	79%	75%	66%
Negative	17%	33%	28%	11%	12%	25%
No contact	6%	11%	16%	11%	12%	9%

TABLE 97

ATTITUDES OF PATERNAL RELATIVES AS
REPORTED BY FATHERS

	Cerebral Palsy	Organic	Mongoloid	Blind	Deaf	Total
Positive	86%	50%	75%	100%	88%	72%
Negative	14%	47%	20%		12%	26%
No contact		3%	5%			2%

This procedure permitted the tabulations of four sets of data. Each parent rated his own relatives as well as those of his spouse. These data were obtained on 275 mothers and the 118 fathers (Tables 94-97).

Maternal Relatives

When mothers were asked to rate their own relatives the overall finding across the five groups reflects a majority opinion on the positive side. Only one fourth of the total group indicated that the maternal relatives were critical. The mothers of the cerebral palsy group presented the highest percentage of positive feelings among relatives.

The discrepancy toward the optimum in this group suggests the possibility that the child with cerebral palsy and the parent of such a child may be viewed by relatives as less subject to criticism as to their handling of the child than any of the other diagnostic categories. Perhaps the parent is held less accountable for the child's problem and the behavior. In the other four groups the percentages are relatively similar in their distribution.

When fathers were asked to rate their wife's relatives the feelings were essentially the same. Three fourths of the fathers presented a positive image of the wife's relatives. Among the father groups the eight fathers in the blind group were unanimous in the positive view. The fathers of the mongoloid group were second in their positivism, with the other three groups being somewhat reduced, but similar.

The highest extent of negativism perceived among maternal relatives was expressed by the fathers of organics. In six organic and five cerebral palsy cases, the father reported the maternal relatives as negative while the mother reported positively. In the mongoloid group the situation was just reversed. Five mongoloid group fathers saw their wife's relatives as positive while the wife reported them negatively.

The discrepancies between husband and wife ratings of maternal relatives represented only 12 per cent of the total study population. Consequently, the agreement between husband and wife on the question of the attitudes of the maternal relatives is very high and indicates that both parents perceive the maternal relatives in the same manner.

Paternal Relatives

Only the fathers of the blind presented an unanimous feeling of positivism in regard for their own relatives in the same manner as they had for the wife's relatives. The fathers of the cerebral palsy and the deaf groups perceived their own relatives in a more positive view than they perceived the maternal relatives even though both sides were perceived positively.

In the organic and mongoloid groups the fathers reported a higher incidence of negativism among their own relatives than they had stated for their wives' relatives. The mothers of the deaf and blind groups showed greater incidence of positivism among their husband's relatives than they had reported for their own relatives. The mothers of the other three groups tended to rate their husband's relatives less favorably than they had rated their own.

In eleven cases fathers indicated a negative perception of their own relatives while wives' reported positively and in eight cases fathers were positive while wives were negative. The discrepancies between mother and father ratings on paternal relatives represented 11 per cent of the total sample.

General Feeling

Of the total study group 88 to 89 per cent were in mother-father agreement on the rating of both maternal and paternal relatives. Husbands were inclined to rate their own relatives more positively than their wives' relatives and, conversely, the wives saw their own relatives somewhat more favorably than their husband's relatives.

In 11 per cent of the cases the discrepancy between husbands and wives on the perceptions of relatives might be viewed as a potential source of friction between the couple in the normal course of living. Considering those cases, therefore, to be a difference in perception between husband and wife and eliminating them from full consideration in the matter of the impact of relatives upon the child-rearing milieu, the general feeling is that the negativism of relatives represents a problem to only a small percentage of the parents of handicapped children. While in individual cases the critical attitudes of relatives may present additional anxieties to the mother and father of the handicapped child, the majority of these parents enjoy a very positive and accepting climate in regard to family relatives.

The general area of adult family relationships is depicted mainly as a supportive and helping one by these parents, and may be considered as an asset for therapeutic planning. In those cases where the parent complains of negativism and interference from relatives on either side of the family, the dynamics are probably unique unto that case and no generalizations related to the handicap will suffice to explain the problem. The explanation probably lies more directly in areas unrelated to the child's handicap.

PARENT ORGANIZATIONS

During the past fifteen years there has been a significant increase in the formation of groups of parents of handicapped children into organizations with considerable stature in local communities and in some instances with national stature. The United Cerebral Palsy and National Association of Retarded Children are but two examples of national organizations that were founded through the efforts of dedicated groups of parents interested in promoting the welfare of children with specific forms of disabilities.

Throughout the nation the energetic efforts of these parents have resulted in the intensification of public education programs, inauguration of new community services, beneficial changes in legislation and, perhaps, most important of all, have offered a convenient vehicle for parents with common problems to meet together to share experiences and through the medium of expert lecturers to learn more about the nature of their child's problem.

In some communities these parent organizations under inspired leadership have risen to a high position of influence in rehabilitation efforts within that community. In other communities the leadership has not been highly effective and the parent group may be struggling to survive as an organization. If a survey were to be conducted nationally, it is very likely that one of the major problems faced by these organizations is the matter of attracting to membership *all* the parents within the community having a child with the disability identification of the organization.

Since the Milwaukee County area has been quite prolific in the organization of parent groups, it was of interest to determine the extent of membership among the parents who participated in this study. Parents were asked whether they belonged to a parent organization, and how they happened to join it, and whether they regularly attended meetings.

Only those organizations which have officially identified themselves as open to parents of children with specific handicaps, and whose purpose for existence is to promote the development and expansion of services for that particular handicap by united effort in the form of committee activities and regular meetings, were included in the tabulations. In the Milwaukee County area six organizations have been organized for such purposes (Table 98).

TABLE 98

PERCENTAGE OF PARENTS INDICATING
MEMBERSHIP IN PARENT ORGANIZATIONS

Parent Group	Cerebral Palsy	Organic	Mongoloid	Blind	Deaf
Association for retarded	7%	22%	44%		
Parents of Visually Handicapped	2%			79%	
Society for Brain-injured	2%	31%			
Cerebral Palsy Parents League	38%	2%			
Milwaukee Hearing Society					38%
Alexander Graham Bell Parents Group (Deaf)					37%
Do not belong to a parent organization	51%	45%	56%	21%	25%

The parents in the blind group showed the highest percentage of group affiliation. Eleven of the fourteen study cases belonged to the organization of Parents of Visually Handicapped Children. Two mothers of mildly involved children with cerebral palsy also belonged to that group because their children also had a visual problem but were not blind. The parents of the deaf group also showed a high percentage of group affiliation with 75 per cent belonging to one of the two organizations devoted to various causes for deaf children.

The parents in the mongoloid group either belonged to the Association for the Retarded or held no group membership. In the organic group slightly more than half of the parents held memberships in parent organizations with some belonging to the Society for Brain-Injured and others to the Association for the Retarded. In the cerebral palsy group half of the cases did not belong to any organization.

Three out of four parents in the deaf and blind groups had joined a parent organization as compared to one in every two cases in the other three groups. These data do not allow for any conclusions to be drawn from the findings of a higher incidence of group affiliations in the deaf and blind groups than for the other three.

When the parents were asked whether or not they regularly attended the meetings of those organizations slightly more than one third (38 per cent) indicated that they were regular in attendance. Although the blind group indicated the highest percentage of group membership they indicated the least regularity in attendance. The mongoloid group showed the highest extent of regularity in attendance. The general impression gained is that while the parents in the deaf and blind groups show a greater extent of group memberships the other three groups appear to show a greater extent of participation in the activities of their respective groups.

While this area was not probed in any depth the possibility that variations among the organizations in terms of program energy, group leadership, projects underway, etc., may account for more or less interest and participation must be entertained.

A few parents indicated a membership in more than one group but this was a negligible percentage.

According to the parents who held membership in these groups the principal method for seeking out membership was in response to a recommendation from their physician, a psychologist or a social worker. This method accounted for 59 per cent of the parents who had joined a parent organization. The second highest incidence of joining occurred as a result of being personally recruited by another parent who already held membership (39 per cent). For a small percentage their joining was prompted by the urging of their child's classroom teacher. Three indicated that they had joined after reading

TABLE 99

PERCENTAGE OF PARENTS STATING THEY REGULARLY
ATTENDED MEETINGS OF PARENT GROUPS*

Cerebral Palsy	Organic	Mongoloid	Blind	Deaf
38%	44%	63%	18%	50%

*Based upon number of cases who had joined

some publicity releases pertaining to the activities of the group in the daily newspaper (Table 99).

It would appear from this, that referral by a professional constitutes the major resource for parent group membership and, consequently, the percentage of parents in any given group in comparison to the total eligible within a community might well reflect the state of awareness among community professionals. It is also significant that personal recruiting by a parent member represents a reasonably productive recruiting process. Parent organizations may give careful consideration to these two methods if they wish to expand their membership to a higher percentage of representation of the specific handicap.

While these findings must be interpreted as a local phenomenon and offer only a suggestion to those interested in the parent organization movement, the clinical implications here are clearly in the direction of urging clinicians to be aware of the existence of pertinent groups and to refer parents to membership. Once referral has been made, however, the organization itself must seek ways to hold the interest and participation of the parent.

COMMENTARY

The majority of parents in all five groups reported that they experienced no difficulty in explaining their child to the community. It seems obvious that some parents experienced greater embarrassment than others and this, in part, was determined by the social attitude of the questioner. In the main, these parents talked freely about their child's problem. Most parents also indicated that they felt that people were usually sincere in their questioning.

Neighborliness, according to the data, seemed unrelated to the presence of a handicapped child in the family. In general, none of the five groups was more or less neighborly than any of the others. Differences were felt to be due to other factors such as recent arrival, distance, etc. There was no indication that the parents had acted differently towards neighbors because of this child nor that the parents felt that their neighbors had a negative attitude because of this. The impression was gained that neighborliness was probably no different in these parents than among other populations. Some people are neighborly and some are not.

Clinical files reveal a number of instances where a group of neighbors was openly hostile to the family containing a handicapped child including the organizations of petitions demanding their removal. In such cases the family lived on an island with great psychological distances between themselves and the neighbors. Some neighbors expressed that the handicapped child was a "maniac," a "deviate," a "case," or some other negative term and refused to allow their children to play with *this* child. There are people who hold such attitudes. Fortunately such cases are rare. Most neighbors are accepting of the handicapped child and the total family.

While the majority of parents in each group enjoy positive attitudes towards *this* child from both maternal and paternal relatives, each group reported some incidence of both sides of relatives who were critical of parental rearing procedures or openly rejected the child. This must be regarded as a secondary social burden with which the parents must contend. The highest incidence of relational negativism fell upon the parents in the organic group from both the mother's relatives and those of the fathers. Fathers tended to offer a more positive appraisal of both sides of relatives than did the mothers.

The findings in regard to parental affiliation with officially organized community parent organizations formed in the interest of specific disability groups must be regarded as primarily holding a local significance. Most communities do not have six different parent groups in existence. If, however, some speculation may be offered it would seem that 50 per cent of the parents of handicapped children do not belong to a parent organization because they do not wish to belong. Some parents resist the idea of joining such a group because they feel that they or their children have little to gain from such membership. Some parents are not joiners.

All parents were aware of the existence of the groups and those who had not joined pleaded a variety of reasons for their failure to join. Of those who joined the groups only about 50 per cent attended meetings regularly. Essentially the parent organizations seem to regularly attract the participation of only 20 to 25 per cent of the parents eligible for the groups. Perhaps other communities have a higher incidence than this study suggested in the Milwaukee County area.

The parent organizations offer the mother and father of the handicapped child the opportunity to meet and talk with other parents facing the same general set of problems. Such meetings may provide a parent with child-rearing suggestions and the chance to hear a variety of professional commentaries in area of parental interest.

Only half of these parents found such an affiliation to have value for them. All five groups had joiners and nonjoiners.

These parents talked freely about their child and did not hide the story. They were neighborly. They had relatives with positive attitudes. Such unanimity did not hold true in regard to their own attitudes towards parent organizations.

Chapter 12

SCHOOLING AND EXPECTATIONS FOR THE FUTURE

THERE ARE TWO major areas of concern in the development of the handicapped child once the early period of diagnostic anxiety has passed. Each parent must be somewhat anxious about how the child will fare in school from age five to eighteen years and also have some concern about the eventual adult life of this child. For those parents in this study whose children were enrolled in school some response to the current situations could be obtained. However, all parents in this study had from ten to seventeen years stretching ahead of them before the child would be an adult and therefore could only express their *expectations* for the future.

During the clinical interview a series of questions related to school and expectations for the future were posed to each parent.

SCHOOLING

School Information

The parent of a handicapped child rarely has a choice in the matter of obtaining educational services for their child. In most instances the school authorities designate that the child requires a specialized form of education in some setting (where other children with similar problems are grouped together) other than the neighborhood school. Often this involves a bus or taxi transportation to and from school for the child.

In this manner the values attendant upon peer interaction in play in the neighborhood, similar interests, common identifications, common referrents are lost to the handicapped child because he attends a *different* school. The parent is also faced with a problem in PTA identification since many of the special units do not have organized parent associations related to the program. These two considerations among others must be construed to bring about some home-school-family relationships which might conceivably be different in families having a handicapped child.

Do these parents feel that the present placement is the best possible school arrangement for this child? What is their opinion of their child's teacher? How does the child feel about school? Do parents help with homework? These and other questions pertaining to school were directed at parents during the clinical interview.

Opinions on School Arrangements

Almost all parents whose children are enrolled in some form of public school placement feel that the child's present school situation represents the best possible school arrangement that could be obtained. Only in the organic group was there a sizable incidence of parents who felt that some other arrangement might be more desirable, or an expression of uncertainty as to whether the present situation was best for the child. In the cerebral palsy, blind and deaf groups one parent expressed a negativism toward the child's school arrangement. Since none of the mongoloid group were enrolled in school the question did not apply (Table 100).

When one considers the general problem of the organically damaged child as an educational entity, and the dilemma which confronts educators in providing profitable educational programs for this group, it is not surprising that parents would express some uncertainty about their child's placement. It is likely that the same degree of uncertainty might be expressed by educators if a survey on the same question were taken.

TABLE 100

MOTHERS' EVALUATIONS OF SCHOOL ARRANGEMENTS
AND PLACEMENT OF THE HANDICAPPED
CHILD IN FREQUENCIES

	Cerebral Palsy	Organic	Mongoloid	Blind	Deaf
Feels arrangement is best possible	22	11		10	18
Feels arrangement is not good and some other placement should be made	1	5		1	1
Undecided		9			1
Child not enrolled in community school program	30	40	25	3	1
No. in group	53	65	25	14	20

For the physically handicapped, blind and deaf youngsters a stable traditional class organization has become an accepted social pattern with special curricula and teaching skills brought together in the best interest of the child.

The general impression gained from the parental response to this question is that parents are accepting of the present school arrangements for their children.

Parent Opinion of Teacher

The next step in shading in the picture of the parental attitude toward school was to ascertain how the parent regarded the child's present teacher. Verbatim statements were analyzed and grouped into three categories. Statements which expressed positive feelings were set in one category and statements which contained expressions of criticism were grouped in a second category. Some parents indicated that they had not had sufficient contact with the teacher to form an opinion or that they did not want to formulate a value judgment concerning the teacher. These responses were placed in a category of "undecided."

The majority opinion was clearly on the positive side (Table 101). Only a few parents expressed negative feelings toward the teacher. These negative expressions took the form of mention of a teacher's impatience, rejection of the child and lack of understanding of the child's needs. Whether or not these critical comments had any basis in fact is not within the scope of this study. These few parents perceived their child's teacher negatively and this negative perception may well have influenced their attitude toward their child's schooling.

TABLE 101

MOTHERS' EVALUATION OF THEIR CHILD'S PRESENT
CLASSROOM TEACHER IN FREQUENCIES

	Cerebral Palsy	Organic	Mongoloid	Blind	Deaf
Expressed positive feeling toward teacher	19	16		10	19
Expressed negative feeling toward teacher	3	2		1	
Undecided	1	7			1
Child not in school	30	40	25	3	
No. in group	53	65	25	14	20

The few parents who were critical of teachers were not necessarily critical of the school arrangement. In fact, parents differentiated between the two comments. The arrangement may have been acceptable according to their perception but they were negative toward the teacher. In the organic group, however, the same parents who expressed uncertainty about their child's placement also hesitated to make any evaluative comment about the teacher.

In general, the parents as a group expressed favorable opinions of the child's teacher.

Help With Schoolwork

While the incidence of homework assignments for those children enrolled in school was very slight, it was of interest to ascertain whether parents shared any responsibility for helping the child with his school work or whether such task was the responsibility of one parent (Table 102). Where parents indicated that neither of them helped their child with school work they offered one or the other explanation. Either the child received no home assignments from the teacher or the child managed whatever assignments were given without recourse to parental help.

Where homework assignments of some form did occur, the parents reported in the majority that both of them participated in helping the child. This was done periodically by one or the other parent, almost on a "taking turns" basis. In no case was the business of helping the child with school work reported to be the province of the father. Several cases in each group, however, did report that the mother was the only parent who offered help.

TABLE 102

INCIDENCE OF HELP GIVEN TO CHILD BY PARENTS IN
COMPLETING SCHOOL ASSIGNMENTS IN THE HOME

	Cerebral Palsy	Organic	Mongoloid	Blind	Deaf
Mother helps but father does not	3	5		3	3
Father helps but mother does not					
Both parents help	12	9		8	15
Neither parent helps	8	11			2
Not applicable	30	40	25	3	
No. in group	53	65	25	14	20

Generally speaking, if home assignments were given fathers tended to help as much as mothers did but a few fathers in each group could be declared nonparticipants in this area. The extent and type of help given was not ascertained.

Opinions on Strictness

A generalized question asking parents to comment on strictness among teachers in schools today was asked as a general documentary bit of datum. It was very interesting to note that none of the parents felt that teachers of today are too strict. Since this was a general question the total population response was tallied (Table 103).

TABLE 103

MOTHERS' OPINIONS OF EXTENT OF STRICTNESS
AMONG CLASSROOM TEACHERS IN PERCENTAGES

	Cerebral Palsy	Organic	Mongoloid	Blind	Deaf
Strict enough	66%	38%	40%	57%	65%
Not strict enough	15%	20%	32%	36%	30%
Too strict					
Undecided	19%	42%	28%	7%	5%

The distribution of responses varied among and between all groups. The mothers in the cerebral palsy group expressed a majority viewpoint that teachers were generally "strict enough." The remainder of the group were divided among those who felt that teachers were "not strict enough" and those whose response was evasive and noncommital. In the organic group nearly half of the mothers made nonevaluative comments but one fifth of that group expressed the feeling that teachers were not strict enough.

No majority opinion characterized the organic group. Lack of majority opinion was also found in the mongoloid group. The only other group to express a majority feeling was the deaf group who felt for the most part that teachers were strict enough. The least amount of indecision was found in the deaf and blind groups. These mothers expressed definite pro or con opinions. In the mongoloid, blind and deaf groups one third, three out of ten expressed, a concern that teachers were not strict enough with their pupils.

The opinions of 177 mothers of handicapped children on the question of whether the teachers of today are strict enough with their pupils reflected a small majority expression that teachers were exercising a sufficient degree of strictness but a strong minority expression that teachers should be stricter was found. The general attitudes expressed regarding strictness among teachers is generally concordant with parental attitudes on strictness which parents expressed in relation to questions regarding their own disciplinary practices with their own children.

Commentary on Parent and School

These data on the parental perceptions and attitudes in relation to school unfortunately pertain to only 44 per cent of the total sample with only the blind and deaf groups having a major percentage of children in school. This distribution is largely due to the recruiting process employed in securing the populations. The blind and deaf groups were recruited from public school classes while the other three groups were secured from clinical case files in private agencies.

Although the data are only partially representative there is still some merit in discussing the school data. While the responses were placed in various categories via the mechanics of information coding, the comments of the parents clearly indicated a considerable amount of naiveté regarding the educational program of the child. There was almost an expression of faith in the schools which seemed based upon a belief that this child had been placed in the best possible situation because "that's what schools do for these kinds of children."

Few parents seemed to have any real understanding of the nature of difference in curriculum between the special group and a regular classroom other than what might be a rather obvious difference such as electronic amplification devices, therapists, etc. Parents also seemed to have faith in the fact that teachers assigned to such classes are properly trained and qualified for this kind of work.

Even though the sample was small, a distinct impression was gained that parents have little real understanding of "what goes on in school" other than an assumption that it is similar to school in general, with some specific activities peculiar to the handicap of the child. "School is school" as far as parents are concerned and there is apparently a great lack of awareness of the nature of difference between regular and special education. Parental notions of special education are essentially a remodeled perception of what regular schooling was for them as children or for their siblings.

The interpretation of the rationale, curriculum and specialized techniques of special education has not been brought to parents in any degree of depth. This is an area of parental need.

EXPECTATIONS

Parental Expectations for Their Child's Future

The responsibility for rearing the child in our society quietly terminates when the parents announce the wedding plans for their son or daughter and their child then assumes a complete adult identity repeating the cycle of the race in his or her own marriage and eventual parenthood. Usually the formal schooling years have been completed by this time and some vocational direction has been attained.

Within the past quarter century a number of modifications have been noted in the traditional school-job-marriage sequence. The incidence of marriage occurring at an earlier age is gradually increasing. Family size averages are pressing beyond the two child family. College trained adults become more frequent in the job market with each passing year. Demand for skills in the vocational world becomes more intense with each passing year.

In the normal course of events a parent can anticipate the termination of child-rearing responsibility between eighteen and twenty-five years after giving birth to the child and quietly sit back to await their cues to respond in the role of grandparents. In ordinary conversation parental boasting of grandchildren, pride in the economic success of their married child, pride in the educational accomplishments of their college youngster, all are expressed frequently and continuously.

A mother's ambition for a glamorous and romantic marriage for her daughter has been advertised and fictionized in books and magazines for many years. A father's aspirations for high-level vocational attainments for their sons and daughters has also been the subject of much fiction.

Within this general cultural framework of expectancy the parent of the handicapped child must view the adult future for his or her child according to the actual or presumed limitations which may alter this normal course of events.

What dreams, aspirations and goals are held by the parents of handicapped children? Do they look forward to marriage for their child or anticipate a continuation of dependence into the adult years? Do they expect their child to obtain a college education or some skill training as a craftsman or tradesman? Do they anticipate any problems in the employment market?

Although the children represented in this study were ten to twenty years distant from the customary age ranges for college-employment-marriage and parenthood, it was felt that a set of questions related to future expectations might add an interesting nuance into the general portrait of parenthood.

Within the series of questions pertaining to school information parents were asked to respond to the query, "How far do you think *this* child will be able to go in school?" In the final stages of the interview the following questions were asked: *"All parents give some thought to what their children will be like as adults. What do you expect of this child's future in regard to employment? How about marriage and parenthood?"*

Marital Expectations

The responses given to the question of parental expectations for marriage and parenthood were distributed into four categories. Those statements which conveyed the belief that the parent anticipated eventual marriage for the child were placed in the "normal" classification. Those responses which expressed doubt or clearly negated such possibility were classified as "not likely." If the parent stated an uncertainty related to some hope that progress might occur or conveyed the general thought of "Who can tell what will happen in the next twenty years," such statements were categorized as "doesn't know." If a parent denied having any form of consideration to the question before having it posed in the interview such denial was classified as "given no thought" (Table 104).

The distribution of maternal responses across the five populations reflects a great deal of variability. Most mothers in the blind and deaf groups anticipate a marital future for their child. Three mothers

TABLE 104

PARENTAL EXPECTATIONS OF MARITAL FUTURE FOR THIS CHILD

	Cerebral Palsy		Organic		Mongoloid		Blind		Deaf	
	M	F	M	F	M	F	M	F	M	F
Normal	34%	40%	25%	39%	92%	11%	71%	63%	85%	92%
Not likely	30%	43%	37%	28%	8%	74%	21%	25%	15%	8%
Don't know	25%	12%	28%	33%		11%	8%	12%		
Given no thought	11%	5%	10%			4%				

in the blind group felt that it would be highly improbable that their children would marry and definitely negated the possibility. Several mothers in the deaf group stated that they were hoping that "time would tell." All of the mothers in these two groups agreed that they had thought about such questions occasionally.

Several mothers in the mongoloid group indicated a hope that "something might happen" in the next twenty years so they really couldn't say what the possibilities might be, but the vast majority in this group expressed a negative expectation. It was in the cerebral palsy and the organic groups where the greatest dispersion took place. The general breakdown in both of these groups was relatively comparable. One third of the mothers in the cerebral palsy group and one fourth of the organic group expected their children to face no significant problems in this area but the remainder were not so confident. Only in these two groups was there any incidence of denial that the mother had given any thought to this matter.

When the responses of the fathers who were interviewed were compared to the mothers' expectations on this question there was a general similarity across the five populations. Fathers and mothers tended to agree of the negative or positive possibilities of a marital future for their children. Some minor differences, however, were noted. Fathers in the organic group were somewhat more optimistic than the mothers and all of the fathers admitted that they had considered the possibility. Several fathers in the mongoloid group stated that they saw no reason why their child might not eventually marry. In the blind and deaf groups there was close agreement on an optimistic outlook. The fathers in the cerebral palsy group were more definite than the mothers on this question.

Further analysis of the proximity of their expectations to the current state of knowledge on these matters, and the extent of their child's handicap and the levels of intelligence, will be discussed later in this section.

Agreement on Marriage Expectations

On the question of whether or not the parents agree in their expectations for their child in regard to eventual marriage, the responses of the fathers who had been interviewed were matched with the responses of their wives on this question. In the first comparative inspection of each pair only the count of agree-disagree was considered. No evaluation was made initially of the direction of disagreement or the reality of either parent's expectation (Table 105).

Three out of four couples in the mongoloid, deaf and blind groups were in agreement on their marital expectations for their child. The cerebral palsy and organic groups showed a higher incidence of disagreement. The percentage of disagreement in these two groups on this question represented a radical increase in the agreement-disagreement ratio which was found on all other questions where the percentage of agreement had consistently been high. Fathers and mothers in these two groups appear to have distinctly different perceptual sets on this question.

TABLE 105

EXTENT OF AGREEMENT ON MARRIAGE EXPECTATIONS
BETWEEN MOTHERS AND FATHERS

	Cerebral Palsy		Organic		Mongoloid		Blind		Deaf	
Agree	16	46%	19	41%	14	74%	6	75%	9	75%
Disagree	19	54%	28	59%	5	26%	2	25%	3	25%
	35		47		19		8		12	

The entire group of couples who were in agreement on the question of marriage were those whose children were severely handicapped and severely retarded. In the organic group those who were in agreement did not represent any particular kind of child in terms of intellectual level, behavior, etc.

The generally high extent of agreement found between mother and father responses throughout the investigation was not reflected in the findings on this particular question.

Employment Expectations

Parental expectations in regard to their child's future as a jobholder in adult society produced a distribution of responses which could be scaled in the same manner as the replies to the question on marriage. In general, the statements of the fathers were more precise and definite on this question than those of the mothers. One might expect that fathers would be more likely to evaluate employment potential on a more direct basis because of their experiential background.

The majority of parents in the blind and deaf groups made statements indicating that they expected that their child would experience no major problem in finding a productive place in the vocational world. Only one mother and father in the blind group felt that it was very unlikely that their child could make his way in the world of work (Table 106).

In the cerebral palsy group a considerable percentage of fathers and mothers anticipated a successful vocational future for their child but there was more doubt among the mothers as to what the future might hold vocationally. The fathers in this group showed more negativism than the mothers in regard to employment potential.

In the organic group the mothers were slightly more optimistic than the fathers, while more fathers felt they could make no judgment at this time and considered various changes which might take place during the next ten to fifteen years. A surprising number of fathers and mothers in the mongoloid group looked forward to a normal adult employment situation for their children.

Only one third of the fathers and a lesser percentage of mothers in this group did not expect that their child could find an independent vocational niche. While mothers presented a highly optimistic outlook the fathers did not negate this but rather indicated a "time will tell" or "times might change" feeling in regard to employment.

As a general rule mothers expressed a greater extent of optimism in regard to employment than the fathers did. Except for the cerebral palsy group there was little difference between mothers and fathers in the percentage of those who felt that their child would not become a productive worker. The mothers' optimism stands in contrast to the higher percentage of expressions of unwillingness to commit themselves among the fathers.

When the distributions on Table 104 and Table 106 are compared, it seems clear that parental expectations in regard to employment are toward what might generally be classified as a "normal vocational adulthood" while their expectations for a normal marital future do not reach the same extent. More parents anticipate employment than anticipate marriage for their children. Parents also appear to

TABLE 106

PARENTAL EXPECTATIONS FOR ADULT EMPLOYMENT FOR THIS CHILD

	Cerebral Palsy		Organic		Mongoloid		Blind		Deaf	
	M	F	M	F	M	F	M	F	M	F
Expects normal employment	43%	37%	66%	59%	52%	32%	86%	75%	95%	83%
Does not expect employment	19%	37%	15%	16%	28%	32%	7%	12%		
Don't know	30%	26%	14%	22%	12%	36%	7%	12%	5%	17%
No thought	8%		5%	3%	8%					

TABLE 107

PARENTAL EXPECTATIONS IN REGARD TO POTENTIAL EDUCATIONAL ATTAINMENT OF THIS CHILD

	Cerebral Palsy		Organic		Mongoloid		Blind		Deaf	
	M	F	M	F	M	F	M	F	M	F
College	23%	34%	14%	24%			64%	38%	75%	50%
High school graduate	18%	20%	11%	14%	4%		14%	50%	15%	42%
Special school		8%	5%	12%	20%	21%	14%			
Eighth grade	17%	9%	16%	16%		9%		12%		
None	2%	9%	2%	7%	4%	16%				
Don't know	40%	20%	52%	27%	72%	47%	8%		10%	8%

be more certain in their responses about employment than they are about the question of marriage.

The same small percentage that denied having previously considered the marriage question also denied having thought of employment potential.

School Expectations

Among the fathers the deaf group expressed the highest level of educational aspiration for their children with half the group indicating that they felt that their child would go to college, and with one exception the other half felt the child would at least complete a high school. One father in this group stated that he "didn't know how it would all come out but he'd take it as it comes" (Table 107).

Half of the fathers in the blind group indicated that they thought a secondary education would be the upper limit for their blind children but several looked forward to collegiate training and one indicated that he "would settle for his boy getting through eighth grade."

The predominant opinion among the fathers of the mongoloid group was one of doubt with expressions, "I have no idea," "Who can tell," "Time will tell," and other statements in a similar vein. Some fathers felt that the child would receive no schooling and others stated that a special school for the retarded would be the highest possible level.

The level of aspiration among the fathers in the organic group showed no significant concentration at any point. One fourth anticipated collegiate training and one fourth made statements similar to those described above which could be classified as "don't know." The other half of the group distributed themselves along the continuum with some expecting high school graduation, some expecting specialized schooling for the retarded and some expressing a willingness to settle for an eighth-grade education.

The fathers in the cerebral palsy group were definitely looking toward high school and college educations for their children with few expecting a limitation of specialized schooling or no schooling.

In the blind and deaf groups the mothers expressed a greater extent of college aspiration for their child than did the fathers. Fathers in these two groups were apparently viewing a secondary education as the upper limits while the mothers held higher expectations. Only a few cases in these two groups felt that their expectations would have to be held pending further developments.

In the other three groups the major percentages of expression fitted into the category of doubt and uncertainty with regard to schooling. This finding was most pronounced among the mothers in the mongoloid group where three out of four felt that they could not even venture a guess as to what limits might be considered for schooling. One mother in this group felt that her child would be able to complete a high school program and one mother thought that her child would never be able to go to a school of any kind. Fathers in this group were less inclined to express doubt and uncertainty.

The mothers in the organic group expressed opinions that distributed among all possible categories. The fathers in this group were slightly more optimistic than the mothers and less inclined to express uncertainty. Half of the mothers stated that they had no idea of what future years might hold in the way of schooling for their children. The fathers in the cerebral palsy group were also somewhat more optimistic than the mothers and less uncertain.

The general impression gained from these findings is that the mothers of the sensory-handicapped children held higher aspirations than the fathers, with opposite finding holding true among the other three groups. One or two parents in the first three groups admitted that they held no expectations for their child's admission to school. All other parents either expected some level of attainment in school or expressed the feeling that they had no idea of how the school question might turn out.

EXTENT OF REALITY

Since the present state of research and demonstration programming in the area of vocational services and employment potential indicates that there is little likelihood that the child at subtrainable or trainable intellectual levels will achieve vocational independence, and the general impression is that few, if any, of the children at these intellectual levels marry and produce children, any statement of optimism for either employment or marriage for such children was classified as "unrealistic."

The expanded emphasis upon vocational rehabilitation for the retarded and congenitally physically handicapped which has occurred in this country within the past decade has brought about an increased possibility that the child within the educable mentally retarded range of intelligence may be placed in competitive community commerce or industry or at least remain productively employed in a sheltered workshop setting.

In regard to marriage and parenthood for the educable mentally handicapped the statistics and the research are sparse and vague. However, there have been enough cases of marriage and parenthood reported to place this potential within the realm of possibility despite opinions, beliefs and attitudes to the contrary.

The child with average intelligence with a mild orthopedic or sensory disability appears to experience little difficulty in achieving vocational independence and marriage and parenthood status. Consequently, parents of children with mild physical handicap or sensory disability, whose intellectual level was found to be average or at educable mentally retarded level, were judged to have a "realistic" expectation if they indicated a positive projection for marriage and employment for their child. Conversely, those parents whose children fitted in this category who indicated a negative projection for the future were considered to be "unrealistic."

While the problem of a severe physical handicap undoubtedly is a major factor in achieving vocational success and marriage, the number of live examples of successful cases at adult levels clearly indicates that if intellectual functioning is at average levels or above, a constructive vocational and marital future is a realistic possibility. Consequently, the parents of such a child have as much right to hope for attainment in these areas as any other parents.

Such factors as job availability, the employment market, sympathetic employers, job skills, etc., are all important in the fulfillment of such a parental goal, but the parent who projects a positive statement in this area from the remote perspective of early childhood must still be considered as having realistic aspirations. The circumstances within a given community at a given point in time may negate such aspirations, but social and economic factors rather than the status of intelligence, or the severity of physical disability, may account for such negation.

Using this type of reasoning, a three point scale was devised to categorize the parental responses to the two questions regarding employment and marriage expectations. The distribution of responses for the five study groups were defined as: (1) realistic with cause; (2) unrealistic with cause, and (3) unrealistic without cause. Table 108 reflects the distribution into two categories of "realistic-unrealistic" according to the scaling described above.

When the ratings of realistic-unrealistic were made on each couple according to a composite of expectations in regard to potential for schooling, marriage and adult employment, the mothers in the mongoloid group were found to be the most unrealistic group among the five groups of mothers, and the fathers in the mongoloid group were the most unrealistic among the fathers. Only the deaf group could be classified as 100 per cent realistic for both mothers and fathers.

This group was followed closely by the blind where unanimity was not present among either the mothers or fathers but only one father and one mother could be classified as unrealistic. Fathers in the cerebral palsy group were more realistic than mothers. Mothers and fathers in the organic group showed matching percentages in the realistic-unrealistic categories. Fathers in the mongoloid group were only slightly more realistic than mothers. In general, fathers appeared to be more realistic than mothers in regard to these three expectations.

Considering these three questions as a composite, the extent of agreement in terms of reality is very high for all groups except the mongoloid, and the findings suggest that most parents in these five groups have realistic aspirations for their child's future.

Most parents in these groups have given thought to what the adult future might be for their child in spite of the present young age of the child. Some expressed a high level of aspiration with reasonable justification. Some seemed to be underestimating their child's potential and some were overestimating their child according to present knowledge in the field. Many expressed the feeling that the current day-by-day problems of the child were such that they, as parents, could not project what the future might hold.

Most parents were judged to be realistic and this finding suggests a revision of popular clinical thought which runs along the lines

TABLE 108

PERCENTAGES OF MOTHERS AND FATHERS RATED AS EXPRESSING
REALISTIC OR UNREALISTIC ASPIRATIONS IN REGARD TO
MARRIAGE EMPLOYMENT AND SCHOOL POTENTIAL
OF THIS CHILD

	Cerebral Palsy		Organic		Mongoloid		Blind		Deaf	
	M	F	M	F	M	F	M	F	M	F
Realistic	79%	89%	75%	72%	48%	58%	93%	87%	100%	100%
Unrealistic	21%	11%	25%	28%	52%	42%	7%	13%		

that parents of handicapped children are unrealistic in their aspirations for the child's eventual adulthood. There was a considerable amount of recognition of a continuing dependency into adulthood. Fathers seemed to be more realistic on employment and marital aspirations, while mothers held a slight edge on the realistic appraisal of a school potential.

This does not seem to be the problem area that it has been believed to be. Daily living with a handicapped child seems to force a parent to face the reality of the future. Many parents seem to be quite confused about the future because they cannot relate their child's present behavior to future criteria. Clinicians can well afford to spend considerable time helping uncertain parents to understand present behavior in the light of the future. This is a major source of anxiety for many parents.

There are a number of areas that were covered in the investigations of child-rearing practices which might be regarded as incidental but they are nonetheless deserving of commentary. The presentation of a full treatment on these topics is believed to be unnecessary but they cannot be ignored.

A Hobby and Activity form (see Appendix) was presented to each parent in the group series in an attempt to determine whether these parents reported any degree of restriction upon their personal recreation and personal freedom because of the presence of a handicapped child in the family.

The tabulation of these results clearly indicated a wide range of interests among the total group. Some mothers reported memberships on bowling teams, card clubs, sororal organizations, and political organizations. Some others emphasized their interest in hobbies such as gardening, flower arrangement, dressmaking, painting and other activities within the home. Fathers showed a similar range of affiliations and home activities such as bowling, golf, fishing, hunting, lodge membership, union affairs, home workshops, etc. A few mothers claimed that the size of their family and household duties scarcely afforded them any opportunity to move within or out of the home in the expression of any interests other than those directly related to the family. Several fathers noted that their own work or business schedule gave them little time for other affairs.

The families differed from one another in range and frequency within and among the five groups. Some couples could be classified as joiners and participants in activities outside the home. Some were homebodies but had hobbies and interests which were personal expressions. In some instances the husbands and wives participated in recreation as a couple and in other cases each parent pursued an independent course.

There was no indication that the presence of a handicapped child proved to be a significant deterrent to parental freedom. Those who were joiners joined. Those who held interest in athletic participation did so. Those who enjoyed home-hobbies found time for such. Some had little else but household responsibilities and work. Whatever was reported to be the situation by the mother and the father was felt to be unrelated to the problem of their child. Where restriction was suspected further investigation clarified the point that this father or mother were like that before the arrival of *this* child. No patterns of similarity or difference existed between the groups.

The popular conception of parents curtailing their own social interests to dedicate themselves to their child or to hide in embarrassment or shame could not be supported in a single instance among 275 parents. If they were, by experience and background, activity oriented they managed to express this orientation, despite the "presumed burden they bear."

A response somewhat similar to this was gathered from the responses on the form called Family Social Practices (see Appendix). Whether parents visited relatives, went on picnics, held family get-togethers, took the children on vacations, and so on, was specific to an individual family. Some families were constantly on the go and some families were comparatively home oriented.

The family patterns, however, seemed to have little or no relationship to the handicapped child. The most severely physically handicapped were bundled into the car and taken on a picnic if the family was a picnicking family. The most hyperactive organic child was taken along to visit relatives if the family was a visiting family. In only rare instances was there evidence of family social restriction because of this child and where it did occur the restriction was attributable to the personal dynamics of a mother or a father to the extent that an atypical situation existed.

Clinical experience suggested that many handicapped children were afraid of animals and this appeared to be a possible area in which some differences might be found among or within the five groups. The investigation into this area was cast as a series of statements offered for checking if the item applied to a particular family (see Appendix).

The incidence of fearfulness in the presence of animals was notable only within the blind group where four out of ten were reported to be afraid of animals. In all other groups a few scattered cases were reported to be afraid. Some of those who were afraid had to contend with the presence of a pet in the family, principally among the blind.

In the cerebral palsy, blind and organic groups the families were approximately evenly divided between those who had pets and those who did not. However, only one in four families in the deaf and only one in three among the mongoloid group owned pets.

Most of the parents were in accord in their feeling that children should have pets, with the mothers of the organic and the blind revealing the highest extent of such belief. For a variety of reasons, however, not all parents gave life to such belief by having a pet within the household. In some cases the husband was against the presence of a pet and in other cases the mother was against it. Some stated that they intended to wait until the child became older. Some said that their living quarters or tenancy restrictions did not permit them to house a pet. Whatever their reasons might have been, the suggestion here is that while the majority of parents are favorably inclined to the belief that children should have pets, the number who actually have pets in the household represents a sharp drop-off in incidence.

In each group of parents some cases reported that they obtained a pet with the idea that the presence of a pet in the household might prove beneficial to the child in some manner. This was most pronounced in the blind group where eight of the fourteen cases indicated such reasoning. The next highest incidence occurred in the organic group where 26 per cent of the mothers stated that they had obtained a pet in the hope that it would help the child.

Chapter 13

PATTERNS OF DISCIPLINE

Society charges each parent with the responsibility of conveying the rules and regulations of social conduct to each of their children. The newborn infant is completely unaware of the behavioral expectancies which lie before him. Parents are charged with the shaping and modeling of the child's day-by-day experiences so a figurative society might look in upon him at any given time and pass judgment as to whether or not the child is developing along the lines society has defined.

As has been previously noted the announcement that a child is handicapped, at best grants a postponement to the parent but it does not grant an absolution. Each parent is expected to bring their child to a sustained level of behavioral conformity. The welfare of any society resides in the ability of all parents to carry out this obligation.

In carrying out the societal obligation to teach a child the lessons of behavioral conformity each parent must develop patterns of discipline. Even though the dictionary definition of the word discipline reads: "Instruction and exercise designed to train to proper conduct or action," the usual parental concept of discipline is one of various forms of punishment utilized when a child does not conform to expectancy.

Clinical experience for many years has continued to point out that parents equate the word *discipline* with the word *punishment*. When any parent is asked, "How do you discipline this child?" the response is not given in terms related to guidance but rather in terms related to spanking, deprivations and so on. So, despite the entymology of the word, custom and usage have shaded the definition in the direction of punishment.

The parent is placed in the constant position of defining boundaries and limitations. There is always an occasion to say "No" or "Stop." There are objects and places to be avoided as well as objects and places to be encouraged. The parent must protect and at the same time push out to subject the child to an expansion of his behaviors. The parent must allow freedom and at the same time inhibit freedom. The wise parent comes to understand which role to take at which time.

Some limitations must be placed upon exploratory freedom. While the child has a great deal to gain from freely moving about in a field of curiosity, investigating heights, depths, planes, enclosures, open terrains and so on, the parent must stand by to set boundaries of safety upon such exploring. Some areas of explorations must be encouraged and permitted—some areas must be forbidden. Each child must incorporate into his own scheme of action a code of behavior containing two columns, the "Dos" and the "Don'ts" of action. Whatever fancy professional labels may be applied to these two columns the net result is always a dual list of the *permitted* and the *forbidden*.

The two lists of "permitted" and "forbidden" are organized for the child by the action of the parent in the daily business of family living. The listing process begins early in the life of the child and continues in some form until adult independence is achieved. The items for each column are derived from several sources. The major source can be called the "societal expectancies." These are the conformity behaviors set forth by the rules and regulations of each society to govern the conduct of its members. Such things as breaking and entering, stealing, personal injury, vandalism, public modesty, etc., come under that heading. Each parent is expected by his society to teach their child to enter another person's home only upon invitation, to respect the property of others, to clothe their body appropriately for public transport, to avoid the temptation to unlawfully appropriate the property of someone else as one's own and so on.

At the level of early childhood these lessons are taught by helping the child to understand that his freedom to enter and exit his own home according to his own dictates is a family privilege which can not be extended to the homes of neighbors. The growing flowers, bushes, lawn and yard decorations of the neighbors must be marked off as forbidden territory. Essentially it is socially permissible for a child to pick flowers in his own yard, dig up the grass, pull branches off the bushes and break the decorations in his own yard. The issue is then exclusively the concern of himself and his parents. When the same action is extended to the neighbors' yards the issue becomes societal and curbing practices must be initiated.

The child may scribble with crayon and chalk on the inside or outside walls of the house or garage, or on the sidewalk or driveway of his own property, and the issue is a personal one for his parents. They may permit or forbid this according to their choice. If, however, the child's drawing surface becomes a neighbor's garage wall or driveway, it no longer matters what the parental choice might be—the societal expectancy is for the parent to devise some method to stop such behavior.

The presence or absence of clothing may be a matter of individual parental choice within the confines of the family abode—society has little real concern with standards of modesty in the private home. Such license, however, can not be extended to the neighborhood, street and yard. Appropriate body coverage is a social expectancy. Appropriateness may be defined in various ways according to changes in style but there is always a demand for sex-part coverage.

In his own home a child may take from his brother or sister possessions and treasures which are not rightfully his and the plea of the defendant and the plaintiff will be decided in the personal family court. If, however, his seizure happens to be the bicycle of a classmate, the roller skates of the neighbor boy, the catcher's glove of the child down the block, the candy from the supermarket shelf or the money from the teacher's desk, the issue becomes societal and is not simply a question of sibling argument.

The listing of the societally "permitteds" and "forbiddens" rests squarely upon the responsible shoulders of the parents according to the social scheme. Each parent is expected to help the child learn the distinctions between what may be acceptable within the family and not acceptable according to community rule. There is really no question of whether the parent agrees or disagrees with the societal dictate— the lessons must be taught.

The second major source of "permitteds" and "forbiddens" stems from the personal value systems of each set of parents. Each couple may individually decide the latitudes and longitudes of each listing according to their own beliefs. Individual members of the society may frown upon certain forms of parental permissiveness or prohibitiveness but this territory of discipline is idiosyncratic to the parent.

Each parent is free to set his own criteria of conformity within the home. The amount of rough play, noise tolerance, and boundary for play can be set by each parent. The freedom to argue, bicker and fight with parents or siblings is an individual family matter. The type and extent of table and eating manners is defined by parental tolerance. The enforcement of bedtime, bathing, clothes hanging, care of toys, orderly storage of equipment, household task responsibilities and so on are all individually determined. Respect for the property of others, prohibitions regarding invasion of privacy and sublimation of personal demands to join a common cause are established by parental directions. The lessons of politeness, temporal delay, waiting one's turn, sharing with others, following instead of leading, performing less preferred tasks, regulating time and responding appropriately and promptly to directives are all taught in the family tutorial situation.

For most children a third source of derivation of "permitteds" and "forbiddens" comes from what might be called an "ethnic-religious" background. Under that heading are listed all those behaviors which are permitted or forbidden because of a cultural heritage or a religious belief. These permissions and prohibitions are historically given and predate the parent. These are the many behaviors which are expected and permitted because one is a Catholic, Protestant or Jew, Polish, Hungarian, Greek, Italian, German, Irish and so on. This is a category of historically defined behaviors. Each parental couple may emphasize or deemphasize the contribution of this source to the building of a composite code of behavior in the child but they will somehow have to account for this factor.

Those who emphasize will use this historical background to motivate the child to certain patterns of conformity by calling attention to this heritage or to explaining the rules according to these biases. Those who deemphasize this factor will have to find ways to dismiss such thinking from consideration.

Three sources, societal expectancies, unique parental values and ethic-religious heritages probably represent the major elements from which a parent derives a code of behavior to be progressively composited in the child.

Employing those three sources each parent is faced with the task of defining which lessons are important and which are not, which are critical at which age, and which serve as foundations for other patterns to follow. Defining this scheme is rarely a carefully planned strategy developed before the live model is present. Characteristically, parents develop that schema in the laboratory of child-rearing on a day by day, step by step basis.

A far more crucial problem which confronts the parent is the matter of defining the techniques to be used in achieving the desired goals. Setting the goals seems to come readily to the parent. If the child unhesitatingly conforms to the desires of the parent, simple verbal directives become the only necessary technique. If the child is momentarily unwilling, the parent is forced to select some technique to achieve compliance.

No parent ever has a problem in defining what a child *should* do. Every parent can readily sketch out a listing of behaviors which he or she considers desirable. The real problem lies in finding a way to get an egocentrically directed child to give up his immediate desires, demands and behaviors in order to conform. Unlike the chapter devoted to the setting of restrictions the concentration is now focussed upon the specific methods utilized by the parent to achieve compliance. A parent may set a countless series of goals for the child, all of which are universally agreed to have value, but the critical issue is whether or not the parent can find a way to make the goals become achievements.

Do parents use the same disciplinary techniques with their handicapped child that they use with their other children? Do these parents regard themselves as strict or lenient? Do mothers and fathers agree on disciplinary techniques? Which techniques are reported as most effective? Does each group go about this differently?

These and several other questions regarding discipline were asked of these parents. Interview and questionnaires were utilized to complete the investigation of this area.

PERCEPTION OF DISCIPLINARY DIFFERENCE

The first question asked of these parents requested them to comment on whether they disciplined *this* child differently from their other children. Only in the organic and mongoloid groups were their

majority responses of a difference in disciplinary approach (Table
109). The deaf and the cerebral palsy groups were approximately
evenly divided among those who perceived a differential versus those
who did not. Among the parents in the blind group there was a
majority opinion of similarity in disciplinary approach between siblings and *this* child.

TABLE 109

RESPONSES OF MOTHERS TO PERCEIVED DIFFERENCES IN THEIR
DISCIPLINE OF THE HANDICAPPED CHILD AND OTHER CHILDREN

Responses	Cerebral Palsy	Organic	Mongoloid	Blind	Deaf	All Groups
Yes	52%	72%	76%	29%	45%	55%
No	44%	22%	24%	64%	55%	42%
Not ascertained	4%	6%		7%		3%
	100%	100%	100%	100%	100%	100%

It is likely that popular belief would favor the notion that the
parents would be inclined to impose a different set of disciplinary
techniques upon their relationship to the handicapped child than they
did upon their normal siblings. Only two of the groups, the organic
and the mongoloid, fell in line with this popular notion. In the blind
group the popular belief was essentially negated and the other two
groups seemed equivocal on both sides of the issue. When the entire
group was considered as a single population of parents of handicapped
children, there seemed to be an equal division among the parents.

In spite of the sensory deprivation of the blind group where it
would seem, by popular notion, that a different approach to discipline would naturally be evoked due to the condition of the child,
the mothers were quite emphatic in their expression of similarity to
sibling practices. The reason why parents in the blind group seemed
to be so emphatic in their expression of similarity is not clear from
the data and any attempt to speculate on this finding must be postponed.

Among those parents in each group who saw a necessity for a
different approach there was a uniform expression of concern for
the child's handicap. As their responses were probed in the interview
situation it became clear that those parents who felt that *this* child

required a different approach based this differential upon the fact that the child did not understand language as well, had a lowered tolerance for frustration and had a different personality from the siblings. Essentially they based their differential upon the handicap.

This emphasis was one of the few instances among the composite of responses where the actual handicap of the child might truly be considered to have significantly influenced child-rearing practices. Here, for a change, the parents did not equate the siblings and the handicapped child. The exact nature of the difference was not ascertained but it is clear that a significant percentage in each group perceived a need for a discipline differential.

Whether such a perception would be justified by the child evidence in each case the point in question here is the perception of the individual parent. If the parent saw some reason for difference, justifiable or not, the difference probably existed as the parents initiated the day-by-day effort to achieve desired conformity.

From interview probing it was apparent that the organic group based their belief of difference primarily upon the hyperactivity of the child with many parental expressions such as, "He is wilder than any of my other children" and "He doesn't grasp as well" being representative explanations. In the mongoloid group references to the child's retardation, and his concurrent difficulties in remembering, discriminating and processing language, seemed to account for the need for a different approach.

The general impression gained from this set of responses favored the belief that the area of discipline brings the nature and characteristics of the handicap into a sharper focus than any other area of behavior. Since those parents who perceived a need for difference were emphatic in attributing this need to the nature of the child's handicap there is some possibility that the parental attempt to achieve conformity behavior becomes the principle vehicle for building parental awareness of the total impact of deviation upon the development of their child. It may be that this area of parent-child interaction is most critical.

The fact that nearly half of the total group saw no need for a differential may be interpreted along a dual course. On the one hand it suggests that these parents were insensitive to a need for a differential and on the other hand it suggests that a different system may not necessarily be required. Either interpretation could be used.

Inspection of the probed inquiries on this question provided no significant resolution of this dilemma. Whatever the reasons might be, some parents see a need for a differential and others do not. While the emphasis varies each group expressed a difference of opinion on this topic.

Only a small percentage of parents considered *this* child to be less difficult to discipline than his siblings. In the mongoloid and deaf groups none of the parents regarded the handicapped child as less of a problem (Table 110).

TABLE 110

MOTHERS' RATINGS OF DIFFICULTY IN DISCIPLINING
HANDICAPPED CHILD COMPARED WITH SIBLINGS

Responses	Cerebral Palsy	Organic	Mongoloid	Blind	Deaf	All Groups
More of a problem	35%	69%	76%	50%	65%	59%
Less of a problem	6%	5%		21%		7%
The same	47%	17%	16%	21%	25%	25%
No other siblings or siblings too young	12%	9%	8%	8%	10%	9%
	100%	100%	100%	100%	100%	100%

When those cases who had no siblings are removed from consideration, the majority opinion across all groups indicated that *this* child was regarded as more of a discipline problem to the parents than were his siblings. Only in the cerebral palsy group was there a sizable incidence of parents who regarded *this* child as about the same amount of problem as the siblings. The other four groups seemed clearly convinced that *this* child was more difficult to discipline. Those mothers who reported *this* child to be less of a problem expressed a uniform opinion that the child "tried harder and actually occasioned less problems." This was particularly true in the cerebral palsy group where lack of ambulation was a factor in behavioral management.

Those who reported their child to be more of a problem than his siblings explained this difference in terms of the child being "spoiled," "stubborn," "harder to manage," "having less ability to learn" and "harder to reach." In the cerebral palsy group who regarded *this* child as more difficult to manage the terms "distractibility" and "hyperactivity" were often given as reasons. Among the organic group where such terms might be expected to be commonplace the terms were rarely used.

The question regarding discipline methods employed with the handicapped child as compared to those used with siblings was not introduced until the cerebral palsy group had completed their interviews (Table 111). Consequently only four groups can be considered in summarizing this question. Each population revealed a difference of opinion on this topic. The blind and deaf groups were about equally divided among those who said they used similar techniques and those who used different techniques. The organic and mongoloid groups favored different techniques.

TABLE 111

MOTHERS' COMPARISONS OF TECHNIQUES AND METHODS OF DISCIPLINE USED ON THIS CHILD AND THEIR OTHER CHILDREN

Responses	Cerebral Palsy*	Organic	Mongoloid	Blind	Deaf
Use same techniques on all		26%	36%	50%	50%
Use different techniques on this child		65%	56%	43%	40%
No other siblings or siblings too young		9%	8%	7%	10%
		100%	100%	100%	100%

*Question not asked

In summary of these first three questions it is clear that the mothers in the mongoloid and organic groups tended to perceive the handicapped child as more of a problem than her nonhandicapped children, and also expressed a need to employ different disciplinary methods. Even though the blind and the deaf groups tended to perceive their handicapped children as more of a problem than the siblings, this perception did not necessarily compel them to employ different techniques.

Those in the blind and deaf groups who reported the use of different techniques represented a distribution of mothers who said the child was less of a problem, more and about the same. Some had responded affirmatively on the question of sibling difference simply on the basis that visual signs and/or auditory signals could be used with the handicapped children but did not intend to convey a difference in practice. However, there were a small number of parents in the deaf and blind groups who definitely and emphatically conveyed an idea of difference.

In general it must be concluded that the parents of the deaf and blind children reported in the majority that they used the same techniques on all of their children while the organic and mongoloid emphatically reported that they used different techniques with *this* child. The differences were based upon factors related to handicap in the latter groups. The former groups were apparently not influenced by the sensory deprivation.

SELF-APPRAISAL OF STRICTNESS

A small percentage of mothers in each of the four groups (excluding cerebral palsy) rated themselves as being too strict in their disciplinary relationship to their handicapped child when they were asked to give a self-appraisal on this question. Another small percentage felt unable to make an appraisal. The majority in each group, however, split somewhat evenly between those who rated themselves as being "just right" and those who perceived themselves as "not strict enough."

Since the rating was a forced choice proposition each mother was confronted with the task of formulating her own operational definition of strictness as it applied to her disciplinary tactics. Under this vague stimulus the distribution of the four groups indicated that some similarity of definition was operating nonetheless. Essentially the find-

TABLE 112

MOTHERS' SELF APPRAISALS OF THEIR LEVEL
OF STRICTNESS IN DISCIPLINING
THEIR HANDICAPPED CHILD

Responses	Cerebral Palsy*	Organic	Mongoloid	Blind	Deaf	All Groups
Too strict		8%	8%	14%	25%	14%
Just right		35%	40%	43%	50%	42%
Not strict enough		49%	48%	43%	25%	41%
Can't discriminate		8%	4%			3%
	—	100%	100%	100%	100%	100%

*Question not asked

ings are equivocal. None of the groups actually differed from the others. Each contained three levels of ratings.

To gain some perspective on the attitude held by the fathers in relation to the strictness of the mother each mother was asked to indicate what she felt her husband's attitude was to her extent of strictness.

The mothers in the deaf group reported that their husbands were evenly divided between those who regarded the mothers as not strict enough and those who felt that the mothers were too strict. Only a small percentage of fathers in the deaf group seemed to regard the strictness level of the wife as just right. The fathers in the blind group were reported as in majority agreement with their wives' level of strictness with one third apparently believing that the wives were not strict enough. The mongoloid group also reported a sizable percentage of concordance (50 per cent) but showed a one third incidence of an attitude that they were not strict enough. Fathers in the cerebral palsy and organic groups seemed to believe that their wives were not strict enough but each of these two groups contained fathers who regarded their wives as too strict or just right.

Taking the entire group as a composite fathers distributed their attitudes at three levels. The usual clinical belief is that fathers tend to regard their wives as not strict enough. The finding that 18 per cent of the fathers regarded their wives as too strict came as a surprise. The findings from this question indicate a considerable amount of disagreement between mothers and fathers on the question of the extent of maternal strictness (Table 113).

TABLE 113
MOTHERS' ESTIMATES OF FATHERS' ATTITUDE
TOWARD LEVEL OF STRICTNESS EMPLOYED
BY MOTHER IN DEALING WITH THIS CHILD

Response	Cerebral Palsy	Organic	Mongoloid	Blind	Deaf	All Groups	All Groups Except Cerebral Palsy
Too strict	20%	14%	13%		42%	18%	17%
Just right	20%	27%	50%	61%	11%	34%	37%
Not strict enough	46%	47%	33%	31%	42%	40%	38%
Other—erratic, inconsistent		2%					1%
Can't discriminate	14%	10%	4%	8%	5%	8%	7%
	100%	100%	100%	100%	100%	100%	100%

When the perceptions of their husbands' evaluation of their levels of strictness are compared with the rating the mother gave herself some interesting comparisons are possible. In the organic group only the mothers who rated themselves as not strict enough reflected that their husbands held the same attitude about them. A few husbands in that group rated their wives as too strict in contradiction to their wife's rating of herself. In the mongoloid and blind groups the fathers were kinder in their ratings than the mothers had been to themselves. In the deaf group, however, the fathers seemed to have quite a different rating of their wives' strictness than the wife had accorded herself. The mothers in the deaf group rated themselves as essentially just right but few of their husbands agreed.

The mothers in the organic and mongoloid groups who reported that their husbands regarded them as too strict felt that their judgment was based upon a belief that the mother was expecting too much of the child. The father perceived the child as less capable and the mother regarded the child as more capable.

Whether either of the parental perceptions of capability was realistic is not the question here. The father's perception of less capability in the child caused him to regard the mother as being overly strict. Another explanation offered by the mothers was their opinion that the father lacked an understanding of the child's problem and consequently did not recognize a need to be strict. Here the mothers were implying that the child's problem necessitated strictness and they were only reacting to this necessity. One other explanation was offered. Several mothers in the organic and deaf groups indicated that their husbands disliked the entire concept of discipline and in their rejection regarded any effort as too strict.

The net impression gained from these explanations is that the mothers who were criticized by fathers as being too strict blamed the fathers' mistaken evaluation on the basis of his imperception of the child. He did not understand. He underestimated the child. They were also reporting, amidst these explanations, the belief that the husbands were judging them unfairly (Table 114).

Those mothers who were criticized as not strict enough presented two principal explanations: (1) The father had a higher level of expectancy and is more strict himself, and (2) the father was critical

TABLE 114

EXPLANATIONS GIVEN BY MOTHERS FOR HUSBANDS'
CRITICAL OPINION OF STRICTNESS LEVEL
EMPLOYED BY MOTHERS

Responses	Cerebral Palsy*	Organic	Mongoloid	Blind	Deaf
			Mother Too Strict		
Husband doesn't understand child or relationship: the need to be strict			33%		49%
Husband believes wife expects too much		78%	67%		25%
Husband's dislike of discipline		11%			13%
Other		11%			13%
Total responding		100%	100%		100%
			Mother Not Strict Enough		
Husband expects more; is more strict; judges differently		37%	63%	25%	63%
Husband feels wife is inconsistent, doesn't follow through		40%	12%	50%	25%
Husband feels wife favors this child because of handicap		20%	25%	25%	
Other		3%			12%
Total responding		100%	100%	100%	100%

*Question not asked.

of the mother's lack of consistency. The strictness of the father was cited as a factor in criticism by the mongoloid and deaf groups and the inconsistency criticism was cited by the organic and blind groups. None of the wives who were criticized as not severe enough commented on their husband's lack of understanding of the child and his problem. That possibility was cited only by those mothers who had been criticized as too strict. In the mongoloid, organic and blind groups one fourth of each group indicated that their husbands believed that the mothers favored this child because of the handicap and therefore was too lenient.

On this question of strictness a speculation might be offered to account for the mother's deprivation of her own rating. Faced with the daily expressed judgment of the father in criticism at either extreme this opinion became her rating of herself when confronted with a questionnaire. Some mothers were undoubtedly influenced by such a factor, but it must be remembered that a sizable percentage of disagreement between paternal judgment and the mother's ratings were noted across the board. It would seem therefore that the majority of the mothers had given a true self-appraisal and were not necessarily influenced by their husband's opinion.

To attain some balance on this question of strictness the mothers were asked to rate the level of strictness employed by the fathers (Table 115). Only a small percentage regarded their husbands as being too strict. The majority opinion of the mothers accorded a rating of "just right" to the fathers across the five groups. Some mothers felt that the fathers were not strict enough. This was most notable in the blind group where approximately one third gave that rating to their husbands.

TABLE 115

MOTHERS' RATINGS OF LEVEL OF STRICTNESS
EMPLOYED BY FATHERS

Response	Cerebral Palsy	Organic	Mongoloid	Blind	Deaf	All Groups
Too strict	13%	16%	13%		5%	10%
Just right	68%	41%	58%	61%	58%	57%
Not strict enough	19%	24%	16%	31%	21%	22%
Other—erratic; inconsistent		17%	13%	8%	11%	10%
Can't discriminate		2%			5%	1%
	100%	100%	100%	100%	100%	100%

On this general topic of strictness the mothers were less critical of their partners than were the fathers. Many mothers expressed comments such as, "He's not around enough to really know what it's like all day," "He expects me to be stricter but when he's around he's not very strict himself." If either partner is inclined to be critical of the other the direction of criticism is toward "not strict enough." In general it seems that there is more of a state of agreement in attitude on this topic than there is a state of disagreement. In some cases the agreement is upon an equalized amount of criticism directed at each other.

Two findings seem to stand out among these data. The mothers and fathers in the deaf group seemed to be in the highest state of disagreement in rating each other's level of strictness and the mothers and fathers in the blind group do not see either party as too strict.

Other than these two findings the distribution across groups is quite similar.

PARENTAL AGREEMENT

Each parent relates to the child in a context of discipline and is a permission granter, a prohibitor, a critic, an admonisher, a directive-giver, a chastizer, a cautioner and a stopper. Each is forgiving and each is loving. The context of any family living situation is a variable one and probably every child ever born has had to find out in one way or another whether both of his parents think the same way on a given issue which is important to him. The time honored notion that each child must test the limits of a situation, must try to manipulate his parents, must seek to play one against the other, is just as applicable to handicapped children as it is to nonhandicapped. Whether or not parents stand united on behavioral issues is a query which each young child throughout the ages has found it necessary to resolve in the daily milieu of the family.

Each parent couple exists in a state of agreement or disagreement as to the best way to handle disciplinary situations as they arise. They may be in accord on major issues and have many differences of opinion on minor issues. A father may contradict a maternal directive and vice versa. The child may become aware of the fact that his parents disagree on certain issues and develop a system of asking the favorable parent when some permission is desired. Issues between parents may flare up in open conflict in the presence of the child, or be camouflaged by silent hostilities which are saved until later. It is a common parental situation.

Mothers were asked to comment on the extent of agreement between themselves and their husbands as to the best way to handle *this* child. Four categories were established to group the responses: "Complete agreement" was assigned when the mother indicated that there was a state of complete harmony between both parties on every issue; "moderate agreement" was rated when there was some evidence of disagreement on minor issues at various times but this was sporadic and of little real significance in the total process. When the state of affairs seemed to be one of more disagreement than agreement, but the issues were minor, the general feeling tone was assigned to a negative category of "moderate disagreement." When the parents seemed to be locked in a continual state of debate, the rating of "marked disagreement" was assigned to the parental response (Table 116).

TABLE 116

MOTHERS' VALUATIONS OF MOTHER-FATHER
AGREEMENT ON BEST WAY TO HANDLE CHILD

Response	Cerebral Palsy	Organic	Mongoloid	Blind	Deaf	All Groups
Complete agreement	6%	25%	21%	15%	16%	17%
Moderate agreement	64%	24%	50%	31%	37%	41%
Moderate disagreement	26%	33%	17%	54%	37%	33%
Marked disagreement	4%	16%	12%		10%	9%
Could not discriminate		2%				
	100%	100%	100%	100%	100%	100%

The mothers' evaluations varied across the five groups. The highest incidence of agreement was reported in the cerebral palsy and mongoloid groups where 70 per cent and 71 per cent of the couples were reported on the positive side of the ledger of this count. The other three groups reflected an approximate split of 50/50 on the positive and negative sides. Only one or two families in each group could be classified as being in marked disagreement (the blind group showed no incidence here). Complete harmony was not the rule, nor was complete disharmony prevalent. Most of the families seemed to reflect a picture of some disagreement between the mother and the father on questions of child management. Such a finding is perhaps typical of the entire nation of child-rearers.

When a disciplinary situation arises and both parents are present, one of the parents must assume the role of initiator of action. This may well be a question of which parent is nearest to the child, or which one has noticed the breach first, but if action is to be taken *one* must take the initiative. In many homes the mother may call the breach to the attention of the father, expecting the action to come from him, and in other homes the father will note the behavior for the mother to take action. A question of this nature was posed to the mothers in this study to ascertain how these families would respond in such a situation.

The general distribution of results across the five groups showed that the mothers generally assumed the role of initiator. In all groups except the blind there was an incidence of about one-third response that either party would take the initiative and that no prevalence could be noted (Table 117).

TABLE 117

MOTHERS' STIPULATION OF FATHER-MOTHER
ASSUMPTION OF DISCIPLINARY ROLE WITH
THIS CHILD WHEN BOTH PARENTS ARE PRESENT

Responses	Cerebral Palsy	Organic	Mongoloid	Blind	Deaf	All Groups
Mother disciplines	48%	38%	46%	54%	47%	47%
Father disciplines	23%	30%	17%	31%	16%	23%
Either	29%	32%	37%	15%	37%	30%
	100%	100%	100%	100%	100%	100%

While there was some incidence of father initiative in each group only the organic and blind groups showed a significant representation of fathers taking the initial step. Even though the mothers reported a sizable percentage of cases wherein both parties might take the first step to act, the role of the mother as the activator of discipline seems to be clearly the majority case. This was usually explained by the mother as being due to the fact that she spent more time with the child and therefore had more opportunity to work out techniques. The distribution is essentially balanced across the five groups. The type of disability seems to have little to do with this question. This is more a matter of the relationship between the husband and wife.

The fact that the mother appeared to be the primary actor in initiating discipline was not necessarily a matter of practice during the father's absence at work. Some mothers commented that they continued to be the initiators even during "after-work" hours because they felt protective toward the child and wished to prevent the harsh treatment from the husband. They felt that their maternal approach was easier and gentler and created less turmoil.

In each group the majority of mothers approved of the disciplinary techniques that were employed by their husbands in relation to this child (Table 118). Each group, however, also contained a sizable percentage of mothers who disapproved of their husbands' practices, led by the organic group where four out of ten voiced some objection. Least disapproval was shown in the blind group.

TABLE 118
MOTHERS' APPROVAL-DISAPPROVAL OF DISCIPLINARY
TECHNIQUES USED BY FATHERS

Responses	Cerebral Palsy	Organic	Mongoloid	Blind	Deaf	All Groups
Approve: Husband does nothing objectionable	72%	59%	71%	85%	68%	71%
Disapprove: Certain of husband's practices are objectionable	28%	41%	29%	15%	32%	29%
	100%	100%	100%	100%	100%	100%

The incidence of disapproval suggested some merit to probing these objections during the course of the interview in order to seek clarification. As the mothers discussed their objections in greater detail it became clear that they did not object to the husband's technique as a technique but were rather concerned with the manner in which he enacted the technique. For example, they agreed that the child needed to be scolded at a given moment, but they objected to the violent language the father employed in conducting the scolding. They did not object to scolding but felt that the husband should not select the mealtime as a scolding situation for the entire day.

Mothers were not concerned that their husband might spank the child, but objected if they regarded the husband as being violent in his spanking. They also objected to striking the child on the head or in the face. These objections were focussed upon the punitive actions of the fathers but some mothers objected to the fact that these husbands threatened the child with all sorts of punishment, and then did not follow through on his threats when the child transgressed. Other husbands were scored as negative on the basis of inconsistency.

Only in rare instances did the mother feel that the punitive action or threat was unwarranted. The objection came from questions of degree of force, time of punishment, etc.

In accounting for this set of objections mothers attributed the violence to the fact that their husbands were short-tempered and explosive as a general characteristic and not only in relation to child discipline. Others attributed the exaggeration to the fact that "he is tired after working all day." When the mother objected to the husband's practice of inconsistency or indulgence she related this to his "special feelings toward *this* child because he is handicapped."

Among those mothers who objected to their husbands' disciplinary behavior only half of this group admitted they had expressed their objections openly to the husband in discussions and in arguments. Their voiced objections had apparently brought about no significant change but there was a note of perseverance in the comments of the mothers and a continuation of such arguments is probably in progress (Table 119).

The other half of the objecting group expressed a general feeling of resignation. They had made suggestions with varying degrees of success but saw no possibility of real change in their husbands. They

TABLE 119

MOTHERS' RESPONSES TO FATHERS' DISCIPLINE
SEEN AS UNACCEPTABLE AS REPORTED
BY THE OBJECTING MOTHER

Responses	Cerebral Palsy	Organic	Mongoloid	Blind	Deaf	All Groups
Mother later discusses or argues with husband about the discipline	65%	80%	86%	50%	50%	66%
Goes along with husband; does nothing	14%	8%		50%	33%	20%
Mother tries to avert occurrence of situation	21%	8%	14%			10%
Mother "makes it up" to the child later		4%			17%	4%
	100%	100%	100%	100%	100%	100%

essentially resigned themselves to the situation. Rather than trying to bring about change in the husband their efforts were directed toward decreasing the number of possibilities for the husband to be involved. Hence these resigned mothers were more likely to move into action first when discipline seemed to be called for.

The objecting group was in the minority. Most of the mothers were in accord with their husbands' tactics. It was also clear from the maternal comments that only in a few instances were their objections to the husband's tactics localized upon his relationship to the handicapped child. Most objecting mothers generalized their criticism to the father's relationship to all children in the family. When the mother felt that the objectionable behavior was unique to the handicapped child, she said so in the interview.

Those mothers who objected to the husband's handling of the handicapped child and attributed his behavior to some special feeling toward the child objected to his leniency—never to degree of punitiveness. If any of the mothers believed that a father's violent attitude stemmed from some deeper feelings of rejection, denial or disgust they did not voice such opinions in the interview.

MATERNAL PERCEPTION OF CONTROL

Each parent must experience some level of confidence in considering whether they have the situation of discipline *under control* or whether they are floundering in a sea of uncertainty. They must perceive themselves to be in charge, perceive the child to be in charge or perceive a teeter-totter arrangement of uncertainty.

The mothers in the cerebral palsy, deaf and blind groups asserted a majority opinion of confidence that they felt that they had the situation well in hand when the child misbehaved. The mongoloid and organic groups did not express the same level of confidence (Table 120). Slightly more than half of these two groups expressed high confidence while the other half of the groups either admitted to a low confidence level or said that their controls were variable.

Only in the deaf group were the mothers either confident or not confident. All other groups reported some incidence of fluctuation in control calling it a "sometimes thing." As a generalization across the groups one in five mothers admitted that they did not have control

TABLE 120

MOTHERS' RATINGS OF THEIR BEING IN CONTROL
OF MISBEHAVIOR SITUATIONS INVOLVING
THE HANDICAPPED CHILD

Responses	Cerebral Palsy	Organic	Mongoloid	Blind	Deaf	All Groups
Yes	82%	57%	56%	72%	80%	69%
No	12%	25%	32%	21%	20%	22%
Sometimes	6%	18%	12%	7%		9%
	100%	100%	100%	100%	100%	100%

of the situation. As a total population finding the majority of the mothers gave themselves a vote of confidence in this area. The mothers viewed themselves as competent and capable.

In an attempt to shed light upon this issue among those mothers who admitted to a low level of confidence a special effort was made to secure more information. Unfortunately this special effort was not included in the interview process until after the cerebral palsy group had completed its sequences. Therefore the data shown in Table 121 do not properly reflect the cerebral palsy group. However, since a number of parents from that group had voluntarily amplified their responses without structured probing and had therefore met the intent of the probe, it was decided to incorporate their data in the table to add to the general picture. It must be remembered that the data in Table 121 serve to clarify the accounting for feelings of inadequacy in only one in five mothers in the total sample. The table therefore represents only thirty-nine cases but the distribution of responses conveys some valuable information.

The mothers in the blind group accounted for their feelings of inadequacy on two bases: (1) The ineffectiveness of the techniques they did employ, and (2) a feeling of helplessness in not knowing what to do in response to the child's misbehavior. Ineffectiveness was scored because their techniques did not serve to reduce the misbehavior. In spite of the mothers' effort the misbehavior was repeated. Helplessness stemmed from the mother's reaction to the handicap.

Those mothers who felt helpless in discipline felt helpless in the knowledge of blindness and could not think of a way to rid the child of his behaviors. Since only three cases were represented it was possible to obtain details regarding the feelings of inadequacy. In

TABLE 121

KINDS OF REASONS FOR PERCEPTIONS OF INADEQUACY
GIVEN BY MOTHERS REPORTING THEMSELVES NOT IN
CONTROL OF DISCIPLINARY SITUATIONS

Responses	Cerebral Palsy*	Organic	Mongoloid	Blind	Deaf	Except Cerebral Palsy†
Discipline is not effective; mischief repeated	11%	18%	27%	50%	75%	42%
Mother at loss as to what to do		25%	9%	50%		21%
Mother loses control of herself	22%	11%	27%			10%
Mother doubts if child understands		21%	37%			14%
Child gets extremely upset	22%	11%			25%	9%
Not ascertained (Mother couldn't say or inadequate information)	45%	14%				4%
	100%	100%	100%	100%	100%	100%

*This question not asked of cerebral palsy population.
†Tabulations included were obtained from voluntary amplified responses cerebral palsy group made in answering whether they felt they had the situation under control when their child was naughty.

one case the mother seemed clearly overwhelmed by the blindness of her child. In the other two cases the children exhibited a variety of behaviors generally classified as "blindisms" and the parent did not know how to rid the child of these. In relation to these blindisms these mothers can be joined by many professional workers in the field of the blind who are often equally helpless in devising effective techniques to accomplish diminution.

In the deaf group the low confidence mothers were mainly concerned that the techniques they did use failed to achieve desired results. If the parent applies a method and the results do not change behavior then another method, and another, must be tried. If the success ratio is low the confidence level of the mother declines. Those who regarded themselves as ineffective expressed the belief that, "I keep trying—but nothing really seems to work—because he does it again, anyway." A small percentage in this group felt helpless in the disciplinary situation because they described the child as having a violent upsetting reaction to discipline. In the face of such extreme upset from corrective measures the mothers were reluctant to try any method for fear of producing the violent reaction. This behavioral response caused them to be very cautious and essentially to appear helpless.

A few mothers in the cerebral palsy, organic and mongoloid groups regarded discipline as a very difficult area for them because of their own loss of emotional control in the face of misbehavior. They spoke of "going to pieces" if they had to punish their child or of "becoming excessively punitive" which they later regretted. They referred to themselves as too emotional and claimed they could not be rational at those times. In the mongoloid and organic groups a few mothers attributed their feelings of inadequacy to the belief that the child had difficulty in understanding and that they as mothers had not been able to find a way to reach the child.

The major reason for a mother's feeling of incompetence was the repetitive ineffectiveness of her efforts. Whatever methods she employed the child did not desist from his misbehavior. To a certain extent it is likely that every parent in the nation experiences some degree of failure in this respect. These mothers, however, regarded this as personal failure due to some personality inadequacy. It is probably true that all the mothers who felt that they were in control had many moments of ineffectiveness also but viewed their failures as "part of the game."

Two types of response to this question can be considered to have bearing upon the nature of the handicap. When the mothers moved cautiously and dubiously because of fear of upsetting the child and occasioning a violent reaction, this response on the part of the child was felt to be unique to the handicapped child. When the mother referred to herself as being at a loss this was also felt to be related to the child's handicap.

Feelings of inadequacy among these thirty-nine mothers stemmed from two sources. For some, a general personality dynamic, perhaps best designated as a "negative self-concept," was the prime reason for ineffectiveness or helplessness. For others the unique behavior of the handicapped child, characteristic to the form of his handicap, accounted for the feeling of inadequacy. Professional clinicians and therapists who have attempted to control some of these cases in the testing or therapy situation can well empathize with the feelings of these mothers.

Since the vast majority of mothers regarded themselves as competent and confident, the significance of the findings on this small percentage must be treated with caution. It must be remembered that each mother was rating *herself*. Actual success, as might be defined by some professionally oriented criteria, was not possible to evaluate. If a mother regarded herself as being in control her perception was accepted.

DISCIPLINARY TECHNIQUES

The tools of discipline available to the parent are many. It is possible to conceive of an historical listing of all disciplinary techniques ever used by parents as a composite imaginary library from which each parent may draw out a technique for temporary use to determine effectiveness. If it proves effective the "loan" may be renewed indefinitely. If it does not, it may be returned and another drawn out for inspection. All of these techniques may be thought of as available on the disciplinary shelf; each measured with some degree of historical effectiveness. Some volumes are regrettably missing from the shelves.

There are no volumes specifically titled *Disciplinary Techniques for Handicapped Children*. The historical practices refer to the non-handicapped. Therefore the parent of the handicapped child is forced to sample the usual techniques, remodel as necessary, discard the inappropriate and somehow, during the course of time, formulate a battery of tried and .rue techniques which prove effective in *their particular situation*.

Having no specific prior reference point of experience as the parent of a handicapped child each parent is essentially a disciplinary prospector, testing out techniques before investing full effort into their use. This study has clearly discovered that the principal reference system for the parents of handicapped children is the backlog of disciplinary experience gained from their nonhandicapped children. They draw upon that system in evolving an approach to the child with a handicap. How specialized and effective they become will be considered in the discussion to follow.

As Sears (1957) has pointed out, disciplinary techniques can be divided into two distinct types, *positive* and *negative* sanctions. Positive sanctions take the form of rewards for good behavior in the general belief that a verbal or tangible reward will not only cause the desired behavior to occur but also cause the behavior to be repeated. Rewarded for his behavior the child will repeat the behavior again and again. This is essentially a positive approach of encouraging expected or desired behaviors as producing a climate of "nice circumstances." This course is available to parents in achieving desired change.

Negative sanctions impose some form of penalty for undesirable behaviors. Here the belief is that the child will seek to avoid repetitions of the penalties by learning the behavioral lesson. He will behave as desired in order to escape the penalty. This course is also available. All parents probably employ both types of sanctions in varying amounts but it is likely that negative sanctions are the more popular choices for most parents.

While there are many ways of providing positive sanctions only two types were investigated in this study. The extent of usage of tangible rewards seemed to offer an approach which would be easiest to clarify. Two questions were incorporated into the individual interview requiring the parents to comment on the use of money as a tangible reward and the use of symbols such as stars, pictures, check marks, etc.

Sears (1957) has previously reported that 86 per cent of the kindergarten mothers in his study used some form of a monetary reward system with their children as one means of obtaining desired behavior. The mothers of the handicapped children reported little use of this technique (Table 122). This was used to some extent in the blind and deaf groups, where 50 per cent and 40 per cent indicated that they used monetary rewards for effort, but was totally denied by the mongoloid group. One fourth of the cerebral palsy and organic groups expressed some use of this concept, but the general impression was gained that this technique was not favored by the majority.

This group finding is in sharp contrast to the reports of the mothers

TABLE 122

MOTHERS' REPORTS OF USE OF MONETARY
REWARDS TO OBTAIN GOOD BEHAVIOR

Responses	Cerebral Palsy	Organic	Mongoloid	Blind	Deaf	All Groups
Yes	25%	28%		50%	40%	29%
No	75%	72%	100%	50%	60%	71%
	100%	100%	100%	100%	100%	100%

of nonhandicapped kindergartners. The discrepancy in these findings cannot be accounted for on the basis of either set of data. The discrepancy is interesting but defies a meaningful interpretation. To some extent the absence of this technique in the mongoloid group may be related to the maternal belief that the child's mental retardation would preclude any appreciation of the meaning of money, and therefore have little value in securing positive change.

Those who used monetary rewards did so in exchange for household labor or errands. None of the mothers admitted to paying the child for each act of good behavior although several mentioned that they occasionally gave the child money for the general behavior of "being a good boy."

None of the parents who provided ways for their child to earn money described any action of withholding the wages if the action was not satisfactorily completed, nor of evolving a forfeiture of earned monies when behavior was undesirable. In this respect the mountains of data being compiled in the area of reinforcement theory should be of great value to parents of the future.

Another tangible reward system which may be employed by mothers is the awarding of points, stars on a chart, rulers to measure heights, etc., as a way of assessing the achievement of desired behaviors. This usually takes the form of a chart on the kitchen or bedroom bulletin board and may be used to reward brushing of teeth, taking of baths, drinking of milk, eating a full meal or any number of other behaviors.

When the mothers were asked to declare the extent of usage of such systems there was a surprisingly overwhelming denial of any use of the system. Only among the deaf group was any incidence noted (Table 123).

In the other groups a total of three mothers reported their use of this technique and two of these admitted they had discontinued

TABLE 123

MOTHERS' REPORTS OF USE OF SYMBOLIC
REWARDS TO OBTAIN GOOD BEHAVIOR

Responses	Cerebral Palsy	Organic	Mongoloid	Blind	Deaf	All Groups
Yes	8%	8%			30%	9%
No	92%	92%	100%	100%	70%	91%
	100%	100%	100%	100%	100%	100%

their effort because it had no effectiveness. The mothers in the deaf group who used this technique regarded it as effective. No interpretation can be offered for the difference of the deaf group from the others.

It is concluded, therefore, that the 177 families represented in this study tended to reject the use of tangible rewards as a system for motivating desired behavior. While some of this rejection may have been due to concerns with inability to appreciate the values of money, inability to understand the meanings of stars and so on, such reasoning was felt to apply in only a few cases. The general impression was gained from the parental comments that these parents simply did not regard such tangible rewards as having value for *this* child or for his siblings.

The possibility exists that these parents used many forms of positive sanctioning which were not included in the two questions in the interview. Since no further questioning was considered in this area, this report must be considered as only a partial coverage of positive sanctioning.

Attention turned next to negative sanctions which seem to be a more popular approach to disciplinary methodology. To cover this area ten questions or statements of negative sanctions were arbitrarily selected as "probably most popular" and offered to the parents for their checking. Parents were asked to evaluate each statement in terms of whether that particular method was "never" used by them, "rarely" used, "occasionally" used or "frequently" used. They were also asked to indicate whether they regarded the technique as effective or ineffective.

Table 124A indicates the distribution among the five groups on the use and effectiveness of slapping the child when misbehaviors occurred.

A negligible percentage of the total population used the technique of a sharp quick slap to achieve desired behavior with any degree of frequency. About one third of each of the four groups (except cerebral palsy) indicated that slapping was used by them occasionally. The mongoloid group indicated that more than half of their group used slapping to control behavior. Nearly half of the blind group said they never slapped their child. Each of the other three groups reported some percentage who *never* used that technique. The majority of parents in the organic, blind and deaf groups, and about 50 per cent of the mongoloid group reported that they used the technique of a sharp, quick slap rarely, occasionally or frequently. The largest percentage was accounted for in "occasional" frequency and the smallest percentage in the "frequently" category. Most of the parents regarded it as an effective technique for accomplishing desired results.

Only one or two parents in each of the five groups indicated that they never had *spanked* their child (Table 124B). The large majority in each group admitted the spanking had been a technique in their disciplinary repertoire. Some parents spoke of this behavior in the past tense and stated that they had used it when the child was younger but no longer felt compelled to resort to this technique. Only a small total percentage across the groups indicated that they resorted to spanking with any degree of frequency.

The majority used spanking occasionally or rarely and explained that there were certain behaviors which sporadically occurred which, in their opinion, required the drastic measure of a spanking if the behavioral lesson were to be learned. The parents in the deaf group seemed most convinced that spanking was an effective technique but they were not alone. The majority of parents in each group who spanked their children occasionally also regarded it as an effective technique.

If the parent spanks the child occasionally in reaction to misbehavior it is then possible to utilize the threat of a spanking as a negative sanctioning behavior. The child remembering the experience of spanking presumably changes his behavior for the better in the face of his threatening parent (Table 124C).

The first interesting finding is reflected in the comparison of Table

125 and Table 126 which shows that some parents who indicated they had never spanked their child did nonetheless use the threat of a possible spanking to obtain cessation of undesirable behavior. Threatening the child with spanking was used by 90 per cent of the deaf group, 88 per cent in the mongoloid, 83 per cent in the blind, and 81 per cent in the organic group. In the cerebral palsy group 62 per cent indicated that they threatened the child, leaving 32 per cent who said they never threatened the child. Since only 9 per cent of this group had refrained from ever spanking the child, one fourth of these parents conveyed the belief that, if they believed a spanking was called for, they spanked, and did not waste time with threats. The other four groups, however, contained some parents who threatened but apparently never got around to carrying out their threats.

Again the deaf group seemed more convinced than the others that threatening a spanking was an effective technique. This conviction is compatible with the finding that 90 per cent of that group regarded spanking as an effective tool. All groups considered threatening the child with spanking to be a less effective technique than actually spanking the child. The organic and mongoloid groups had a divided group opinion on the effectiveness of threat. The cerebral palsy and deaf groups were convinced that threat served their purposes, and the mongoloid group regarded it as an ineffective approach. Parental opinion on the effectiveness of threat in obtaining desired behavior was scattered and certainly less convincing than their attitudes towards the effectiveness of the actual spanking.

Popular observation of maternal disciplinary action and some historical notions of child-rearing suggests that many mothers threaten the child with the promise that negative behaviors will be reported to the father when he returns to the home after working hours. This threat is intended to imply consequences far more severe than the mother might be able to conjure up at the moment of transgression.

The majority opinion of the four groups of mothers who were asked this question (Table 124D) indicated that this practice was rarely or never used by these mothers.

Some parents indicated that on rare occasions they had threatened to inform the father but hastened to add that this had occurred once

TABLE 124
MOTHERS' EVALUATIONS OF SPECIFIC DISCIPLINE TECHNIQUES AS TO FREQUENCY OF USE AND EFFECTIVENESS

FREQUENCY

A. Technique: Slapping Child

	Cerebral Palsy*				Organic				Mongoloid				Blind				Deaf			
	N	R	O	F	N	R	O	F	N	R	O	F	N	R	O	F	N	R	O	F
Not applicable					23%				16%				46%				30%			
Ineffective						11%	10%	2%		4%	20%				8%			5%	15%	
Effective						26%	26%	2%		16%	36%	8%		8%	30%	8%		5%	35%	10%

*Frequency not asked

B. Technique: Spanking Child

	Cerebral Palsy				Organic				Mongoloid				Blind				Deaf			
	N	R	O	F	N	R	O	F	N	R	O	F	N	R	O	F	N	R	O	F
Not applicable	9%				12%				8%				8%				5%			
Ineffective		9%	21%	6%		9%	11%	3%		4%	16%	4%		8%	8%				5%	
Effective		15%	27%	13%		23%	34%	8%			44%	24%			51%	25%		10%	70%	10%

C. Technique: Threatening Child

	Cerebral Palsy				Organic				Mongoloid				Blind				Deaf			
	N	R	O	F	N	R	O	F	N	R	O	F	N	R	O	F	N	R	O	F
Not applicable	38%				19%				12%				17%				10%			
Ineffective			6%	2%		3%	29%	7%			20%	36%		17%	25%	8%		5%	20%	25%
Effective		2%	15%	37%		8%	24%	10%		12%	12%	8%			8%	25%		10%	30%	25%

D. Technique: Threatening to tell Father

	Cerebral Palsy				Organic				Mongoloid				Blind				Deaf			
	N	R	O	F	N	R	O	F	N	R	O	F	N	R	O	F	N	R	O	F
Not applicable	75%				53%				72%				69%				60%			
Ineffective		2%	8%	2%		16%	7%	5%		12%	13%	12%			8%	8%		15%	5%	10%
Effective		4%	8%	9%		8%	11%			4%	8%				8%	15%		5%	5%	

E. Technique: Sit on Chair - Corner

	Cerebral Palsy				Organic				Mongoloid				Blind				Deaf			
	N	R	O	F	N	R	O	F	N	R	O	F	N	R	O	F	N	R	O	F
Not applicable	75%				58%				67%				84%				68%			
Effective		2%	8%			2%	5%	3%		4%	13%	4%			8%			11%	5%	11%
Ineffective		4%	8%	21%		8%	24%			4%	8%	4%			8%			5%		

F: Sending Child to Room

	Cerebral Palsy				Organic				Mongoloid				Blind				Deaf			
	N	R	O	F	N	R	O	F	N	R	O	F	N	R	O	F	N	R	O	F
Not applicable	56%				25%				50%				42%				40%			
Ineffective		4%	8%	21%		12%	8%	2%		13%	16%	13%			8%	17%				15%
Effective		11%	8%			16%	25%	12%		8%	16%				8%	25%		10%	20%	15%

G. Technique: Put Child to Bed

	Cerebral Palsy				Organic				Mongoloid				Blind				Deaf			
	N	R	O	F	N	R	O	F	N	R	O	F	N	R	O	F	N	R	O	F
Not applicable	75%				67%				84%				84%				75%			
Ineffective		4%	2%	4%		13%	3%	3%		4%	8%	8%			8%			5%	5%	10%
Effective		11%	2%	4%		7%	7%			4%	4%				8%			5%	5%	

KEY

N—Never
R—Rarely
O—Occasionally
F—Frequently

*Frequency not asked

TABLE 124 (Continued)

MOTHER'S EVALUATIONS OF SPECIFIC DISCIPLINE TECHNIQUES AS TO FREQUENCY OF USE AND EFFECTIVENESS

H. Technique: Withholding Affection

	Cerebral Palsy				Organic				Mongoloid				Blind				Deaf			
	N	R	O	F	N	R	O	F	N	R	O	F	N	R	O	F	N	R	O	F
Not applicable	75%				80%				68%				54%				74%			
Ineffective		11%	2%	4%		3%	10%	2%				4%		15%	23%	4%			5%	5%
Effective		8%		4%		3%	2%	2%		12%	12%	4%				8%		11%	5%	5%

I. Technique: Depriving Child

	Cerebral Palsy				Organic				Mongoloid				Blind				Deaf			
	N	R	O	F	N	R	O	F	N	R	O	F	N	R	O	F	N	R	O	F
Not applicable	48%				38%				64%				36%				40%			
Ineffective		10%	4%	4%		8%	18%	2%		8%	8%			7%	7%	7%		25%	5%	
Effective		11%	6%	17%		10%	18%	6%			8%	20%		14%	29%	7%			5%	30%

J. Technique: Explain Wrong in Behavior

	Cerebral Palsy				Organic				Mongoloid				Blind				Deaf			
	N	R	O	F	N	R	O	F	N	R	O	F	N	R	O	F	N	R	O	F
Not applicable	11%				3%				8%				7%				10%			
Ineffective		8%	14%			2%	6%	21%		8%	13%	17%		7%	7%			15%	5%	
Effective		6%	14%	47%			21%	47%		4%	13%	37%			14%	65%			15%	55%

*Frequency not asked.

KEY

N—Never
R—Rarely
O—Occasionally
F—Frequently

or twice a year. Only a negligible percentage in each group regarded this practice as being an effective one. Those who used it frequently regarded it an ineffective technique. The technique of threatening to report transgressions to the father was uniformly rejected by the vast majority in each group as a relatively useless procedure to obtain desired results.

In clinical practice a number of parents through the years had reported the use of a punishment corner or a punishment chair as an effective technique. To determine the range and efficiency of such a practice the question was included in this survey. Few parents in any of the five groups used this technique (Table 124E).

Only in the organic group did the parents report any extent of effectiveness in gaining desired behavior by sending the child to sit in the corner on a punishment chair to contemplate the error of his ways. Among those parents who used the technique only a few found it to have value. Each group, however, had some incidence of parents who had tried such a technique. Most parents had never given it consideration as a possible technique.

Another method of negative sanction may be designated as the "banishment technique." This technique takes the form of sending the child to his room for a period of solitary confinement assuming that such action will cause the child to contemplate his misdeed and mend his ways. This brings about a cessation of whatever he was doing, and deprives him of companionship and the excitement and interest of the family situation. In this same category the practice of sending or putting the child to bed as a punishment technique must also be regarded as a banishment.

The distributions of results on these two topics are contained in Tables 124F and 124G. Because of the similarity in the general concept both techniques will be discussed simultaneously.

The parents in the cerebral palsy group were evenly divided on the question of using the technique of banishing the child to his room, and those who did so regarded it to be an effective technique. Only one fourth of that group used the procedure of sending the child to bed as a punishment, and those who did were divided on the question of whether this was an effective method.

The majority in the organic group employed the banishment technique of sending the child to his room and regarded it to be an effective measure. The same group, however, made little use of the technique of putting the child in bed to punish him and those who did use it were divided on the question of efficiency.

The mongoloid group was also evenly divided in their use of sending the child to his room. Most of the parents in this group who did so considered it to be a valuable tool. The mothers in this group reported little incidence of sending the child to bed as a punitive measure and the few who did resort to such tactics felt it did not accomplish the desired goal.

Sending the child to his room was a technique of most of the parents in the blind and deaf groups. While the blind group was divided on the question of value of the practice, the deaf group seemed convinced of its effectiveness. Both of these groups reported a small incidence of punishment by sending the child to bed and even among these small percentages there were few who regarded this to be an efficient method.

On these two questions which were concerned with the use of banishment, either by sending the child to his room or sending the child to bed as a punishing method, the general incidence across the five groups was consistent. Each group was evenly divided on the use of banishment to the child's room and each group seemed to reject the method of punishment by sending the child to bed. Only the organic group showed a significant difference. Parents in that group made more use of the technique of sending the child to his room. Among the parents who used either technique there was more confidence recorded in the use of banishment to his room than in sending the child to bed.

The parent may also choose to withhold affection as a technique for gaining conformity. To employ this technique the parent must deliberately refuse the child's approach, be frigid toward him for a time, make no effort to smile at subsequent behavior and make no effort to kiss or pat the child. This denial of affection is intended to convince the child that he has lost something as a result of his behavior and that only sincere repentance, resolution of amendment and conforming behavior can regain what has been lost.

All five groups indicated that this approach was not employed by the majority. Only in the blind group was there a division of opinion on this matter of any consequence—54 per cent to 46 per cent (Table 124H).

Opinion as to the effectiveness of withholding affection as a technique to attain desired behaviors was divided among the parents who used it. The mongoloid and blind groups showed some favorable opinion but the other three groups were equivocal.

Another technique which could be classified as a standard parental procedure in discipline comes under the heading of deprivation. Here the parent seeks to gain conformity by depriving the child of a favored toy, a dessert, a promised visit, etc. The particular items or events varied from parent to parent but the technique was employed by the majority of parents in each group except the mongoloid, where the majority did not use it. The blind, deaf and organic groups showed the highest incidence of use. The deaf group was equally divided in their appraisal of the effectiveness of deprivation (Table 124I). The blind group expressed the highest level of confidence in the technique. Generally those who used this approach were impressed with its effectiveness.

The final technique listed concerned the use of verbal behavior as a method for attaining changes in behavior. Here the parent uses words to "explain the wrongness" of the child's behavior hoping that the child will get the message. The responses of the parents to this question are of particular interest in view of the number of cases who had language problems of a receptive nature or were mentally retarded. There was certainly enough evidence to suggest that many of the parents would experience difficulty if they were to rely upon a verbal approach. The findings reflect an almost unanimous reliance upon verbal explanation as a principal disciplinary approach (Table 124J). The majority in each group regarded verbal explanations as an effective tool in shaping behavior.

Only in the mongoloid group was there any significant indecision regarding the effectiveness of the verbal approach. It is likely that the child's difficulty in receiving and interpreting language accounted for this equivocal appraisal of effectiveness. In each group there were some parents who felt that their verbal efforts were ineffective. Language difficulties on the part of the child were reported to be the reason for the inefficiency.

Since spanking appeared to be a favored technique, and since the mothers seemed to be the primary initiators of discipline, there was some interest in the part the fathers played in the administration of spankings. Mothers were asked to note the frequency with which fathers spanked the children. Table 125 shows a comparative breakdown of the frequency of spankings administered by mothers and by fathers.

When all groups were considered collectively the mothers were more likely to administer spankings than the fathers. In all groups except the deaf the mothers' efforts were clearly more frequent than the fathers. Since the deaf group seemed to hold a higher level of confidence than the others in the value of spankings it is not surprising that the fathers in this group were more active in spankings than the others.

Parental Follow-Through

One final question was necessary to add to the perspectives on discipline. Since the use of threats was regarded by these parents as a critical tool to obtain desired behavior the consistency in following through on expressed threats could reflect some measure of whether these parents only talked or actually talked and acted.

Each child must come to know there is a constancy and a predictability in his environmental surround. When he is threatened with some form of punishment if his misbehavior continues—the continuation of that behavior must result in punishment if he is to be able to predict a cause and effect relationship. If, however, the threats are made and not carried out then his predictability ratio is in jeopardy. Under such conditions each succeeding threat is likely to be given less and less weight by the child.

To ascertain the distribution among these five groups the same question used in the Sears (1957) study was asked of these mothers: *"How often do you tell X that you're going to punish him and then for some reason do not follow through?"*

Twenty-four per cent of the total group of mothers claimed that they always followed through on their threats (Table 126). The mothers in the cerebral palsy group reported the highest incidence of consistency and the mongoloid group indicated the lowest incidence of consistency. The majority in the organic, mongoloid and deaf

TABLE 125

COMPARISONS OF FREQUENCY OF SPANKING
BY MOTHERS AND FATHERS
REPORTED BY MOTHERS

	Cerebral Palsy		Organic		Mongoloid		Blind		Deaf		All Groups	
	M	F	M	F	M	F	M	F	M	F	M	F
Never	9%	19%	12%	10%	8%	21%	8%	24%	5%	10%	8%	17%
Rare	24%	55%	32%	55%	4%	29%	59%	68%	10%	37%	26%	49%
Occasionally	48%	11%	45%	30%	60%	46%	33%	8%	75%	37%	52%	26%
Frequently	19%	15%	11%	5%	28%	4%			10%	16%	14%	8%
Total	100%	100%	100%	100%	100%	100%	100%	100%	100%	100%	100%	100%

TABLE 126

MOTHERS' REPORTS OF FOLLOWING THROUGH
ON THREATS OF PUNISHMENT

	Cerebral Palsy	Organic	Mongoloid	Blind	Deaf	All Groups	Sears' Study (1957)
Always follows through	43%	20%	8%	29%	20%	24%	13%
Sometimes do not	20%	61%	64%	42%	70%	51%	56%
Often do not	29%	17%	28%	29%	10%	23%	27%
Never comes up	6%					1%	2%
Not ascertained	2%	2%				1%	2%
Total	100%	100%	100%	100%	100%	100%	100%

groups admitted that they sometimes did not follow through. The blind group admitted to some inconsistency in four out of ten cases.

Three out of ten in the cerebral palsy, mongoloid and blind groups admitted that they were often guilty of not following through. Only a few parents in the organic and deaf groups admitted to some constancy of inconsistency.

Although the same question was scored differently in the Sears study it is possible to consider a comparison between the two studies if certain liberties are taken with the Sears' scoring categories. Combining the Sears' categories of "quite often" "quite often—practically every day" into one unit and combining the "occasionally" and "frequently" categories of this study will permit a comparison for illustrative purposes.

The mothers of the handicapped groups in every case except the mongoloid group claimed a higher degree of consistency than did the mothers of the nonhandicapped kindergartners in the Sears' study (24 per cent to 13 per cent). Those who admitted to inconsistency in both studies were fairly evenly matched. The two extreme claims of the cerebral palsy and the mongoloid groups distorted the comparison. The admission of the mongoloid group and the claim of the cerebral palsy group do not seem to be in keeping with the responses of these two groups throughout the sereis of discipline questions. The reasons for these discrepancies are not open to interpretation.

COMMENTARY ON DISCIPLINARY TECHNIQUES

For the composite group there was a division of opinion on the question of whether the parents employed the same or different discipline techniques with this child as compared to siblings. Where there seemed to be a definite opinion of difference further investigation revealed that the actual differences were not as noticeable in practices as they were reported to be by the parental global perceptions.

Most mothers regarded their handicapped child as being a greater problem to them in discipline than their other children except for those who had cerebral palsied children, where a surprising number regarded the physically handicapped child as no more of a problem than their other children. No specific reason could be ascertained for this differential.

About half of the mothers regarded themselves as holding a "just right" amount of strictness in dealing with this child and the other half regarded themselves as too lenient. The mothers' attitude towards the fathers' level of strictness ran the same course as their own. Only a few mothers regarded themselves or their mates as being too strict

The mothers presented a general picture of their husbands as not understanding the child and being critical of them for demanding too much of the handicapped child. Most couples were presented as having some extent of disagreement about the value of certain disciplinary tactics in dealing with the handicapped child. The mother was clearly presented as the leader in disciplinary activity and about one third objected to the way their husband handled the child. The mothers were more likely to spank the child than the fathers were.

Only a small percentage of mothers seemed to have any question about their own competency in dealing with the child. These feelings of inadequacy seemed to stem from two sources: (1) A negative self-concept on the part of the mother, and (2) bewildering behavior on the part of the child.

A small percentage of parents employed an approach of positive sanctions. The usual approach was one of negative sanctioning.

Ten techniques which were arbitrarily selected as standard approaches to discipline were presented to the parents requesting them to comment on the frequency of use and the relative effectiveness of each.

The incidence of usage of each of the ten techniques can be used to establish a rank order of preference as reported by the total population of 177 sets of parents of handicapped children. While some degree of variation might be noted within an individual group this total population reported the following preferences:

1. Explaining the wrongness of behavior (90 per cent plus).
2. Spanking (90 per cent).
3. Threatening spanking (80 to 85 per cent).
4. Sending child to his room (50 to 70 per cent).
5. Depriving the child (40 to 60 per cent).
6. Withholding affection (25 to 50 per cent) equivocal.
7. Threatening to tell father (30 to 35 per cent) ineffective.
8. Slapping (25 to 30 per cent) effective.

9. Sit on chair in corner (20 to 30 per cent) equivocal.

10. Put child to bed (20 to 30 per cent) equivocal.

There is little doubt that the primary technique employed by nearly all parents was a verbal approach to reasoning and explaining to the child the error of his ways. The emphasis upon this appeal to reason was regarded by the majority of parents as the most effective technique in their disciplinary repertoire.

The verbal approach emphasis did not imply that each parent calmly sat down with the child and patiently explained the pros and cons of a given piece of behavior. These findings rather convey the notion that these parents used a verbal approach to control of behavior. The degree of patience, the language used and types of situations which might be included were unfortunately not investigated. Guidance of behavior by verbal suggestion casually given, a sharp admonition spoken in a commanding voice, a verbal barrage amounting to an oral spanking, and the setting of definite boundaries by using oral symbols of limitation were all regarded as having variable incidence in the verbal approach. How the mother felt while using words, what words were used and the quantity of words employed are possible areas of interest for future researchers interested in the child-rearing process.

The fact that a child may be deaf, mentally retarded, physically handicapped, receptively confused, auditorially inattentive and visually unaware appeared to have little significance in this matter. These parents, perhaps like most parents living in a highly verbal nation, relied primarily upon a system of talking the child out of undesirable, and into desirable, behavior.

In order of incidence these parents regarded spanking as a close second in effectiveness for gaining desirable responses. This form of "shock therapy" signals to the child that his behavior has been grossly deviant from parental expectations. Any popular notions which may be held regarding the likelihood that the presence of a handicap is a significant deterrent to a parental desire to corporally emphasize a point in behavior must certainly be dispelled by these findings.

There is always the possibility that the parent finds the spanking process a way of venting his or her own emotional outrage and that the disciplinary intent is actually secondary. There is also the possibility that the delivery of the spanking may be an impassionate procedure rationalized as "strictly to the benefit of the child." It is likely that both types of consideration as well as variants between these two opposites were randomly distributed throughout the entire sample. The nature of the transgressions which were perceived to warrant spankings, the length of time involved and the lightness or heaviness of the blows was not studied.

In this preliminary effort consideration was given only to the question of incidence and preference. The many details of circumstance and dynamics are left to future investigators. The parents clearly indicated that they have spanked, and do spank, their handicapped child as a technique to achieve a modification of behavior.

Once having established such a preference it is not surprising that these first two preferences of verbal reasoning and corporal punishment should lead to a third ranked technique of threatening the child with a prospect of a spanking. When the child is aware of "spankingness" a verbal threat of such possibility may be sufficient to have him quit an undesired action. Some parents, however, expressed the belief that the threat was not nearly as effective as the actual spanking. Spanking is an abrupt, immediate, on-the-spot action. Threatening a spanking allows the parent the leeway to act or not act. This process then becomes a matter of whether the parent actually follows through on a threat or dismisses it.

Those three techniques must be regarded as the major tools of discipline for these parents. The other seven techniques studied show a rapid rate of incidence decline and must be regarded as significantly of less value to the parent. Two additional techniques can be listed in the preferential ranking even though less used. Banishing the child to his room, and depriving him of something he wants, stand as fourth and fifth ranked techniques.

These first five techniques must be regarded as the basic pattern of discipline for this total sample. The other five techniques are included in the repertoire of less than one third of the total group and even those who use the techniques are divided in their evaluation of the effectiveness of each. It is probably true that some parents apply these lesser techniques with a certain amount of comfort and confidence, and therefore achieve results, while others were less convinced of the effectiveness at the outset. The parental supply of techniques is not abundant. No parents suggested categories of technology which departed from the basic list.

A basic limitation exists in considering the actual effectiveness of these various techniques. The nature of the questioning limits the interpretation of these results to the extent that the findings reflect the perceptions of the parents and not necessarily the actual state of affairs. The true effectiveness of each technique can only be judged by studying the impact of each technique upon the positive shaping of the child's behavior. That study is also assigned to some future research.

These parents were emphatically on the side of negative sanctioning in devising methods for shaping their child's behavior in the direction desired. Positive sanctioning was minimally reported.

An inspection of the rank order of preferences in each of the five groups will help to delineate any possible deviations from the total group pattern which might bear some relationship to the peculiarities of a given disability. Two of the ten techniques were not included in the study of the cerebral palsy group and these have arbitrarily been assigned to ninth and tenth order for that group.

Cerebral Palsy

1. Spanking.
2. Explaining the wrong in behavior.
3. Threatening a spanking.
4. Depriving the child.
5. Sending him to his room.
6. Put the child to bed.
7. Sit on chair in corner.
8. Withholding affection.
9. Slapping.
10. Threatening to tell father.

The first two techniques are ranked in accord with the total sample but the mothers in this group did not rely as much as others upon the use of threats of spankings. They apparently took more direct action. Sending the child to his room was also not as widely used in this group. This reduced incidence was probably due to the locomotive abilities of some of the cases. This group spanked, explained and deprived in that order of preference. Techniques requiring mobility on the part of the child were less favored. The locomotive status of the child apparently is an influential factor in the parental choice of techniques.

The organic group was much in accord with the rankings of the total sample except that more reliance was placed on slapping than among other groups.

Organic

1. Explaining the wrong in behavior.
2. Spanking.
3. Threatening a spanking.
4. Sending child to his room.
5. Slapping.
6. Depriving the child.
7. Sit on a chair in the corner.
8. Threatening to tell father.
9. Put the child to bed.
10. Withholding affection.

These parents seemed to prefer a quick slap as a means of gaining results over the total sample rank of depriving the child. Withholding affection was less used by this group than any of the others. This group also showed a higher incidence of putting the child to bed as a punitive measure than any other group and also sent the child to his room oftener than other groups.

This group showed the greatest incidence of sampling all techniques and, in general, seemed less confident in the effectiveness of their set of techniques than did the others. There is the likelihood that perceptual and language problems frequently associated with organic problems, characteristics of hyperactivity, perseveration, distractibility, disinhibition, and so on, have a net effect of thwarting parental techniques and necessitating a wider sampling on the part of the parents to find a suitable technique.

The mongoloid group was the most convinced of the five groups that a quick slap was an effective tool and found it to be far more useful than sending the child to his room.

Mongoloid

1. Explaining the wrong in behavior.
2. Spanking.
3. Threatening a spanking.
4. Slapping the child.
5. Sending the child to his room.
6. Sit on the chair in the corner.
7. Depriving the child.
8. Withholding affection.
9. Threatening to tell father.
10. Put the child to bed.

Considering the probability that traditional understandings regarding the intellectual and language levels of a mongoloid group would tend to place this group of children at a two to three year level of efficiency, the parental reliance upon a verbal approach suggests a milieu of language confusion. These parents, however, regarded the verbal approach as most effective of all. Putting the child to bed was considered by these parents to be less effective than other groups considered it to be. Depriving the child was also considered as far less effective than other groups had found it.

The first four techniques listed constituted their primary system. They expressed little confidence in the other six. They found greater value in the use of a punishment corner than the others did. They seem to have been influenced by the retardation factor at certain points and to have ignored it at others.

The blind group was the most emphatic of the five groups in declaring their preference for the verbal approach. There was no indication of hesitancy because of a receptive language problem or degrees of retardation.

Blind

1. Explaining the wrong in behavior.
2. Spanking.
3. Threatening a spanking.
4. Depriving the child.
5. Sending the child to his room.
6. Slapping.

7. Withholding affection.
8. Threatening to tell father.
9. Sit on a chair in the corner.
10. Put the child to bed.

They were less inclined to the quick-slap approach than any of the other groups but were the most inclined of the five to use withholding of affection as a technique. Putting the child to bed and using a punishment chair were significantly less used by these parents than by the other four groups. In general, this group conformed to the first five selections of the total sample.

The deaf group also conformed with a considerable amount of confidence to the first five techniques of the total sample. Here again the heavy reliance placed upon a verbal approach seems to be at odds with the traditional picture of the deaf child and his problems in understanding oral language. Since these parents had previously been noted to engage in less language modification than might be expected, the parental belief in the effectiveness of a verbal technique suggests that they did, in fact, find a way to reach the child in spite of the acoustic handicap.

This group also provided a significant incidence of sampling all approaches in their effort to find a comfortable and effective way.

Deaf

1. Spanking.
2. Threatening a spanking.
3. Explaining the wrong in behavior.
4. Slapping.
5. Sending the child to his room.
6. Depriving the child.
7. Threatening to tell father.
8. Sit on a chair in the corner.
9. Withholding affection.
10. Put the child to bed.

On the question of disciplinary techniques the net conclusion is that these parents were not influenced to any significant degree in their choice of method or frequency by the fact or the nature of the child's handicap. While some parents in each group suggested that the child's handicap had to be given consideration this was not a common reflection. It is also true, that although more than half of the total group indicated that they disciplined *this* child differently from their other children there were nearly as many parents who denied a difference. The nature of the difference, for those who professed a difference, was not reflected as a choice of unusual techniques but was rather a matter of quality and quantity. The techniques were the same as those used with siblings.

This finding is taken to imply that parents of handicapped children have not creatively developed new techniques but tend to rely upon standard techniques used by all parents.

Chapter 14

THE PARENT AND RELIGION

It is historically true that in times of great crisis people turn to religion to find comfort and security. It is also true that individuals experiencing personal trauma may find great comfort in religion. Turning to religion may well represent a highly significant coping strategy for the parents of handicapped children.

The popular press is continually pointing out a great concern that declining moral standards in this society may stem from failures to hold and practice religious beliefs. Billboards, signs and various other forms of advertising media grow more numerous with slogans and religious messages urging people to practice their religious beliefs as a hope for reducing many of the negative social statistics on divorce, crime, immorality, etc.

The 177 families in this study, with few exceptions, identified themselves as being affiliated with a religious belief. When religious beliefs are translated into actions it can easily be seen that a great deal of child-rearing content may be related to religion. The practices of attending church, praying, receiving instructions, holding minor religious ceremonies within the home are all methods which are communicated to the child and can be subscribed under the heading of a child-rearing practice area.

More than half of the total study population were Catholic and with the mongoloid and blind groups showing the highest percentage. Six per cent were Jewish and 3 per cent were of other religions while approximately 40 per cent were Protestant. Only 1 per cent of the total group indicated that they held no religious belief.

An additional shading may be added to the general family portrait by an investigation into certain questions related to religion. Some data in this area were obtained from the Family Social Patterns questionnaire and some from several questions that were included in the clinical interview.

The first focus of investigation was directed at ascertaining the regularity with which these parents practiced their religious convictions in the form of church or synagogue attendance at services.

A poll of church attendance during 1963 conducted by the American Institute of Public Opinion in New Jersey revealed that two Protestants out of every five, 71 per cent of the Catholics, and one out of four of the Jewish faith in the United States attended a church or synagogue in a typical week. The midwestern section of the country showed a 48 per cent weekly attendance. According to the Gallup survey women had a better church attendance than men did; 51 per cent of women compared to 41 per cent of men attended church in a typical week.

The findings among the mothers and fathers of handicapped children in this study reflect a higher incidence of regular weekly church attendance in both the mothers and fathers than the national average. Of the mothers, 74 per cent were regular in their weekly church attendance and 54 per cent of the fathers. Across the five groups the blind group reflected the highest percentage in both the mother and father groups. The other groups reflected an essentially similar but reduced percentage. A small percentage of fathers and mothers did not attend church at all (Tables 127 and 128).

The constancy of the similarity in religious belief over a period of two generations was also checked. The finding was nearly the same for the mothers and the fathers; three fourths of the parents held the same beliefs as had been held by their own parents. Only 4 per cent of the total group indicated that both the mother and father of the handicapped child practiced a different religion than had been held by either of their parents. In the remaining 21 per

TABLE 127

FREQUENCY OF CHURCH ATTENDANCE AMONG
MOTHERS IN PERCENTAGES

	Cerebral Palsy	Organic	Mongoloid	Blind	Deaf	Total
Once or more weekly	69	76	77	85	63	74%
Twice a month	11	6	8	5	12	7%
Monthly or several times per year	11	11	7	10	4	11%
Not at all	3	3			8	3%
Nots ascertained	6	4	8		13	5%

TABLE 128

FREQUENCY OF CHURCH ATTENDANCE AMONG
FATHERS IN PERCENTAGES

	Cerebral Palsy	Organic	Mongoloid	Blind	Deaf	Total
Once or more weekly	56	51	53	63	54	54%
Twice a month	17	17	5		28	15%
Monthly or several times per year	19	16	26	17		16%
Not at all	3	4	16	20		6%
Not ascertained	3	12			18	9%

TABLE 129

CONSTANCY OF RELIGIOUS BELIEF OVER
TWO GENERATIONS OF THE PARENTS

	Mother and Her Parents		Father and His Parents	
	f	%	f	%
Same	136	76	93	72
Different	42	24	36	28

cent of the cases one of the parents had changed their religion from that of their parents (Table 129).

When those families who reported that either the mother or father, or both, were not regular in church attendance were compared, irregularity was more pronounced among the fathers than the mothers. In half of the families in the cerebral palsy, mongoloid and blind groups one parent or both did not attend church regularly. The highest incidence of irregular attendance occurred in the deaf group followed closely by the organic. The organic and deaf groups differed significantly from the other three groups in the number of families in which both the mother and the father were irregular in their church attendance.

The mothers in the blind group reported the highest incidence of frequent family rituals of a religious nature while the deaf group were least frequent and showed the highest absence of any rituals (Table 130). Nearly half of the families in the mongoloid and deaf reported that they never held any family rituals of a religious nature. The general finding is that most parents reported in the negative on this question. While there was a general impression of religious participation being a standard the expression of religiousness did not extend

TABLE 130

FREQUENCY OF FAMILY RITUALS OF A RELIGIOUS NATURE

	Cerebral Palsy	Organic	Mongoloid	Blind	Deaf	Total
Frequently often	30%	25%	26%	47%	13%	27%
Rarely—sometimes	41%	28%	23%	32%	21%	30%
Never	22%	37%	44%	16%	45%	33%
Not ascertained	6%	10%	7%	5%	21%	10%

to the organization of and conduct of religious rituals as family affairs.

Frequency of church attendance as a family group was highest among the blind but all others reported that at least four out of ten families went to church as a family unit. As a composite finding, one fourth of the families never attended church as a family group. In this matter the entire group seemed to be equally divided between families who frequently went to church together and those who rarely or never did so (Table 131).

Gathering the members of the family together to listen to the father or some other designated member read aloud from the Bible was not a frequent practice for any of the five groups. One third of the families indicated that there were some occasions on which such might occur but that such occasions were rare. The general finding was that oral reading from the Bible as a family group was not a part of the manner in which these families gave expression to their religious beliefs (Table 132).

TABLE 131

FREQUENCY OF CHURCH ATTENDANCE
AS A FAMILY GROUP

	Cerebral Palsy	Organic	Mongoloid	Blind	Deaf	Total
Frequently—often	40%	40%	44%	79%	45%	44%
Rarely—sometimes	34%	24%	28%	5%	21%	26%
Never	24%	31%	23%	11%	17%	25%
Not ascertained	1%	4%	5%	5%	17%	5%

Another way in which beliefs might be expressed is by family prayer other than at mealtimes. The majority of parents in all groups except the blind indicated that they rarely or never did this. The blind group contrary to all others reported in the majority that this was a frequent family practice (Table 133).

TABLE 132

FREQUENCY OF FAMILY ORAL BIBLE READING

	Cerebral Palsy	Organic	Mongoloid	Blind	Deaf	Total
Frequently—often	8%	8%		10%		6%
Rarely—sometimes	39%	22%	36%	42%	38%	32%
Never	50%	62%	59%	37%	45%	55%
Not ascertained	3%	8%	5%	10%	17%	7%

TABLE 133

FREQUENCY OF FAMILY PRAYER OTHER THAN AT MEALTIME

	Cerebral Palsy	Organic	Mongoloid	Blind	Deaf	Total
Frequently—often	39%	21%	23%	58%	17%	28%
Rarely—sometimes	43%	33%	41%	32%	50%	38%
Never	17%	37%	28%	5%	17%	27%
Not ascertained	1%	9%	8%	5%	17%	7%

Almost all of the parents indicated that their handicapped child received some form of formal religious instruction (Table 134). It should be noted that a very energetic movement among several church groups in Milwaukee County during the past five years has resulted in a network of Sunday school programs for the retarded and physically handicapped. Many of the children represented in this study are enrolled in such programs.

TABLE 134

PERCENTAGE OF CHILDREN IN EACH
GROUP REPORTING THAT CHILDREN
RECEIVE RELIGIOUS INSTRUCTION

Cerebral Palsy	Organic	Mongoloid	Blind	Deaf
86%	83%	91%	86%	83%

Cases were classified as "high religious" if they frequently or often attended church as a family group, prayed together at times other than meals, read aloud from the Bible, practiced family affairs at holiday periods in accordance with their religious beliefs and attended church services on a regular weekly basis.

Those families who were irregular in church attendance or did not attend at all, did not conduct family practices in accord with religious beliefs at holiday or special periods, seldom or never prayed and who reported that neither prayer nor religion had been helpful to them in their adjustment were categorized as "low religious."

According to this scale approximately half of the families in each group rested somewhere in between both ends of the scale with variations in the extent of their religious practices which do not allow for either a high or low rating. The blind group revealed the highest incidence of high-religious followed by the cerebral palsy group (Table 135). These same two groups showed the least incidence of low-religious.

TABLE 135

PERCENTAGES OF HIGH-LOW RELIGIOUS FAMILIES

	Palsy Cerebral	Organic	Mongoloid	Blind	Deaf
Highly religious	45%	20%	32%	64%	25%
Low religious	9%	31%	20%	7%	20%

Understand About God

Parents were asked to respond to the question, Does your child understand about God? as a part of the general series of items which could be related to the topic of religion. Most of the parents expressed the belief that their child did understand about God (Table 136). Some stated that the child learned whatever understanding was held from the formalized Sunday school or church instruction sessions. Others said that they had personally taught the child to hold some understanding of God.

TABLE 136

DISTRIBUTION OF RESPONSES ON QUESTION,
"DOES YOUR CHILD UNDERSTAND ABOUT GOD"

	Cerebral Palsy	Organic	Mongoloid	Blind	Deaf
Understands	75%	57%	80%	79%	67%
Does not understand	25%	43%	20%	21%	33%

As a general rule the families that reported that their child had no understanding of God were also among the families who had been classified as low-religious. This reported lack of understanding of God held no significant relationship to the professed religious affiliation of the parents, the intellectual level of the child or the degree of severity of the handicap.

Individual interpretation on the part of each parent as to the meaning of the word "understand" undoubtedly influenced the distribution of responses. Some parents of severely retarded children commented that their child had some vague idea of a Higher Being and while they felt there was some form of understanding they would feel hard pressed to detail the nature of that understanding.

Conversely some parents with children of average intelligence expressed the feeling that their children did not hold any real understanding of God. Despite the fact that the question was really quite vague and allowed a wide latitude of individual interpretation it is interesting to find that, with two exceptions, the parents who stated that their child did not understand about God fell within the low-religious classification. This suggests that the degrees of latitude afforded by the question were not nearly as expansive as one might think at first glance. Low religious participation by the parent may well reduce the number of opportunities to earn this understanding from the home situation and perhaps decrease parental sensitivity to this area of instruction.

Help of Prayer

The parent of the handicapped child is confronted with a need to adapt to the anxieties of diagnostic searching, therapy sessions, a probable negative prognosis, persistent questions about the adequacy of their child's present and future behavior, school potential, their own perception of the seriousness of the child's problem, spouse reaction and empathy and many other problems during the child's growing years. Faced with this kind of problem, do these parents find comfort and support from their religious convictions? In time of stress have they turned to religion and prayer?

Two questions were set in the clinical interview which directly asked the parent whether religion and prayer had been helpful to them in their adjustment to their general problem of having a handicapped child. In the early pilot interviews the question had been asked as a unit but it was soon discovered that some parents were differentiating between religion and prayer and indicating that only one or the other had been helpful. Consequently, the questions were separated in the final interview form.

The majority of parents in each group responded affirmatively to the question of whether religion had been of help to them in adjusting to this problem (Table 137). Only in the organic and the deaf groups was there a sizable incidence of those who denied that religion had helped.

TABLE 137

PERCENTAGE OF CASES WHO FELT RELIGION
WAS HELPFUL IN ADJUSTING

	Cerebral Palsy	Organic	Mongoloid	Blind	Deaf
Yes	94%	74%	84%	93%	79%
No	6%	26%	16%	7%	21%

Those who felt that their religion had been and was helpful to them made statements such as the following:

"It's something to lean on."

"I can find comfort and consolation in my religion."

"Religion makes things a little brighter and it gives you hope."

"Going to church seems to relieve the pressure."

"It gives you strength and patience."

Those who denied that religion had helped stated a blunt "No" to the question. Despite the fact that some parents could be classified as low-religious when the extent of active expression and participation were taken into account the high-low classification was not significantly related to whether the parent found religion to be helpful.

As a general rule those parents who were affirmative about the supportive character of their religion were also affirmative in regard to prayer (Table 138). Several cases in the deaf, mongoloid and organic groups, however, attributed a helpful quality to prayer but denied that religion *per se* had helped. They felt that prayer was personal and individual while religion implied the more formal, collective aspects of a belief and therefore claimed that their comfort and support should more properly be attributed to prayer.

The following expressions were typical of those made by parents who indicated that prayer had been helpful to them:

TABLE 138

PERCENTAGE OF CASES WHO FELT THAT
PRAYER HAD BEEN HELPFUL

	Cerebral Palsy	Organic	Mongoloid	Blind	Deaf
Yes	94%	78%	96%	93%	85%
No	6%	22%	4%	7%	15%

"Prayers are a way of unloading misery and unhappiness."

"Gives you patience and courage."

"Reassures me of God's help."

"Helps me to accept God's will."

"Helps me over the rough spots."

"It's a great source of relief.

Some parents felt that prayer had been an integral force in helping the child to make progress. Many stated that their prayers had been answered in the child's success in overcoming certain obstacles. Several mothers explained that prayer had probably saved their marriages. Almost all of the parents prayed. Only the global question was asked. No detailing of type and extent of prayer was questioned.

COMMENTARY ON RELIGION

Mothers in these groups attended church services with a greater regularity than the fathers. Three fourths of the mothers were regular churchgoers but only half of the fathers were reported to attend church regularly. The parents of these handicapped children had a higher percentage of religious participation than reflected in the national average. (Tables 136 and 137). Only three cases in 177 were reported to never attend services.

In comparing the mother and father incidence of "no church attendance," this finding did not pertain to any single couple. At least one parent went to church regularly or periodically. In the general sense of the word every home in this study could be considered to have some religion and in most cases this was represented by an active regular participation in services.

In three fourths of the cases the mother practiced the same religion as her parents had practiced, and a similar incidence of holding the same religion as his parents was true of the father. Only a small percentage of families in each of the five groups admitted that both the father and mother were irregular in their church attendance. Family rituals such as evening sessions of Bible readings, joint family prayer other than mealtime, family rosary, special religious practices within the home, and so on, were not of significant incidence except among the blind group where nearly half of the group indicated a frequency of personal family religious practices. The majority of families in each other group rarely or never held any form of religious rituals within their own home.

Despite the fact that the majority of these families expressed their religious beliefs in some extent of regular attendance at church services few of these families had organized any formal family practices which they considered under the heading of religious rituals. The practice of oral family Bible reading was reported to be a rare event, or never to have occurred, in the vast majority of families in each of the five groups. No group showed a meaningful incidence of such a practice. Few families prayed together other than at mealtimes.

The popular advertising slogan which announces that, "The family that prays together—stays together" carries with it the suggestion that parents and children should attend church as a family unit. The practice suggested was mainly incidental in the blind group but all other groups reported nearly half of their families to engage in this practice. It was not possible to ascertain the reasons why some parents rarely or never included the entire family in this practice, but some obvious reality considerations must be taken into account.

The presence of an infant in the family, the severely physically handicapped child, the wild, hyperactive, neurologically impaired child, the fact that some mothers and fathers were themselves infrequent attendants, are all possible reasons for the family infrequency. There is also the possibility that the handicap of the child became some form of influence against such a practice. All of these reasons and none of these reasons may have been applicable. The questioning and the data were insufficient to permit any conclusions on this score.

Within recent years there has been an increased effort on the part of all religions to offer specialized religious instruction to handicapped children, or to extend an invitation to these populations to join in children's services which are regularly scheduled. Nearly all of the children in each group were reported to be receiving or have received some extent of formal religious instruction.

Despite the fact that a mother or a father may have been irregular attendants at church services it seems clear that the parents somehow made certain that the child received some instruction. The high incidence of such instruction for the children in the mongoloid group was directly attributable to a very energetic and dynamic effort on the part of some religious authorities in the Milwaukee County area who were particularly devoted to developing religious instruction programs for the mentally retarded.

In spite of the sporadic distressing behaviors of some of the organic group children their parents had persistently made some attempt to involve their children in instructional programs. The cerebral palsy group enrolled their children in a program if it was at all possible to bring the child to the service. As far as could be ascertained the blind and deaf groups enrolled their children in regular programs. Those cases who did not receive some exposure to formal religious instruction were the most severe physical or behavioral problems in each group. On this question of religious instruction for the handicapped child all five groups were uniformly and emphatically affirmative.

The rating of low religiousness was given to about one third of the families in the organic group and only a few families in that group merited a ranking of high religiousness. The blind group had the highest incidence of high religiousness but in all other groups at least half of the families were clustered between these two extremes.

Despite the inherent difficulties in defining criteria for an affirmative response to the question, Does your child understand about God? all five groups responded with a majority affirmative. The uncertainty of criteria may well have been randomly distributed to the extent that the negative influence of indefiniteness was diminished.

The vast majority of parents in each group reported that both religion and prayer had been helpful to them in adjusting to their role as the parent of a handicapped child.

In general summary it is clear that the presence of a handicapped child in the family neither decreased or increased the religiousness of a family. Farber (1959) has reported that Catholics in crisis (having a severely retarded child) receive a greater degree of emotional support than do non-Catholics. His study also indicated that there was no significant relationship between the regularity of church attendance and the marital integration of the parents. He concluded as part of his final summary that religious associations could be regarded as supportive to the parents with a retarded child at home. While Farber was referring only to the parents of retarded children it seems clear that the parents of all five groups in the present study affirm that belief.

Most children represented in this study had some exposure to formal religious instruction regardless of retardation, acuity loss or physical handicap. The majority of families were rated as being of average religiousness.

This particular area of the parental portrait appears to be a comfortable well-defined area for a great majority. There was no indication of degree of difference on any of the questions covered which could significantly be attributed to the nature of the child's handicap. The presence of a handicapped child in the family was felt to hold some form of positive relationship to religiousness but the data were too thin to weight such a conclusion. Barring evidence to the contrary, however, the tendency toward the positive must be suspected from these data.

From the standpoint of child-rearing practices most parents set their child a good example in this area, made every effort to expose their child to religious training and to some degree incorporated prayer into family life. Religion must be regarded as a significant brush stroke in forming the parental portrait.

Chapter 15

THE PARENTS PERCEPTIONS
AND ATTITUDES

THERE ARE A variety of topics which were covered during the group testing sequence and the clinical interview which constitute a sort of miscellany that can be loosely grouped under the heading of parental attitudes. Many of the areas already covered have delineated attitudes of various kinds and there is no wish to suggest that this section ignores all of those. It is rather that this chapter is devoted to a number of areas which seem to logically cluster under the title of attitudes.

SOURCE OF CHILD-REARING INFORMATION

During the past decade American parents have been exposed to a wide variety of child-rearing information from a number of sources. Popular magazines have featured "expert" articles related to child development and behavior in a constant stream. Favorite commentators and advisors have emerged to promote a greater understanding of what has been learned about children in scientific observations and laboratory study of behavior. Booklets and pamphlets covering various phases of development are readily accessible to parents in commercial form or as free handouts from public relations offices associated with industry.

Concurrently with this rapid literary and counseling expansion on child information has come the accusing finger of an aroused professional society directed at the parent failure in delinquency, emotional disturbance, underachievement, etc. "Tender, loving care" has become a prescriptive slogan in parent-child relations to rival many of the catch phrases of commercial advertising. Ancient proverbs related to child-rearing handed down through the ages have been replaced with psychological cliches of "frustration," "permissiveness," "neurosis," etc. Sociologists decry the disintegration of family unity; and "togetherness" becomes the slogan and goal for the American family. Considering the changing complexities of family life with all the ramifications of psychological and sociological filtration to a literate society, we were intrigued by the question of child-rearing sources of information in these selected populations.

A number of questions quickly came to mind. Would parents of handicapped children rely more heavily upon professional advice, written or spoken, for ideas on child-rearing practices? Could parents identify the source of their learning about children and the devising of rearing techniques? Would any differences be evident among the five groups which might relate significantly to the particular nature of the child's disability? Since the question in this area would be directed at both mothers and fathers, what state of agreement might be discerned in the various groups? These and many other questions prompted the inclusion of this area into the question sequence of the clinical interview.

The parents were asked to respond to the question, *When you consider the entire business of rearing a child from which source do you feel you learned the most about rearing children, such as from your mother, from books, from watching others, etc.?*

While the phrasing of the question selectively sets a perceptual frame it was felt that such a structure was justifiable in establishing an initial entry into this area of investigation. Although many of the parents indicated several sources such as "parental model" and "peer observation" or other combinations within the categories, the responses were coded on the basis of *primary* source as expressed by the parent even though other sources were seen as contributory.

Inspection of the responses suggested that five categories could be employed to distribute the data. More than half of the total groups offered responses which could be broadly classified under the term "experience." Included in this category were responses referring to the learning of child-rearing on the basis of trial and error approaches, or through the multiple unit system of learning by experience with one child and progressively becoming more secure in parent techniques as more children were born into the family.

Other responses related to adolescent experiences as a baby-sitter, or some form of care for siblings, as being a primary source of child-rearing learning were also included in this category. Those expressions which seemed to imply that such knowledge was merely a matter of common sense and required no special knowledge and those which suggested that such knowledge was a natural endowment were also defined as experience. The following verbatim responses of mothers will serve to illustrate the range of comments included under the heading of experience.

I didn't learn anything—I acted by instinct like a dog. I try to use common sense and apply it to my own child.

It's day after day—you learn through your mistakes.

It comes from everyday living. Every day is different.

Something I just picked up myself in taking care of others' children—baby sitting.

From my own experience. I had different ideas before I had them—I have learned.

From experience—I did housework for people who had small children and I observed them.

A lot from my own experience—you feel around to find out.

I really feel—I doubt any book—if you don't feel that way you won't do it. It's something you learn from observation all your life.

Just plain common sense and being a registered nurse helps.

Automatically picked it up myself. I like my job. I used to wonder when I was younger if I could do a good job of being a mother. I learned—it worked out okay.

The comments of some of the fathers are also useful in illustrating the experience category:

I just use my common sense.

My wife and I worked together and learning the hard way—through experience.

I guess experience—we have six.

Just muddled through—we don't subscribe to magazines or books. Just treat children as we think they should be raised—just common sense.

Practical experience of raising children—I don't believe in books.

The use of "parental models" represented the next longest cluster of responses, with comments related to using similar techniques as were used by their own parents in their upbringing. The general theme of these comments was the imitation of patterns of rearing which they experienced in their own childhood. A few comments can serve to illustrate this theme:

> From my mother. We had a large family and she trained us well.
>
> From my mother. She raised up five and I always wanted to do that.
>
> I try to reflect on my parents.
>
> I follow my mother's footsteps.

While the majority of responses classified here were expressions of positive model, a number of parents indicated that the parental model was a negative one in which they were now trying to avoid the faults they perceived in their parents.

The next highest percentage of responses fell within a general category which could be defined as "peer observation." These comments expressed the learning through observation of the way other parents dealt with their children and copying those techniques. Many expressed a selective viewpoint indicating that by observing other parents they learned what *not* to do as well as what *to do*.

Reliance upon printed materials such as books and pamphlets was cited infrequently by these parents as a primary source of child-rearing information. Only 12 per cent of the total group of mothers indicated that reading about child-rearing had served as a source. The comments of the fathers reflected a lesser incidence (7 per cent of "book learning" than did the mothers. Several parents' responses in relation to books are of interest.

The mother of a five year old mongoloid stated:

> Mostly trial and error—we tried to get information from books but have found our own experience of growing up helped us.

The mother of a nine year old in the organic group expressed another perspective on books:

> From my own experience. Sometimes you read books but it doesn't always pertain to you.

The least incidence was found in the category of "professional" where parents expressed reliance upon physicians, psychologists and social workers who had specifically discussed child problems and parental techniques with them on a personal basis. Only two mothers and two fathers (not pairs) indicated a professional source.

The findings indicate a high degree of similarity in the distribution of various sources among the four diagnostic groups who responded to this question. (The item was not included in the interview at the time the cerebral palsy group was studied.) The only point of variance was found in the mothers of the deaf where parental models seem to hold a more favored position.

The general tone of the responses is a note of random activity in child-rearing with day by day trial and error processes gradually developing a composite which a parent may classify as a child-rearing repertoire. There is also a lack of direction, and an expression of searching contained throughout the records expressed in the two comments listed below:

> For the most important job in the world—women are ill-equipped. Very little from my own mother—from a combination of books, observations and, of course, through parent participation and counseling here.
>
> It should be taught.

The possibilities which appear vibrant under the surface of these limited response patterns to this initial question hold promise that a more detailed study in this particular area might prove fruitful. The exploration in depth on the axis of positive and negative parental modeling, asking parents to more specifically link present practices to those employed by their own parents with them, seems laden with all sorts of potential.

The investigation of modifications in child-rearing because of lessons learned with the first child, with a probing of the rationale for such changes, also holds promise of adding significant information to an understanding of parent-child dynamics. It is recognized that the single question included in this study barely nicked the surface but its principal intent was to prospect a new vein and merely examine the area for potential.

The findings were essentially the same for each group and no differences were found which might suggest a significant difference between any two or more groups. Since the question pertained to child-rearing practices in general, and did not specifically ask for the origin of practices used with the handicapped child, no direct relationship can be drawn regarding sources employed in any differentials between practices of the siblings and the handicapped.

The data in this study have consistently reflected a minimum of differences in child-rearing practices, however, and as a consequence the source of specific child-rearing practices related directly to the handicapped child might be expected to be very vague. Perhaps the same general distribution would have been obtained.

Some parents have initiated changes or modifications of practices with the handicapped child on a trial and error basis learning from their own experience. Some have tried to do things as they think their own mothers and fathers might have done. Some may have benefited from parent organization meetings of a peer group (other mothers of similarly handicapped children) where there was some opportunity to exchange child-rearing recipes and evaluate successes and failures. A small percentage have undoubtedly found valuable suggestions in pamphlets, articles and books written for or about parents of specific types of handicapped children.

The net impression gained indicates that the majority of the parents develop their own models and seem to be only minimally influenced by the vast amount of professional research which has been conducted for the past century. Each parent devises some curriculum of child-rearing from a variety of sources—the least of which is the professional body of information on child development. It would appear that a course of instruction to teach parents the extensive and valuable findings which have accrued related to the dynamics of parent-child interaction is significantly lacking on the American scene.

If the void is present in the general domain of child-rearing it can scarcely be expected that the parent would find a more favorable situation when he tried to develop a methodology as a child-rearer of a handicapped child. Since he is essentially without support, he relies upon the same general set of sources to work out his own model for the handicapped child. It is not surprising that the two approaches turn out to be nearly identical.

DECISION MAKING

In the day-by-day business of family living there are many occasions in which decisions have to be made. The matter of whether or not family finances will permit an expenditure for new furniture, new clothes, a power-mower, music lessons for the children, extent of insurance coverage, special educational costs, new cars, additional rooms, purchase of a new home, family vacations—these are some examples of the situations in which one or both parents must make negative or positive decisions. While the whole question of decision-making in a family offers an intriguing area for investigation on a comprehensive basis, only a surface approach to this question was included in this study.

To gain some impression of whether these five groups showed any differences among the groups, and to ascertain the general distribution of decision-making responsibilities, two questions were posed during the interview sequence. The questions were stated:

"We are wondering who makes the main decisions about the children. In some families it is the father; in others the mother. How does this work out in your family?

How about health matters, such as calling the doctor or keeping this child indoors for the day? Who decides that?

The parental responses to the question pertaining to main decisions regarding the children indicated that the deaf group tended to share these decisions either by having the mothers and fathers mutually participate in each decision, or to each make decisions as necessary independently, but be unable to define which parent had major responsibility in this area. When parents described the fact that they shared responsibility but may have acted in a given situation without conferring with the other partner, they explained that they "knew" what the other would have wanted them to do and that such decisions were always followed by a conference to discuss the situation further and thereby achieve a mutual understanding (Table 139).

In the blind group the mothers tended to make the main decisions,

TABLE 139

DISTRIBUTION OF RESPONSES OF MOTHERS ON QUESTION
"WHO MAKES THE MAIN DECISION IN THE FAMILY"

	Cerebral Palsy	Organic	Mongoloid	Blind	Deaf	Total
Mother	35%	24%	37%	50%	9%	31%
Father	29%	31%	26%	12%	25%	28%
Shared	36%	45%	37%	38%	66%	41%

but the other three groups showed a distribution into thirds with some
cases defining the mother as the major decision-maker, some the
father and some the mutual process of parent-sharing. There was a
tendency noted among the organic group toward sharing such responsibilities on an overall basis across the groups none of the three possible
conditions was markedly different from the other two.

Decision-making situations pertaining to health matters on a day-
by-day basis such as determining whether a child should stay home
from school because of illness, whether a doctor should be called,
whether the child should be kept indoors, etc. are clearly the province
of the mothers in all five groups. All groups showed a sharp reduction
in the parent-sharing process and the incidence of paternal decision-
making when the question of daily child health was introduced
(Table 140).

TABLE 140

DISTRIBUTION OF MOTHER RESPONSES ON QUESTION
OF WHICH PARENT MAKES DECISIONS IN HEALTH
MATTERS PERTAINING TO THIS CHILD

	Cerebral Palsy	Organic	Mongoloid	Blind	Deaf	Total
Mother	51%	67%	79%	63%	66%	64%
Father	20%	9%	5%	25%	9%	12%
Both	29%	24%	16%	12%	25%	24%

Commentary

Parents seem to have divided the world of decision-making into two
spheres. In the majority of families the question of province on matters
of health is the clear domain of the mother. Where such province
has been reported as paternal domain the percentage of incidence is
small. When it comes to decisions other than health the fathers appear
to take a more active role. Since no effort was made to obtain details
of matters on which decisions were made the results are based upon

the global impressions of the mothers. To some extent such other decisions might be considered as economic and therefore likely to call upon the father's decision-making province.

Across the groups however it was quite clear that in some families the mothers made almost all of the family decisions or there was a mutuality. The incidence of the father as the main decision-maker was in the minority. Only the deaf group showed a significant difference in the direction of more mutual sharing than the other groups.

The finding that the mother is the provincial guardian on decision-making related to the children is in keeping with a national trend and can perhaps be related historically to the ageless role of the mother. She has always been the principal manager of children. These families are no different than other families in this respect.

There was no evidence obtained from parental comments, interviewers' observations or clinical notes to suggest that this decision-making province was in any way related to the presence of a handicapped child. It was felt that this question would have been answered similarly by these parents if they had not had a handicapped child. These provincial jurisdictions were set by the way each man and woman conceived of their roles as parents.

PARENTAL PERCEPTIONS OF CHANGES

No parent is ever prepared in advance for the advent of a handicapped child. The arrival of such a diagnosis either at birth or later places the family in some form of crisis. The crisis may be a grave one thrust upon the family with an immediacy or it may cumulatively grow through time. Each couple has to cope with this crisis in some manner. Clinical case files across the nation are filled with many variations in coping behavior among parents. Clinicians will attest to the fact that some parents are changed for the better and some for the worse.

Farber (1959) included a series of questions related to perceptions of personality change on the part of fathers and mothers in his study of parents of severely retarded children. Since the particular series in the Farber study contributed to composite marital integration index no direct comparisons can be made with the effort in this study.

There was some interest in ascertaining what extent of difference might be reflected in this study related to each parent's perception of change in personality organization since the birth of this child. Were they more or less patient? More or less religious? More or less nervous? Angered more or less easily? Happier or less happy?

To gain information on this topic from the five groups of mothers and fathers involved in this study the question series employed by Farber were slightly modified to permit each parent to evaluate themselves and their mates. The forms were a part of the clinical interview sequence and each parent completed two series, one pertaining to their own perception of change within themselves and the second pertaining to change which they perceived to have occurred in their mates (see Appendix).

Each item allowed for three possible choices, one which indicated a negative, one a positive and a neutral change. A simple scoring system based upon a 2-0-1 rating was used to derive a total score for the form. Ten items from the form were selected for scoring and three were deleted because they did not pertain to the scoring scheme. On this basis a total score of twenty would indicate that a negative rating had been checked on each item. If all positive items were checked a score of zero would reflect this rating. A score of ten would indicate that no change for the better or worse had been perceived. None of the parents checked a consistent rating on all items.

To ascertain the variability on this perception among all five groups mean scores were obtained for each group. Tables 141 and 142 indicate the mean scores for fathers' perceptions of self-change and spouse change and the mothers' similar perceptions.

As a general finding the fathers tended to perceive little negative

TABLE 141

MEAN SCORES MEASURING PERCEIVED CHANGES IN PARENT
SINCE BIRTH OF CHILD

Changes in Mother as Seen by Self			*Changes in Mother as Seen by Husband*	
	Mean	*SD*	*Mean*	*SD*
Blind	9.69	3.2	9.4	3.22
Deaf	7.78	2.50	8.55	2.70
Cerebral Palsy	7.78	3.48	9.03	3.24
Mongoloid	8.86	3.43	8.62	3.57
Organic	9.19	3.46	9.26	3.15

(Higher score indicates more detrimental change)

TABLE 142

MEAN SCORES MEASURING PERCEIVED CHANGES IN PARENT
SINCE BIRTH OF THE CHILD

| | Changes in Father as Seen by Self | | Changes in Father as Seen By Wife | |
	Mean	SD	Mean	SD
Blind	8.88	2.47	8.75	2.44
Deaf	7.06	3.37	9.13	3.02
Cerebral	7.91	2.90	8.68	2.52
Mongoloid	8.37	3.01	8.89	3.09
Organic	8.65	3.31	10.06	3.29

(Higher score indicates more detrimental change)

change to have occurred in their personality since the birth of this child. Fathers in the deaf group rated themselves as least negatively changed among the five groups, and the fathers of the blind group reported the most negative change in themselves. The five groups were quite similar in self-rankings of fathers with most of the negative scoring contributed by items related to less patience, more worry, and more nervousness.

As a total group the fathers tended to perceive more detrimental change in their wives than they had among themselves, except for the blind group who accorded their wives nearly the same rating they had given themselves. The fathers in the organic, deaf and cerebral palsy groups felt that their wives had been considerably more detrimentally affected by the birth of this child than they had been.

The mothers in the deaf and organic groups admitted to more detrimental change than the fathers but the other three groups reflected a similarity in self-ratings. When these means are analyzed to compare the ratings of spouses, the organic and deaf group mothers gave their husbands a higher negative rating of detrimental change than the fathers had accorded to them. In the blind and cerebral palsy groups the fathers ranked their wives as more negatively changed than their wives had rated them. The mongoloid group accorded each other about the same amount of negative change.

Although the total population clustered quite closely on all four possible rankings there are a number of tentative generalizations which might be listed:

1. As a general finding the total population saw themselves and their spouses as having undergone both positive and negative changes since the birth of the handicapped child.

2. Fathers regarded themselves as less negatively affected than mothers.

3. Spouse ratings were split with some mothers seeing greater negative change in fathers and some fathers seeing greater negative change in mothers.

4. The highest extent of negative change was found among the fathers in the organic group as rated by their wives. Similarly the fathers in the organic group saw more negative changes in their wives than any of the other groups of fathers had noted.

5. The fathers and mothers in the deaf group perceived comparatively little change in themselves but each attributed considerably greater change to their spouses.

6. Using the mother's admission of her own rating and a matched perception of her by her husband as a reflection of some accuracy, the mothers in the blind and organic groups manifested the highest amount of negative change.

Commentary on Perception of Change

The treatment of these data has been principally directed toward reflecting group characteristics and the revelation of differences which might be noted between groups. The patterning of perceived changes in personality since the birth of this child is variable within groups and among groups to the extent that only restricted generalizations may be offered. There is enough variation within each group to suggest that this topic is better studied on an individual basis.

It is interesting to note however that the vast majority of couples perceived some degree of detrimental change within themselves and each other since the birth of the handicapped. None of the families attempted to imply that only positive changes had occurred nor that there was no perception of change. None of the parents regarded themselves or their mates as "being the same as before." All indicated that something had changed in their general attitudinal structure.

Whether the changes reported, both negative and positive, can safely be attributed to the advent of the handicapped child into the family is questionable. Although the title of the questionnaire attempted to establish a perceptual set in each parent of rating on the basis of "since the birth of this child," and therefore suggested that either positive or negative changes were somehow associated with attitudes pertaining to the child, there were enough parents who volunteered commentary on this form to introduce a cautionary note in interpreting these findings.

A number of mothers indicated that they had regarded the form as simply referring to a point in time and noted negative or positive change whether or not they felt it was related to the incidence of a handicapped child. One attributed the change as resulting from the "death of his mother"; another dated the change from the time when "his business failed"; another indicated that the negatives were all due to a sexual conflict between husband and wife. Some fathers felt that the negative changes were due to "too many kids around the house."

There can be little doubt that every parent perceived some change. It is unlikely however that such change can simply be attributed to the mechanical incidence of the handicapped child. A composite of events and experiences in the fabric of five or eight years of family living certainly contains some strands and fibers which are derived from adapting to the role of being the parent of a handicapped child. But such an event is only one form of crisis, or one form of stress, which can occur in the lives of parents over a span four to ten years. The crisis of the child is interwoven but not necessarily an isolated cause.

Despite the restrictions placed upon interpretation by this form it is interesting to note that, even within a composite set of reasons, there is a high extent of similarity among 177 families. Sources of marital friction are suggested in perceptual discrepancies between mothers and fathers which might have great significance in individual families.

These findings do suggest that a more profound investigation into this area might prove extremely profitable in delineating a clearer professional picture of the handicapped child.

The general "buckshot approach" employed throughout this study was intended to discover spots where further investigation held promise. The area of changes in attitude which accompany the advent in the child, and the respective dual perceptions of those changes which exist in each parent, certainly deserve further study. The simplicity of the questionnaire employed in this study can only be regarded as a small scratch on the surface of this area. A single study employing more complex and detailed information holds great promise of making a significant contribution to parent psychology.

FATHER PARTICIPATION IN CHILD-REARING

Combining the mother and father responses to questions concerning the participation of the father in diapering, bathing and feeding the infant with responses to questions about the father's role in bedtime and toilet training, and other questions related to activities of the father with this child in recreation, school, motor development, etc., it was possible to devise a four point scale of distribution to indicate high or low levels of participation among the five groups of fathers. Information for such ranking was obtained from both the mother and father interviews (Table 143).

TABLE 143

EXTENT OF PARTICIPATION OF FATHERS IN DAY
BY DAY CHILD-REARING PROCEDURES

	Cerebral Palsy	Organic	Mongoloid	Blind	Deaf
Continuous high-level participation	60%	38%	89%	75%	58%
Only during infancy	6%	5%			9%
When child older but not during infancy	20%	41%	11%	12%	33%
Continuous low-level participation	14%	16%		12%	
	100%	100%	100%	100%	100%

If there was a general pattern of participation in each of the areas investigated, i.e., the father had diapered and fed the infant, put him to bed, helped with toilet, tried to teach, helped with school work, etc., this was classified as continuous high level participation. The fathers of the mongoloid and blind groups dominated this category.

If the protocol indicated that the father was quite active during the infancy of this child but seemed to have progressively diminished, his participation the category of "only during infancy" was employed. A negligible percentage of fathers were placed in that category.

A third possibility existed if the father appeared to become progressively more active as the child grew older but was minimally active during the infancy period. This was particularly true of the fathers in the organic group and about one-third of the deaf group.

Some fathers had to be classified as rarely involved in the child-rearing process according to reports and considered as exhibiting a continuous low level of participation. Several fathers in the cerebral palsy, organic and blind groups were so placed.

On the basis of this composite only a few fathers were currently *not* actively participating in the child-rearing process, with the mongoloid and blind group fathers reported to have been the most consistent through the years.

For the vast majority of these families there was a clear indication that the child-rearing responsibilities were a joint undertaking of both parents. The high percentage of fathers in each of these groups who participated in this study can be taken as further evidence of the fact that the fathers of these children actively participate in their rearing. Whether the father leads or follows, assists or directs, advises or enacts—he is a part of the child-rearing process not only during infancy but throughout the childhood.

A small percentage of the fathers did not become actively involved until the child was older. A very small percentage seem to have dropped out of active relationships after the infant period passed. The small minority who were reported to have been relatively inactive in this respect represent a set of special cases. The explanation for this minority group is obscured.

SPOUSE'S ATTITUDE TOWARD CHILD

During the course of the clinical interview each parent was asked, "What do you feel your husband's (wife's) attitude is toward this child?" This was injected to gain an elaboration on the level of esteem held by each spouse for the other.

Two broad classifications of response were defined from the verbatim responses. Those responses which stated that the spouse was a very good father or mother, that the spouse loved the child dearly, was affectionate and loving, accepted the child or in some manner conveyed an expression of a favorable attitude were identified as "positive."

When the response stated that the parent felt responsible for the child's condition, gave more attention to the child because of the handicap, was disappointed or felt inadequate in dealing with the child, such statements were classified as "negative."

Table 144 reflects a majority expression of a positive attitude on the part of both mothers and fathers in all groups as stated by their spouses. In general the mothers and fathers were about equally kind to one another in their evaluation of the other's attitude. In the cerebral palsy group there was a tendency for more mothers to rate the husbands on the negative side, and among the deaf there tended to be a greater number of mothers rated by their spouses toward the negative side. The greatest extent of positivism was attributed to the mothers of the cerebral palsy group while the mongoloid and deaf mothers showed the least percentage of positivism as a group.

TABLE 144
RATING BY SPOUSE ATTITUDE
BY MOTHERS AND FATHERS

	Cerebral Palsy	Organic	Mongoloid	Blind	Deaf
Percentage positive rating fathers gave to mothers	86%	70%	67%	71%	63%
Percentage positive rating mothers gave to fathers	74%	74%	68%	76%	72%
Percentage negative rating fathers gave to mothers	14%	30%	33%	28%	37%
Percentage negative rating mothers gave to fathers	26%	26%	32%	24%	28%

As a group phenomenon both the husband and the wife presented their spouses in a favorable light on the question of attitude toward this child. While some question might be raised about a parental desire to acquiesce and make favorable statements about their spouses, there were apparently from one fourth to one third of some of the groups who felt no hesitancy about ascribing a negative attitude on the part of their spouse to this child.

The findings reported in this table may almost be taken as a characteristic reflection in these groups. There was a rather consistent finding of 20 to 30 per cent in almost every table who seemed to depart from the majority opinion of any given topic. Careful inspection of the full records of both mothers and fathers suggested that about seventeen couples in the total group could be classified as being in an extreme state of marital crisis with massive evidence of rejection of the child, open hostilities expressed by both mothers and fathers and an obvious state of disagreement apparent at every opportunity. These seventeen families consistently appeared in the minority percentages on issue after issue.

This group, however, did not account for the total one-fifth to one-third who were at variance with the majority throughout the study. Analysis of the records failed to yield any kind of patterning within that minority group. The identity of the families varied from tabulation to tabulation. Item by item, each group had a small percentage who held a different belief but the variance from the majority were not the same parents each time.

Likewise, within this tabulation of perceptions of negative attitudes in spouses, there was no significant incidence of both the mother and father perceiving each other negatively. While this was true for a small number of cases, the understanding of this mutual negativism lies within the dynamics of those individual sets of parents, and cannot be inferred to be characteristic of a minority sample in each of the five groups.

It is of interest to note, however, that the fathers in the cerebral palsy group revealed the lowest incidence of ascribing a negative attitude toward this child on the part of the mothers. The other four groups of fathers rated from 28 to 37 per cent of the wives on the negative side. The mothers in each group had approximately an equalized incidence of regarding the fathers to be negative in his attitude toward this child.

Perhaps the most frequent complaint of the fathers came in the form of criticizing the mother for ignoring the needs of the other children while she catered to the needs of the handicapped child. The greatest complaint of the mothers revolved around the concern for the lack of interest shown by the fathers. Fathers criticized mothers for over-indulgence and mothers criticized fathers for apathy.

Similar complaints were registered in each of the five groups in relatively equal amounts so it cannot be said that this form of criticism is more true of one group than another. When the spouse-critical parents were checked to determine if such criticism was more prevalent among parents of severely handicapped versus moderately handicapped, retarded versus average, boy versus girl, none of the pairings yielded any form of distribution which could be considered meaningful. Instead, it simply seemed to be a matter of individual perception on the part of each parent and may have been influenced to some extent by the presence of the handicapped child, but was more likely a case of critical evaluation regardless of this child.

While the negative perceptions were present, the majority accorded each other a positive attitude.

Use of Formalized Scales

The bulk of the data obtained in this study was obtained from clinical interview and nonstandardized questionnaires designed and developed specifically for this investigation. Two existing standardized instruments held possibilities for providing some objective measures of attitudes and personality among the parents—the Parent Attitude Research Instrument developed by Schaefer and Bell, and the California Psychological Inventory (Gough, 1960). The California test was comparatively new at the time it was included in this investigation. There was some thought at the time that these five populations might make some general contribution to the normative process for this test.

It was also felt that both tests would yield profiles which might then be related to specific responses or clusters of responses on the interview and questionnaire series. Both tests presented some problems in analysis because of errors and omissions in the parental effort to complete the forms. Although 275 mothers actually took the two tests the usable records finally available are somewhat reduced from that number because of errors.

THE PARENT ATTITUDE RESEARCH INVENTORY

Many professional writings both theoretical and experimental have been stimulated by the premise that maternal attitudes are important factors in child-rearing. While studies in the area purport to demonstrate relationships only, there is implicit and often explicit, the notion of causality in the discussion of these relationships. This type of reasoning is particularly noticeable in studies investigating the relationship between maternal attitudes and conditions characterized by emotional disturbance such as schizophrenia wherein the psychological component of the handicapped is most apparent. On the other hand, in those handicapping conditions such as cerebral palsy or blindness wherein the physical defect is manifest, the handicap is generally considered the causal factor in the development of the attitudes.

The present discussion is oriented toward the latter approach under the assumption that if child-rearing attitudes develop in response to the advent of the handicapped child then the intensity with which the attitude is held might be related to the severity of the handicapped. A second hypothesis based on a study by Merrill (1946) suggests itself also.

Merrill observed a control and an experimental group of mother-child pairs as they interacted in a free-play situation. The experimental mothers were told that the children had not shown full realization of their capacities. The control group, who were not exposed to this mild criticism, did not vary the play patterns during a second session. However, the experimental group showed significant increases —directing, interfering, criticizing and structuring changes in activity.

Merrill concluded that middle class mothers tend to react to mild criticism of the adequacy of their children by implementing an authoritarian control of the child's behavior. Hence, in generalizing to the present study, it seems likely that it may not be the severity of handicap but the fact that the child has been diagnosed as different or deficient in some respect which triggers an authoritarian attitudinal pattern on the part of the parent.

A number of limitations existed in the study of the Parental Attitude Research Instrument (PARI). However the target population is defined, whether it be all the handicapped in Milwaukee, or even all the handicapped from only middle class families in Milwaukee, it would be very difficult to argue that these five samples are truly representative of the five subpopulations. In essence these are "hard road samples" or samples determined by availability.

Considerable evidence has accrued to the effect that the universe of parental attitudes toward child-rearing can be parsimoniously described in terms of two orthogonal dimensions. Schaefer's (1959) circumflex model based on factor analysis of the Parental Attitude Research Instrument and the Fels Parent Behavior Scale identifies the two axes as autonomy—control and hostility—love.

Zuckerman's (1958) work with the PARI on diverse groups has indicated an invariant factor structure for this instrument with the two main factors being identified as authoritarian control and hostility rejection.

Oppenheim (1963) at the Maudsley Hospital in London, had developed inventories for child-rearing attitudes and parental behavior. Upon factor-analyzing this data, he found the two main factors, which he identified as autocracy and acceptance, accounted for most of the variance.

A study of Milton (1958) has suggested that the two types of discipline defined by Sears (1957), i.e., object-oriented and love-oriented techniques are closely related to the two attitudinal factors described by Zuckerman and Schaefer. Chorost (1962) in turn has argued convincingly that Aaronfreed's extinction (or assaultive) and induction (guilt-inducing) techniques are constructs similar to those of Sears, Zuckerman and Schaefer.

Finally, Loevinger (1962) in developing her Family Problems Scale, identified the two main item clusters as authoritarian family ideology and conventionality-anxiety. She noted the similarity between these clusters and the two dimensions identified by Zuckerman. A schematic summary of the construct similarity among these workers is shown in the following figure (Fig. 1).

Using this summary of construct similarity an attempt was made to characterize the attitudes of mothers of these five handicap groups. That is, the analysis allowed the placement of each group in one of the four quadrants defined by the two attitudinal dimensions. The

FIGURE 1. Schematic summary of construct similarity.

Shaefer	*Zuckerman*	*Oppenheim*	*Sears*	*Aaronfreed*
I. Autonomy —>control factor	Authoritarian —>control factor	Autonomy factor	>Object oriented techniques	->Extinction techniques
II. Hostility —>love factor	Parental ——>warmth factor	Acceptance factor	>Love oriented techniques	->Induction techniques

instrument which was used to index the attitudinal dimensions was the Parental Attitude Research Instrument.

As an additional point of interest, the five groups were collapsed and broken out into a moderate-severe dichotomy. These two categories were then identified in the two-dimensional space (Fig. 2).

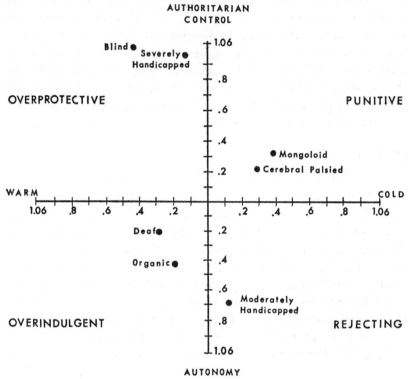

FIGURE 2. Identification of child-rearing attitudes of mothers of selected groups of handicapped children.

In utilizing the proposed two-dimensional schema, the four quadrants align themselves with the four categories of child-rearing attitudes suggested by Schaefer (1959) and Zuckerman (1959). That is, as defined by the interaction between the two dimensions these categories are: punitive attitudes (high authoritarian control and low parental warmth), over-indulgent attitudes (low authoritarian control and low parental warmth), and over-protective attitudes (high authoritarian control and high parental warmth).

Since this model has not been used to differentiate between attitudes of parents of handicapped children, hypotheses-making did not seem appropriate. Rather, the intent was straightforward description with post hoc speculation occurring later. Medical diagnosis determined the placement of the children in the various categories. In addition, the medical person rated the severity of the handicap in terms of functional impairment along a mild-moderate-severe continuum. Independent ratings by two psychologists of the children on a five-point scale in ten areas of functioning had yielded a bimodal total score distribution which coincided, except for two cases, with the physician's rating of mild-moderate and severe. Thus, on the basis of the physician's ratings, 107 children were considered mildly or moderately handicapped, while seventy were severely handicapped.

Method

The Parental Attitude Research Instrument, a Likert-type test developed by Schaefer and Bell (1958) was administered to the mothers in small groups of five to ten people. As a result of a preceding interview, the set of the mothers was towards their handicapped child. To obtain measures of the authoritarian dimension, ten scales (2, 4, 10, 11, 12, 15, 16, 18, 19, 20) from the PARI were summed. Other workers (Zuckerman, *et al.*, 1958) as well have found that these scales loaded most heavily and clearly on what has been identified as the authoritarian-control factor. The previous studies and this factor analysis of PARI have also shown that scales 7, 9 and 13 provided the best measure of the warmth of hostility-love dimension.

Results

Previous work done by Zuckerman *et al.* (1958, 1960) and Garfield and Helper (1962) have shown that PARI scores were markedly influenced both by the mother's age and her education. An analysis of these data using a median test demonstrated no significant relationship between these two variables and the warmth scores (X^2 1.00; $X^2 = 4.03$, p .10). However, while age was not significantly related to the authoritarian scores ($X^2 = 5.84$, p .20), the mother's education *was* highly related to the authoritarian scores ($X^2 = 19.36$, p .01). Therefore, in testing differences between authoritarian score means covariance analysis was used to partial out the effects of education.

The warmth and authoritarian scores were not significantly related ($X^2 = 3.29$, p .05).

Table 145 a and b, presents the source table for the analysis of the authoritarian scores when the effects of maternal education had been removed. Differences among the handicapped groups were highly significant ($F = 7.29$, p .01) as was the difference between severity of handicap ($F = 249.31$, p .01). The means shown on the table are adjusted means with the effect of education removed. The common within classes regression coefficient was used for this purpose.

As shown in Table 146 a and b, significant differences were not found in the warmth scores for the handicapped groups nor for the severity breakout.

The group means obtained on the two dimensions were transformed to standard scores using the square root of the error terms as an estimate of the standard deviations. Using these standard scores, each group's position in the two-dimensional space was identified and

TABLE 145
SOURCE TABLE FOR ANALYSIS OF VARIANCE OF
AUTHORITARIAN SCORES WITH EFFECTS OF
MOTHER'S EDUCATION REMOVED

a. *Source*	*df*	*SS*	*MS*	*F*	*P*
Between	4	703	175.8	7.29	<.01
Within	168	4049	24.1		
Total	172	4725			

Adjusted group means:

	Cerebral Palsy	Organic	Mongoloid	Blind	Deaf
	114.3	111.6	115.4	118.7	112.9

b. *Source*	*df*	*SS*	*MS*	*F*	*P*
Between	1	2817	2817.0	249.31	<.01
Within	171	1935	11.3		
Total	172*	4752			

Adjusted group means:

	Mild/Moderate	Severe
	110.4	118.6

TABLE 146

SOURCE TABLE FOR ANALYSIS OF VARIANCE
OF WARMTH SCORES

a. *Source*	*df*	*SS*	*MS*	*F*	*P*
Between	4	385	96.3	2.67	$<.05$
Within	173	6231	36.0		
Total	177	6616			

Group means:

	Cerebral Palsy	Organic	Mongoloid	Blind	Deaf
	44.2	41.9	44.4	40.3	41.0

b. *Source*	*df*	*SS*	*MS*	*F*	*P*
Between	1	32	32.0	—	NS
Within	176	6584	37.4		
Total	177	6616			

Group means:

	Mild/Moderate	Severe
	43.1	42.2

entered in the respective quadrants as shown in Figure 1. Within the schema proposed, and using the labeling system of Schaefer and Zuckerman, it would seem that the mothers comprising the five diagnostic and two severity groups were characterized by the following attitudes:

Blind—over-protective attitudes

Deaf—over-indulgent attitudes

Mongoloid—punitive attitudes

Cerebral palsy—punitive attitudes

Organic—over-indulgent attitudes

Mildly handicapped—rejecting attitudes

Severely handicapped—over-protective attitudes

It is questionable, though, how much weight one can put on the quadrant assignment of the groups. The spread along the warmth axis was minimal so that a slight shift in the point of intersection due to, for instance, inclusion of a group of normals or emotionally disturbed in such an analysis, could easily result in a different quadrant designation for these five groups.

However, if one considers the authoritarian dimension alone, important differences and similarities did exist between the groups. For instance, a strong authoritarian orientation characterized the mothers of the severely handicapped. Furthermore, when compared to the deaf and organic mothers, the mothers of the cerebral palsy, mongoloid and blind groups also showed a strong authoritarian orientation toward child-rearing practices.

Using a method suggested by Cox, significant differences were found between the deaf and organic as a group, and between the mongoloid and cerebral palsy as a group, as well as between the latter group and the blind.

Discussion

In line with the original intent of the analysis, the child-rearing attitudes of mothers of five groups of handicapped children were located in the four quadrants defined by the interaction of the two attitudinal dimensions of authoritarian-control and of warmth. However, to develop or explicate the differential identification of the maternal attitudes seems a little premature, for the differences among the groups on the warmth dimension were minimal. Thus, minor variations from the present study, such as an increased number or inclusion of another group, could easily shift the interjection point on the warmth axis, thereby changing the quadrant identification of the present groups. This qualification regarding the five handicapping conditions applies equally well when the quadrant identification of the moderate and severe breakout is considered.

Another limitation in the interpretation of this data is apparent from recent work with the PARI by Zuckerman and others who have demonstrated that the response sets of social desirability and acquiescence exert a marked influence on scores obtained on this instrument. These effects were not handled in any way in this study, so the findings must be interpreted with this limitation in mind.

The study has shown, however, that the major differences of opinion concerning child-rearing among the groups examined was clearly in relation to the amount of authoritarian-control condoned by the mothers. The most authoritarian attitudes were evidenced by mothers of blind, followed by the mongoloid, cerebral palsied and deaf, with the mothers of the organics having the least authoritarian attitudes. When the five groups were combined and dichotomized into mothers of the moderately and of the severely handicapped, the mothers of severely handicapped held by far the more authoritarian attitudes.

Consideration of these findings leads to the conclusion that attitudes of authoritarian control in child-rearing may vary as a function of the degree to which a child's capacities are perceived to deviate from the normal. The manner in which five groups positioned themselves along the authoritarian continuum suggested that the genesis of this perception may lie in the visibility of the handicap. Since a more subtle perceptual definition of deviation can occur as a result of semantic labeling, the diagnostic endeavors of the professional might well be considered a factor also, particularly when one moves into the area of emotional disturbances.

It must be admitted that the literature provides but equivocal experimental support for the position that perceived inadequacies in the functioning of the child issues in extreme attitudes of authoritarian control. Margolis (1961) found no significant differences in the PARI performance of a group of mothers of chronic asthmatic children and a comparable group. On the other hand, Moll and Darley (1960), using the PARI, concluded that mothers of articulatory-impaired children had high standards and were more critical of their children's functioning than were mothers of non-speech-impaired children. In addition, Oppenheim (1963), using an inventory other than the PARI, found that mothers of psychotic and mongoloids were less autocratic than a comparable group of normal mothers.

In the area of emotional disturbances, Zuckerman *et al.* (1958) found no differences in authoritarian control scores between mothers of schizophrenics and a control group of mothers. However, Tolor and Rafferty (1963) in replicating Zuckerman's study concluded that mothers of hospitalized patients expressed more authoritarian attitudes than mothers of normals. Zuckerman, Barrett, Bragiel (1960) found that the authoritarian factor was not related to a child's diagnosis within a clinic group, and also did not yield marked differences between clinic parents and a control group of parents.

While the extent of relationship between attitudes and overt behavior remains unclear, a laboratory-type study by Merrill provides support for the contention that perceived inadequacies in a child result in an increase in controlling and interfering behavior on the part of the mother.

In our culture, at the present time, authoritarianism as opposed to autonomy in child-rearing tends to be a negative attribute. Yet one wonders how much choice the mother of the severely handicapped child has with regard to her child-rearing problems. Meeting the needs of such a child she must of necessity be controlling and structuring so that the child might, at a minimum, survive. It is perhaps a truism that activities persistently engaged in are valued insofar as they become a part of the individual's self-perception. Thus, after some four to ten years of implementing the regime of child-rearing characterized by structuring and directing the activities of a severely handicapped child, one would expect that items describing this type of behavior would not be completely denied by these mothers in spite of some cultural pressure to do so.

THE CALIFORNIA PSYCHOLOGICAL INVENTORY

At an early stage in the analysis of the data for this project, it was realized that the findings would not be amenable to an unambiguous interpretation. For instance, given a clearly defined child-rearing practice, it was very unlikely that this practice would have a uniform effect *on all* childrens' behavior, in *all* situations as administered by *all* mothers (or fathers). Furthermore, it was very apparent that the survey or descriptive nature of the project would not allow a *partialling out* of the influences of these various factors in a precise manner.

Also, since the child-rearing practices were not determined in fact, nor even specified situationally in most questions, one was left with a verbal description in response to a general question. That the personality structure of the respondent with its attendant needs, wishes and desires would account for much of the variance in the content of the responses seemed like a reasonable surmise. It was of some interest then to ascertain, in at least a general way, some notion of the similarities and differences which might exist in the personality structure of the respondents.

The California Psychological Inventory (Gough, 1960) was administered to 246 mothers and 124 fathers. A descriptive analysis of the profiles of the 370 parents will be given. Neither *a priori* nor *post priori* hypotheses were made. Rather, descriptive comments based on the results of a discriminant analysis of the 370 profiles comprise the body of this section, with inferential hyperbole being minimal.

Analysis

The raw scores obtained on the eighteen CPI scales were transformed to T-scores so that both male (fathers) and female (mothers) profiles could be compared in terms of a common metric. The T-scores were then punched on IBM cards with one subject per card. These data were analyzed using the Control Data Corporation 1604 computer in the Numerical Analysis Laboratory at the University of Wisconsin. The program used (CO-OP ID: G6 WIS DISCR) computed the statistics required for discriminant analysis. The print-out of this routine comprised the following:

1. Covariance matrices for total and within groups.
2. Mean of each variable for each group.
3. Discriminant function for each group.
4. Matrix of D-squares, one value for each pair of groups, and
5. An associated matrix of F values to test the significance of differences between groups.
6. The discriminant function of each individual for each group.
7. The distribution of the number of individuals classified into each group.
8. An overall test of lambda.
9. A test of the lambda for each variable.

The approximate chi-square and F tests of significance are those developed by Rao (1952) as reported by Sampson (1962).

Results

Since the focus was upon the discrimination of many groups with multiple variates (CPI scales) an overall test of mean values for the several populations was needed before additional analysis would be warranted. The obtained lambda of .508 yielded an F-ratio of 1.51 which with 162 and 2.795 df was significant at better than the .01 level. A test for each variable across all groups is shown in Table 147. Significant F-ratios were found on only two scales, sociability (p .01) and femininity (p .05).

TABLE 147

TEST OF LAMBDA FOR EACH OF THE 18 CPI *SCALES (df 9.343)*

Scale	Lambda	F-ratio
1. Dominance	.974	1.01
2. Capacity for status	.970	1.18
3. Sociability	.920	3.32*
4. Social presence	.983	0.65
5. Self-acceptance	.962	1.49
6. Sense of well-being	.962	1.50
7. Responsibility	.955	1.78
8. Socialization	.978	0.84
9. Self-control	.987	0.52
10. Tolerance	.963	1.47
11. Good impression	.992	0.32
12. Communality	.982	0.69
13. Achievement via conformance	.981	0.75
14. Achievement via independence	.969	1.21
15. Intellectual efficiency	.991	0.34
16. Psychological-mindedness	.956	1.77
17. Flexibility	.960	1.59
18. Femininity	.941	2.39†

*significant at .01 level
†significant at .05 level

Inspection of Table 148 indicates that the variability among the groups on these two scales was a function not of diagnostic groups but of sex. As would be expected mothers scored higher on femininity ($\overline{X}$=55.4) than did the fathers ($\overline{X}$=50.7) with both parents scoring somewhat higher than the general mean of 50.0. On the other hand, the fathers scored a little higher ($\overline{X}$=47.8) than did the mothers ($\overline{X}$=44.7) on sociability with both groups being significantly lower than the general mean (allowing for SEm of .63 and .90 with group Ns of 246 and 124).

As pointed out previously, the main concern of this section was to indicate, if possible, similarities and differences in the personality patterns of the parents. The generalized distance function (D^2) developed by Mahalanobis (cited in Rao, 1952) provides an index of the resemblance between the profiles of two groups. One can thus speak of a generalized distance between two groups and compare the distances between any two pairs of groups. It is possible therefore to sort out clusters of groups in terms of their closeness in what, mathematically, is conceived as a multidimensional space.

The generalized distances separating the profiles of all ten groups (mothers and fathers) are shown in Table 149. Examination of the table indicates that all the significant and most of the near significant

TABLE 148

MEAN T-SCORES ON C.P.I. SCALES OF MOTHERS AND FATHERS OF HANDICAPPED GROUPS

CPI Scales	Cerebral Palsy		Organic		Mongoloid		Blind		Deaf	
	M	F	M	F	M	F	M	F	M	F
1. Do	46.7	52.8	46.4	54.9	44.3	52.3	44.4	43.9	48.1	52.5
2. Cs	44.6	48.1	45.4	51.6	42.3	50.7	40.0	45.5	43.0	49.4
3. Sy	46.7	48.3	47.5	50.4	43.3	49.6	41.7	41.4	44.1	49.1
4. Sp	47.2	52.1	47.6	53.3	44.5	52.1	42.4	48.1	45.6	55.1
5. Sa	48.0	54.5	47.9	54.9	46.2	52.7	44.7	49.0	48.7	59.1
6. Wb	47.6	49.4	48.8	52.6	45.9	54.9	45.9	48.9	47.8	53.0
7. Re	48.9	51.5	49.2	50.7	52.8	48.6	47.3	44.6	50.5	47.5
8. Po	48.1	49.5	46.5	48.6	48.1	52.5	48.5	50.5	47.5	50.0
9. Sc	48.8	50.7	50.4	50.6	50.5	52.0	51.0	47.6	51.0	44.8
10. To	46.0	50.0	47.6	49.0	47.0	48.4	43.6	45.5	49.0	45.7
11. Gi	46.1	48.8	47.5	49.5	45.9	48.5	46.6	43.9	46.0	45.0
12. Cm	50.8	52.9	49.9	52.0	49.6	55.1	51.8	50.9	50.9	58.0
13. Ac	44.4	50.8	46.0	50.3	44.7	52.5	45.1	44.9	45.9	47.3
14. Ai	47.8	53.7	51.7	52.9	50.1	52.5	47.9	46.0	52.6	47.9
15. Ie	44.6	49.0	45.3	49.6	42.5	49.8	42.2	43.5	46.1	48.6
16. Py	46.7	51.7	51.0	53.5	48.9	55.3	43.9	48.1	50.4	51.2
17. Fx	49.5	48.9	50.5	49.7	52.3	50.9	42.4	50.0	47.2	42.3
18. Fe	54.6	52.1	56.4	51.4	59.0	52.5	54.7	52.9	52.4	44.7

TABLE 149
D-SQUARES FOR EACH PAIR OF GROUPS FOR MOTHERS AND FATHERS OF FIVE GROUPS OF HANDICAPPED CHILDREN

		Organic		Blind		Deaf		Mongoloid		Cerebral Palsy	
		M	F	M	F	M	F	M	F	M	F
Organic	M	—	1.39*	1.42	2.61	1.14	6.05*	0.88	2.38*	0.56	1.68*
	F		—	2.13	2.03	1.57	2.94	2.61*	1.00	1.43†	0.64
Blind	M			—	2.84	0.85	5.37†	2.15	3.65	0.96	1.67
	F				—	2.88	3.45	3.10	1.92	1.90	2.44
Deaf	M					—	4.80†	1.58	3.28†	1.09	0.97
	F						—	7.70*	3.54	5.09*	3.32
Mongoloid	M							—	3.98*	0.95	2.24*
	F								—	2.71*	2.03
Cerebral Palsy	M									—	1.54†
	F										—

*significant at .01 level
†significant at .05 level

D²s are those indexing the distances between the profiles of the mothers and of the fathers. Within a given sex group, no significant D²s were found. It is apparent that the mothers as a group presented considerably more homogeneous personality profiles than did the fathers. Furthermore, consideration of the fathers' D² only, indicates that the group with the most divergent profile were the fathers of a deaf child.

Conclusions

An analysis was undertaken of the patterning of T-scores obtained on the eighteen scales of the CPI by groups of mothers and fathers of children with one of five handicapping conditions. The salient results were considered to be the following:

1. When compared with the general population on which the test was standardized, both the mothers and the fathers of a handicapped child scored significantly lower on the sociability scale. This conclusion must be considered tentative since equated groups of parents of a nonhandicapped child were not administered the test under the same circumstances. However, the large divergence from the expected score does suggst that these ten parent groups tend *not* to be the "kind of person who enjoys group activities and likes to be with and work with other people" (Gough, 1960). Furthermore, the mothers demonstrated considerably less of this trait than did the fathers.

2. When group personality profiles over the eighteen CPI scales were indexed by the generalized distance function, sex differences accounted for two rather distinct profile clusters, i.e., mothers and fathers.

3. Mothers demonstrated more homogeneous personality profiles than did fathers. Fathers of a deaf child possessed the most divergent personality profile among the fathers groups.

Chapter 16

THE HANDICAPPED RANKING SCALE*

THERE IS PROBABLY more awareness of child handicaps among the general citizenry during the past several years than at any other time in history. The following represents an attempt to study one aspect of this awareness and may hopefully inspire other investigators to probe more deeply. The parents of handicapped children are the focus of this discussion.

Clinical counseling experiences with the parents of handicapped children during the past ten years at the Easter Seal Center in Milwaukee have consistently revealed comparative expressions from parents on the topic of other forms of handicap than the one represented in their child. Parents have expressed sympathetic utterances for mothers observed to have children in wheelchairs, or whose children are amputees, and so forth. The comments were always of the nature of "I'm glad I don't have that problem." These and other comments seemed to suggest that these mothers held some form of unspecified ranking attitude as they considered their plight in relation to other mothers.

When a full-scale investigation of child-rearing patterns among parents of handicapped children was initiated in 1959, the research team decided to devise a simple ranking scale to be included among the general set of questionnaires in the investigation sequence which might reflect this presumed unconscious ranking process observed in clinical counseling. The scale was devised by the author on a simple, straightforward basis by listing ten handicapping conditions and providing associated spaces for indicating a numerical rank.

The terms epilepsy, brain-injury, mental retardation, blindness, deafness, polio, diabetes, cerebral palsy, heart trouble, and mental illness were selected because they represented labels with which the

---

*This chapter appeared as an article in *The American Journal of Public Health,* December 10, 1965. It is reprinted here with their permission.

parents might be expected to be familiar. More or less serious conditions bearing polysyllabic medical labels were eliminated from consideration on the basis that the parents may never have become acquainted with such semantics.

The project on child-rearing patterns included sample populations of mothers and fathers of children with cerebral palsy, brain damage, mongolism, deafness, and blindness. Consequently, the five terms related to the problems of their children had to be listed. The other five terms were arbitrarily selected.

Three basic questions were of interest in asking for the rankings:
What differences in rankings might be obtained from five groups of parents representing varying handicaps?

What ranking would the parents assign to their child's problem?

What differences might exist between mothers and fathers on this scale?

In the course of reviewing the first set of parent data from this form the research staff expressed interest in the possibility of sampling a wide variety of populations for comparative reference. What might be the relative positions of these handicaps among a group of parents of nonhandicapped children? What differences might exist among various professional groups whose daily work centered around providing services to handicapped children? What differences could be ascertained in the relative rankings of students who are preparing for professional therapy or teaching, and those who are experienced professionals in the same fields?

Other questions were suggested by the possibilities of multiple samplings. What variance exists between parents of a particular type of handicapped child and those professionals who work with such a child?

To pursue the answers to these questions the scale was administered to occupational, physical, and speech therapists actively employed and to college students preparing for these professions, to public health nurses, registered nurses and nursing students, and to various special education teachers, elementary and secondary teachers, and respective undergraduates. Female undergraduates in a liberal arts college, a group of Catholic nuns, optometrists, psychology students, mothers and fathers of nonhandicapped children, and two groups of professional fund raisers and program planners were also included. In all, twenty-two reasonably homogeneous groups were obtained.

Procedure for Administering the Scale

The methods of administration in all cases were similar. Directions were read aloud to all groups. Directions for clarification were all met with the same response from the examiner—that the ten conditions be ranked in severity according to each subject's perception.

No effort was made to ascertain the reasoning of the subjects in setting the rank order. As much of a unified perceptual set as was felt possible was obtained by the common directions. Analysis was directed toward differences and similarities among groups, and variations in perception were considered as chance factors in a large sampling.

Difficulties in administration of the scale were most frequently encountered in the professional groups where the sophistication of training and background occasioned much discomfort in reacting to diagnostic labels without benefit of various nuances of severity, multiplicity, and complexity. Despite some discomfort, all of the professional groups complied with the instructions. Since the reaction was a common one across all professional groups, regardless of specific discipline, the perceptual dilemma was regarded as a uniform factor.

None of the nonsophisticated groups—parents, nonprofessional, college students, or others—offered any objections to complying with directions, as stated.

With the exception of approximately twenty-five mothers and fathers, who, because of interview schedules performed the ranking scale in individual sessions, all other participants completed the scales in a group session. The cooperation of various instructors was obtained to allow undergraduate and graduate college students to accomplish the scale during class periods.

The scales were obtained from all practicing professional groups as a part of one of their annual professional group meetings. The mothers and fathers of nonhandicapped children were brought into the project through PTA meetings. Parents of handicapped children were those participating in the Child-Rearing Practices study, and they completed the ranking scale during a group session (five to ten parents) along with a battery of other pencil and paper forms related to the general study.

The following directions were read aloud to the group: *"Ten handicapping conditions of childhood are listed. Please rank these, from one to ten, according to your own feelings on the basis of severity. Which handicap do you feel is the most severe problem a child could have? Which handicap do you feel is second most serious? Which do you feel is the third most serious, and so forth. Consider only the child and his problems in adjustment."*

GENERAL POPULATION SAMPLE AND FINDINGS

In addition to the 189 mothers and 122 fathers of handicapped children, the ranking scales were obtained from twenty-two reasonably homogeneous groups. The total sample consisted of 2,375 scales obtained principally from people residing in the state of Wisconsin. Whether or not similar findings might be obtained from other geographical areas is open to question.

A criterion of 90 per cent, or more, responding in a given way to any group, was set for the judgment of a within-group rank. The same criterion was set when all groups were combined.

The general findings indicate that the total sample of approximately 2,400 individuals are in close accord in defining their judgment of the relative severity of these ten handicapping conditions. The rank order of severity, as judged by the total sample, is as follows:

1. Cerebral palsy
2. Mental retardation
3. Mental illness
4. Brain-injury
5. Blindness
6. Epilepsy
7. Deafness
8. Polio
9. Heart trouble
10. Diabetes

The first five ranks and the last two are clearly established, but blindness, epilepsy, and polio are interchangeable at the sixth, seventh, and eighth level between the parents of handicapped children and all other groups. There seems to be little doubt that polio is no longer regarded as the dire threat it once was, and that both diabetes and heart trouble are considered as relatively insignificant problems in the perceptions of this study population.

Parents of Handicapped Children

There was a marked concordance among all of the mothers and fathers of handicapped children in ranking cerebral palsy, mental retardation and mental illness as the first, second, and third most severe problems which could be inflicted upon a child.

It is interesting to note that the parents of deaf children and the parents of blind children tend to view their own child's problem as relatively mild in comparison to their perception of levels of seriousness. Although the parents of cerebral palsied, organically damaged, and mongol children seem to feel that someone else's problems are more serious than their own, they still rank their own problem relatively high in seriousness.

Parents of Nonhandicapped Children

The rankings of 35 fathers and 323 mothers of nonhandicapped children were obtained from PTA type groups (Table 150). Fathers gave the first four positions to cerebral palsy, mental illness, mental retardation and blindness, while the mothers gave the first four positions to cerebral palsy, mental retardation, mental illness and brain-injury.

Although the number of fathers of nonhandicapped children represents a small group for comparison with the 122 fathers of handicapped, the total group of fathers (157) were concordant in their rankings. The mothers of the handicapped (189) showed a slight difference in rank order from the mothers of the nonhandicapped, giving first place to cerebral palsy versus third rank among the mothers of the nonhandicapped, the first four places were given to the same handicaps in both groups (512).

A high level of agreement in the ranking of the first four handicaps and the last four handicaps was found in the combined groups of 736 mothers and fathers.

TABLE 150

FIRST, SECOND, AND THIRD RANKINGS AMONG MOTHERS
AND FATHERS OF HANDICAPPED CHILDREN AND RANKED
POSITION OF THEIR OWN CHILD'S HANDICAP

	First	*Second*	*Third*	*Rank of Own Child's Problem*
Mothers of cerebral palsied	Mental retardation	Cerebral palsy	Mental illness	2
Fathers of cerebral palsied	Mental illness	Mental retardation	Cerebral palsy	3
Mothers of organics	Cerebral palsy	Mental retardation	Mental illness	4
Fathers of organics	Cerebral palsy	Brain injury	Mental retardation	2
Mothers of mongols	Cerebral palsy	Brain injury	Mental retardation	3
Fathers of mongols	Cerebral palsy	Mental retardation	Brain injury	2
Mothers of deaf	Mental retardation	Cerebral palsy	Brain injury	6
Fathers of deaf	Mental retardation	Brain injury	Cerebral palsy	6
Mothers of blind	Mental retardation	Mental illness	Brain injury	5
Fathers of blind	Mental illness	Mental retardation	Brain injury	5

Teachers' Groups

A total sampling of 594 persons, active teachers and undergraduates in the field of education, was asked to complete the Handicap Ranking Scale. As indicated in Table 151, the sample consisted of seven different groups. Actively employed special and secondary teachers considered mental illness as the most serious handicap a child could have. Elementary teachers were more impressed with brain-injury and cerebral palsy, and relegated mental illness to third rank in their scale.

Undergraduates, in both elementary and secondary education, seemed to be equally concerned about cerebral palsy and mental illness. Teachers of mentally retarded and teachers of cerebral palsied ranked the child problem with which they are most intimately concerned in fourth position, bearing out again the contention that intimate, first-hand knowledge of the problem tends to diminish the perception of relative severity.

When the total sampling of teachers was considered as a single

TABLE 151
FIRST FOUR RANKINGS AMONG TEACHER GROUPS

	No				
Orthopedic teachers	24	BI	MI	MR	CP
Elementary teachers	147	BI	CP	MI	MR
Elementary undergraduates	170	CP	MI	BI	MR
Secondary education undergraduates	53	MI	CP	BI	MR
Secondary teachers	104	MI	CP	BI	B
Graduate students in education	37	CP	MI	B	BI
Teachers of MR	59	MI	BI	CP	MR
For all teachers	594	MI	CP	BI	MR
For elementary employed	147	BI	CP	MI	MR
For secondary teachers	104	MI	CP	BI	B
For special teachers	83	MI	BI	CP	MR
For elementary and secondary students	200	CP	MI	BI	MR

group, mental illness was judged to be the most severe handicap with cerebral palsy, brain-injury and mental retardation following in that order. Educators as a group appeared to be far more impressed with the relative severity of mental illness than were any of the other groups in this study.

The intensive emphasis on emotional disturbance which has been promoted in educational periodicals, convention programming, seminars, lectures, inservice training meetings, and the like, during the past five years, may account for this heightened perception of severity. It may also be that increased sensitivity in this area has led to the recognition of more children in American classrooms with emotional disturbance.

Nursing Groups

Ranking forms were obtained from 295 registered nurses, public health nurses, and nursing students. It was felt that this population represented a particular form of sensitivity to handicap problems among children. The registered nurses were all active in pediatric services in Milwaukee hospitals and came in frequent contact with the ten types of disabilities. The public health nurses in their home visits became personally aware of such conditions at a preschool level, or for those children who might be so severely involved as to preclude school acceptance. The student nurses were all in training at Milwaukee Children's Hospital where all of these problems are daily occurrences.

In general, the rankings of the first five positions were essentially similar to those of the total study sample (Table 152). For some reason, which at the moment defies explanation, registered nurses and public health nurses introduced blindness into third position in their rankings. No other group ranked blindness higher than fourth. Their younger "sisters"—the student nurses—ranked blindness in the fifth position in consonance with the general rankings for all subjects. This was particularly interesting in view of the fact that these were two totally different groups of women.

TABLE 152

FIRST FOUR RANKINGS OF NURSING GROUPS

	No				
Student nurses	135	CP	BI	MI	MR
Registered nurses	99	CP	BI	B	MI
Public health nurses	61	CP	BI	B	MI
Total	295				

Professional Therapists

In the general field of child rehabilitation, the three therapeutic disciplines of physical, occupational, and speech therapy occupy traditional team roles. These professionals, working in child therapy clinics, are most familiar with the complexities in child development occasioned by some handicap and represent a professional group which might be expected to have an essentially uniform perceptual set when requested to establish a rank order of seriousness. Their formal academic training and their internship affiliations expose them to extensive lecture and practical coverage of child problems.

The 235 therapists who responded to this study represent a sampling of fourteen different universities in terms of origin of academic background, fifty-one different clinical settings in terms of present operational practice, and twelve different states in terms of geographical location.

The inspection of the ranking scales for the total therapist group shows a surprising agreement on the first and second ranking for the four groups listed in Table 153. While there is a slight variation

TABLE 153

FIRST FOUR RANKINGS OF THERAPIST GROUPS

	No				
Physical therapists	20	BI	CP	MR	MI
Occupational therapists	59	BI	CP	MI	MR
Speech therapists	83	BI	CP	MR	MI
Student speech therapists	73	BI	CP	MI	MR
Total	235				

among the groups on the question of third and fourth rank, the findings for the total group show a consistency in the assignment of the four highest levels: brain-injury, cerebral palsy, mental retardation, and mental illness.

In general, one might expect that the neuromuscular problems of the cerebral palsied child represents the highest demand on a day-by-day basis for these professionals to exercise the knowledge of their discipline, with the problems manifest in the brain-injured, retarded and emotionally disturbed being principally on a behavioral level. In recent years, the general problems of these three types of children have increasingly been incorporated into the active caseloads of the child-therapy clinics, and the therapists have been challenged to devise techniques within their own disciplines for meeting the needs of the children. In consideration of the major emphasis recorded in the literature, on the problems of hyperactivity, impulsivity, distractibility, and so forth, in the brain-injured children, the number one rank may well represent the dilemma of all of these professionals in their day-by-day contact with the organic child.

Miscellaneous Groups

Rankings were elicited from 315 students at a private, parochial college for young women, ranging from the freshmen to the senior year group. The students ranked mental retardation (second) as more serious than did the total population (fourth), but their first four choices were in agreement with all other groups.

From the same school, eighty-eight Catholic nuns submitted rankings which were highly consistent with the order of the total group, except for the ranking of epilepsy in fourth place. Since no other group ranked epilepsy any higher than sixth on the scale, this represented a specialized finding. It is not possible to indulge in any speculations related to this discordant rank.

Four other small homogeneous groups were included in the final tabulations: thirty-two practicing optometrists from the state of Wisconsin; forty-two staff members of the National Society for Crippled Children and Adults; fifty-one staff members of the United Cerebral Palsy Association, and fifty-five male junior and senior undergraduate students majoring in psychology at two local universities. For these four groups, the ratings were consistent with those of the total population.

SUMMARY

Analysis of the rankings for the total population of nearly 2,500 subjects indicates a consensus on severity. A surprisingly small amount of variance was encountered between and within groups. There is good reason to believe that the findings would be relatively similar throughout the population.

If this sample is viewed as tentative evaluation of the manner in which society generally grades the severity of certain childhood handicaps, there seems to be an expression that the child with cerebral palsy is perceived as being most in need of help. Why mental retardation, as a distinctive entity, is ranked in fourth position in the perception of the public according to these findings remains obscure.

At this point, only speculations can be expressed. The ranking of polio in sixth position appears to be consonant with a general diminution of anxiety and dread in relation to this disease since the advent of the vaccines. The American public may now be expressing a readiness for an educational approach on cerebral palsy, brain-injury, mental illness, and mental retardation which might be explored intensively to the advantage of research and programming in these areas.

A number of speculations may be offered on a post hoc basis from the data at hand as follows:

1. Intimate regular contact with a specific disability group, as in ordinary, daily family life, or through therapeutic contact in a clinic or school setting, appears to diminish the relative severity of that disability in the eyes of the perceiver. The oppor-

tunity to live with the problem, either professionally or parentally, softens the perception.

2. The clinical finding, derived from parent counseling experience, which indicated the possibility that parents of handicapped children perceive other child handicaps as more severe than those of their own children, is tentatively confirmed in these data. If the true perceptual set of the parents might be divined on a post hoc basis, it is possible that parental rankings of severities were based upon thoughts which might be stated as, "I know what my child's problem is, and what it is like to live with it, but some other unknown problem might be more difficult to manage than the one I have." There is an old saying that "the grass on the other side of the mountain always looks greener," which does not seem to hold true in terms of perception of severity in other disabled children.

3. The rankings of professionals may well have been determined by the relative ease with which each group managed a specific disability child in clinical or classroom practice, i.e., children who were most difficult for them to manage were perceived as more serious than those whom they managed with comfort by virtue of experience, training and/or inclination. Despite the instructional set to define the rankings in terms of the child, it seems entirely possible that the rankings are more properly a reflection of the "capability perception" of the respondent.

Several tentative implications arise from these data. First, familiarity with a given handicap by virtue of living in close contact with it softens the perception of seriousness and may bring about a higher level of acceptance. The tendency to segregate handicapped children, clinically and educationally, may unknowingly serve to maximize severity perception among the normal population. Greater efforts to integrate these children into normal groupings at all levels may soften the negative societal perception of deviation.

Second, further exploration in the area of parental perception to uncover underlying motivations and attitudes guiding the relegation of their child's own handicap to lesser rank looms as a promising vein of investigation.

Third, the further probing of the public health nurses' and the registered nurses' discrepant ranking of blindness might reveal some interesting findings.

Fourth, these data suggest that the further study of perception of deviation among various social groups appears laden with all sorts of possibility for a significant contribution to the full understanding of disability on the American scene.

Chapter 17

SUMMARY: CRITIQUE AND A PROPOSAL

A BROAD SURVEY HAS been made of child-rearing practices among parents of handicapped children. Many areas have been covered and a number have been omitted. The data were obtained from two sources, a lengthy clinical interview and a series of group administered questionnaires. The data were obtained from a middle class population of mothers and fathers whose handicapped children ranged in age between four and ten years old. Five populations, cerebral palsy, organic, mongoloid, blind and deaf comprised the sample.

The data which have been presented allow for two forms of observation. On the one hand, the findings suggest some common behaviors which seem to characterize the total population studied, irrespective of the nature of the child's handicap and his or her intellectual level. On the other hand, some observations can be made on specific disability groups wherein a particular behavior seems more pronounced than among other groups. First, to the general observations.

GENERAL OBSERVATIONS

1. *There was a general tendency towards similarity in child-rearing practices among these five groups with only scattered evidence of variations which might be attributed to the nature of the child's handicap.*

This finding suggests several possible explanations. First, some consideration must be given to the possibility that the phrasing and selection of questions in both the group questionnaire sequences and the clinical interview were lacking in the sensitiveness required to call forth the differences which might exist.

Secondly, one must consider the possibility that no actual differences exist between these five groups on the question of child-rearing practices. Those who are clinically convinced that a difference is

[341]

inevitable will be inclined to be critical of the investigative approach. The data of the study, however, seem to clearly demonstrate that all these parents went about the business of child-rearing in the same manner regardless of the handicap of their child.

2. *Most of the differences which were found between and within groups was felt to be due to dynamic factors related to parent personalities rather than to the fact that the mother or father were parents of a specific type of handicapped child.*

Dotted throughout the study is a variable incidence of difference ranging from 15 to 35 per cent of the parents in each group who reported a different technique from the other parents in their own group and in other groups. On certain types of practices the differences were obviously reality-oriented and would be inevitable for anyone who was charged with rearing a blind child or a severely muscularly involved child. These obvious techniques were not subject to parental interpretation—they were directly related to the child's handicap. When a child is a severe spastic quadriplegic with the involvement carried over to the tongue the mother is forced to a certain form of procedure in feeding regardless of her own desires to initiate a more advanced practice.

Such differences can be classified as reality-oriented and as such are not really pertinent to the differential referred to in this conclusion. When differences occurred which could not be classified as reality-oriented, they were not felt to be related to the fact or nature of the child's handicap but seemed more precisely attributable to a specific parent's attitude toward *this* child or to be a part of the personality organization of an individual parent. The explanation for the difference, since it was usually a minority finding, is more likely to be delineated by a study more directly focussed upon the personality of the parent rather than upon child-rearing practices *per se.*

3 *The general tendency to characterize parents of handicapped children as guilt-ridden, anxiety-laden, overprotective, and rejecting beings is unfortunate. While it is true that such cases exist, the majority of the parents are unduly stigmatized by this generalization.*

Even though this study did not involved a specific effort to ascertain the personal dynamics of each parent, the clinical relationship with these parents before, during and after the study strengthened the conviction that the traditional adjectives which have been applied to these populations are not an inevitable consequence of having a handicapped child. Some parents are burdened with feelings of guilt. Some are overprotective and some reject their children.

To establish an automatic image of this constellation of dynamics sets forth the notion of a one to one ratio castigating all parents before an attempt is made to understand them as individual people. This has the effect of diagnosis without benefit of examination and denies to the parent his individual right to have his own feelings on the matter.

This type of preconceived notion calls forth a preconceived approach to a therapeutic relationship which almost defies the patient to escape from the generalization. It is possible to bear a handicapped child without rejecting him or becoming overprotective or guilt-ridden. Some parents manage to escape such pathology.

4. *In none of the cases was there any evidence that the parents had buried themselves into a social isolation as a result of having a handicapped child. Most of the parents held outside social interests which regularly engaged their time and attention such as clubs, recreational activities, etc. Where this was not true of a particular parent the evidence did not suggest that the limitation of social activity held a significant relationship to the fact that the family contained a handicapped child. Some people are "joiners" and some are "loners."*

In most cases the parents moved about freely in the community engaging in no shameful hiding of the fact that they had a handicapped child. They talked freely to neighbors and relatives about their child. While they made no particular effort to advertise this fact there was also no evidence of hiding. They took the child with them as they moved about the community and explained as was necessary. When clinicians are confronted with parents who have isolated themselves in some form of hermitic containment because they have a handicapped child this is probably an unusual situation and not typical of the reactions represented in this study.

5. *The child-rearing practices employed with these handicapped children did not differ significantly from those used with their siblings.*

There is no manual conveniently available to guide a parent in becoming an effective parent of a handicapped child. For that matter there is no manual available to guide any mother and father to an effective parenthood for any child. These parents defined four sources of child-rearing efficiency and probably voiced the sentiments of all parents.

First, they relied upon their own personal experience as a child-rearer and essentially learned as they went along. Second, they recalled their own upbringing and borrowed liberally from their own parents those techniques which they felt had been meritorious in their own child development. Third, they observed their peers and discussed and copied techniques which other parents seemed to find useful. Finally, as a fourth and least used source some relied upon literature and professional advice.

Since no parent is ever prepared to be a parent of a handicapped child, and since available resources to coach them in a different approach are rare, it is not surprising that they adopt a single child-rearing approach and apply it to all of their children. They may vary language, insistence, time schedules and even expectancies but they do not seem to develop different techniques.

One of the major disappointments incurred in reviewing the present data was the lack of creativity in child-rearing practices. Approximately ninety opportunities were afforded to both mothers and fathers to spell out the manner in which they attempted to solve a particular problem while establishing some pattern of desired behavior. Few parents developed special devices unique to the child's particular motor problem. Few reported any modifications in language, equipment, household furnishings, toys, aids, etc. ingeniously devised to support a special learning in the child. Where devices were reported, these usually were purchasable commercially and were employed by parents in general.

Confronted with children manifesting a variety of perceptual confusions, language deficiencies—both receptive and expressive, various motoric inabilities, etc., the general child-rearing approach reflected in the data is largely one of employing the same techniques with the handicapped child as were used with the normal siblings.

Therapists and teachers take special pride in the matter of finding or designing special devices to motivate the handicapped child, and to facilitate learning by devising some easier way of doing something. Nothing approaching such ingenuity was found among the parents.

The only parents who reported any specialized techniques were those who had participated in a parent education program devoted to exposing parents to special techniques which they might employ in a home setting to aid in their child's learning.

The tentative impression gained from the findings of these parent examples is that the unique complex of the child's handicap does not motivate any special practices. When confronted with a problem involving the handicapped child's daily behavior and learning, the parent appears to rely almost entirely upon techniques employed with their other children.

The factors which may account for this lack are not clear, but it is felt that some consideration must be given to the fact that the general emphasis placed upon the child as a *medical entity* acted as a deterrent to perceiving the child as a learning organism. It appears that parents expect the child to learn in the same manner as other children.

While they make many allowances for the child's inabilities the expectancy for learning is the same. Apparently, if the problem is not solved by employing the same techniques which have proved useful with their other children, they worry about the child's inability, but do not set about the business of trying to teach a desired behavior in a different way.

The fact that so little ingenuity was elicited may well be the fault of the instruments employed and further evaluation may trace this factor to the instrument. However, the frequency with which the parent was asked, "How did you do this?" "What did you do about . . . ?" throughout the interview would be expected to evoke some incidence of ingenious techniques.

Another point which has bearing on this topic is the element of social stress. Each parent faces a certain amount of negative attitude from the society in which they live. Despite the remarkable advancements which have been made on many fronts in American life most of the citizens of this nation have a certain degree of discomfort in the presence of the handicapped and have not yet figured out how to feel in this area. This discomfort is frequently communicated to the parents.

It would hardly seem likely, when one considers the social impact of having a handicapped child, the anxieties which are inevitable attendants upon his development and the many problems which lie in the path of development for any child, that these parents should prove to be models of patience, fortitude and balance. They were little different than other parents. They made it up as they went along.

6. *Parents, generally, seem to be quite naive about modifying their language in keeping with the child's actual ability to process language on a receptive level. They usually give their child credit for understanding a great deal more of their language than is actually the case.*

Although many parents reported that they had to simplify their language in order to reach their child and were in general concordance with diagnostic clinical findings on the presence of a receptive language problem in the child, the modifications which were employed by the parents were trial and error, hit and miss propositions.

As parents were asked to elaborate on their system for modifying language spoken to this child, the general comment was quite similar to a statement made by one mother, "If I see he isn't getting it I try to say it another way and I keep trying until I find a way to say it. I guess most of the time I try to keep it simple." Each parent probably finds his own version of simplicity.

The point of greatest interest centered on the absence of professionally guided techniques. Only a few parents had a significant grasp of the precise difficulties of their child. They held a global impression of difficulties in receiving but could not discuss their child's problem in terms of more or less difficulty when the household was noisy, more or less difficulty if the communique consisted of more than a sentence, more or less difficulty in terms of speed of delivery, etc.

The professional appraisal of receptive language problems in children frequently becomes a comprehensive task of precise delineation of types of errors, types of constructions which pose the greatest difficulty, etc. Clinicians working in language therapy must focus on specific areas of dysfunction—not simply upon the global difficulty in reception. In the course of doing this they have devised many different techniques of modifying expressive language in order to communicate with the child or the patient. These techniques have proven to be effective in economically resolving the receptive dilemma of the problem-receiver.

If the comments of the parents in this study are considered to be representative of the general state of affairs in this area, it is clear that the professionals have not transmitted these effective techniques to the practical laboratory of the parent in the home. In the critical formative language years, when the communication pattern is vital in the establishment of child-rearing practices, the parent seems to operate without benefit of the research and clinical "know-how" which the professional clinician possesses. There would be little argument on the question of the primacy of language in parent-child interactions and all professionals would undoubtedly score the expressive practice of the parent and the receptive level of the child as an extremely critical component in building communication patterns within the home.

It seems imperative, therefore, that knowledgeable specialists in language development and communicative efficiency must address themselves more directly to the language of child-rearing as a significant area of concern. While much has been written about this general field, the delineation of effective patterns of language expression for communication of parental directives seems to have been essentially ignored. It is an area of parent-child interaction which is taken for granted.

Only when one observes the mother of a receptive aphasic child bombarding him with a lengthy series of commands, and sees the bewilderment of the child and the frustration of the mother, does this point take on real meaning. This child, perhaps, has great difficulty receptively managing single words with any degree of efficiency and is persistently placed in a barrage demand.

This illustration may appear too dramatic, but variations on this theme are constantly observable in a rehabilitation clinic serving various types of handicapped children. The nature of aphasia, deafness, and retardation are quite well understood from a communication standpoint by professionals but the messages have not been passed on to the parents.

By the time most parents reach the professional office they have already devised some system of getting through to their child no matter how serious his handicap may be. There is too much "communication space" in family living to wait for a program. The parent does the best he or she can under the circumstances. Language structuring at an earlier level would be a significant assist and a bonus to the child-rearing process.

As a general notation it must be recorded that one of the major by-products of this study has been the steady impression of the chasm which exists between the extensive body of knowledge in child rehabilitation and the minimal awareness of this knowledge on the parental front of child-rearing. There is an obvious need for bridges to be built.

7. *The incidence of significant negative attitudes and behaviors from siblings in relation to the handicapped child is minimal according to these parents. The general picture presented by the parents is that siblings tend to accept the handicapped child and help in various ways.*

The belief that the siblings of a handicapped child suffer adverse psychological effects because of neglect from parents, competition for attention, identification of themselves as tainted, attitudes of inheritability, etc., has been an historical segment of rehabilitation psychology. Sibling rivalry is a well-documented family phenomenon. A number of years ago the middle child rose to prominence as a special psychological entity and the oldest child in the family has been regarded as having special problems (Bossard and Boll, 1956).

Farber (1959) asked the mothers of severely retarded youngsters to rate the oldest nonhandicapped sibling on ten personality traits. He found an adverse influence on the adjustment of normal siblings to be present if the mother regarded the retarded child as highly dependent. If the retarded child was regarded as highly independent, the adversity of the siblings was not found to be significant.

The only group among the five presented in the child-rearing study which could be regarded as totally similar to the Farber group was the mongoloid. Recalling the reporting of this group on the questions of negative-positive attitude ratings of mothers an overwhelming majority (88 per cent) rated the siblings as holding positive attitudes.

It must be noted that these sibling findings for all groups were based upon parental evaluations. A direct approach to the siblings with appropriate investigative instruments might well reveal a somewhat different picture. Whether the parent perceived a true or false state of sibling attitude the parent probably used their own ratings as an operational definition of attitude when it came to child-rearing. A positive picture was presented by the parents in sufficient uniformity across the five groups to suggest that a common bias was operating. Parents in all groups perceived minimal evidence of adverse influence upon siblings.

8. *As a general rule the mothers and fathers were in agreement on their responses to questions about child-rearing practices. Minor disagreements were noted on some points in the protocols of all couples who were interviewed but such disagreements were not on significant issues. Where the extent of disagreement was significant the response patterns of both parties gave indication that the marriage was poorly integrated and that daily living had become a succession of open arguments or a matter of quiet hostility in which both were mechanically going about the business of day-by-day living. Such cases were in the minority.*

The data obtained do not suggest that marital difficulties could be attributed to the presence of the handicapped child in the family. Rather, the day-by-day adjustments to integrating the child into the family could be viewed as a stress factor which served to aggravate a basic problem of discord within either or both parents.

Some parents attempted to portray a pattern of such blissful relationships surrounding the advent and development of the child that the picture was too pretty. When several such cases were analyzed *in toto* this veneer showed various discrepancies which suggested that the family situation was not quite as glowing as they wished to portray.

Only a few parent couples in this study gave any evidence of significant marital discord. This is not too surprising however when one considers that the study population was both a captive and a volunteer group and those parents who were deeply involved in discord were less likely to volunteer themselves to such exposure. The 177 families who presented their stories painted a picture of a considerable amount of agreement between the husband and wife on the majority of issues. Significant disagreements were in the minority. A cursory analysis of father interview protocols tends to support the maternal contentions of family harmony.

In all fairness to these parents relatively few tried to depict an idyllic state. They were open and frank in describing areas of disagreement and the underlying reasons (in their perception) for such lack of agreement. Whether the findings of child-rearing practices reported in this text can be considered as truly representative of the total population of parents of handicapped children throughout the nation is certainly open to debate.

There undoubtedly are many practitioners in agencies, clinics and schools who can cite families where the total child-rearing composite may be warped by the marital discord of the parents and therefore at great variance with the generally favorable state of affairs reflected here. At the same time there are probably cases which can be cited as being even more harmonious than those included in this study.

It must be concluded, however, that a significant number of parent couples having a handicapped child in their home reported a high state of agreement between the mother and father. Differences of opinion existed at times with all of these couples but the prosaic batting average was definitely on the favorable side.

A somewhat negative shadow was cast upon the family portrait by the incidence of cases where the father was depicted as immature and irresponsible.

There was a general impression among all of the interviewers that most of the fathers were immature and only moderately responsible people. Most fathers do not become engrossed in the suffering process associated with the initial concern and progressive awareness. They seem to adopt a little boy role or a brother role in relation to the problem, and conveyed the idea that they were removed from the situation—not by choice, but by circumstance. Many felt lonely and excluded—wanting to be involved but not quite accepted into the "buffering circle." Many plunged themselves into intensive preoccupation with the business of making a living. As one father expressed it, "They called me in and gave me the facts about our boy but I quickly got the idea that I was supposed to go out and earn a living while my wife and the therapist went to work on the kid."

While the mother receives the opportunity to change by continual contact with professionals, the father seldom is given the same opportunity. Consequently, the perceptual gap grows wider as the mother experiences change and actually gets ahead of the father on the timetable of change.

If the feelings of the fathers are being interpreted correctly in this analysis they were clearly pleading for an identified role in the general picture.

This is not to say that such an impression necessarily detracted from a general finding of spouse agreement. A favorable state of affairs in regard to agreement can be maintained simply by having the wife recognize this fact and assume the major share of responsibility. Once the responsibility had been assumed those fathers who might be characterized as immature were quite willing to accept a secondary role thereby preserving a high state of agreement.

A number of observations can be offered without commentary since they have been discussed in some detail in the body of the text and are simply noted here as general points of recapitulation.

1. The area of sex training was generalized by these parents to be no different than it might be for any child, but parents tended to place such considerations on the calendar of the future and saw the area as one of minor import at this age level.

2. Most parents tended to be realistic in their expectations for marriage, level of possible schooling, and adult employment. While some parents seemed to overestimate their child's potential for the future some of them read the signs of limitation quite realistically.

3. Parents tended to have positive attitudes towards their child's teacher and the manner in which the community school system has arranged for their child's education.

4. Only a small percentage of the parent population had allied itself with an organization of parents devoted to the cause of

their child. If they did join, this was usually upon recommendation from some professional.

5. The vast majority were church-going people although not rigidly regular in this attendance. Most of them made some form of arrangement for their child to receive religious instruction.

6. The often discussed "diagnostic shopping expeditions" which are inferred to be a characteristic of parents of handicapped children were of minimal incidence in these groups.

Two more observations can be included in this general summary before directing attention to some specific findings of difference.

1. *There are only minimal indications that the rearing of a handicapped child significantly alters a parent's child-rearing concepts.*

These parents gave very little evidence to suggest that any significant changes occurred in their general concepts regarding child-rearing simply because they had a handicapped child in the family. It would appear that what they believed about child-rearing they *believed*. They all seemed to have set about the business of rearing the handicapped child according to whatever set of beliefs they held about child-rearing in general and few of them changed their basic set of beliefs even in the face of difficulties encountered in their day by day practices.

2. *The total investigation sequence had therapeutic significance for most of the parents.*

Throughout the conduct of the study the research staff became more and more impressed with the fact that the sheer mechanics of inventory had a therapeutic significance. The organization structure of the questionnaires and the clinical interview were openly cited by many parents as the "first time they had ever had a chance to systematically review the what and why of their daily relationship to their handicapped child."

Although the fathers and mothers were interviewed separately the fact that each covered the same territory caused many couples to spend many evening hours reviewing their respective answers to individual questions. For many couples this was the first time they had actually sat together to review their practices and their attitudes. Both mothers and fathers volunteered comments to the effect that they had never been aware that their spouse felt a particular way about some issue—because they had never discussed it.

Perhaps the major effect was one of creating an awareness within these parents of the total composite called "child-rearing." In the prosaic hustle and bustle of child care, social obligations, work schedules, bills, installment payments, need for school clothes, dental appointments, music lessons, therapy sessions, religious instructions and an apparently endless series of child emergencies, it is likely that few parents take the time to sit in quiet discussion to analyze their attitudes and practices.

Most were impressed with the immensity of their child-rearing task simply by the multiplicity of questions which were included in the process. Often mothers returned to a subsequent interview session to add a postscript to a previous response or to edit a response given earlier because "she had been thinking it over and wished to more accurately state her position on the matter." Some couples repaired misunderstandings which had plagued the intimacy of their relationship to each other for years.

While there was no intention within the design of the project to obtain personal insight, this became a bonus benefit for a considerable number of the parents as a result of the interview. Some mothers reported that the emphasis suggested by the questioning had helped them to reevaluate the emphases which existed in their own practices, and to recognize the fact that they were personally emphasizing minute and significant details while ignoring some more important aspects.

Parents of the blind and deaf groups had experienced considerably less number of clinical contacts than the other three groups and had a variable reaction to the process. In both of these groups two kinds of parents were represented. There were those who seemed ill at ease in the interview and conveyed the impression that they were somewhat stiff and formal and quite unaccustomed to sharing so much detail with a professional. They were generally more cautious, guarded and reserved. On the other hand, each of these two groups contained parents who seemed to have been impatiently awaiting the opportunity to tell their story.

There are probably advantages and disadvantages to the procedure of being a master reporter to clinicians because of frequent experiences versus being a complete novice at the task of divulging so much detail. The parents in these two groups were obviously less schooled in telling their stories.

The therapeutic effect was so impressive that clinicians in rehabilitation settings might well consider the possibility of employing some of these questionnaires in a routine manner. Often parents serve mainly as agents of transportation to deliver and fetch their child to and from therapy appointments spending a good deal of time in a waiting room. The period of waiting could be used by the parent to complete many of these questionnaires and a dual purpose would be served. The information could be added to the case file to aid in understanding the parent, and the parent would have the opportunity to systematically consider various aspects of the child-rearing process.

There is something positive to be said about the mere process of subjecting a parent to the task of verbally defining the answers to this inventory. Areas of child-rearing are systematically organized for consideration in a manner which most parents would be unlikely to organize at a personal level. The experience also helped parents to organize a retrospective evaluation of past practice and achieve some semblance of an efficiency rating for their own benefit.

Above and beyond the data-giving process the entire experience was judged to have a positive therapeutic value for the majority of parents in this study. The implications for parent workers are clear.

It must also be noted that the decision to provide such "therapeutic space" for the parents within the interview situation proved a dilemma in the early period of the study. The initial dedication was clearly in the direction of regarding the parent primarily in terms of data procurement.

It was clear during the early stages of the project that these parents were also seeking clarifications, a listening person and a sounding board. The temptation to remain exclusively dedicated to the research objective and to clinically force the parent to remain diligent to the task was forceful. The parental expression of need was also forceful. In retrospect the decision to try to achieve both goals may have been detrimental to the objective procurement of the data but beneficial to the parents. It was a choice which had to be made and it was made. What may be lacking in data deposit seems to be more than amply balanced by the positive impact of this experience upon the parental dynamics of those people who were involved. The strategy was wise from one standpoint and unwise from another. Each position has its own merits.

SPECIFIC OBSERVATIONS

The general course of the study reflected a great deal more in the way of similarity than it did to an exposition of difference within or between groups. There are, however, a number of specific points which deserve special mention.

1. The medical nature of the child's problem is a far less influential factor in child-rearing than the child's level of intelligence. Problems in communication and learning present more dilemmas to the parent than the sensory loss or the physical handicap.

2. The deaf and the blind group conveyed the greatest extent of general ease in child-rearing but it must be pointed out that, in this sample, there was only minor incidence of reduced intelligence among these groups, whereas mental retardation was of significant incidence in the other three groups.

3. Toilet training presented the greatest problem to the mongoloid group in terms of time span for achievement.

4. While the general tendency towards realism in levels of aspiration for marriage, schooling, and employment held for all groups, the mongoloid group showed the highest incidence of unrealistic aspirations.

5. The organic group experienced the lengthiest delay in arriving at a diagnosis. The peculiarities of diagnostic certainty in this area continue to be a major problem to parents and professionals throughout the nation.

All other specifics of difference were attributable to the idiosyncrasies of a given set of parents and there seemed to be no way to link these to the peculiarities of a given handicap. These differences have been elaborated upon in the individual sections on rearing practices and need no further summation.

In general the family lives of these children seemed to be little different from what one might expect to find in any population. Variations were certainly apparent when the child was classified as a severe case within his own disability group but there is no evidence contained in this study to suggest that, because a child's diagnostic label places him within a given category, he is therefore automatically subject to a different set of child-rearing practices. His diagnostic label *per se* seems to have little bearing.

It is rather a question of the severity of his disability, the extent of intellectual immaturity, the degree of language dysfunction—and above all, the particular idiosyncrasies of his particular set of parents. It seems logical to suppose that special considerations must accompany each disability—these parents have raised doubts about this logic.

METHODOLOGICAL SUMMARY CONSIDERATIONS

In utilizing the interview and group questionnaires at data-gathering devices, one is inevitably faced with the question of the accuracy with which events have been recalled. It would indicate considerable naiveté to assume the parental reports as factual. On the other hand, to assume the reports to be a total distortion of what has transpired would indicate a degree of cynicism not in accord with the reality of the situation. Rather, it would seem that the veridicality of parental perceptions would vary with the event, and that the probability of error might be specified. A review of the pertinent literature and a small investigation was undertaken to clarify to some extent the reliability of parents' retrospective reports.

A number of studies consistently suggest that large errors do exist in mothers' retrospective reports of child-rearing practices. Skard (1960) found that hard fact data, such as length of child at birth, were recalled best, while general wishes and attitudes were recalled with least accuracy over a period of six years. Time was not related to the degree of distortion. The general conclusion was ". . . anamnestic material did not reflect their early experiences and attitudes so much as their current picture of the past." They further observed that when anxiety was associated with the actual experience, agreement recall was facilitated.

Goddard, *et al.* (1961) compared the retrospective account of twenty-five mothers with hospital records after a period of four to five years. In their summary, they indicated that:

> The results show that mothers do not report gestation time reliably, that many mothers are incorrect when they state that forceps were not used in the delivery, that few mothers can report accurately the immediate

difficulties at the delivery of the infant. Feeding history revealed many discrepancies in nursing and knowledge of formula composition. Many mothers forget or overlook a significant number of illnesses. On the other hand, the mothers' evaluation of difficulty of labor and delivery agrees with that of the physician; facts concerning weight at birth and at subsequent yearly intervals, and details of motor development are reported with accuracy.

Wenar (1961) analyzed the interview responses of twenty-five mothers who, three to six years earlier, had brought their children to a therapeutic nursing school. He found that 43 per cent of the statements were different from previous interviews, and that 40 per cent of these statements were extremely distorted.

MacFarlane (1938) investigated the accuracy of maternal recall twenty-one months from the time of the child's birth. He found that marked unreliability was evidenced in the recall of physical condition during pregnancy, use of instrument or not, illnesses, and various developmental factors. Labor was recalled with an average discrepancy of three and a half hours. Weight at birth, however, was reliably reported.

The above studies suggest that anamnestic data may have adequate reliability only insofar as it pertains to relatively objective evidence, such as birth weights, pregnancy terms, length of baby, Rh factor and so forth. It would seem that in interpreting these data it is necessary to limit one's range to talking about the phenomenology of the mother and father at the time of the interview, of their reported perceptions and feelings occurring at that time. Only at some risk can causal relations be inferred from these data as they have been collected. Typically, however, this contemporary phenomenology of the mother, whether or not accurate historically, is the substance which the interviewer in a clinical setting must interpret and utilize in order to understand the client. Indeed, these feelings, and perceptions of the mother, without undue emphasis on their objective validity, are part of an area in need of investigation. A few studies of a variable-finding nature have been done.

Radke-Yarrow (1963) has reported some sex-linked factors in the parents' retrospections. She reports that:

> . . . on descriptions of the child's aggression, 31 per cent of the mothers' reports on boys were rated identically from the initial and recall date, compared with only 15 per cent of the reports on girls. The tendency

to recall boys as *more* aggressive and girls as *less* aggressive than described on initial measures appears but is not significant in the exploratory sample. There *is* another sex-linked trend: for their sons, mothers *recall* greater sharing by the father in the discipline role than was reported initially; for daughters the shift is to recall less sharing by the father than appeared initially.

In addition, MacFarlane (1938) found that mothers tended to make their children more precocious than they actually were. Chess (1960) indicated that distortion occurred in the direction of socially acquired concepts of optimal functioning, while McCord (1961) found that cultural stereotypes molded the parents' reported perceptions of family life. Social desirability, a response set which has been shown to have a pervasive influence on responses to attitutional and personality test items, apparently influences to some extent recall of past events. Another response set, acquiescence, has been demonstrated to be a pervasive influence in the data of this present project (Cook, 1962). That is, those mothers high on acquiescence in the PARI and CPI were also high in the personal interview.

There is no question that the perceptions of mothers and fathers are subject to a wide range of coloration from many sources but, since this has been found to be a typical finding in parent research, it is likely that these particular parents were no more, or no less, subject to such perceptual distortion. As has been noted earlier the perceptions of the professional and the perceptions of the parent occur in two quite different matrices. It is probably true that no parent can ever observe and report on any of his or her children with the objectivity desired by the researcher.

The only true course of investigating child-rearing practices would require some system of on-the-spot coverage, but such a course would also be subject to the awareness of "on-stageness" in the parent which would undoubtedly influence the practices in some way. At this stage of development in parent research the emphasis continues to rest upon the parental reporting of what they say they do. Despite the superficiality in some the areas of this study, the clinical impression was continuous that most of the parents were sincerely interested in giving an honest report. Whatever distortions may be present do not appear to negate the report but rather convey the notion that such distortions are an integral part of the child-rearing milieu.

In retrospective analysis an effort was made to determine which areas of the interview, or which specific questions, appeared to have produced the highest levels of anxiety among the parents. While such an effort was, undoubtedly, subjective in character there was a unanimous agreement among all project personnel that six questions stood out as the most disturbing inquiries for almost all of the parents. Most parents were quite distressed by the request to formulate a description of their spouse. This request caused the longest delay before answering and the greatest difficulty with sentence structure. The distress was equally noted when they were asked to formulate a description of themselves. Another upsetting question was phrased, "Who is more dominant—you or your husband?" Parents also found themselves hard pressed to describe the impact of this child upon them. The definition of their expectations for their child's future in regard to schooling, employment, marriage, and parenthood was a painful area of consideration. Finally, their concern with the attitudes of other people towards them, proved to be a difficult problem of response.

While individual parents were distressed by various questions because of unique personal problems, the six referred to above were difficult for all and appeared to have a generally unsettling effect upon all parents who were interviewed.

OMISSIONS

Inspection of the full series of instruments contained in the Appendix will reveal that some areas of investigation have been omitted from discussion within this text. Two reasons can be given to account for these omissions:

1. In some instances the form or the question which had been presumably carefully contrived for clarity of thought and semantic organization *before* the study began proved to have been ambiguous and confusing when the responses were tabulated. Any effort to find some meaningful method for setting categories of response, for sorting purposes became a frustrating experience which eventually generated a decision to forego the data in that area. In spite of the fantastic number of words which are available in the English language the selection of a few simple words cast

in a sentence, or a question, which would result in an equalized perception of meaning and intent among 300 adults proved to be a very complicated task. The blame for the loss of some data rests upon an inability to properly phrase questions to produce desired results. Future researchers might well take these losses into account when plotting questions and statements.

2. Some data still remain carefully stored and tabulated neatly in filing cabinets awaiting the necessary working over to bring them to final form for publication. The most sizable portion of these data lie with the full-scaled interview given to the fathers. These protocols are deserving of a more penetrating analysis than can currently be developed. It is a significant project for the future, particularly in view of the fact that fathers generally have rarely been research subjects. The loss to this present text has not been total. Throughout the recounting of the child-rearing practices the father's viewpoint and attitude have been interwoven into the narrative wherever it has been possible to do so.

A number of other areas can also be classified in this "limbo-position" of prepublication stage and will be prepared in the months and years to come. The entire series of clinical interview questions 165-206 covering manifesting of affection and dependency on the part of the child, marital integration, husband and wife dislikes for one another, maternal and paternal temperament, perception of severity, etc., are yet to be translated into narrative form.

The entire project was enormously "data wealthy" but unfortunately "time poor" from the standpoint of interpretation time. It will take many years to wisely spend the data in service to the parents who so faithfully and willingly contributed to the deposit.

METHODOLOGY

The original design of this study entertained no formal hypothesis. A straightforward search for answers to the simple question, "What practices do the parents of handicapped children employ?" was the basic intent. From the outset this study was simply intended as a preliminary of rearing techniques. There was no profound intent to probe parental motivations, anxiety levels or relationships between personal dynamics and a particular technique. To subject these data to such a probing analysis is not a comfortable task. If such profundity had been a part of the original design the instruments of measure would have been conceived differently and presented less casually.

As a consequence of original design there are many points where those clinicians who seek a more psychologically oriented analysis will be disappointed. This study must be viewed as a first tilling of parental soil. The hoped for crop must be patiently awaited as other researchers cultivate and refine these preliminary findings with more sophisticated styles of research design.

The initial prospecting is now completed. No dramatic bonanza was uncovered. Perhaps the probing was attempted in areas where other investigators may not have chosen to search. Perhaps the penetration was not deep enough. Some veins were found which hold promise for better equipped prospectors in the future to find rich ores of understanding. Some probes yielded nothing. There will doubtless be many veterans of research diggings who will feel that the wrong stones were turned. Others will probably feel that too many stones were turned, causing the true veins to be obscured by the dust. Each prospector, however, reads his own signs and interprets the map in his own unique fashion. If the net result of this venture has simply piqued the curiosity of some other prospectors who will try the same field with better instruments, more precise maps and refined engineering, it will have served an important purpose.

While new discoveries in medicine, physiology, biology, biochemistry, and other fields are constantly improving the health potential of our society almost on a daily basis, the number of parents who leave the practitioner's office or the hospital with their doubts and anxieties crystallized in the awesome label of a handicap word for their child, continues to be an impressive figure. They deserve the best information that can be obtained to help them in the child-rearing process.

After months of reflection and contemplation on the meaningfulness of the composite study there is the obvious conclusion which has now become a cliche—more research needs to be done. Above and beyond the cliche a more significant and pressing conclusion has forcefully emerged from the experience of this project. This conclusion has been conceptualized as a Project for Tomorrow—The Parent Counselor.

THE CONCEPT OF THE PARENT COUNSELOR

The greatest obstacle to widespread and significant advancement in the field of special education has been the failure of community school systems to find a mutually comfortable technique for successfully incorporating the parent of the special class child into a reinforcing role of value to the child's learning advancement. It would be difficult to find any assembly of teachers of retarded, blind, deaf, aphasic, etc., who do not vocalize freely about unrealistic aspirations of parents, lack of understanding, refusal to accept the child's limitations, over-dependency, over-solicitiousness and a host of other negative comments. Like the weather, everybody talks about parents but nobody does anything about them.

The extensive influence of psychiatric theory upon education has helped to create the impression that parents of handicapped children are guilt-ridden, anxiety-laden, rejecting beings who are inclined to be troublesome to professionals in clinics and schools. Many school people complain that parents have little or no understanding of what the school is trying to do for their child. Many feel that parents fail to accept their child's need for special help. The list of complaints against parents is lengthy. The amelioration of all such problems is left in the hands of the classroom teacher or, in some cases, private casework agencies in the community may come to the teacher's rescue and accept parent referrals.

Parents with handicapped children seldom have any awareness of what schools have to offer their child until the child reaches school age and some placement is necessary. Seldom do they concurrently receive an orientation to the totality of the special education department so they might learn how their community school system has been organized to meet special needs. They often come to the schools laden with anxieties built during the first five years of a child's life by less than adequate diagnosis, or a confusion of diagnostic terminology which they do not understand.

The formality of schooling, regular or special has traditionally been a major technique for transmitting the cultural heritage of the nation to its citizens and a preparation for productive adult citizenship. The parent also bears the same two basic responsibilities. Parents and educators by virtue of their chosen roles accept a mutual responsibility toward the child.

Many years ago it was felt that this unity of purpose in seeking the best possible educational milieu for each child might be fostered by formation of a Parent-Teacher Association devoted to the principle of mutuality and togetherness. Every school has one of these, much in the same manner that every family has a car. Unfortunately most of these become vehicles of operation for a few dynamic parents in leadership roles with a perpetual annual campaign to entice a better turnout for each monthly meeting.

Program chairmen in local communities struggle desperately to find speakers or panels who might bring pertinent information to the hardy group of rugged parents who painfully brave whatever elements may exist on the monthly meeting night to continue to search for the nebulous togetherness between teacher and parent. Few communities contain enough professionals capable of standing before an audience and helping parents understand some critical point in child development or education to sustain a PTA over a period of several years.

As a result, program chairmen find themselves scheduling a speaker to regale the group with a silent-picture-lecture version of his canoe trip along a distant river. This is scheduled in the hope that such a program will attract more of the fathers. Because no program chairman wishes to be accused of overlong meetings, and the custodians wish to close the building early, this venture into educative mutuality is usually limited to a thirty-minute burst followed quickly by a social hour of coffee and cookies.

It is not at all unusual to find the teachers of the school clustered in a group as if providing an insulation to each other against possible infiltration from some intrepid parent. Little effort is actually devoted to the togetherness of teacher and parent at the PTA meeting since the parent literally gets his turn at the teacher at the annual "open house" and the periodic teacher conferences.

In some quarters where some form of special class may be located in the elementary school, it is considered highly desirable to integrate "these parents" with the "regular" parents for PTA purposes. In other quarters the attempt may be made to have two PTA's within a single school because the needs and problems of the two sets of parents are different.

This effort on the part of most schools represents the major process of parent-relationships other than some compulsory system of reporting at intervals on a child's progress. Even in this matter of reporting periodically to parents there are staunch advocates for each of twenty to thirty different ways of accomplishing this.

Many administrators will now rise up in arms to proclaim the fact that school systems all over the country are increasingly employing more and more psychologists and school social workers to meet this very need. Unfortunately each school system contains enough children with "acute" adjustment problems which are of immediate concern and which quickly monopolize the full schedule of these special people.

The demands for immediate attention scarcely leave any time to be concerned with the parents whose children present no unusual adjustment problems, and seem to go along "in a nice typical way" from September to June. For the most part these specialists are unavailable to the average parent because the emergency waiting-list far exceeds their time allotments.

Consequently most American parents talk to their child's teacher once, twice or three times each year unless they happen to warrant further attention by virtue of acute problems in their child. Some parents have never personally talked with their child's teachers during an entire elementary school experience. Somehow or other most parents seem to have a blind faith in the school, believing that everything is "going along fine in the way it's supposed to go—unless I hear to the contrary."

The teacher who is empathically identified with the child often finds herself in the position of the gardener who has so painstakingly hoed and raked his ground, carefully planted his seeds in neat rows and, standing back in a state of satisfaction, muses on the wonders of the future which will come into blooming beauty from his careful work, only to be abruptly dismayed by an errant child galloping over the hallowed ground and ruining the tender handiwork. It is frequently the *parent* who is perceived by the teacher as the culprit who disturbs the handiwork she has wrought in the child. Like the gardener, the teacher has only one recourse—to hoe and rake and plant again.

The teacher's business is child learning. She has been trained for this in four or five years of academic and internship training and has probably matured in progressive competence by virtue of her efforts with hundreds of children who have passed through her classroom. Her obligation to the child is, by cultural and national objective, so vital and compelling that it is unfair to demand that she incorporate the additional role of a parent counselor into her chosen profession. She was not trained to do this and if the private comments of hundreds of teachers can be considered representative, she tends to regard this aspect of her job with a high degree of anxiety.

In the field of psychotherapy there seems to be a universal agreement that the therapist who works with the patient cannot become the therapist for the mother. There cannot be a conflict of empathies. In political life a conflict of interests is regarded as a barrier to efficiency and loyalty. When it comes to parents and school, however, the relationship is regarded as prosaic, routine and a necessary, albeit unhappy, component of a teacher's role. Nobody else seems to think that the parents are a vital ingredient in proper education so why should the teacher? The parents may suddenly become important when a problem arises or when this parent becomes a voter who must be wooed for the upcoming referendum.

None of the theories of personal dynamics which now guide workers on all fronts of human welfare stemmed from the study of dynamics among parents of handicapped children or for that matter from the study of *any* kind of parents. It is a most interesting phenomena to observe the ease with which clinicians of various orientations and dynamic creeds can take a single item in behavior, or a cluster of behaviors, and conveniently identify and allocate these to positions on the trunk of some theory.

If the parent and the special class teacher are both to fulfill their obligations to the child, some new considerations must be given to novel approaches to parent education. The business of parenthood is child-rearing, while the business of the special class is to teach specific skills and behaviors to aid the child to manage progressively more complex formal learning materials. The two goals are separately assigned but are not mutually exclusive. They are also not interchangeable. Parents who try to become professional teachers with flash cards, word drills, reading lessons, etc., usually do a poor job. Teachers who try to become substitute mothers usually do a poor job. Neither the parent nor the teacher should attempt to usurp or assign each other's role. If each carries out the traditionally assigned role the unity of purpose is gained.

There are literally hundreds of behaviors which must be established by parents which are completely outside the purview of the classroom. The more that schools are baited into the trap of fulfilling parental responsibilities, the more dependent become the parents upon the schools to expand services into noneducational areas of behavior. At the opposite pole, the attempt to turn the family kitchen table into an extension of the classroom is an intrusion into family living.

If the class curriculum is so extensive that it cannot be managed except by extending the child's exercises to the kitchen table for overtime in the form of homework assignments then perhaps the school day should be lengthened or the curriculum reorganized.

The family home can be viewed as a laboratory for learning a system of moral values, interpersonal living, table manners, prayers, personal hygiene, leisure-time skills, household responsibility, respect for property, and countless other lessons. All of these can be taught to children using the same *principles of learning* employed by the teacher in the arithmetic lessons.

The parent in the home may help the child to generalize from his classroom learning into family activities of daily living. This task, of and by itself, offers the parent a lengthy list of possible activities which are so numerous that to pause in parenthood to teach number combinations represents a diversion from the basic obligation.

Let each laboratory be concerned with its own set of behavioral experiments and explore their respective areas in depth. Each might be interested in the work of the other and remain acquainted with particular results and problems but content themselves primarily with their own work.

If such a dichotomy has any validity it follows that a new type of professional is called for on the educational scene. Somehow a procedure must be developed to acquaint the parent with principles of learning and the obligations and techniques of child-rearing. A procedure must also be found to help the parent understand the mutualities as well as the separations. The professional specifically conceived to fulfill such an obligation is a *parent counselor.*

The parent counselor would function as a member of the staff of the Special Education Department of a community school system and carry a full time responsibility for the development of parent counseling relationships. To fulfill a preventive role he would serve as a referral resource to community physicians and clinics for parents of infants and young children who have been diagnosed as handicapped and may eventually require the services of special education units.

Where a community provides clinical services to parents in the process of treating the young child such as a community cerebral palsy clinic, a preschool retardation clinic, etc., the parent counselor would relate himself cooperatively to those programs for the purpose of initiating a school-relationship with the parents at the earliest possible date. If no such facilities exist within a community, the parent counselor would relate himself directly to the parents in an individual counseling relationship. This will permit the counseling relationship to develop at the early moments when parents are developing their attitudes toward the child and seeking to identify their own roles in relation to the handicapped child.

At the same time he would relate himself to the existing special class units in that particular school system. Through an intake-interview process, and in consultation with the respective special class teachers, the parent counselor would make some analysis of the needs of the individual parents and, from this analysis, determine the most effective way of serving the parents. A number of possibilities can be devised. Where the needs of the parents dictate, the counselor could establish an individual counseling relationship with regular sessions. Others may be organized into groups for regular weekly sessions. Others may be organized into units which could meet on a bi-weekly or monthly basis.

Since most children assigned to special class units tend to remain in these units from the early elementary years to the early teen years, the relationships with parents can be viewed as a long term proposition. Intensive initial relationships with parents would progressively become less intense through the years.

Part of the parent counselor's responsibility would be to make home visits to become acquainted with the totality of the family in its own milieu. Meetings would be held in the school building. For greatest effect the installation of a classroom observation window would allow parents unobtrusively to observe activity with accompanying commentary from the parent counselor.

The parent counselor would serve as the principal liaison agent to community clinics, agencies, physicians and other professionals who might become involved with the problems of a given family. He could represent the school in various agency or clinic staffings.

More progressive units of special education might also consider the possibility of providing group counseling experiences to parents of preschool handicapped children who will eventually become members of special classes at a later age. Such a program would enable educators to acquaint parents with the various criteria established for special classes, to orient parents expectancies of behavior to be achieved by the age of admission, to help parents devise techniques for achieving such preschool behaviors, and could serve as a means of obtaining valuable developmental data on a cumulative basis long before the child must be assigned to a classroom.

The preschool counselor might be considered as a second step in developing an adequate approach to the parents of handicapped children, but the parent counselor in the special class structure is nominated for the top priority. School administrators and special education supervisors might do well to give some serious consideration to the initiation of a program of parent counseling. This is not a luxury item to be rejected because of budgetary limitations. Careful consideration of the long-range benefits to special education will reveal it to be an economy and a significant concept for advancing curriculum.

The parent counselor, as an integrated member of the special education team in a community school system, could:

1. Serve to establish an early counseling relationship with the parents of handicapped children during the infancy and preschool years helping them to define roles, set positive attitudes and develop home climates which would contribute to the optimal development of the child prior to special class admission.

2. Serve as a sensitive interpreter of school functions and potential to community physicians and clinics.

3. Serve to encourage various community resources to expand services to provide a network of preschool services to handicapped children.

4. Serve as a vehicle for reporting on and discussing child progress in the classroom in consultation with the teacher.

5. Serve the purpose of systematically discussing the purposes and objectives of special class curriculum and allow for discussion of particular methodologies employed by the teacher to reach those objectives.

6. Serve to permit scheduled observation of classroom activity under the direct guidance of the parent counselor so that pertinent behaviors might be pointed out to illustrate discussion material, or heighten parental sensitivity to certain behavioral patterns in children generally, or specific patterns in a single child.

7. Serve as a continual feedback to the teacher on the manner in which classroom learning is becoming manifest in the child's family-community life as well as to provide a source of information for the teacher regarding significant family dynamics and behaviors which would allow her to integrate such data into her day-by-day relationships to the benefit of the child's development. This feedback would come about in regularly scheduled sessions between the teacher and the parent counselor where individual cases would be reviewed, and specific objectives set, for future effort. The teacher would provide the parent counselor with child learning data while the parent counselor would provide

significant family data obtained from analysis of parental comments and behavior. During this exchange of data, case planning and educational objectives would be set for both the child *and* the parent.

8. Provide the parent with the opportunity to clarify questions, rumors, medieval myths and legends regarding her child's handicap and that of others.

9. Provide a community orientation for parents to acquaint them with various diagnostic and therapeutic public and private agencies, existing within the local community or nearby, which might in some manner be pertinent to their particular problem.

10. Provide a continuing orientation to special education philosophy of the particular school system, and the panorama of special services arranged for children beyond that with which the parent might be personally familiar because it serves her particular child.

11. Serve as a sounding board for reaction to various administratively or professionally contemplated modifications in special programs. It might also serve as a vehicle for generating enthusiastic support for programs of broad community orientation to the special programs, or for referendum matters which must be eventually be acted upon by the community voters.

12. Serve as a learning situation for parents in which they might gain a broader and deeper understanding of the particular nature of their child's handicap and the relationship between that handicap and problems in learning.

13. Serve as a method for helping the parents learn sound and proven principles of child learning which they might employ in their daily relationships with their child and siblings.

14. Serve as a method for developing the reinforcement of classroom learning in the home situation by helping the parents specifically to structure learning opportunities in the home and family settings, and also routines which *will help the child to generalize* from his classroom learning into daily family and community life. The effort here would be devoted to finding ways in which the child-rearing practices of the parent could be geared to the same set of learning principles used by the teacher for academic progress, i.e., the welding of practices of parents

operating in *their* sphere of influence and the practices of the teacher operating in *her* sphere.

The next problem becomes the matter of defining the professional characteristics of the parent counselor. Such a professional must have, (1) an adequate understanding of educational methodology in all types of special education, (2) a deep understanding of the nature and dynamics of various child handicaps and (3) a solid background in personal dynamics.

Most professionals associated with education qualify on only one of the three characteristics, but this is a starting point. Until university programs can be organized to offer specialized training, school systems courageous enough to initiate such a program will have to rely upon existing personnel converted to such assignments, and supplement and support their work with available course work in areas of deficiency.

A general survey of university and college programs across the nation reveals that social work training programs cover many areas of preparation but little or no attention is directed towards the counseling of parents of handicapped children. Only a few of the teacher preparation programs in the field of special education cover any material related to parents of the handicapped. Training programs in occupational, physical, and speech therapy devote little attention to the parent problem. Generally, elementary education sequences offer little content related to parents. Programs of school counselor preparation usually minimize concern for the handicapped child and his parents. Only in the Family Life Education program is there an emphasis upon group education of parents towards improving child-rearing practices and parental attitudes.

Rarely do students majoring in special education enroll in courses in counseling theory and, vice versa, rarely do majors in counseling and guidance take course work in special education. A review of counselor education training programs in colleges throughout the country indicates that there is practically no effort to assist counselors in gaining a sensitivity to the needs of students with handicapping conditions. Neither field has expanded to enrich the student in training.

The parent of the handicapped child has not been a popular subject for research. The parent of the emotionally disturbed child has been studied from many viewpoints, but the parent of the mentally retarded, deaf, blind, visually handicapped, physically handicapped and neurologically impaired have not fared as well.

The studies conducted by Farber at Illinois on parents of severely mentally retarded, those of Spriestersbach on parents of cleft palate children, and those of Barsch on child-rearing practices among parents of handicapped children, represent the major efforts in this area.

Less elaborate studies of isolated traits of phenomena among parents of various handicap groups are dotted throughout the literature, but rarely have any studies of parents been initiated and developed in the setting of a public school special education program. Where reports *have* appeared about counseling efforts with groups of parents of handicapped children they have been private agency oriented.

In recognition of the paucity of information in this general area of special education, and out of a sense of great concern for the total optimizing of special education, it is felt that an effective demonstration should be conducted in the training of parent counselors to meet such needs. Whether such a program is located in a university or college setting, in a private community agency or initiated exclusively by a school system, a set of objectives for such a training program can be defined:

1. To conduct orientation seminars and institutes for special education personnel regarding various topics pertinents to the *parenthood of the special child.*

2. To develop a graduate training program leading to specialization as a *parent counselor.*

3. To provide a vehicle for the stimulation of research study in the field of *parentology.*

4. To define a unique set of concepts pertient to the joint needs of special education and counseling psychology.

5. To establish the concept of *parentology* as the study of parenthood in terms of child-rearing practices.

6. To develop a new concept of a coordinate professional specialization in the fields of special education and counseling.

7. To determine the values of such a professional specialist in improving the efficiency of the special education matrix in a community school system.

8. To establish a vehicle for bringing research findings on parenthood of the special child to the attention of special class teachers through a program of conferences and institutes.

9. To unify appropriate content from social work, psychology, medicine, special education, sociology, physical, occupational and speech therapy into a professional background for parent counselors.

10. To study and analyze the detailed dynamics of the interpersonal reactions between individual counselors and parents.

11. To define the content of the parent discussion sessions as a child-rearing curriculum, integrating the current appropriate insight gained from research in child development.

12. To establish a clinically oriented physical environment to study the most effective way of introducing this concept in architectural terms into the community school buildings.

In a three step process the concept of the parent counselor could be introduced into the entire field of child rehabilitation. The first step could be initiated with the community school program. The second step could introduce this concept as a preschool and community clinic level, and the third step could bring such a professional into the maternity ward or the infant clinic of the local hospitals to assist the parents during the critical period of initial concern and action.

This type of a professional would rightfully establish the import of the parent and balance the rehabilitation scale. It is a bold concept and may even be regarded by some as unrealistic.

It is, however, a concept derived from clinical experience, and the conviction of its validity has been immensely strengthened by the outcome of this study. The parents of handicapped children conveyed the message in hundreds of ways throughout the study—and the chorus is clear. If our nation wishes to optimize the development of its handicapped children, increase their potential for contribution, strengthen the family model and insure a condition of health—the plea of these parents should be heeded. A way *must* be found to understand and help. There is no choice.

BIBLIOGRAPHY

AARONFREED, J.: Internal and external orientation in the moral behavior of children. Paper read before American Psychological Association, September, 1959.

CHESS, S.; THOMAS, A.; BIRCH, H.G., and HERTZOG, M.: Implications of a longitudinal study of child development for child psychiatry. *Amer J Psychiat, 117*:434-441, 1960.

CHOROST, S.B.: Parental child-rearing attitudes and their correlates in adolescent hostility. *Genet Psychol Monogr, 66*:49-90, 1962.

CLARK, S.M., and FARBER, B.: The handicapped child in the family. A working draft prepared for conference on the cerebral palsied individual in the family, Urbana, Ill., Sept. 1962.

COLEMAN, J.C.: Group therapy with parents of mentally deficient children. *Amer J Ment Defic, 57*:700-704, 1953.

COOK, JOHN J.: Acquiescence in the PARI, CPI and the interpersonal interview. Accepted by *Ont Psychol Ass Quart*, 1963.

COOK, JOHN J.: Family limitation subsequent to the birth of the cerebral palsied child. *CP Review, 24*:8-9, 1963.

COX, D.R.: *Planning of Experiments*. New York, Wiley, 1958.

CRONBACH, L.J., and GLESER, G.C.: Assessing similarity between profiles. *Psychol Bull, 50*:456-473, 1953.

FARBER, BERNARD: Effects of a severely mentally retarded child on family integration. *Monogr Soc Res Child Develop, 24*, No. 2, (Serial No. 71), 1959.

GARFIELD, S.L., and HALPER, M.M.: Parental attitudes and socio-economic status. *J Clin Psychol, 18*:171-175, 1962.

GODDARD, R.E.; BRODER, G., and WENAR, C.: Reliability of pediatric histories. A preliminary study. *Pediatrics, 23*:1011-1018, 1961.

GOLDSTEIN, H.: Report Number Two on Study Projects for Trainable Mentally Handicapped Children. Springfield, Ill., Superintendent of Public Instruction, 1956.

GOUGH, H.G.: *Manual for the California Psychological Inventory*. Palo Alto, Consulting Psychologists Press, 1960.

GREBLER, ANNA MARIE: Parental attitudes toward mentally retarded children. *Amer J Ment Defic, 56*:475-483, 1952.

HAGGARD, E.A.; BREKSTAD, A., and SKARD, A.G.: On the reliability of the anamnestic interview. *J Abnorm Soc Psychol, 61*:311-318, 1960.

HOLT, K.S.: The influence of a retarded child upon family limitation. *J Ment Defic Res, 2*:28-36, 1958.

JOHNSON, P.O., and JACKSON, R.W.B.: *Modern Statistical Methods*. Chicago, Rand McNally, 1959.

[375]

KATZ, G.H.: Should the child be sent to an institution. *Nerv Child, 5*:172-177, 1946.

KOCH, HELEN L.: The relation of certain family constellation characteristics and the attitudes of children toward adults. *Child Develop, 26*:13-40, 1955.

MACFARLANE, J.W.: Studies in child guidance. I. Methodology of data collection and organization. *Monogr Soc Res Child Develop, 3*, No. 6 (Serial No. 19), 1938.

MARGOLIS, M.: The mother-child relationship in bronchial asthma. *J Abnorm Soc Psychol, 63*:360-367, 1961.

McCORD, J., and McCORD, W.: Cultural stereotypes and the validity of interviews for research in child development. *Child Develop, 32*:171-186, 1961.

MERRILL, B.: A measurement of mother-child interaction. *J Abnorm Soc Psychol, 41*:37-49, 1946.

MESSICK, S.: Separate set and content scores for personality and attitude scales. *Educ Psychol Measurement, 21*:912-923, 1961.

MILTON, G.A.: A factor analytic study of child rearing behaviors. *Child Develop, 29*:381-382, 1958.

MOLL, K.L., and DARLEY, F.L.: Attitudes of mothers of articulatory impaired and speech retarded children. *J Speech Hearing Dis, 25*:377-384, 1960.

NUNNALLY, J.: The analysis of profile data. *Psychol Bull, 59*:311-319, 1962.

OPPENHEIM, A.N.: Inventories for child-rearing attitudes and parental behavior. Unpublished paper, 1963.

POPE, L.: Religion and class structure. In R. BENDIX and S.M. LIPSET (Eds.): *Class, Status and Power*. Glencoe, Free Press, 1953, pp. 316-323.

RABBAN, M.: Sex-role identification in young children in two diverse social groups. *Genet Psychol Monogr, 81*:158, 1950.

RADKE-YARROW, M.: Problems of methods in parent-child research. *Child Develop, 34*:1963.

RAO, C.R.: *Advanced statistical methods in biometric research*. New York, Wiley, 1952.

Report on Study Projects for Trainable Mentally Handicapped Children. Springfield, Ill., Superintendent of Public Instruction, 1954.

ROE, H.: The psychological effects of having a cerebral palsied child in the family. Unpublished doctoral dissertation, Columbia Univ, 1952.

ROHRER, W.C., and SCHMIDT, J.F.: *Family Type and Social Participation*. College Park, Maryland, Agricultural Experiment Station, Univ. of Maryland, 1954, Misc. Publ. 196.

ROSEN, L.: Selected aspects in the development of the mother's understanding of her mentally retarded child, *Amer J Ment Defic, 59*:522-528, 1955.

SAMPSON, P.: *Manual for Users. Numerical Analysis Lab.*, Madison, Univ. of Wisconsin, 1962.

SCHAEFER, E.S.: A circumplex model for maternal behavior. *J Abnorm Soc Psychol, 95*:226-235, 1959.

SCHAEFFER, E.S., and BELL, R.Q.: Parental Attitudes Research Instruments:

Normative Data. Bethesda, Maryland, Nat. Inst. of Mental Health (undated mimeographed pamphlet).

SEARS, R.R.; MACCOBY, E.E., and LEVIN, H.: *Patterns of Child Rearing.* Evanston, Row-Peterson, 1957.

SHERE, MARIE: An evaluation of the social and emotional development of the cerebral palsied twin. Unpublished doctoral dissertation, Univ. of Illinois, 1954.

STENDLER, C.: Six years of child training practices. In *Sociological Studies of Health and Sickness.* New York, McGraw-Hill, 1960, pp. 40-55.

STONE, MARGUERITE M.: Parental attitudes to retardation. *Amer J Ment Defic, 53*:363-372, 1948.

THORNE, F.C., and ANDREWS, J.S.: Unworthy parental attitudes toward mental defectives. *Amer J Ment Defic, 50*:411-418, 1946.

TOLOR, A., and RAFFERTY, W.: The attitudes of mothers of hospitalized patients. *J Nerv Ment Dis, 136*:76-81, 1963.

WALKER, GALE H.: Some considerations of parental reactions to institutionalization of defective children; *Amer J Ment Defic, 54*:108-114, 1949.

WARDELL, WINIFRED: Case work with parents of mentally deficient children. *Amer J Ment Defic, 52*:91-97, 1947.

WEINGOLD, J.T., and HORMUTH, R.P.: Group guidance of parents of mentally retarded children. *J Clin Psychol, 9*:118-124, 1935.

WENAR, C.: The reliability of mothers' histories. *Child Develop, 32*:491-500, 1961.

ZUCKERMAN, M.; BARRETT, B.H., and BRAGIEL, R.M.: The parental attitudes of parents of child guidance cases. *Child Develop, 31*:401-417, 1960.

ZUCKERMAN, M.; BARRETT-RIBBACH, B., and MONASHKIN, I.: Normative data and factor analysis of the PARI. *J Consult Psychol, 22*:165-171, 1958.

ZUCKERMAN, M; OLTEAN, M., and MONASHKIN, I.: The parental attitudes of mothers of schizophrenics. *J Consult Psychol, 22*:307, 310, 1958.

APPENDIX

MOTHER INTERVIEW*

(To be filled in by interviewer)

Boy............ Girl............

Child's Name

(CR 21-3)   1. If any miscarriages:

	1st	2nd	3rd	4th	5th

1a. Year
1b. Month (gestation)
1c. Severity
1d. MD opinion
1e. Hospitalized
1f. Do you have your own opinion of what probably caused the miscarriages? ....

(CR 21-4)   2. If any stillborn:

	1st	2nd	3rd	4th	5th

2a. Year
2b. Month (gestation)
2c. Severity
2d. MD opinion
2e. Hospitalized
2f. Do you have your own opinion of what probably caused the stillbirth? ....

(CR 21-4)   3. If any premature:

	1st	2nd	3rd	4th	5th

3a. Year
3b. Month (gestation)
3c. Severity
3d. MD opinion
3e. Hospitalized
3f. Do you have your own opinion of what probably caused the prematurity? ....

(CR 21-4)   4. If any abortions:
(Please explain) ....

---

*Interview Form IMI

[379]

(CR 21-5a)   5. If any falls:
        5a. At what month? _____
        5b. Did you rest in bed after the fall? _____
        5c. Did the doctor order you to rest? _____
        5d. Did you decide to do this on your own? _____

(CR 21-5b)   6. If a temperature at any time during pregnancy:
        6a. For how many days? _____
        6b. Were you very sick? _____
        6c. Did a doctor treat you at that time? _____

(CR 21-5c)   7. If measles during pregnancy:
        7a. At what month? _____
        7b. For how long? _____

CR 21-5d)   8. If any virus infections during pregnancy:
        8a. At what month? _____
        8b. For how long? _____

(CR 21-5e)   9. If any menstrual bleeding during pregnancy:
        When—what month? _____
        9a. At your regular period? _____
        9b. Was this severe? _____

(CR 21-5f)   10. If false labor pains during this pregnancy:
        10a. At what month? _____
        10b. For how long a period? _____
        10c. What did your doctor say about these? _____
        _____

(CR 21-5g)   11. If on any diet during this pregnancy:
        11a. Did you decide this on your own? _____
        11b. Why? _____
        11c. Did your doctor prescribe it? _____
        Why? _____

(CR 21-5i)   12. If any long trips during this pregnancy:
        12a. How? _____
        12b. At what month? _____
        12c. Did this seem to affect you in any way? _____
        _____

(CR 21-5j)   13. If doctor set any special limitations on daily activities during
        this pregnancy:
        Explain: What limitations? _____
        Why? _____
        _____

(CR 21-5k)   14. If set any special limitations on yourself during this preg-
        nancy:
        What? _____
        Why? _____

(CR 21-5l)   15. If spent any unusual amount of time in bed during preg-
        nancy:
        15a. Why? _____
        _____
        15b. At what month? _____

(CR 21-5m)   16. If any question of a blood problem during your pregnancy, such as Rh:

16a. Did you know about this before you became pregnant?

_____

16b. Did you discuss it with your doctor? _____

16c. Before the pregnancy? _____

16d. During the pregnancy? _____

16e. Did you get regular blood checks? _____

(CR 21-5n)   17. If under any nervous strain or unusual emotional upset during pregnancy:

Please explain: _____

_____

(CR 21-5p)   18. If any operations or other illnesses during this pregnancy:

18a. For what? _____

18b. At what month? _____

18c. Were you hospitalized? _____ How long? _____

18d. Was there any question on the baby's welfare?

_____

(CR 21-5q)   19. If worried about your pregnancy?

19a. Why? _____

_____

_____

(CR 21-5r)   20. If any medicine during your pregnancy:

20a. What for? _____

20b. What kinds? _____

20c. For how long? _____

20d. What effect? _____

(CR 21-6a)   21. If checked *more problems* in this pregnancy:

Please explain: _____

(CR 21-9a)   22. If received medicine during labor: What type? _____

_____

_____

(CR 10a-b)   23. If "very worried" or "somewhat worried" regarding delivery is checked ask: Why and what fears did you have? _____

_____

_____

_____

(CR 21-11a-d)   24. If delivery regarded "very easy" or "very difficult":

Please explain _____

_____

_____

(CR 21-12a)   25. If received anaesthesia during delivery: What? _____

_____

_____

(CR 21-13a-b)   26. If "easiest" or "most difficult" delivery is checked:

Please explain: _____

_____

_____

(CR 21-14b-c)   27. If "premature or postmature" checked:
27a. Pre_____weeks
27b. Post_____weeks
27c. What explanation did the doctor offer to account for the pre/post maturity? _____
_____
_____

27d. What did you think caused the pre/post maturity?
_____
_____

(CR 21-16 yes) 28. If any other cesarean: Which one(s) _____
_____

(CR 21m-18a)   29. If X was jaundiced—please explain: _____
_____

(CR 21m-18b)   30. If blue or discolored—please explain: _____
_____

(CR 21m-18c)   31. If oxygen—for how long? _____

(CR 21m-18f)   32. If misshapen—please describe: _____
_____
_____

(CR 21m-18g)   33. If physically disfigured—please describe: _____
_____

(CR 21m-18h)   34. If "other" complications—please describe: _____
_____

(CR 21-19a)   35. If "obstetrician" checked:
Did a specialist also deliver your other children?

35a. *(If no)* Why did you want a specialist for X's delivery?
_____

(CR 21-19c)   36. If delivered by "other"—Who? _____
Why? _____

(CR 21-20 yes) 37. If doctor concerned about X's development—What did he say? _____
_____
_____

(CR 21-21a)   38. If pediatrician attended delivery—Why? _____
_____
_____
_____

(CR 21-22a) 39. If feeding problem—Describe: _____
_____
_____

39a. Did this worry you? _____
_____
_____

39b. How long did it take before the feeding problem straightened out? _____

39c. How did you go about solving this problem? _____
_____
_____

(CR 21-22b) 40. If sleeping problem—describe: _____
_____
_____

40a. Did you worry about this? _____
_____
_____

40b. How long before this sleeping problem straightened out? _____
_____

40c. How did you go about solving this problem? _____

(CR 21-23a) 41. If any other children a feeding problem—please explain:
_____

41a. How solved? _____

(CR 21-23b) 42. If any other children a sleep problem—please explain:_____
_____

42a. How solved: _____
_____

Initial Concern and Action

43. When did you first become concerned about X? _____
44. What did you notice? _____
_____
_____
45. Did your husband recognize this too? _____
How did he react? _____
46. Did he agree with you about your concern? _____
_____

47. Whom did you talk to about your concern? _____

48. To whom did you take the child? _____

49. What were you told by this doctor? _____
_____

50. How did you feel—about this?_____
_____

51. How many times did this doctor see you to explain the problem? _____

    51a. How much time did he spend with you? _____
52. What was his attitude (sympathetic, impatient, etc.)? _____

53. Did the doctor suggest some form of help for X?   Yes   No
    53a. What? _____

54. Did your husband go to the doctor with you?   Yes   No
55. Did you go to anyone else to find out what was wrong with X?
    Yes   No
    55a. If yes—*(probe number of intermediate contacts, reaction, motivation).*
_____
_____

56. When do you feel that you got the diagnosis of X's problem?
    Age of child: _____

57. From whom? _____
58. What were you told? _____
_____

59. How did you feel when you found out the nature of X's problem? _____
_____
_____

60. How many times did this doctor see you to explain the problem? _____

61. What was his attitude? _____

62. Did the doctor suggest some form of help for X's problem? _____
    62a. What? _____
63. Did your husband go to the doctor with you? _____
64. Has your husband ever talked to the doctor about X's problem? _____
_____
_____

65. Does he accept what the doctors have said about X? _____
_____
_____

Motor Development

66. At what age were you able to put X in the middle of the floor and have him sit by himself? _____

67. Did you help X in learning to walk? _____
    How? _____

68. How did you teach him to dress himself? _____
    _____

69. How did you teach him to feed himself? _____
    _____

70. How did you teach him to wash himself? _____
    _____

71. Was it harder to teach X these things than it was to teach your other children? _____ Why? _____
    _____

Toilet Training

72. How did you go about bladder training this child? _____
    _____
    _____

    72a. How did it go? _____
    _____

    72b. How many time did you attempt training? _____
    72c. How about staying dry at night? _____
    _____

73. How did you go about bowel training? _____
    _____
    _____

    73a. How did it go? _____
    _____

    73b. How many times did you attempt training? _____

74. How long was it before X was trained:
    74a. Bowels _____
    74b. Bladder _____

(CR 28-2)   75. If *not yet dry* at night—What did you do about it last time X wet at night? _____
                   75a. What is X's reaction to wetting at night? _____
                   _____

(CR 28-4)   76. If bladder trained *earlier* or *later*—Why? _____

(CR 28-5)   77. If bowel trained *earlier* or *later*—Why? _____
                   _____

               78. We know that it can be very upsetting when children "forget" after they are mostly trained. What was your usual reaction to these "slip-ups"? _____
                   _____
                   _____

               79. What part did your husband play in the toilet training of this child? _____
                   _____

(CR 28-10)   80. If toilet training was "learned *slower*"—Why do you feel this was so? _____

_____

(CR 28-12)   81. If started training "too soon" or "too late"—Why do you feel this was so? _____

_____

(CR 28-13a-d)   82. If in toilet training you were *"much too strict"* or *"much too lenient"*—Why do you feel this was so? _____

_____

_____

(CR 28-14a)   83. If "different way"—What was different? _____

_____

Sleep and Rest Patterns

84. How is your husband involved in putting X to bed? _____

_____

85. Does X's problem cause you to do anything differently with him at bedtime than you might do with your other children? _____

_____

86. What does X take to bed at night? _____
    86a. How do you feel about this? _____

    86b. Is this or was this true of your other children? _____

    _____

87. Is there anything unusual about X's sleep pattern (such as nightmares, restlessness, etc.)? _____

_____

88. Once X is in bed for the night does he bother you? _____

    88a. What have you done about this? _____

(CR 25-11a)   89. If *"tires more easily"*—Why do you feel this is so?_____

_____

(CR 25-12)   90. *(Whichever checked)* Why? _____

_____

(CR 25-13)   91. *(Whichever checked)*—Why? _____

_____

Infancy Care and Feeding

(CR 31-3)

92. If breast fed—for how long? _____

93. If bottle fed—check if any breast feeding? _____

Why did you stop? _____

_____

94. If *bottle fed only*—How did you happen to decide to use the bottle? _____

_____

(CR 31-4)

95. If other children fed differently—Why?_____

_____

_____

96. How did X react when taken off the bottle? _____

_____

(CR 31-6)

97. Whichever checked: Why do you feel this is (was) so?

_____

(CR 31-8cde)

98. If "began regular menu" after 24 months—please explain:

_____

(CR 31-9ab)

99. If eats *more* or *less* than other children—Why do you feel this is so? _____

_____

(CR 31-10a)

100. If "more of an eating problem"—Why do you feel this is so?

_____

Child Complaints

101. On all items checked *yes*—What seems to bring these on?

_____

_____

_____

Childhood Illness

(CR 22-12e)

102. If convulsions or seizures at infancy—which?

Conv. Seiz. What age? _____

102a. What did doctor say about this? _____

_____

102b. How often did these occur? _____

(CR 22-12f)

103. If seizures or convulsions since age two:

Please describe what happens: _____

_____

103a. How frequently? _____

103b. Under MD care? _____

103c. Type medication? _____

104. Is X now receiving medication to "calm his nerves"?
     Yes   No
     104a. If yes—What type? _____
     104b. Does it help? _____

_____

Vision and Hearing

Present Form 24M then—

(CR 24-6)   105. If Yes on 6, and no doctor checked:
             What was your concern? _____

_____

(CR 24-8)   106. If Yes on 8—Where was hearing tested? _____

_____

Child Therapy Form

107. On each type therapy checked—*(probe)*
     Do you feel this helped X?
     (Evaluate response and rank)

Type therapy _____	Type therapy _____
_____Great benefit	_____Great benefit
_____Some benefit	_____Some benefit
_____Minimal benefit	_____Minimal benefit
_____No change or got worse	_____No change or got worse
Type therapy _____	Type therapy _____
_____Great benefit	_____Great benefit
_____Some benefit	_____Some benefit
_____Minimal benefit	_____Minimal benefit
_____No change or got worse	_____No change or got worse

108. How does X get along with his brothers and sisters?

_____

109. With which child does X get along best?
                 Code: _____Oldest
                         _____Youngest
                         _____Nearest chronlogic sib

                         _____
                         _____Does not apply

     109a. Why do you feel this is so? _____
     _____
     _____

110. With which child does he fight most often? _____

                 Code: _____Oldest
                         _____Youngest
                         _____Nearest sib

                         _____
                         _____Does not apply

111. Do you give more attention to X than your other children?

_____

111a. If *more* or *less*—Why? _____

_____

112. Do you find yourself making comparisons between your children?
Yes   No
112a. What sort of comparisons? _____

_____

_____

113. Do you tend to favor one child?   Yes   No   00
113a. If yes, which, and why? _____

_____

114. Does your husband favor one child? Yes   No   00
114a. If yes, which, and why? _____

_____

115. How about grandparents favoring one child?
　　　　　Maternal   Yes   No   00
　　　　　Paternal   Yes   No   00
115a. If yes, which, and why? _____

_____

_____

116. Which of your children is brightest for his age? _____

_____

117. How do your other children seem to feel about X's problem?

_____

118. How do they explain X to their friends? _____

_____

119. How have you explained X's problem to your other children?

_____

_____

_____

120. Do you feel that your other children cooperate with you in teaching X various things? _____
　　　　　Code: _____Very cooperative
　　　　　　　　_____Somewhat cooperative
　　　　　　　　_____Minimally cooperative
　　　　　　　　_____Not cooperative
　　　　　　　　_____Does not apply
120a. If cooperative—How do they help? _____

_____

121. At some time or other, every child experiences a rejection by some adults who for some reason or another may not like him at the moment. When this has happened to your child, what has X done? _____

_____

122. One frequently hears that children can be very cruel. Children may refuse to allow others to play with them or

in some other way directly reject a child. When this happens, what does X do? _____
_____

123. When you consider the entire business of rearing a child, from which source do you feel you learned the most about raising children, such as, from your mother, from books, from watching others, etc.? _____
_____

127. How would you describe X, so that a person like myself who doesn't know X, would get an idea of what kind of child X is? _____
_____
_____

Discipline

128. Do you feel that X has to be disciplined differently than other children?   Yes   No
If yes—why? _____
_____

(CR 30M-1ab)   129. If *more or less* of a discipline problem—why do you feel this is so? _____
_____

(CR 30M-2b)   130. If *different* techniques in discipline—Why? _____
_____
_____

131. In general, how well would you say you and your husband agree about the best way to handle X? _____
_____

132. Does he ever think you are too strict or not strict enough?
     Code: _____Too strict
            _____Not strict enough
            _____Just right
            _____Don't know how he feels
            _____Other *(probe)*

     132a. If *too strict* or *not strict enough*, why does he feel this way? _____

133. When X has to be disciplined, who usually does it, you or your husband (assuming both of you are there)? _____
_____

134. How strict is your husband with X?
     Code: _____Too strict
            _____Not strict enough
            _____Just right
            _____Don't know how he feels
            _____Other *(probe)*

135. Does your husband ever do anything in disciplining that you would rather he would not do?   Yes   No
135a. If yes, what? _____

135b. If yes, why does he do this? _____

135c. If yes, what have you done about this? _____
_____
_____

Interview Series To Accompany Discipline Form CR 30M

How do you feel about your results with each of these discipline techniques?

		Very Effective	*Somewhat Effective*	*Minimally Effective*	*Ineffective*
(4a)	136.	Depriving child			
(4b)	137.	Threaten to tell father			
(4c)	138.	Slapping			
(4d)	139.	Spanking			
(4e)	140.	Withholding affection			
(4f)	141.	Using threats			
(4g)	142.	Other			
(4h)	143.	Sending to X's room			
(4i)	144.	Sat on chair			
(4j)	145.	Putting to bed			
(4k)	145yl.	Explain behavior			

146. How often does your husband spank X? _____
        Code: _____ Never
                _____ Rarely
                _____ Occasionally
                _____ Frequently
    146a. How does X react when spanked—does it seem to hurt his feelings, make him angry, or what? _____
    _____

147. How often do you tell X that you're going to punish him and then for some reason dont follow through? _____
_____
        Code: _____ Never
                _____ Rarely
                _____ Occasionally
                _____ Frequently
    147a. What keeps you from following through? _____
    _____

148. Do you have any ways in which X can earn money? Yes No
148a. If yes—what? _____
_____

149. During the past year, have you tried to get good behavior by points, gold stars, charts, etc.?   Yes   No

  149a. If yes—which? And what for? _____

  _____

  _____

  _____

150. Do you feel you have the situation pretty well under control when X is naughty? _____

  150a. If no—why? _____

  _____

151. How much freedom do you allow X in moving about in the neighborhood? _____

  _____

  _____

152. Have you ever talked with professionals with regard to understanding your child or yourself better (psychologist, socialist worker, psychiatrist)?   Yes   No

  If yes 152a. Where? _____

          152b. For how long? _____

          152c. What happened? _____

  _____

  _____

Special Series on Mongolism

1. What is your understanding of what Mongolism is? _____

  _____

  _____

2. Have you seen any other mongoloid children?   Yes   No
   Where? _____

  2a. If yes—How do you feel X compares with them? _____

      Code: _____Better

             _____Worse

             _____About the same

3. Do you feel your child is getting better as time goes on?
   Yes   No _____

  3a. If yes—in what ways? _____

  _____

      Code: _____Much improved

             _____Somewhat improved

             _____Slightly improved

             _____Not improved

4. If menopausal mongol—What are the attitudes of your grown children towards X? _____

  _____

  _____

School Information

(Ask 153 through
158a only if X
in school)

153. Where does X go to school? _____
_____

    153a. Is he in any type of special class? _____

154. Do you feel that this is the best school arrangement for X?
Yes   No
154a. If no—Why not? _____
_____

155. What is your impression of his present teacher? _____

156. Is X learning as much as you thought he would? _____

157. How long did it take X to get used to school? _____

158. How does X get along with other children in his class?
_____

    158a. How do you judge this? _____

(Ask 159 & 160
in all cases)

159. Some people say that teachers in general are not strict
enough with their pupils. How do you feel about this?
_____
_____

160. How far do you think X will be able to go in school? _____
_____

161. Do you help X with his school work?
Code: _____Never   _____Occasionally
          _____Rarely   _____Frequently

162. Does your husband ever help with school work? _____
Code: _____Never
          _____Rarely
          _____Occasionally
          _____Frequently

163. Have you done this on your own or at the suggestion of the
teacher?   _____Own_____Teacher

164. In general, how would you say X feels about school? _____
_____
_____

Affection and Dependency

165. Do you feel that X is an affectionate child; for instance,
does he often want to be kissed and hugged? _____
Code: _____Never
          _____Rarely
          _____Occasionally
          _____Frequency

166. Besides kissing and hugging, in what other ways do you and your husband show your affection for X? _____
_____

167. What do you think your husband's attitude is towards X?
_____

168. Let's talk about some things your husband does with X in which you have no part. For instance, does he try to teach X things?   Yes   No
    168a. If yes—What things? _____
    _____
    _____

169. What sort of things do X and your husband enjoy doing together? _____
_____

170. Does your husband do things with X that he does not do with the other children?   Yes   No   00
    170a. If yes—what things? _____

171. What things do you feel X dislikes about your husband?
_____
_____

172. We are wondering who makes the main decisions about the children. In some families it is the father; in others, the mother. How does this work out in your family? _____
_____

    172a. How about health matters, such as calling the doctor or keeping X indoors for the day—Who decides that? _____
_____

173. Who decides how much X should help around the house, with cleaning, dishes, etc.? _____

174. Do you feel that your husband cooperates with you as much as you would like in raising X? _____

175. What sort of a person is your husband? _____
_____
_____

176. How would you describe yourself? _____
_____
_____

177. Do you or your husband tend to be more dominant?
    M   F

178. How do you feel about this? _____
_____

179. In what ways are you and your husband alike? _____

180. Would you rather have X take after you or your husband? M F

     180. In what ways? _____

181. Whom does X like more, you or your husband? M F
    181a. Why do you say this? _____

182. Does X behave better for you or your husband? M F
    182a. Why do you think this is so? _____

183. Do you criticize or praise more often? _____
    183a. How about your husband? _____
184. What kinds of things do you praise X for? _____
185. Do you get angry with X sometimes?   Yes   No

186. When you're tired or not feeling well, are you irritated by X?

187. How do you generally react if X demands attention when you're busy? _____
    187a. How about if X asks you to help him with something, yet you think he could probably do by himself? _____

    187b. Do you think X demands more attention from you than is usual for a child of this age? _____
188. What do you think X dislikes about you? _____

189. In what ways do you get on each other's nerves? _____

190. Do you show your affection toward each other quite a bit, or are you fairly reserved? _____
191. Do you worry a good deal about things related to X? _____
192. How serious do you feel your child's problem is? _____

193. Do you feel that the circumstances surrounding X's birth and infancy influenced the way you have reared X? _____
    In what way? _____

194. Does your child understand about God?   Yes   No
    194a. If yes—How did X learn this? _____

195. Has religion been of help to you in adjusting to this problem?   Yes   No
    195a. If yes—In what way? _____

196. Has prayer been of help to you?   Yes   No
     196a. If yes—In what way? _____

     _____

197. Does X fit into your family? _____
198. Who has helped you to understand your child's problems?

     _____

     198a. How have they helped you? _____

     _____

199. When you are worried, whom do you confide in most?

     _____

200. Do you find that it helps you to talk over your problems
     and worries with someone?   Yes   No
     200a. If yes—How does it help? _____

     _____

201. In the general course of daily living, do you feel that
     people often disappoint you?   Yes   No
202. Would you describe yourself as easygoing or domineering
     in your relationship with X? _____ Easy _____ Domineering
     202a. Why? _____

     _____

203. Many times, we know, parents have their own ideas of what
     really caused their child's problem, despite what the doctors
     have said. What do you think caused X's problem? _____

     _____

204. What effect do you feel X has had upon your marriage?

     _____

205. What effect do you feel X has had upon you? _____

     _____

     _____

206. Do you think people generally understand your problem?
     Yes   No
     206a. What makes you feel this way? _____

     _____

207. How important do you think it is for a boy of X's age to
     act like a real boy (for a girl to be lady-like)? _____

     207a. *(For boys)* How about playing with dolls and that
           sort of thing? _____
     207b. *(For girls)* How about playing rough games and that
           sort of thing? _____
208. How do you feel about allowing X to run about without any
     clothes on? _____

     _____

209. What have you done about it when you have noticed him
     playing with himself? _____
     209a. Do you feel it is important to prevent this in a child?
           Yes   No
     209b. If yes—Why do you feel it is important? _____

     _____

210. How about sex play with other children—has this come up yet?　Yes　No
210a. If yes—What happened and what did you do about it?

---

211. What about children wanting to look at each other, or go to the toilet together, or giggling together—How do you feel about it when you notice this sort of thing going on among the children? _____

---

212. When X is upset, what are some of the ways you have learned to comfort him? _____

---

213. Do you feel that X does better when events are routine, regular and organized?　Yes　No
If yes—Why do you feel this is so? _____

---

214. Did X's problem have anything to do with your desire for more children?　Yes　No
If yes—please explain: _____

---

215. Since X was born, do you feel that the attitudes of friends and neighbors have changed toward you?　Yes　No
If yes—How? _____

---

216. In general, are you concerned about what others think of you?　Yes　No　_____

217. All parents give some thought to what their children will be like as adults. What do you expect of X's future in regard to employment? _____

---

218. How about marriage and parenthood? _____

---

219. Part of the business of having a child with a problem is the matter of consulting a number of professional people in your search for help. Do you feel that the professional people to whom you have taken X are genuinely interested in your problem? _____

219a. Do they seem to know what they're talking about?
Yes　No　_____

220. One final question:
Do you have any suggestions as to what else might have been included in this study to help us understand your particular situation better? _____

FATHER INTERVIEW*

Boy _____
Girl _____

As you may know we are interested in all aspects of how parents deal with their children. We are just as interested in fathers as we are in mothers. As you can see we have many questions to ask. Let's begin with this one.

Infancy Feeding and Care

1. Now will you think back to when _____ was a baby. Was X easy to take care of when he was a baby?

_____

2. Who took care of him mostly then? _____
   (If someone other than mother) please explain: _____

_____

3. How much did you do in connection with taking care of X when he was a baby? _____

3a. Did you ever change the baby's diapers?	Yes	No
3b. Feed him?	Yes	No
3c. Give a bath?	Yes	No

4. Did you care for your other children in the same way?   Yes   No
   4a. (If no) Why were you different with X? _____

_____

Initial Concern and Action

5. When did you first become concerned about X? _____

_____

6. What did you notice? _____

_____

7. Did your wife recognize this too? _____
   How did she react? _____
8. Did she agree with you about your concern? _____

_____

9. Whom did you talk to about your concern? _____

_____

10. To whom did you take the child? _____
11. What were you told by this doctor? _____

_____

12. How did you feel about this? _____

_____

13. How many times did this doctor see you to explain the problem? _____

_____

13a. How much time did he spend with you? _____

_____
*Interview Form IFi

14. What was his attitude (sympathetic, impatient, etc.) _____

15. Did the doctor suggest some form of help for X? _____
    15a. What? _____

16. Did you go to anyone else to find out what was wrong
    with X?   Yes   No
    16a. If yes— *Probe number of intermediate contacts, re-*
    action, motivation. _____

    _____

    _____

    _____

    _____

17. When do you feel that you got the diagnosis of X's problem?
    Age of child _____. _____

    _____

18. From whom? _____
19. What were you told? _____

    _____

20. How did you feel when you found out the nature of X's
    problem? _____

    _____

    _____

21. How many times did this doctor see you to explain the
    problem? _____

    _____

22. What was his attitude? _____

    _____

23. Did the doctor suggest some form of help for X's problem?
    23a. What? _____
24. Does your wife accept what the doctors have said about X?

    _____

    _____

Toilet Training

Now we would like to consider toilet training.

25. At what age was toilet training started with X?
    25a. Bowel _____
    25b. Bladder _____
26. Did you agree with your wife on the time of starting train-
    ing?   Yes   No
    26a. (If no) Why did you disagree? _____

    _____

27. Was this the same time as your other children were started?
    Yes   No

27a. (If later) Did you and your wife discuss starting later with this child? _____
_____

28. How did you help with the toilet training? _____
_____

29. Does X wet the bed? _____
29a. (If yes) How do you feel about this? _____
_____

29b. (If yes) What have you done personally to help X with this bedwetting problem? _____
_____

30. Did you help along with the toilet training of your other children.   Yes   No   00
31. How long was it before X was trained? _____
31a. Bowels _____
31b. Bladder _____

Sleep and Rest Patterns

32. How are you involved in putting X to bed? _____
_____
_____

33. Does X's problem cause you to do anything differently with him at bedtime than you might do with your other children? _____
_____
_____

34. What does X take to bed at night? _____
34a. How do you feel about this? _____
_____

34b. Is this or was this true of your other children? _____
_____

35. Is there anything unusual about X's sleep pattern (such as nightmares, restlessness etc.)? _____
_____

36. Once X is in bed for the night does he both you? _____
_____

36a. What have you done about this? _____
_____

(CR 25F-10a)   37. If "tires more easily"—Why do you feel this is so? _____
_____
_____

Childhood Illnesses

38. Did your child have any convulsions or seizures during infancy?   Yes   No

38a. Which? _____

38b. At what age? _____

38c. What did the doctor say about this? _____

_____

38d. How often did these occur? _____

_____

39. Did your child have any convulsions or seizures after the age of two?   Yes   No

39a. Which? _____

39b. At what age? _____

39c. How frequently? _____

39d. Under MD care? _____

39e. Type medication? _____

40. Is X now receiving medication to "calm his nerves"? Yes   No

40a. If yes, what type? _____

40b. Does it help? _____

Vision and Hearing

41. Have you ever thought there was something wrong with this child's eyesight?   Yes   No

41a. What was your concern? _____

_____

42. Have you ever thought there was something wrong with this child's hearing?   Yes   No

42a. What was your concern? _____

_____

Child Therapy Form

(CR 27f)

43. On each type therapy checked—*(Probe)*

Do you feel this helped X?

(Evaluate response and rank)

Type Therapy _____	Type therapy _____
_____Great benefit	_____Great benefit
_____Some benefit	_____Some benefit
_____Minimal benefit	_____Minimal benefit
_____No change or got worse	_____No change or got worse
Type Therapy _____	Type therapy _____
_____Great benefit	_____Great benefit
_____Some benefit	_____Some benefit
_____Minimal benefit	_____Minimal benefit
_____No change or got worse	_____No change or got worse

44. How does X get along with his brothers and sisters? _____

_____

45. With which child does X get along best?
   Code: _____Oldest
          _____Youngest
          _____Nearest chronologic sib
          _____
          _____Does not apply
   45a. Why do you feel this is so? _____
   _____
   _____

46. With which child does he fight most often? _____
   Code: _____Oldest
          _____Youngest
          _____Nearest sib
          _____
          _____Does not apply
47. Do you give more attention to X than your other children?
   _____
   47a. If *more* or *less*—Why? _____
   _____

48. Do you find yourself making comparisons between your
   children? _____
   _____
   48a. What sort of comparisons? _____
   _____

49. Do you tend to favor one child?   Yes   No   00
   49a. If yes, which, and why? _____
   _____

50. Does your wife favor one child?   Yes   No   00
   50a. If yes, which, and why? _____
   _____

51. How about grandparents favoring one child? _____
   Maternal   Yes   No   00
   Paternal   Yes   No   00
   51a. If yes, which, and why? _____
   _____
   _____

52. Which of your children is brightest for his age? _____00
   _____
   _____

53. How do your other children seem to feel about X's problem?
   _____
   _____

54. How do they explain X to their friends? _____
   _____

55. How have you explained X's problem to your other children?
   _____
   _____

56. Do you feel that your other children cooperate with you in
   teaching X various things? _____

Code: _____Very cooperative

_____Somewhat cooperative

_____Minimally cooperative

_____Not cooperative

_____Does not apply

56a. (If cooperative) How do they help? _____

57. At some time or other, every child experiences a rejection by some adults who for some reason or another may not like him at the moment. When this has happened to your child, what has X done? _____

_____

58. One frequently hears that children can be very cruel. Children may refuse to allow others to play with them or in some other way directly reject a child. When this happens, what does X do? _____

_____

59. When you consider the entire business of rearing a child, from which source do you feel you learned the most about raising children, such as, from your father, mother, from books, from watching others, etc.? _____

_____

63. How would you describe X, so that a person like myself who doesn't know X, would get an idea of what kind of child X is? _____

_____

_____

Discipline

64. Do you feel that X has to be disciplined differently than other children?   Yes   No

64a. If yes—Why? _____

_____

(CR 30F-1ab)   65. If *more* or *less* of a discipline problem—why do you feel this is so? _____

_____

(CR 30F-2b)   66. If *different* discipline techniques—why? _____

_____

67. In general, how well would you say you and your wife agree about the best way to handle X? _____

_____

68. Does she ever think you are too strict or not strict enough?

Code: _____Too strict

_____Not strict enough

_____Just right

_____Don't know how she feels

_____Other *(probe)*

68a. If *too strict* or *not strict enough,* why does she feel this way? _____

69. When X has to be disciplined, who usually does it, you or your wife (assuming both of you are there)? _____

70. How strict is your wife with X?
    Code: _____Too strict
    _____Not strict enough
    _____Just right
    _____Don't know how she feels
    _____Other (probe)

71. Does your wife ever do anything in disciplining that you would rather she would not do?   Yes   No
    71a. If yes—What? _____

    71b. If yes—why does she do this? _____

    71c. If yes—what have you done about this? _____

Interview Series To Accompany Discipline Form CR 30F

How do you feel about your results with each of these discipline techniques?

		Very Effective	Somewhat Effective	Minimally Effective	Ineffective
(4a)	72.	Threaten to tell			
(4b)	73.	father			
		Slapping			
(4c)	74.	Spanking			
(4d)	75.	Withholding			
(4e)	76.	Depriving child			
		affection			
(4f)	77.	Using threats			
(4g)	78.	Sending to X's			
		room			
(4h)	79.	Sat on chair			
(4i)	80.	Putting to bed			
(4j)	81.	Explain behavior			
(4k)	81yl.	Other			

82. How often does your wife spank X? _____

    Code: _____Never
    _____Rarely
    _____Occasionally
    _____Frequently

83. How does X react when spanked—does it seem to hurt his feelings, make him angry, or what? _____

_____

_____

84. How often do you tell X that you're going to punish him and then for some reason don't follow through? _____

_____

Code: _____Never
_____Rarely
_____Occasionally
_____Frequently

84a. What keeps you from following through? _____

_____

85. Do you have any ways in which X can earn money?
Yes   No
85a. If yes—what? _____

_____

86. During the past year, have you tried to get good behavior by points, gold stars, charts, etc.?   Yes   No
86a. If yes—which? And what for? _____

_____

87. Do you feel you have the situation pretty well under control when X is naughty? _____
87a. If no—why? _____

_____

88. How much freedom do you allow X in moving about in the neighborhood? _____

_____

89. Have you ever talked with professionals with regard to understanding your child or yourself better (psychologist, social worker, psychiatrist)?   Yes   No
(If yes) 89a. Where? _____
89b. For how long? _____
89c. What happened? _____

_____

_____

Special Series on Organics

1. The brain is a very mysterious thing. What do you think has actually happened to the brain in X's case? _____

_____

_____

2. Have you seen any other children with brain-injury?   Yes   No

2a. If yes—How do you feel X compares with them? _____
_____
_____
_____

    Code: _____Better
            _____Worse
            _____About the same

3. In what way does X show that he is brain-injured? _____
_____
_____
_____

4. Do you feel your child is improving as time goes on?   Yes   No
4a. If yes—In what ways? _____
_____
_____

    Code: _____Much improved
            _____Somewhat improved
            _____Slightly improved
            _____Not improved

School Information

(Ask 90 through 95a only if X in school)

90. Where does X go to school? _____
90a. Is he in any type of special class? _____

91. Do you feel that this is the best school arrangement for X?
    Yes   No
91a. If no—Why not? _____

92. What is your impression of his present teacher? _____

93. Is X learning as much as you thought he would? _____

94. How long did it take X to get used to school? _____

95. How does X get along with other children in his class?
_____
_____

    95a. How do you judge this? _____

(Ask 96 and 97 in all cases)

96. Some people say that teachers in general are not strict enough with their pupils. How do you feel about this?
_____

97. How far do you think X will be able to go in school?
_____

98. Do you help X with his school work? _____

Code: _____Never
_____Rarely
_____Occasionally
_____Frequently

99. Does your wife ever help with school work? _____
    Code: _____Never
    _____Rarely
    _____Occasionally
    _____Frequently

100. Have you done this on your own or at the suggestion of the teacher?   _____Own   _____Teacher

101. In general, how would you say X feels about school? _____
    _____
    _____

Affection and Dependency

102. Do you feel that X is an affectionate child; for instance, does he often want to be kissed and hugged? _____
    Code: _____Never
    _____Rarely
    _____Occasionally
    _____Frequently

103. Besides kissing and hugging, in what other ways do you and your wife show your affection for X? _____
    _____
    _____

104. What do you think your wife's attitude is toward X? _____
    _____
    _____

105. Let's talk about some things you do with X in which your wife has no part. For instance, do you try to teach X things?   Yes   No
    105a. If yes—What things? _____
    _____
    _____

106. What sort of things do you and X enjoy doing together?
    _____
    _____

107. Do you do things with X that you do not do with the other children?   Yes   No   00
    107a. If yes—What things? _____
    _____
    _____
    _____

108. What things do you feel X dislikes about your wife?
    _____
    _____

109. We are wondering who makes the main decisions about the children. In some families it is the father; in others, the mother. How does this work out in your family? ....
_____

109a. How about health matters, such as calling the doctor or keeping X indoors for the day—Who decides that?
_____

110. Who decides how much X should help around the house, with cleaning, dishes, etc.? _____

111. Do you feel that your wife cooperates with you as much as you would like in raising X? _____

112. What sort of a person is your wife? _____
_____
_____

113. How would you describe yourself? _____
_____
_____

114. Do you or your wife tend to be more dominant   M   F
115. How do you feel about this? _____

116. In what ways are you and your wife alike? _____

117. Would you rather have X take after you or your wife?
       M   F

117a. In what ways? _____

118. Whom does X like more, you or your wife?   M   F
118a. Why do you say this? _____

119. Does X behave better for you or your wife?   M   F
119a. Why do you think this is so? _____

120. Do you criticize or praise more often? _____

120a. How about your wife? _____
121. What kinds of things do you praise X for? _____

122. Do you get angry with X sometimes?   Yes   No

123. When you're tired or not feeling well, are you irritated by X?
_____

124. How do you generally react if X demands attention when you're busy? _____

    124a. How about if X asks you to help him with something, yet you think he could probably do by himself?

_____

_____

    124b. Do you think X demands more attention from you than is usual for a child of this age? _____

125. What do you think X dislikes about you? _____

126. In what ways do you get on each other's nerves? _____

_____

_____

127. Do you show your affection toward each other quite a bit, or are you fairly reserved? _____

128. Do you worry a good deal about things related to X?

_____

129. How serious do you feel your child's problem is? _____

130. Do you feel that the circumstances surround X's birth and infancy influenced the way you have reared X?
  Yes   No
    130a. If yes—In what ways? _____

131. Does your child understand about God?   Yes   No
    131a. If yes—How did X learn this? _____

_____

132. Has religion been of help to you in adjusting to this problem?   Yes   No
    132a. If yes—In what way? _____

_____

133. Has prayer been of help to you?   Yes   No
    133a. If yes—In what way? _____

134. Does X fit into your family? _____

135. Who has helped you to understand your child's problems?

_____

    135a. How have they helped you? _____

136. When you are worried, whom do you confide in most?

_____

_____

137. Do you find that it helps you to talk over your problems and worries with someone? Yes No
137a. If yes—How does it help? _____
_____
_____

138. In the general course of daily living, do you feel that people often disappoint you? Yes No

139. Would you describe yourself as easygoing or domineering in your relationship with X? _____Easy _____Domineering
139a. Why? _____
_____

140. Many times, we know, parents have their own ideas of what *really* caused their child's problem, despite what the doctors have said. What do *you* think caused X's problem? _____
_____
_____
_____

141. What effect do you feel X has had upon your marriage?
_____

142. What effect do you feel that X has had upon you? _____
_____

143. Do you think people generally understand your problem? Yes No
143a. What makes you feel this way? _____
_____
_____

144. How important do you think it is for a boy of X's age to act like a real boy (for a girl to be lady-like)? _____
_____

144a. *(For boys)* How about playing with dolls and that sort of thing? _____
144b. *(For girls)* How about playing rough games and that sort of thing? _____

145. How do you feel about allowing X to run about without his clothes on? _____
_____

146. What have you done about it when you have noticed him playing with himself? _____
_____

146a. Do you feel it is important to prevent this in a child? Yes No
146b. If yes—Why do you feel it is important? _____
_____

147. How about sex play with other children—has this come up yet? Yes No

147a. If yes—What happened and what did you do about it? _____

_____

148. What about children wanting to look at each other, or go to the toilet together, or giggling together—How do you feel about it when you notice this sort of thing going on among the children? _____

_____

149. When X is upset, what are some of the ways you have learned to comfort him? _____

_____

150. Do you feel that X does better when events are routine, regular and organized?   Yes   No
150a. If yes—Why do you feel this is so? _____

_____

151. Did X's problem have anything to do with your desire for more children?   Yes   No
151a. If yes—Please explain: _____

_____

152. Since X was born, do you feel that the attitudes of friends and neighbors have changed toward you?   Yes   No
152a. If yes—How? _____

_____

153. In general, are you concerned about what others think of you?   Yes   No

_____

154. All parents give some thought to what their children will be like as adults. What do you expect of X's future in regard to employment? _____

_____

155. How about marriage and parenthood? _____

_____

156. Part of the business of having a child with a problem is the matter of consulting a number of professional people in your search for help. Do you feel that the professional people to whom you have taken X are genuinely interested in your problem? _____

_____

_____

156a. Do they seem to know what they're talking about?
     Yes   No

_____

_____

157. One final question:
Do you have any suggestions as to what else might have been
included in this study to help us understand your particular
situation better? _____

_____

_____

_____

SOCIOECONOMIC FORM*

Age and Sex of Siblings

_____

_____

_____

_____

_____

_____

_____

_____

Annual gross income of family (check the correct category)
1. Below $2,500 _____   4. $4,600—$6,000 _____
2. $2,600—$3,500 _____   5. $6,100—$8,500 _____
3. $3,600—$4,500 _____   6. $8,600—$10,000 _____
                                               7. Above $10,000 _____

Own your own home _____ Rent _____
Husband's Occupation: _____

---

*C.R. Group Form 1M

FAMILY HISTORY*

Questions About Mother

1. Mother's place of birth _____
2. Mother's education (circle highest completed)
     1 2 3 4 5 6 7 8 HS1 HS2 HS3 HS4 C1 C2 C3 C4
     Master's Degree
3. Were you raised by your own parents? _____Yes _____No
   (If no—explain) _____

_____

_____

4. Are you currently employed? _____Yes _____No
5. What kind of job? _____
6. How many hours per week?   _____Full time
                                        _____Less than 5 hours
                                        _____5—10 Hours
                                        _____10—20 Hours
                                        _____20—35 Hours

7. Education of mother's parents: (Circle highest completed)
   For mother's father: 1 2 3 4 5 6 7 8 HS1 HS2 HS3 HS4
   C1 C2 C3 C4 Postgraduate
   For mother's mother: 1 2 3 4 5 6 7 8 HS1 HS2 HS3 HS4
   C1 C2 C3 C4 Postgraduate
8. What kind of work did your father do? _____
9. How many _____brothers _____sisters
10. Who was the more dominant member of your family?
    _____Father _____Mother
a. Do you belong to a church or synagogue?_____ Religion?_____
   How frequently do you attend? _____
b. Were your parents of this belief too? _____ If not, what was their
   religious preference?_____
c. Do your children receive religious instructions? _____

*C.R. Group Form 2M, 2F.

FAMILY HISTORY*

Questions About Mother

1. Mother's place of birth _____
2. Mother's education (circle highest completed)
   1 2 3 4 5 6 7 8 HS1 HS2 HS3 HS4 C1 C2 C3 C4
   Master's Degree
3. Were you raised by your own parents? _____Yes _____No
   (If no—explain) _____

   _____
   _____
4. Are you currently employed? _____Yes _____No
5. What kind of job? _____
6. How many hours per week?   _____Full time
                                 _____Less than 5 hours
                                 _____5—10 Hours
                                 _____10—20 Hours
                                 _____20—35 Hours
7. Education of mother's parents: (Circle highest completed)
   For mother's father: 1 2 3 4 5 6 7 8 HS1 HS2 HS3 HS4
   C1 C2 C3 C4 Postgraduate
   For mother's mother: 1 2 3 4 5 6 7 8 HS1 HS2 HS3 HS4
   C1 C2 C3 C4 Postgraduate
8. What kind of work did your father do? _____
9. How many _____brothers _____sisters
10. Who was the more dominant member of your family?
    _____Father _____Mother
a. Do you belong to a church or synagogue?_____ Religion?_____
   How frequently do you attend? _____
b. Were your parents of this belief too? _____ If not, what was their
   religious preference?_____
c. Do your children receive religious instructions? _____

*C.R. Group Form 2M, 2F.

FAMILY SOCIAL PATTERNS*

Directions: Families usually have special things that they do together as a unit. Each family is different. Check each item in the list below according to the way it applies in your case.

	Often	Some-times	Barely	Never	Not Possible
1. We visit my husband's relatives, taking the children along.					
2. We visit my relatives, taking the children along.					
3. When we visit relatives or friends, my husband and I go alone.					
4. When we visit relatives or friends, we take the whole family.					
5. My husband and I go out alone to movies, dinners, plays, etc.					
6. My husband and I go out with a group of people.					
7. We have a regular evening away from the children.					
8. We have family picnics.					
9. We spend our vacation away from home without the children.					
10. The whole family, as a unit, spends the vacation away from home.					
11. We play games in which the whole family joins.					
12. We go to church as a family group.					
13. We pray together as a family group, other than at meal time.					
14. We read aloud from the Bible.					
15. The family enjoys listening to records.					
16. We sing together.					
17. We enjoy taking long auto trips.					
18. We enjoy hiking with the family.					
19. We have friends over to the house to play cards.					
20. We go to sports events as a family group.					
21. "Visitors" stop in without invitation or warning.					
22. We have religious rituals which we conduct with the family, according to our religious beliefs.					
23. We go to the movies with the family.					

24. Other.
25. Add any comments you wish
    which might explain any of above
    answers.

---

*C.R. Group Form 3M, 3MF, 3FF, 3FM.

COURTSHIP AND MARRIAGE*

1. Is this your first marriage?
    1a. _____Yes
    1b. _____No
2. How long had you gone with your husband before you became engaged?
    About _____ months.
3. How long were you engaged? About _____ months.
4. Just before your marriage, did you prefer to spend your leisure time:
    4a. _____At home
    4b. _____Usually at home
    4c. _____Usually on the go
    4d. _____Always on the go
5. Just before your marriage, did your husband prefer to spend his leisure time:
    5a. _____At home
    5b. _____Usually at home
    5c. _____Usually on the go
    5d. _____Always on the go
6. Before the children were born, how much of your spare time did you and your husband spend together in your common interests:
    6a. _____All of it
    6b. _____Most of it
    6c. _____A little of it
    6d. _____Almost none of it
7. How long after marriage had you planned to have your first child?
    7a. _____No special plans
    7b. _____As soon as possible
    7c. _____One or two years
    7d. _____Three or more years
8. The engagement period is often one of doubt. Did you ever have any doubts about your engagement?
    8a. _____Yes
    8a. _____No
9. By whom were you married?
    9a. _____Religious person
    9b. _____Civil ceremony
10. In the first year or so of marriage, did you have any difficulty in adjusting to married life?
    10a. _____Very much
    10b. _____Some
    10c. _____A little
    10d. _____Not at all

---

*C.R. Group Form 4.

11. What was your occupation at the time of your marriage?
12. When you were a child, how happy was your mother in her marriage?
    12a. _____Exceedingly happy
    12b. _____Happier than most
    12c. _____Average happiness
    12d. _____Less than average happiness
13. When you were a child, how happy was your father in his marriage?
    13a. _____Exceedingly happy
    13b. _____Happier than most
    13c. _____Average happiness
    13d. _____Less than average happiness
14. When you were a child, what was your attitude toward your mother?
    14a. _____Very close
    14b. _____Fairly close
    14c. _____Not very close
    14d. _____Not close at all
15. When you were a child, what was your attitude toward your father?
    15a. _____Very close
    15b. _____Fairly close
    15c. _____Not very close
    15d. _____Not close at all
16. Did either your mother or father disapprove of your marriage?
    16a. _____Yes
    16b. _____No
17. In the first year or so of your marriage, how often did you attend church services?
    17a. _____Less than once a month
    17b. _____Two or three times a month
    17c. _____Four or more times a month
18. In the first year of your marriage, how many friends did you and your husband have in common?
    18a. _____Almost none
    18b. _____A few
    18c. _____Several
    18d. _____Many
19. Getting ahead in occupation or place in the community sometimes means that you have to do certain things you may not like. Which of the following things would you be willing to do in order to get ahead?

	Very Willing	Somewhat Willing	A Little Willing	Not at all Willing
For your husband to learn new skills				
Leave your friends				
Keep quiet about political views				
Move around the country a lot				
For your husband to take on more responsibility				
Give up spare time				
Keep quiet about religious views				

NEIGHBOR RELATIONSHIPS*

1. How long have you lived in the neighborhood you are now living in?
   (Please check the appropriate answer to each question.)
   1a. _____less than one year
   1b. _____1-3 years
   1c. _____3-10 years
   1d. _____10-20 years
   1e. _____20 years or longer

2. How many of your friends who live in your neighborhood did you get to know since you or they moved into the neighborhood?
   2a. _____More than two
   2b. _____Two
   2c. _____One
   2d. _____None

3. Do you and any of your neighbors go to movies, picnics or other things like that together?
   3a. _____Often
   3b. _____Sometimes
   3c. _____Rarely
   3d. _____Never

4. Do you and your neighbors entertain one another?
   4a. _____Often
   4b. _____Simetimes
   4c. _____Rarely
   4d. _____Never

5. If you were holding a party or tea for an out-of-town visitor, how many of your friends would you invite?
   5a. _____More than two
   5b. _____Two
   5c. _____One
   5d. _____None

6. How many of your neighbors' homes have you ever been in?
   6a. _____Four or more
   6b. _____One to three
   6c. _____None

7. How many of your neighbors have ever talked to you about their problems when they were worried or asked you for advise or help?
   7a. _____More than two
   7b. _____Two
   7c. _____One
   7d. _____More than two

8. Do you and your neighbors exchange or borrow things from one another such as books, magazines, dishes, tools, recipes, preserves, or garden vegetables?
   8a. _____Often
   8b. _____Sometimes
   8c. _____Rarely
   8d. _____Never

---

*C.R. Group Form 5.

9. About how many of the people in your neighborhood would you recognize by sight if you saw them in a large crowd?
   9a. _____More than half
   9b. _____About half
   9c. _____A few
   9d. _____None

10. With how many of your neighbors do you have a friendly talk fairly frequently?
    10a. _____More than two
    10b. _____Two
    10c. _____One
    10d. _____None

11. About how many of the people in your neighborhood do you say "Hello" or "Good morning" to when you meet on the street?
    11a. _____Six or more
    11b. _____Five or less

12. How many of the names of the families in your neighborhood do you know?
    12a. _____Four or more
    12b. _____One to three
    12c. _____None

13. How often do you have a talk with any of your neighbors?
    13a. _____Often
    13b. _____Sometimes
    13c. _____Rarely
    13d. _____Never

14. Are there neighbors you do not like?
    14a. _____None
    14b. _____A few
    14c. _____Many

15. My neighbors at times disappoint me.
    15a. _____Yes
    15b. _____No

16. What my neighbors think of me does not bother me.
    16a. _____Yes
    16b. _____No

EXPLANATION GIVEN TO NEIGHBORS

We know that at one time or another neighbors may ask about your child and that you give some explanation. The statements listed below cover a variety of possibilities. Check *each* statement that applies to your case.

_____ I explain only when someone asks me directly.

_____ I tell them exactly what the doctors have told us about our child.

_____ I tell them nothing. It's none of their business.

_____ I have told our immediate neighbors, but have not bothered to tell the others.

_____ My neighbors have never talked to me about my child.

_____ I tell my neighbors about my child because I think they should know the troubles we have.

_____ I have explained my child's problem so that the neighbors will be more understanding of him.

_____ I keep my neighbors informed regularly on my child's progress. They are very understanding.

_____ I have no neighbors to talk to.

_____ I've told them that he was sick when he was a baby.

_____ I've told them that we don't know what's wrong.

_____ I've told them there's nothing wrong.

_____ That he'll outgrow it.

_____ I haven't told them anything.

_____ I have given them some literature to read.

_____ I've held a neighborhood meeting to discuss his problems.

_____ I've found it better to make no effort to explain.

_____ I've told them that he needs to learn control of his emotions.

_____ I feel better if I tell people that he is _____.

_____ I feel badly if I tell people he is _____.

_____ I do not use the word _____ in referring to my child.

_____ Add any information which you feel might better help us to understand your particular situation in this area.

CHILD'S ACTIVITIES

_____ Scout troop	( ) weekly	( ) monthly
_____ YMCA program	( ) weekly	( ) monthly
_____ Church social groups	( ) weekly	( ) monthly
_____ Music lessons	( ) weekly	( ) monthly
_____ Dancing lessons	( ) weekly	( ) monthly
_____ Athletic team	( ) weekly	( ) monthly

CHILD'S HOBBIES OR INTERESTS

_____ Builds models (airplanes, cars, etc.)

_____ Collects things _____

_____ Reads for pleasure

_____ Plays phonograph

_____ Plays table games

_____ Watches TV

_____ Plays cowboys

_____ Rides bike

_____ Skates

_____ Visits other kids

_____ Goes shopping for mother

_____ Does chores

_____ Plays dolls

_____ Plays house

_____ Has paper route

_____ Does tasks for neighbors

_____ Does homework

_____ Sets table

_____ Cooks

_____ Practices musical instrument

_____ Cleans own room

_____ Goes to movies

---------- Goes to library
---------- Attends lectures
---------- Does science experiments
---------- Plays with animals
---------- Goes to playground
---------- Plays outdoor games
---------- Goes to church
---------- Hangs around neighborhood business places
---------- Does errands for money
---------- Draws
---------- Colors
---------- Plays in sandbox
---------- Plays with toy cars
---------- Wanders aimlessly—doesn't seem to know what to do
---------- Does silly things which seem to make no sense.
---------- Is too wild to settle down to anything.
---------- Other:

HOBBY, ACTIVITY AND OUTSIDE INTERESTS OF MOTHER

Regularly scheduled activities in which I participate:

---------- Church Social Club	( ) weekly	( ) monthly	
---------- Card Club	( ) weekly	( ) monthly	
---------- Committee work	( ) weekly	( ) monthly	
---------- Bowling	( ) weekly	( ) monthly	
---------- Sorority Group	( ) weekly	( ) monthly	
---------- Volunteer Work	( ) weekly	( ) monthly	----------------------
---------- Church Choir	( ) weekly	( ) monthly	*(Place)*
---------- Dramatic Work	( ) weekly	( ) monthly	
---------- Evening school classes	( ) weekly	( ) monthly	
---------- Sewing Group	( ) weekly	( ) monthly	
---------- Scout leader	( ) weekly	( ) monthly	
---------- Dancing club	( ) weekly	( ) monthly	

Interests which occupy my time:

---------- Knitting
---------- Making my own clothes
---------- Making clothes for my children
---------- Skating
---------- Decorating
---------- Making jewelry
---------- Gardening
---------- Clay modeling
---------- Drawing or Painting
---------- Making hats
---------- Collecting things
---------- --
---------- --
---------- --

HOBBY, ACTIVITY & OUTSIDE INTERESTS OF FATHER

Regularly scheduled activities in which my husband participates:

_____ Church Social Club	(	) weekly	(	) monthly
_____ Card Club	(	) weekly	(	) monthly
_____ Lodge Work	(	) weekly	(	) monthly
_____ Bowling League	(	) weekly	(	) monthly
_____ Fishing trips	(	) weekly	(	) monthly
_____ Hunting trips	(	) weekly	(	) monthly
_____ Church Choir	(	) weekly	(	) monthly
_____ Music Group	(	) weekly	(	) monthly
_____ Dramatic Club	(	) weekly	(	) monthly
_____ Evening School Classes	(	) weekly	(	) monthly
_____ Church Choir or Glee Club	(	) weekly	(	) monthly
_____ Dartball League	(	) weekly	(	) monthly
_____ Baseball Team	(	) weekly	(	) monthly
_____ Basketball Team	(	) weekly	(	) monthly
_____ Scout Work	(	) weekly	(	) monthly
_____ CYO Work	(	) weekly	(	) monthly
_____ Dancing Club	(	) weekly	(	) monthly

Activities which occupy his time:

_____ Working in his home workshop
_____ Special mechanics
_____ Making models
_____ Practicing a musical instrument
_____ Reading
_____ Making furniture
_____ Household repairs
_____ Square dancing
_____ Collections

_____ _____
_____ _____
_____ _____

MY RELATIVES

1. _____ Do not see anything wrong with our child
2. _____ Think he needs a good spanking
3. _____ Never express their opinion one way or the other
4. _____ Think that we make too much of a fuss over this child
5. _____ Think that we're too easy on this child
6. _____ Think that we do not show him enough love
7. _____ Think that we are exaggerating our problems
8. _____ Think that we have more of a problem than we realize
9. _____ Try to be kind and helpful
10. _____ Are very sympathetic to our problem
11. _____ Think we ought to place this child in an institution
12. _____ Feel that he is just a spoiled child
13. _____ Think we ought to take him to another doctor

14. ....Think we are not doing enough for him
15. ....Criticize the way we handle this child
16. ....Feel sorry for this child
17. ....Think this is all my husband's fault
17a. ....Think this is all my fault
18. ....Think that the child's condition was inherited from my husband
18a. ....Think that the child's condition was inherited from me
19. ....Do not visit us because of this child
20. ....Do not invite us to their houses because of this child
21. ....Don't seem to know how to act in the presence of this child
22. ....Tell us about all sorts of homemade cures
23. ....Are completely unaware that we have a problem
24. ....Are seen very seldom
25. ....Are a great help to us
26. ....Have rejected me
27. ....Are not on speaking terms with us
28. ....Are afraid of this child
29. ....Try too hard to be kind to this child
30. ....Don't know how to talk to this child
31. ....Seem to ignore this child
32. ....Have no contact with us
33. ....Do not understand our problem at all
34. ....Are ideal
35. ....Have not been told a thing
Other

MY HUSBAND'S RELATIVES

1. ....Do not see anything wrong with our child
2. ....Think he needs a good spanking
3. ....Never express their opinion one way or the other
4. ....Think that we make too much of a fuss over this child
5. ....Think that we're too easy on this child
6. ....Think that we do not show him enough love
7. ....Think that we are exaggerating our problems
8. ....Think that we have more of a problem than we realize
9. ....Try to be kind and helpful
10. ....Are very sympathetic to our problem
11. ....Think we ought to place this child in an institution
12. ....Feel that he is just a spoiled child
13. ....Think we ought to take him to another doctor
14. ....Think we are not doing enough for him
15. ....Criticize the way we handle this child
16. ....Feel sorry for this child
17. ....Think this is all my fault
17a. ....Think this is all my husband's fault
18. ....Think that the child's condition was inherited from me
18a. ....Think that the child's condition was inherited from my husband
19. ....Do not visit us because of this child
20. ....Do not invite us to their houses because of this child

21. _____Don't seem to know how to act in the presence of this child
22. _____Tell us about all sorts of homemade cures
23. _____Are completely unaware that we have a problem
24. _____Are seen very seldom
25. _____Are a great help to us
26. _____Have rejected me
27. _____Are afraid of this child
28. _____Are not on speaking terms with us
29. _____Try too hard to be kind to this child
30. _____Don't know how to talk to this child
31. _____Seem to ignore this child
32. _____Have no contact with us
33. _____Do not understand our problem at all
34. _____Are ideal
35. _____Have not been told a thing

Other

CHILD BEHAVIOR CHECKLIST*

C.R. Group Form 12

Below is a list of different kinds of child behavior. If your child usually does the things listed, put a circle around the word "yes." If she (he) does not usually do it, put a circle around the word "No."

1. Yes No Free to roam all over house and yard
2. Yes No Walks upstairs without help
3. Yes No Enjoys rough and tumble play
4. Yes No Buttons and unbuttons own clothing
5. Yes No Takes off coat or dress without help
6. Yes No Eats with a fork
7. Yes No Gets a drink of water without help
8. Yes No Puts on coat or dress without help
9. Yes No Permitted to play with scissors
10. Yes No I make frequent trips to child's room to see if he (she) is sleeping quietly
11. Yes No Walks downstairs without help
12. Yes No Washes hands and face without help
13. Yes No Likes to keep things tidy
14. Yes No Will give up immediate pleasures for promise of getting something good later
15. Yes No Goes on little errands near house
16. Yes No Willing to wait his (her) turn
17. Yes No Willing to share toys
18. Yes No Allowed to help set the table
19. Yes No Unlaces and takes off own shoes
20. Yes No I often lie down at night with child until he (she) falls asleep
21. Yes No Once in a while, I put off until tomorrow what I ought to do today
22. Yes No Cares for self at the toilet
23. Yes No Goes about neighborhood himself (herself)
24. Yes No Laces and ties own shoes

25. Yes No Plays competitive games (for example, baseball, football)
26. Yes No Child needs favorite toy or stuffed animal to take to bed
27. Yes No Usually prefers playing with a group of two or three children to playing by himself
28. Yes No Has many fears (dark, dogs, old men)
29. Yes No Uses skates
30. Yes No I allow child to wash dishes
31. Yes No Puts toys away where they belong
32. Yes No Uses table knife for spreading butter
33. Yes No Gets ready for bed without help
34. Yes No Climbs trees, fences, or other high places
35. Yes No Uses tools (for examples, nails wood together, tightens screws)
36. Yes No Goes to bed at night willingly
37. Yes No Sometimes wets at night
38. Yes No Sometimes gets hurt in rough outdoor play
39. Yes No Is a very sensitive child
40. Yes No Insists on being first in everything
41. Yes No Bosses and teases other children a good deal
42. Yes No Uses table knife for cutting meat
43. Yes No Good table manners
44. Yes No Attends school or special classes
45. Yes No Takes a bath without help
46. Yes No Helps with routine household chores (such as sweeping or dusting)
47. Yes No I am afraid that child will be injured in outdoor play
48. Yes No Goes to the store alone to buy milk or bed
49. Yes No Goes by street car or bus alone
50. Yes No Can be left at home all alone
51. Yes No Visits overnight in friends' homes
52. Yes No Must be watched closely because of sickly condition
53. Yes No Catches cold easily
54. Yes No Gets tired easily
55. Yes No I sometimes get angry with my child
56. Yes No I prepare special food if child doesn't want to eat
57. Yes No Complains of aches and pains
58. Yes No Goes to movies alone or with other children
59. Yes No Sometimes, when I am not feeling well, I am cross with my child

PLAY BEHAVIOR WITH OTHERS*

C.R. Group Form 13

Directions:

One of the important areas of development for children is the matter of playing with other children. Listed below are some items about play. Check those items which apply to your child.

1. ....Plays nicely with other children.
2. ....Does not know how to play with others.
3. ....Continually squabbles.
4. ....Domineering (must play *his* way).
5. ....Has one regular playmate.

6. _____Withdraws from other children.
7. _____Has several children that are regular playmates.
8. _____Stands and watches but does not participate.
9. _____Has no one to play with.
10. _____Has never had opportunity to play with children of own age.
11. _____Hangs around the fringes of the group.
12. _____Hits, bites, spits or kicks children.
13. _____Plays well with one other child, but cannot seem to get along with two or more.
14. _____Pushes them around and is rough in attempt to show affection.
15. _____Breaks toys of other children.
16. _____Is destructive with his own toys.
17. _____Seems to spoil the play of other children.
18. _____Refuses to share his toys with others.
19. _____Can only play for short periods of time without becoming upset.
20. _____Refuses to play with others.
21. _____Seems unaware of other children.
22. _____Is preoccupied with a single object which amuses him, such as _____.
23. _____Cannot seem to keep his hands off other children's toys.
24. _____Expects children to come to him.
25. _____Prefers to play with younger children.
26. _____Prefers to play with older children.
27. _____Prefers to play by himself.
28. _____Must be urged to play with others.
29. _____We must continually suggest things for him to do.
30. _____Always wants me to be his playmate.
31. _____Occupies himself well when left alone to play.
32. _____Flits from one activity to another.
33. _____Never carries through on anything he starts.
34. _____Prefers to be with me rather than to play with children.
35. _____Prefers to be with children and doesn't want me around.
36. _____Most of the time he just seems to wander around with no special plan.
37. _____Other.

SIBLING ATTITUDES*

C.R. Group Form 14

Directions:

Brothers and sisters frequently must make some kind of adjustment. This adjustment varies in every family. Check those items which apply to your particular case.

1. _____Brothers and sisters resent attention we have to give to him.
2. _____Brothers and sisters try to understand.
3. _____Brothers and sisters "pick on him."
4. _____They tease him.
5. _____They are too young to be concerned.
6. _____They protect him.
7. _____They take him along with them in their play.
8. _____They complain about having to take him along in their play.
9. _____They ask many questions about what makes him different.

10. _____They bring other children into the house freely.
11. _____They do not bring other children to the home.
12. _____They think he's "nuts."
13. _____They hit him.
14. _____They have no trouble understanding him.
15. _____They refuse to let him play with their toys.
16. _____They help to dress him.
17. _____They feed him.
18. _____They resent his intrusions in their play.
19. _____They try to "teach" him school lessons.
20. _____They explain to their friends that "He is sick."
21. _____They do not seem to "see" anything wrong with him.
22. _____They cannot understand his speech.
23. _____He embarrasses them in the presence of their friends.
24. _____They blame him for their own misdeeds.
25. _____They complain that "he gets away with things."
26. _____They think he is our "favorite."
27. _____They report his misdeeds.
28. _____They are proud of him.
29. _____They attack him.
30. _____They ignore him.

COMMUNICATION FORM

_____ He seems to remember music that he hears better than he remembers words.
_____ Remembers and repeats various catch words from TV commercials.
_____ Prefers to use gestures rather than trying to talk words.
_____ He doesn't seem to remember the things I tell him.
_____ The easiest way to get through to him is by gestures.
_____ One word may have several different meanings to him.
_____ He does not respond when you call his name.
_____ He does not respond to simple directions like "come here," "sit down," etc., unless you also give some hand signal along with it.
_____ Seems there are times when he understands much better than at other times.
_____ He seems confused when somebody talks fast.
_____ Holds his hands over his ears when people talk to him.
_____ Holds his hands over his ears when he hears certain noises.
_____ Only the family seems to be able to understand him when he talks.
_____ He gets so excited when he tries to talk that the words just don't come out.
_____ We talk louder to this child.
_____ We talk slower to this child.
_____ We frequently have to say things several different ways before he understands.
_____ We use shorter sentences when we talk to him.
_____ We talk differently to him than to other children.
_____ We make sure that he's looking at us when we talk to him.
_____ He doesn't listen if he's concentrating on something.
_____ Seems to catch on better if we use gestures when we talk to him.
_____ Seems to understand other children better than he does adults.

---------- Very often it seems that he doesn't hear what I'm saying.
---------- I have to repeat things I say before he seems to catch on.
---------- Doesn't seem to understand anything people say to him.
---------- He must be looking at you while you're talking or he doesn't understand.
---------- Understands nothing that is said to him.
---------- Has no way of letting us know what he wants.
---------- We try to teach him to say words clearly.
---------- We have given up trying to teach him to say words clearly.
---------- He's learning to talk clearly.
---------- Seems as if he's making no progress in speech.
---------- He continually interrupts adult conversations to say something irrelevant.
---------- He talks too loudly.
---------- He talks explosively.
---------- Sometimes he talks so softly that you can't hear what he is saying.
---------- He is very upset if someone whispers to him.
---------- He cannot remember prayers or nursery rhymes.
---------- He has no intelligible words.
---------- He does not try to talk.
---------- He expresses himself in "baby talk."
---------- He seems to talk better when he's angry.
---------- His speech is clearer in the morning than in the late afternoon.
---------- He talks too fast when he becomes excited.
---------- When he becomes excited, his speech is unintelligible.
---------- No matter what he is asked, he has a few pat answers which he gives every time.
---------- He may answer questions, but his answer is not related to the question.
---------- He pesters people with speech sounds persistently, but these are not understandable.
---------- He calls pictures of men and women "daddies" or "mommies."
---------- He calls all animals "doggies."
---------- When we don't understand the words he's trying to say, he points, or shows us what he means.
---------- He makes sounds just as if he were talking, but none of this is understandable.
---------- He gets angry at us when the words don't come out the way he wishes.
---------- He gets angry at us if we don't understand what he's trying to say.
---------- He gets his pronouns all mixed up when he talks.
---------- If he tries to tell us about some event or experience he has had, he seems to get all mixed up.
---------- He gets angry at himself when the words don't come out as he wants.
---------- He keeps repeating the same thing over and over again.
---------- He continually refers to something that happened yesterday or days or weeks ago.
---------- He seems to be a "Little Sir Echo" and repeats exactly what anyone says to him.
---------- He has little sentences or phrases which he says out loud, where the words are clear but they make no sense.
---------- Often he has different names for the same object.
---------- He "talks" in a steady stream, but nobody can understand what he's saying.

.... He talks like a telegram.

.... One minute he may be able to say a word, and the next minute be unable to repeat it.

.... Words seem to be "on the tip of his tongue," but he just can't seem to get them out.

CHORES*

Very often parents feel that it is important for children to do "chores" around the house as a way of helping and learning responsibility.

1. Do you feel that your child should be given regular jobs to do around the house? ....

Here is a list of jobs. Which of these do you expect your child to do *regularly?*

	Yes	*No*	
2.	....	....	Washing dishes
3.	....	....	Drying dishes
4.	....	....	Setting table
5.	....	....	Cleaning own room
6.	....	....	Making bed
7.	....	....	Carrying out garbage
8.	....	....	Feeding dog or other pet
9.	....	....	Clearing toys
10.	....	....	Emptying wastebaskets
11.	....	....	Cutting grass
12.	....	....	Vacuum
13.	....	....	Dust
14.	....	....	Other: ....

15. What allowance do you give your child every week?
      (Circle)   nothing   penny   nickel   dime   quarter   half   dollar
16. Do you insist that he save money each week from his allowance?
      ....Yes   ....No

*C.R. Group Form 16

REACTION TO REJECTION BY CHILDREN

*Group Form 17

One frequently hears that children can be very cruel. Children may refuse to allow others to play with them and in some other way directly reject a child. When this happens what does your child do?

1. ....He bites them
2. ....He hits them
3. ....He spits at them
4. ....He kicks them
5. ....He cries
6. ....He runs away from them
7. ....He tells mother about it
8. ....He does not seem to feel rejection
9. ....He swears at them
10. ....He breaks their toys
11. ....He "steals" something from them
12. ....He throws something at them

13. ....He "takes it out" on somebody else
14. ....He ignores them
15. ....He continues to try to play with them in spite of this
16. ....Other (explain)

THINGS DADDY DOES WITH THIS CHILD

Check each item which applies to activities which your husband carries on with this child in which *you* are not directly involved.

Never   Rarely   Often   Frequently

........Helps him get dressed
........Feeds him
........Bathes him
........Takes him to school
........Stays with child when you are away
........Shows how to use tools
........Plays catch
........Teaches how to bat
........Teaches how to roller skate
........Takes for a ride in the car
........Reads stories to
........Takes to the dentist
........Takes to the doctor
........Takes along on fishing trips
........Takes along on hunting trips
........Takes to baseball or football games, etc.
........Takes to the playground
........Helps with homework
........Specifically tries to teach things
........Takes to his office or shop
........Uses as a helper for workshop
    or home repair jobs
........Takes to church
........Takes to visit friends or relatives
........Takes bowling
........Takes ice-skating, sled-riding, skiing, etc.
........Takes to stores on shopping trips
........Takes to movies
........Teaches prayers
........Visits teacher for teacher
    conference at school
Other:

CHANGES IN MOTHER SINCE BIRTH OF THIS CHILD

C.R. Group Form 19aM

In what ways do you think you have changed since this child was born? Please check one in each of the questions below.

1. I've become
   1a. ....more patient
   1b. ....less patient

    1c. _____about as patient
    1d. _____as I was before
2. I plan
    2a. _____more for the future
    2b. _____I live more from day to day
    2c. _____I plan about as much as I did before
3. I make friends
    3a. _____more easily
    3b. _____less easily
    3c. _____about as easily
    3d. _____as I used to
4. I've become
    4a. _____more deeply religious
    4b. _____less religious
    4c. _____about as religious
    4d. _____as I was before
5. I worry
    5a. _____more
    5b. _____less
    5c. _____about as much
    5d. _____as I did before
6. I've become
    6a. _____more nervous
    6b. _____less nervous
    6c. _____about as nervous
    6d. _____as I was before
7. I get angry
    7a. _____more easily
    7b. _____less easily
    7c. _____about as easily
    7d. _____as I did before
8. In general, I've become
    8a. _____more unhappy
    8b. _____happier
    8c. _____about as happy
    8d. _____as I was before
9. In general I feel I've
    9a. _____changed for the better
    9b. _____changed for the worse
    9c. _____in some respects I've changed for the better and in some for the worse
    9d. _____I haven't changed at all
10. In general I get along _____ with my mate as before
    10a. _____better
    10b. _____less well
    10c. _____about as well
11. When you are worried, whom do you confide in most? (*Check one*)
    11a. _____your mate
    11b. _____your parents

11c. _____your brothers and sisters
11d. _____your children
11e. _____other relatives
11f. _____friends or neighbors
11g. _____minister
11h. _____no one—keep it to myself
11i. _____other person (*please write in*) _____
12. Which group of people do you feel most at ease with or most comfortable to be with?
12a. _____The people my husband works with
12b. _____Other church members
12c. _____My relatives
12d. _____Other parents of retarded children
12e. _____Members of my club (social club, Parent-Teachers Association, bridge club, sorority, etc.)
12f. _____Neighbors
12g. _____Parents who have (normal) children about the same age as mine
12h. _____None of these

CHANGES IN HUSBAND SINCE BIRTH OF THIS CHILD*

C.R. Group Form 19bM

In what ways do you think your husband has changed since this child was born? Please check one in each of the questions below.

1. My husband has become
   1a. _____more patient
   1b. _____less patient
   1c. _____about as patient as he was before
2. My husband plans
   2a. _____more for the future
   2b. _____he lives more from day to day
   2c. _____he plans about as much as he did before
3. My husband makes friends
   3a. _____more easily
   3b. _____less easily
   3c. _____about as easily as he used to
4. My husband has become
   4a. _____more deeply religious
   4b. _____less religious
   4c. _____about as religious as he was before
5. My husband worries
   5a. _____more
   5b. _____less
   5c. _____about as much as he did before
6. My husband finds himself worrying about something about the child.
   6a. _____frequently
   6b. _____sometimes
   6c. _____rarely
   6d. _____never

7. My husband has become
    7a. _____more nervous
    7b. _____less nervous
    7c. _____about as nervous as he was before
8. My husband gets angry
    8a. _____more easily
    8b. _____less easily
    8c. _____about as easily as he did before
9. In general, my husband has become
    9a. _____ more unhappy
    9b. _____happier
    9c. _____about as happy as he was before
10. In general I feel my husband has
    10a. _____changed for the better
    10b. _____changed for the worse
    10c. _____in some respects he has changed for the better and in some for the worse
    10d. _____he hasn't changed at all
11. In general I get along _____ with my husband as before
    11a. _____better
    11b. _____less well
    11c. _____about as well
12. When your husband is worried, whom does he confide in most?
    (Check one)
    12a. _____you
    12b. _____his parents
    12c. _____his brothers and sisters
    12d. _____his children
    12e. _____other relatives
    12f. _____friends or neighbors
    12g. _____minister
    12h. _____no one—keeps it to himself
    12i. _____other person *(please write in)* _____
13. Which groups of people does your husband feel most at ease with or most comfortable with?
    13a. _____the people he works with
    13b. _____other church members
    13c. _____his relatives
    13d. _____other parents of such children
    13e. _____members of his club (social club, Parent-Teachers Association, Bridge club, fraternity, etc.)
    13f. _____neighbors
    13g. _____parents who have normal children about the same age as ours
    13h. _____none of these

ATTITUDES TOWARDS ANIMALS*

*C.R. Group Form 20
1. _____My child is afraid of animals.
2. _____My child is not afraid of animals.

3. _____We have no pets in our home
4. _____We have a
    4a. _____dog
    4b. _____cat
    4c. _____bird
5. _____I do not want any pets around the home
6. _____My husband does not want any pets
7. _____My child ignores animals
8. _____My child is cruel towards animals
9. _____I think children should have pets
10. _____If my child wanted a pet we would get one
11. _____We got a pet for our child because we felt it would help
12. _____My child does not treat animals gently

INDEX